All American

Volume I

Uniting America's Story, Piece by Piece

The Explorers to the Jacksonians

Teacher's Guide & Answer Key

A full year's curriculum in 32 weekly lessons

CELESTE W. RAKES

Dover, DE

All American History: Uniting America's Story, Piece by Piece Teacher's Guide
by Celeste W. Rakes
Vol. I of the All American History series 2nd Edition

Published by Bright Ideas Press
P.O. Box 333, Cheswold, DE 19936
www.BrightIdeasPress.com

This book is the 2nd edition of the All American History Vol. I Teacher's Guide. It is completely compatible with the 1st editions of the Student Reader and the Student Activity Book.

The publisher wishes to thank Melissa Craig for compiling the unit book lists.

ISBN-13: 978-1-892427-14-4
ISBN-10: 1-892427-14-1

Library of Congress has cataloged *All American History: Uniting America's Story, Piece by Piece Student Reader* as follows:

Library of Congress Cataloging-in-Publication Data

Rakes, Celeste W.
All American history / Celeste W. Rakes.
p. cm.
Includes bibliographical references and index.
Contents: v. 1. Uniting America's story, piece by piece : student reader.
ISBN 1-892427-12-5 (hard cover : alk. paper)
1. United States — History — Textbooks. I. Title.

E178.1.R27 2006
973 — dc22 2005021128

16 15 14 13 12 11 6 5 4 3 2 1

TABLE OF CONTENTS

Section One

HOW TO USE ALL AMERICAN HISTORY VOL. I

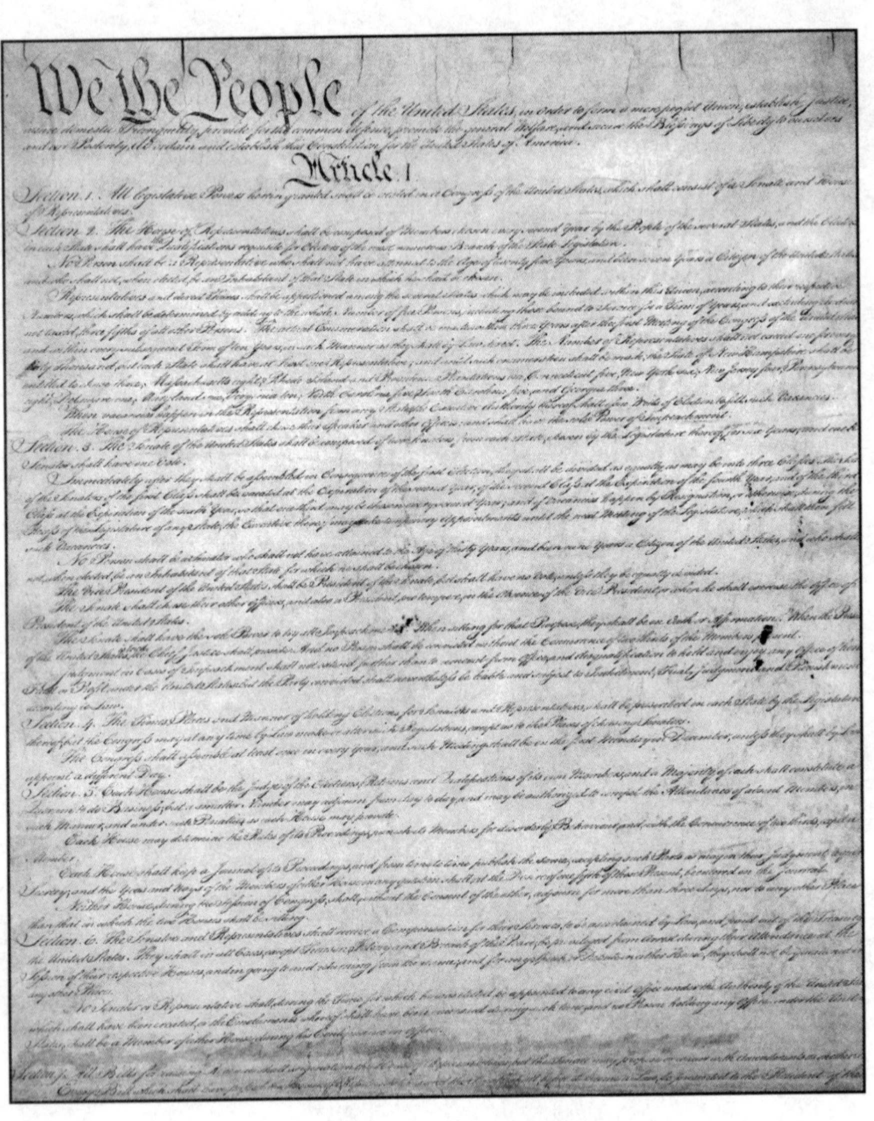

We the People

Article. I

How Do I Get the Most from This Curriculum?

Introduction

All American History Volume I is organized into thirty-two lessons, each of which is designed to provide a week's worth of instruction. An additional four weeks (one at the end of each unit) can be devoted to unit reviews, field trips, and/or completion of special projects. *All American History's* unique features include:

- Adaptability for both younger students and high school students
- Both hands-on activities and strong, challenging content
- Emphasis on social *and* cultural history
- Interactive forms to be used while reading and teaching the lessons
- Context provided for each lesson in the Atmosphere section of each lesson
- Weekly summation of the important points of each lesson

How Do I Use the Student Reader?

The *Student Reader* is designed to be used in tandem with the *Student Activity Book*. Whether the student reads the lesson in the reader independently or has the material taught or explained to him by a teacher, he should be encouraged to work on that lesson's corresponding *forms* (not the For Review or For Further Study questions) in the *Student Activity Book* as he processes the information in the reader. Completing these forms while being introduced to the material in the *Student Reader* provides practice in "note-taking" and helps the student analyze and retain the material better. In the section "How Do I Use This Curriculum with My Co-op?" below, you will find more details concerning how to present the lessons in the reader to students with auditory and kinesthetic learning styles. A strong reader should not struggle with mastering the information in the *Student Reader* and the accompanying pages in the *Student Activity Book*.

How Do I Use the Student Activity Book?

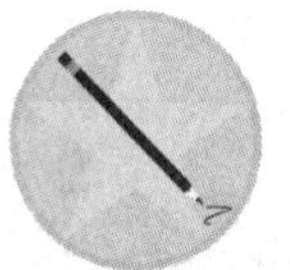

The *Student Activity Book* is not optional. Filling out the forms designed for each lesson will not only improve the student's understanding and retention of the material he has read (or been taught), but it will also provide him with additional information not found in the *Student Reader*. The For Review questions for each lesson (found after the forms in the *Student Activity Book*) were also carefully crafted to ensure that the student has mastered the important information for that lesson.

At the end of each of the thirty-two lessons, the *Student Activity Book* lists four For Further Study questions. In the Section Four answer keys of this *Teacher's Guide*, you will find a great deal of information related to these projects — in other words, the answers! Even if you do not assign these projects to your student, plan on reading the information in Section Four, under "For Further Study Questions and Answers," for each lesson. *A wealth of interesting historical details is contained in this section, much of which you could share quickly and easily with your child if he is not attempting to research the For Further Study Questions on his own.*

How Do I Use the Teacher's Guide?

This *Teacher's Guide* is a tremendous resource, and the wealth of ideas that make this curriculum complete, memorable, and fun can ONLY be found in this *Teacher's Guide.*

Section Two, Teaching Resources, contains the following information, broken down unit by unit:

- Project Possibilities that can be ongoing for the entire eight weeks
- Book List Reminder
- Timeline Dates
- Mapmaking Reminder
- Review Games
- Family Activities
- Checklists

Section Three is filled with annotated book lists of both fiction and nonfiction reading for the primary, middle, and secondary levels. This section is also divided into four units.

Section Four contains directions for the maps found in each of the four units.

Section Five consists of the answers to the For Further Study questions in the *Student Activity Book*, as well as suggestions for adapting these questions for younger students.

Section Six provides the answers to the *Student Activity Book* forms and maps and the For Review questions.

Section Seven has fourteen optional, reproducible forms that your students can use to guide them into further research about significant topics.

Section Eight contains all the reproducible images needed for the *Student Activity Book* forms. These images may also be used for your timelines or review games, or for making other projects/notebooks.

How Do I Use This Curriculum with Fifth – Eighth Grade Students?

This curriculum was created to be used with middle school/junior high students (fifth–eighth graders). However, students in these grades possess a wide range of abilities and a variety of learning styles. The older and more capable the student, the more you should expect in terms of comprehension and retention of the information in the *Student Reader*, degree of completion of the *Student Activity Book* pages, and tackling of the For Further Study questions. Many students in this grade range have become excellent independent readers, but others still struggle with reading on their own and become easily discouraged without verbal interaction and/or hands-on activities. *All American History* was developed to offer learning opportunities to visual, auditory, and kinesthetic learners. Please remember that this is also a high school level course; therefore, be discerning in how much you assign to your fifth–eighth grade student.

Bright Ideas Press also publishes a program called Illuminations. Year 4 of this program is designed to schedule All American History together with literature, bible reading, geography, and language arts. Please visit www.BrightIdeasPress.com for more information.

How Do I Use This Curriculum with High School Students?

All American History, Volume I, is a rich, in-depth course for high school students. For your student to earn an American History high school credit, my recommendations would be to:

- Assign the majority of the For Further Study questions in the *Student Activity Book* (found at the end of each lesson)
- Accomplish some of the Project Possibilities listed in this *Teacher's Guide*
- Require the use of some of the optional forms in the *Student Activity Book*
- Compile the For Review questions (or selections from those questions) in the *Student Activity Book* to use for tests

A separate test packet is available as a digital download from the Bright Ideas website. It includes 8 Tests, each covering four lessons (weeks). The tests consist of multiple-choice, true/false, matching, and map work questions. (An answer key is included.)

How Do I Use This Curriculum with Younger Students?

Bright Ideas Press has developed a special package to help parents adapt this curriculum for younger students – All American History Jr. These materials can be purchased at the Bright Ideas website and include simplified lesson plans, notebooking pages, folderbooks, challenge cards, puzzles, coloring pages, and maps. If you are using AAH Jr. with younger students, you will not need the *All American History Student Activity Book*.

If you decide not to purchase All American Jr., you should still be able to find many activities and projects for younger students in the *Teacher's Guide*, as well as fun learning experiences for the entire family. It is important for you to realize that the Student Reader was not designed to be read word-for-word to younger children (unless they are gifted and working above grade level). However, much of the information in the reader lessons will be very interesting to them if shared in a simple storytelling fashion. The teacher or an older child can re-tell or narrate the lesson to younger students, concentrating on the important people and events and showing them the pictures in the *Student Reader* for that lesson.

You may decide, however, not to narrate the *Student Reader* to your younger students. Rather, you may choose to have them read books related to the topics in the *Student Reader*, while their older sibling(s) are studying the *Student Reader*. For each of the four units, you will find in this *Teacher's Guide* lists of individuals for whom you can find biographies. You will also find annotated reading lists for younger, middle, and high school students. If your younger child enjoys reading or being read to, you should easily be able to locate more than enough books from the library to keep him and/or you busy for the eight weeks of each unit. Don't worry about covering all the people and events found in the *Student Reader* and don't worry about whether your reading is perfectly chronological. Just concentrate on making learning history enjoyable; awaken your younger student's appetite for further study of American history in the years ahead.

If a younger child likes to write or do things with his hands, he may enjoy cutting out the images and flags in the *Student Activity Book* and placing them on the correct forms while an older sibling completes the forms. (Section Seven of this *Teacher's Guide* has all the images for the forms, so you could easily copy some for a younger student.) The younger child doesn't have to fill in all the blanks on the form — just a few of the more important ones. Many younger children would enjoy using colored pencils to draw on the maps found on the back of many of the forms or using a children's atlas to find major places mentioned in the lessons.

Section Five of this *Teacher's Guide* also has lesson-by-lesson suggestions on how to adapt the For Further Study questions for use with younger children. Your older students may enjoy sharing with their younger siblings some of the information that they are learning in these projects. Each lesson also has at least one suggested Family Activity. All of these were designed particularly with the younger members of the family in mind.

How Do I Use This Curriculum with My Family?

The first day or two of each lesson should be spent digesting the information found on the week's topic in the *Student Reader*. Older students will probably be able to read and understand the information and complete the corresponding forms in the *Student Activity Book* on their own. These forms were intended to be used as the student is reading/hearing the information from the *Student Reader*. (If younger children in the family are included in the unit study, the parent should read carefully the previous section on how to use this curriculum with younger students.)

Following the completion of the lesson's required forms, the student can check to see how well he has mastered the material by tackling the lesson's For Review questions. You will probably also want to add the Timeline Dates (which can be found for each unit in Section Two of this *Teacher's Guide*) to your family timeline.

If your state requires a portfolio, a notebook containing the required forms as well as any additional maps, timelines, and your student's Native American and African American notebooks would make excellent portfolio additions.

The remainder of the week should be devoted to other projects chosen by the student and/or parent. Each of the thirty-two lessons in the *Student Activity Book* contains four For Further Study questions related to that week's topic. Some of these projects are research-oriented, whereas others are more hands-on activities. Choose which projects you wish to pursue each week. Providing your junior high student with an opportunity to try his hand at some historical research would be of great benefit to him. If you have younger students, you may choose to use the adaptations of the For Further Study questions created just for them. A high school student should usually do all four of the For Further Study questions every week. To make your job easier, the information that should be gained from working on these questions is included in the For Further Study answers in Section Four of this *Teacher's Guide*. If time does not allow for completion of all four of the For Further Study questions, your student would certainly profit from hearing or reading the brief account of the historical details contained in these For Further Study answers.

The *Teacher's Guide* also contains Project Possibilities that span the entire eight weeks of each unit. If you have children who love to read, supply them with a stack of biographies or historical fiction for each time period. My daughter, who is a voracious reader, read biographies of all the presidents and many other important American historical figures. You might also pick a family read-aloud book for each of the units. Even if your child is not a big reader, try to get him to read at least several books for each eight-week unit. He doesn't have to pick large volumes; I have learned many fascinating historical facts from short biographies and works of nonfiction, and the illustrations and photographs in such books are usually wonderful.

If you have younger children or children who enjoy hands-on learning, look specifically at Lessons 15, 16, 31, and 32 and plan opportunities for them to do some cooking, to listen to music, or to look at paintings. There are also a number of hands-on activities scattered throughout the For Further Study questions in each unit. Don't be afraid to let them write a play or videotape a news report or come up with some other creative way to use the information that they are learning. Some of our most precious homeschooling memories as a family resulted from such attempts.

At the end of each unit you may choose to insert a *bonus* week before beginning the next unit's lessons. This ninth week could be used for field trips, watching related movies, and finishing projects or adding to notebooks. Planning for this *bonus* week is a wonderful stress reducer and provides *catch-up* time if there has been any sickness or other reasons why your student might be behind.

How Do I Use This Curriculum with My Co-op?

The co-op class for which I developed this curriculum met once a week for an hour. During that time period, I shared with the students most of the information found in the *Student Reader* for that week's lesson. I did not read it to them word-for-word. Rather, I attempted to share it with them in a story-telling fashion. Although I didn't memorize the facts of the lesson, I was familiar enough with them that I could tell the story in my own words.

I also tried to make my presentation interactive. Instead of doing all the talking, I came up with questions to get the students involved in discovering some of the information on their own and in forming opinions about what they were learning. I also had them working on their *Student Activity Book* forms in class.

As I talked about a president, students were cutting and pasting his picture to his form and filling in the information about him. I discovered that I didn't need to be afraid to let my students do something with their hands while I was telling the story. This multi-sensory approach really seemed to solidify their understanding of the information that I was sharing. Years later, my son can remember almost everything he learned using this hands-on approach.

During our class time, I also brought in many pictures and photographs to make what we were discussing more real to my students. If I had been teaching just my own child at home, I might not have gone to the trouble of doing that. However, for a classroom of students, I made the effort — and it was well worth it. Looking at the visual depictions of the material that we were studying always raised further questions or provoked other insights, and I ended up learning from my student's reactions to the images. We also did map and timeline work in class.

In some of my co-op classes, we did the For Review questions in the *Student Activity Book* together as a class. One group in particular loved doing this. With other groups, I assigned the For Review questions for them to do at home, and then we went over them as a review at the beginning of the next class period. I have also used the unit Review Games found in the *Teacher's Guide* — sometimes with teams, depending on the size of the group, and sometimes with the opportunity to earn little treats. This is always a big hit!

During the four days that my co-op students were at home, they were encouraged to choose at least a couple of related projects to work on (either from the lesson's For Further Study questions or from the Project Possibilities listed for the unit in the *Teacher's Guide*). In the co-op situation in which I taught, the responsibility for monitoring the students' progress in their work at home was left with their parents. However, I always encouraged my students to bring to class any of their projects that they would like to show me, and I occasionally offered some kind of reward for them to do so. I also planned a special co-op field trip or activity for each of the units.

How Do I Use This Curriculum with My Classroom?

Most of what I shared concerning the co-op classes that I taught would apply in this context as well. The major difference is that you (the classroom teacher) will be supervising the projects that your students work on, rather than their parents at home. You will also have to come up with a means of grading their work. The following are some of the decisions that you will have to make.

- Will you require your students to do any reading other than that from the *Student Reader*? If so, will you require biographies, historical fiction, nonfiction, or a combination? How much reading will you require them to do, and how much choice will you give them in what they pick to read? How will you hold them accountable for what they read — will you have them write a report, give an oral presentation, do a poster, or create some sort of art project?
- Will you require your students to construct any of the suggested notebooks — Native American or African American? If so, which ones? Will you assign any creative writing projects? Will they work on these individually or in groups?
- Will you require your students to do any of the For Further Study questions? If so, how many? Will it be the same number for each lesson?
- Will you assign the same project(s) to the entire class or will you allow the students to individually choose which of the Project Possibilities they would like to do?
- Will you plan review games for the class, or does your schedule allow for field trips or special historical days — complete with food and other hands-on activities?

- Will you give tests on the material? If you desire to do so or are required to do so, the review activities in the *Student Activity Book* would provide a rich resource for test questions.

There are dozens of possible combinations of projects and activities that you could choose for your classes. As their teacher, you'll be the best one to determine which activities are chosen and in what order they are accomplished. That said, here are two *possible* schedules:

Option One
(for classes that meet five days a week)

- Monday — Students read to themselves from the *Student Reader* and/or participate in teacher-led discussion of the information contained in the *Student Reader* along with work on the corresponding forms (including maps) in the *Student Activity Book*
- Tuesday — Timeline Dates and the For Review questions
- Wednesday — Reading day (allowing them time to read supplemental books relating to the time period for that unit or lesson)
- Thursday — For Further Study questions and Review Games
- Friday — Testing day (if you are required to test) and/or more supplemental reading time

Option Two
(for classes that meet three days a week)

- Monday — Students read to themselves from the *Student Reader* and/or participate in teacher-led discussion of the information contained in the *Student Reader* along with work on the corresponding forms (including maps) in the *Student Activity Book* and adding Timeline Dates
- Wednesday — For Review questions, additional reading, begin For Further Study questions
- Friday — Finish For Further Study questions, additional reading, and/or Review Games, testing day (if required)

Detailed Instructions

Forms

This curriculum was developed with the intention of having the students complete the forms in the *Student Activity Book* while reading and studying the lessons in the *Student Reader*. All of the information that I have requested from the students for these forms is included in the lessons of the *Student Reader*. If the information is not included in the *Student Reader* or is not specific enough in the text of the *Student Reader*, that space on that form is filled in for the student. *These forms are NOT intended to be used as quizzes or tests, only as multi-sensory reinforcement of the information from the lessons.* They are also great practice for note-taking.

Optional Forms

In Section Seven of this *Teacher's Guide*, as well as in the *Student Activity Book*, there are fourteen additional forms that may be photocopied repeatedly. Filling in the Notebook Timeline form is one option for your student to use in creating a timeline. The other forms can guide your student in doing additional research and/or creating notebooks. The Optional Forms include:

- Notebook Timeline
- Native American Tribe
- Native American
- African American
- European Explorer
- American Colony
- United States President
- Revolutionary War Battle
- War of 1812 Battle
- Mexican War Battle
- Colonial Family Life/Clothing
- Colonial Culture
- Nineteenth Century Family Life/Clothing
- Nineteenth Century Culture

Images and Flags

The *Student Activity Book* forms were designed to allow removal of the pages from the binding and placement in a three-ring binder, if so desired. The images and flags to be glued onto these forms are all included in the back of each *Student Activity Book*. These images are in the exact order that they will be used. The flags should be colored in, using the appropriate colors for each country. However, your student also has the option of printing color flags to use. You can download these color flags from www.BrightIdeasPress.com.

A majority of the images included in both the *Student Reader* and the *Student Activity Book* were obtained from either the Library of Congress or the National Archives. I have included the reproduction numbers or call numbers in the credit lines of each of these images. If you are interested in doing further research on these topics, both the Library of Congress and the National Archives contain a vast array of visual resources (many of which are available online) that can be searched topically or by these reproduction or call numbers.

All the images and flags have also been included in the back of this book for your use. Feel free to photocopy them before cutting and use them for review games, flashcards, or replacements for your students. Please note that I have chosen to use current flags to represent the countries that were involved in wars and not historical flags of those countries, unless no current flag exists. This was done solely for ease of visual identification.

Maps

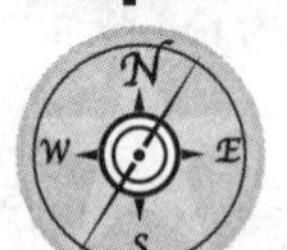

There is a map on the back of most of the required *Student Activity Book* forms. Almost all of these maps are to be completed to match the corresponding maps in the *Student Reader*. Directions for completing the maps in each unit can be found in Section IV of this *Teacher's Guide*.

A legend box has been included on each of the maps so that your student can choose colors and/or patterns to express information as desired. Additional blank maps might be helpful for reviewing the location of cities and countries, states and capitals practice, and illustrations for optional For Further Study questions. Blank maps are also handy for younger students who enjoy coloring, for kinesthetic or visual learners, and for students desiring to do more hands-on practice.

Book Lists

Books can really make history come to life for students of all ages! We have done the work for you in finding a plethora of books. These extensive, annotated book lists are found in Section Three, listed by unit and then by primary, middle, and secondary grade levels. Enjoy yourself — read aloud with your students as much as reasonably possible. Make a point of finding attractive, well-illustrated books for your visual learners. Find books-on-tape for auditory ones. While none of these books are required, they will add depth to your studies.

Timelines

In this *Teacher's Guide*, Timeline Dates are listed, by unit, in Section Two, Teaching Resources. Section Eight, Images for Required Forms, contains many images that are perfect for timelines, as well as for the optional Notebook Timeline form.

Timelines are especially useful for:

- Seeing the events of history in a graphically organized fashion
- Seeing the events of history at a glance
- Seeing relationships between people, places, and events
- Making an abstract concept concrete
- Visual learners

- Kinesthetic learners as they construct their timeline
- Reinforcing the information being studied

There are a number of methods for recording timelines. Here are a few examples:

- On strips of paper along a wall
- On poster board or science project boards
- On a laminated Timeline of World History
- On index cards

Another option (especially appealing to older students) is to have the student create a notebook-style timeline. To that end, we have included in this *Teacher's Guide* a notebook-style timeline form.

An extremely useful website for seeing photos of a variety of timeline styles is www.homeschoolinthewoods.com by Amy Pak, whose illustrations are used in *All American History, Volumes I and II.*

Additional Resources: Atlases, Maps, and Timelines

All of the following atlases and map resources are recommended by and available from Bright Ideas Press.

Atlases

Choose the ones that are right for your students. Both a world and USA atlas are necessary.

- *Rand McNally Atlas of World Geography* (Grades 8–12)
- *Rand McNally Children's Illustrated Atlas of the United States* (all ages)
- *Rand McNally Historical Atlas of the United States* (highly recommended for grades 7 and up)

Maps

- *WonderMaps* (Bright Ideas Press)
- Blank, laminated oversized USA outline map
- Blank, laminated oversized world outline map

Timeline Resources

- *History through the Ages:* America's History timeline figures by Amy Pak — available in both a cardstock version and a CD-Rom version
- Laminated Timeline of World History

Section Two

TEACHING RESOURCES

UNIT ONE
Resources

Project Possibilities

1. Have your student(s) choose a biography of one or more of these explorers from the Age of European Exploration.

    - Leif Eriksson
    - Marco Polo
    - Prince Henry the Navigator
    - Christopher Columbus
    - Amerigo Vespucci
    - John Cabot
    - Vasco Nuñez de Balboa
    - Hernando Cortés
    - Francisco Pizarro
    - Juan Ponce de Leon
    - Ferdinand Magellan
    - Giovanni da Verrazano
    - Jacques Cartier
    - Hernando de Soto
    - Francisco Vasquez de Coronado
    - Sir Francis Drake
    - Sir Walter Raleigh (Ralegh)
    - Henry Hudson
    - Samuel de Champlain

    Ask your student(s) the following questions: Would you have liked to sail with this explorer? Can you provide three reasons why or why not?

2. Have your student(s) pick one or more works of historical fiction to read from the Unit One Book List.

3. Have your student(s) select one or more creative writing projects related to the information learned in Unit One. Projects include writing a poem about an explorer, a journal entry or captain's log entry from a day in the life of an explorer, a newspaper article or a script for a TV news report describing the adventures of one of the explorers, or a drama depicting a significant event from the life of one of the explorers.

    The drama could be performed for an audience or the TV news report could be performed and videotaped.

    Your student(s) can illustrate the writing project or make a mural showing the adventures of one of the explorers.

4. Have your student(s) put together a Native American Notebook. There are data forms in the *Student Activity Book* to copy and use for this purpose. Pages could be added to this notebook while studying Lessons 1, 3, 5, and 8 in Unit One.

Book List Reminder

See the annotated bibliography in Section Three.

Timeline Dates

As you study each explorer, record a key date(s) for his explorations on a timeline.

- 1000: Leif Ericksson (Lesson 1)
- 1272 – 1295: Marco Polo (Lesson 2)
- 1420 – 1460: Prince Henry's Navigators (Lesson 2)

- 1492 – 1504: Christopher Columbus (Lesson 3)
- 1499 – 1504: Amerigo Vespucci (Lesson 3)
- 1497 – 1498: John Cabot (Lesson 4)
- 1513: Vasco Nuñez de Balboa (Lesson 4)
- 1519 – 1521: Hernando Cortés (Lesson 4)
- 1532 – 1533: Francisco Pizarro (Lesson 4)
- 1513 – 1521: Juan Ponce de Leon (Lesson 5)
- 1519 – 1521: Ferdinand Magellan (Lesson 5)
- 1524 – 1525: Giovanni da Verrazano (Lesson 5)
- 1534 – 1536: Jacques Cartier (Lesson 6)
- 1539 – 1542: Hernando de Soto (Lesson 6)
- 1540 – 1542: Francisco Vasquez de Coronado (Lesson 6)
- 1577 – 1580: Sir Francis Drake (Lesson 7)
- 1584 – 1616: Sir Walter Raleigh (Lesson 7)
- 1607 – 1611: Henry Hudson (Lesson 8)
- 1603 – 1612: Samuel de Champlain (Lesson 8)

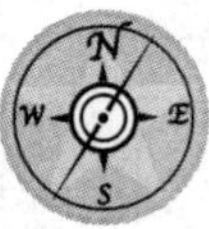

Mapmaking Reminder

Directions for completing the map forms can be found in Section Four of this *Teacher's Guide*.

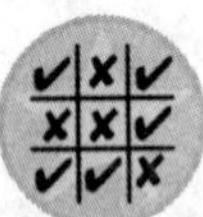

Review Games

For long-term usage and durability, you may wish to either photocopy the images onto cardstock or glue them to a piece of poster board before cutting them out. All of the images, icons, and flags from the *Student Activity Book* have been included in this book for your use.

1. Cut out pictures of each country's flag and each explorer used in Unit One. Place each flag on a table, leaving space beneath it. See if your student(s) can place pictures of the explorers who sailed for that country under each flag. (Note: As some explorers did exploration for more than one country, you will need additional copies of those pictures.)

2. Locate the descriptions of the explorers in the Unit One Final Review. Make a copy of these descriptions. Cut out each description separately, and then mix up the entire set of explorers and their descriptions. See if your student(s) can match up the picture of each explorer with his description.

All of these reviews can be done during each of the lessons of Unit One. Just keep adding flags, pictures of explorers, and/or descriptions as you study them each week or use them as a final review.

Family Activity Ideas

Lesson 1

- Watch the movie *Veggie Tales: Lyle the Kindly Viking*. Compare and contrast its portrayal of the Vikings and their ships with what you have learned.

- The Vikings loved jewelry, and almost everyone in Viking society owned some. The Vikings were skilled craftsmen. Their pieces were intricate, symmetrical, and often made of silver. Make a simple piece of silver-colored jewelry.

Lesson 2

- Prince Henry was known for making great advances in navigation and map-making. Make a map of your room or house. Try to make it as accurate as possible. Which way is north?

- During the Polos' journeys, they saw many riches and brought home treasures and valuable spices. See if you can identify the spices in your home by smell or taste alone.

Lesson 3

- Think about what it was like to live on a ship for months at a time. What things do you use every day that you would not be able to take on board? How would it feel to live without those items? Try living for an entire day with just what you would find on a ship.

- Sailors slept in hammocks, not beds. Take a sheet and tie it up like a hammock. Sleep in it tonight!

Lesson 4

- It took Balboa, his men, and his guides twenty-four days to cross forty-five miles of jungle. Go for a nature hike in the woods and imagine what it would be like to trek through that land if no one had been there before. How would you get through? Would you need a machete? What animals might you see on your walk?

Lesson 5

- One of the sailors' main foods was hard tack. Try making and eating your own. There are a number of recipes; but they all call for flour, water, and salt. Some also include lard. Try this one:

    - 2 cups flour
    - ¾ cup water
    - 2 teaspoon salt (dissolved into the water)
    - 1 tablespoon lard

  Mix ingredients thoroughly. Flatten batter onto a cookie sheet to about one and one-half inch thick. Bake 30 minutes. Cut into squares 3 inches by 3 inches. Pierce each square with a grid of 4 holes by 4 holes. Preheat oven at 400 degrees. Bake for 35–45 minutes. Then flip them and bake until hard.

Lesson 6

- A Spanish seaman's diet consisted of water, vinegar, wine, olive oil, molasses, cheese, honey, raisins, rice, garlic, almonds, hardtack, legumes, sardines, anchovies, pickled or salted meat, and salted flour. Try sardines or anchovies. What do you think? Could you have survived on this diet?

- Why was their meat and flour salted? Salt acts as a preservative and gives flavor. What do these two Bible references mean? Memorize one of them.

    - Matthew 5:13 (NKJV): "You are the salt of the earth; but if the salt loses its flavor, how shall it be seasoned? It is then good for nothing but to be thrown out and trampled underfoot by men."

    - Colossians 4:6 (NKJV): "Let your speech always be with grace, seasoned with salt, that you may know how you ought to answer each one."

Lesson 7

- Explorers had to utilize the stars and planets to determine their location. Go outside on a clear night and try to identify the North Star and the Big Dipper. Can you recognize any other constellations or any planets?

Lesson 8

- During Hudson's day, sand hourglasses were the most reliable means of keeping time. Look at a simple hourglass or sand timer. You may have one in a board game. How does it work? Directions can be found online for making your own.

- Figureheads were common on the prow (front) of ships. Mermaids and dragons were two common designs for figureheads, but many other figures were also used. What kind of figurehead might have been on Hudson's ship? Design or sculpt a figurehead for your own sailing ship.

UNIT ONE
Checklist

Please Note:
SR = *Student Reader*
SAB = *Student Activity Book*
TG = *Teacher's Guide*

Required for Lesson 1
- ❑ Lesson 1 (page 5, SR)
- ❑ Corresponding Required Form (page 1, SAB)
- ❑ Corresponding Map (page 2, SAB)
- ❑ For Review questions (page 3, SAB)

Optional for Lesson 1
- ❑ For Further Study projects (page 6, SAB)
- ❑ Additional Options for Unit (page 13, TG)

Required for Lesson 2
- ❑ Lesson 2 (page 13, SR)
- ❑ Corresponding Required Forms (pages 7 & 9, SAB)
- ❑ Corresponding Maps (pages 8&10, SAB)
- ❑ For Review questions (page 11, SAB)

Optional for Lesson 2
- ❑ For Further Study projects (page 13, SAB)
- ❑ Additional Options for Unit (page 13, TG)

Required for Lesson 3
- ❑ Lesson 3 (page 25, SR)
- ❑ Corresponding Required Forms (pages 15 &17, SAB)
- ❑ Corresponding Maps (pages 16 & 18, SAB)
- ❑ For Review questions (page 19, SAB)

Optional for Lesson 3
- ❑ For Further Study projects (page 20, SAB)
- ❑ Additional Options for Unit (page 13, TG)

Required for Lesson 4
- ❑ Lesson 4 (page 37, SR)
- ❑ Corresponding Required Forms (pages 21, 23, & 25, SAB)
- ❑ Corresponding Maps (pages 22, 24, & 26, SAB)
- ❑ For Review questions (page 27, SAB)

Optional for Lesson 4
- ❑ For Further Study projects (page 28, SAB)
- ❑ Additional Options for Unit (page 13, TG)

Required for Lesson 5
- ❑ Lesson 5 (page 51, SR)
- ❑ Corresponding Required Forms (pages 31, 33, & 35, SAB)
- ❑ Corresponding Maps (pages 32, 34, & 36, SAB)
- ❑ For Review questions (page 37, SAB)

Optional for Lesson 5
- ❑ For Further Study projects (page 40, SAB)
- ❑ Additional Options for Unit (page 13, TG)

Required for Lesson 6
- ❑ Lesson 6 (page 65, SR)
- ❑ Corresponding Required Forms (pages 41, 43, & 45, SAB)
- ❑ Corresponding Maps (pages 42, 44, & 46, SAB)
- ❑ For Review questions (page 47, SAB)

Optional for Lesson 6
- ❑ For Further Study projects (page 49, SAB)
- ❑ Additional Options for Unit (page 13, TG)

Required for Lesson 7

- ❑ Lesson 7 (page 77, SR)
- ❑ Corresponding Required Forms (pages 51 & 53, SAB)
- ❑ Corresponding Maps (pages 52 & 54, SAB)
- ❑ For Review questions (page 55, SAB)

Optional for Lesson 7

- ❑ For Further Study projects (page 57, SAB)
- ❑ Additional Options for Unit (page 13, TG)

Required for Lesson 8

- ❑ Lesson 8 (page 89, SR)
- ❑ Corresponding Required Forms (pages 59 & 61, SAB)
- ❑ Corresponding Maps (pages 60 & 62, SAB)
- ❑ For Review questions (page 63, SAB)

Optional for Lesson 8

- ❑ For Further Study projects (page 64, SAB)
- ❑ Additional Options for Unit (page 13, TG)

Required for Unit One

- ❑ Final Review (page 65, SAB)

Additional Options for Unit

- ❑ Project Possibilities (page 13, TG)
- ❑ Timeline Dates (page 13, TG)
- ❑ Optional Map Review (page 59, TG)
- ❑ Review Games (page 14, TG)
- ❑ Additional Reading from Book Lists (page 39, TG)
- ❑ For Further Study Younger Student Adaptations (page 68, TG)
- ❑ Family Activity Ideas (page 14, TG)

UNIT TWO
Resources

Project Possibilities

1. Have your student(s) choose a biography of one or more of these European colonial leaders or Native Americans who lived during the period of colonization.

    - Captain John Smith
    - Powhatan
    - Pocahontas
    - John Rolfe
    - Captain Miles Standish
    - William Bradford
    - Samoset
    - Squanto
    - John Winthrop
    - Massasoit
    - Roger Williams
    - Ann Hutchinson
    - Thomas Hooker
    - Peter Minuet
    - Peter Stuyvesant
    - William Penn
    - Cecil Calvert
    - James Oglethorpe
    - Jonathan Edwards
    - John Peter Zenger

    Ask your student(s) to decide the strengths and weaknesses of the European colonist or the Native American and list his or her top three accomplishments.

2. Have your student(s) pick one or more works of historical fiction to read from the Unit Two Book List.

3. Have your student(s) select one or more creative writing projects related to the information you learn concerning the period of colonization. Projects include writing a poem about a colonist or Native American, a journal entry from a day in the life of a colonist or Native American, a newspaper article or a script for a TV news report describing an important occurrence in one of the colonies, or a drama depicting a significant time in the establishment of one of the colonies.

    The drama could be performed for an audience or the TV news report could be performed and videotaped.

    Your student(s) can also illustrate the writing project or make a mural depicting the history of one of the colonies.

4. Several of the early colonial settlements (such as Jamestown and Plymouth) have interesting websites to explore. If possible, plan a field trip to visit one of these early settlements in person.

5. If your student(s) is putting together a Native American Notebook, pages could be added to this notebook while studying Lessons 9, 13, and 14 in Unit Two.

6. Have your student(s) put together an African American Notebook. This notebook can span both volumes of *All American History*. As an introduction to this notebook, the student(s) could write a report on the lives of African slaves coming to America during this period of colonization and answer the following questions: Under what conditions did these slaves travel to America? Where did most of them live once they arrived in America? What hardships did they face? Who fought for emancipation of slaves in America during the colonial period?

Book List Reminder

See the annotated bibliography in Section Three.

Timeline Dates

As you study each colony, record the date of its establishment on a timeline.

- 1607: Jamestown (Lesson 9)
- 1620: Plymouth (Lesson 10)
- 1630: Massachusetts Bay (Lesson 10)
- 1622: New Hampshire (Lesson 11)
- 1636: Rhode Island (Lesson 11)
- 1636: Connecticut (Lesson 11)
- 1626: New York (Lesson 12)
- 1664: New Jersey (Lesson 12)
- 1638: Delaware (Lesson 13)
- 1682: Pennsylvania (Lesson 13)
- 1634: Maryland (Lesson 14)
- 1653: North Carolina (Lesson 14)
- 1670: South Carolina (Lesson 14)
- 1732: Georgia (Lesson 14)

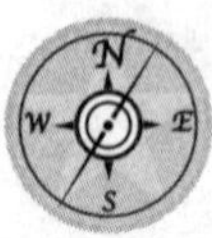

Mapmaking Reminder

Directions for completing the map forms can be found in Section Four of this *Teacher's Guide*.

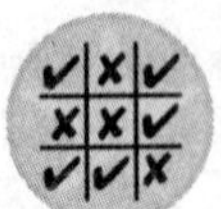

Review Games

For long-term usage and durability, you may wish to either photocopy the images onto cardstock or glue them to a piece of poster board before cutting them out. All of the images, icons, and flags from the *Student Activity Book* have been included in this book for your use.

1. Cut out a picture of each of the key figures from the period of colonization, the flags of the colonizing nations, and the motivation for founding icons. Have students review by placing each of the proper figures on a large outline map of the colonies. For example: On Pennsylvania, the student would place a picture of William Penn, an English flag, and the religious motivation icon (the cross).

2. Trace an outline of each of the colonies onto the front of index cards. Glue the key figure images, motivation icons, and flags of the colonizing nations onto the backs. Use them for review as flash cards.

Family Activity Ideas

Lesson 9

- Dress up as a Native American. Here are directions for an easy and fairly durable fake leather to use for vests, moccasins, etc. It makes a great miniature tee-pee, too! All you need are brown grocery bags, glycerin (from a drug store), and water.
    - Make a solution of 2 parts glycerin to 3 parts water.
    - Cut bags into the size pieces you will need for your project.
    - Crinkle the pieces and dunk them in water. Let dry.
    - Sponge on the solution until the pieces are wet again. Let dry.
- Learn about birch-bark canoes that Native Americans used. Build your own.

Lesson 10

- The colonists were very grateful to the Lord for their arrival at Plymouth. If you are studying this lesson in November, take time to learn more about the first Thanksgiving. For what are you thankful? Memorize Psalm 100 or 111.

- Make an acrostic using the word *thankful* or write a thank-you note to someone special.

Lesson 11

- Rhode Island is, geographically, the smallest state. Its nickname is the "Ocean State." What is the nickname of your state? What is the nickname of New Hampshire? What about Connecticut? Why do you think that they have these nicknames?

Lesson 12

- Try a Pennsylvania Dutch recipe, such as this one for baked oatmeal.

    - 1 cup oil
    - 2 cups sugar
    - 4 eggs
    - 6 cups rolled oats
    - 4 teaspoon baking powder
    - 4 teaspoon salt
    - 2 cups milk

    Combine all ingredients, and pour mixture into greased 9 x 13 pan. Bake at 350 degrees for 30 minutes or until firm in the middle. Eat hot or cold, with or without milk.

Lesson 13

- During this time period, Native American children had more chores and less time to play than you do today, just like the early colonists' children. However, they did have dolls and toys, such as miniature bows and arrows and handheld ball games. Lenape games for teenagers and adults included kicking football games. Here are two simple games that you can play right now:

    - Hand Game — guessing game where an opponent has to guess in which hand an object is hidden. Beans, sticks, or other markers are used to keep score.

    - Moccasin Game — guessing game where an opponent has to guess in which moccasin an object is hidden. Beans, sticks, or other markers are used to keep score. Substitute a pair of sneakers!

- The Swedes introduced the log cabin to North America, building the first ones in Delaware. Build your own log cabin out of pretzel logs and frosting (yummier!) or pretzel logs and a hot glue gun (sturdier!).

Lesson 14

- Watch a children's film version of *Treasure Island. Muppet Treasure Island* (rated G) is a fun, not-too-scary one. Discuss what might be realistic in this movie about a pirate's life. How are pirates different from sailors?

- Here is a Cherokee explanation of the sky that would be interesting to illustrate: The Cherokee believed that the sun was a young woman who lived in the east. The moon was her brother and lived in the west. One story tells how the Redbird was the daughter of the sun. Eclipses were believed to be caused by a giant frog that lived in the sky and tried to swallow them. The lightning and the rainbow were the clothing of the sons of thunder, who lived far in the west above the sky vault.

    Contrast this with your beliefs. Where in the Bible do we learn about the rainbow? Look it up! Draw a picture illustrating this important promise from God.

Lesson 15

- In colonial days, students learned from a hornbook. Make your own hornbook.

    - Cut a piece of cardboard in the shape of a paddle.

    - Cut a piece of paper the size of the big part of the paddle.

    - Write the alphabet in capital letters, then in lowercase letters.

    - Paste it onto the paddle

    - Cover with clear contact paper or plastic wrap.

- Colonists had to make their own butter from cream. You can churn your own butter. Be sure you have several people around to help. This is simple but tiring! Pour heavy cream into a jar and start shaking. Keep shaking until the cream separates and you are left with butter and buttermilk. See how yummy it is on bread and crackers. Can you imagine doing this in a big churn? Churning butter was often a child's chore.

Lesson 16

- Games helped colonial children learn skills that they would need later in life. Games taught children how to aim and throw, how to solve problems, and how to follow directions. Pick one or more of these games to play: puzzles, hoops, kite flying, jump rope, spinning tops, hopscotch, Jacob's ladder, leap frog, bow & arrow, blind man's bluff, see-saw, string games, marbles, swinging, ice sliding, or pick-up sticks
- Quilts were very common during this time. Quilts are blankets made from leftover fabrics stitched together into blocks and then sewn together into a specific pattern. Certain patterns were popular and were used over and over again. Do you have a quilt? Look for popular quilt patterns like the "log cabin." Make your own quilt design out of strips of colored paper.

UNIT TWO
Checklist

Please Note:
SR = *Student Reader*
SAB = *Student Activity Book*
TG = *Teacher's Guide*

Required for Lesson 9
- ❑ Lesson 9 (page 101, SR)
- ❑ Corresponding Required Form (page 69, SAB)
- ❑ Corresponding Map (page 70, SAB)
- ❑ For Review questions (page 71, SAB)

Optional for Lesson 9
- ❑ For Further Study projects (page 72, SAB)
- ❑ Additional Options for Unit (page 19, TG)

Required for Lesson 10
- ❑ Lesson 10 (page 113, SR)
- ❑ Corresponding Required Forms (pages 73 & 75, SAB)
- ❑ Corresponding Maps (pages 74 & 76, SAB)
- ❑ For Review questions (page 77, SAB)

Optional for Lesson 10
- ❑ For Further Study projects (page 81, SAB)
- ❑ Additional Options for Unit (page 19, TG)

Required for Lesson 11
- ❑ Lesson 11 (page 127, SR)
- ❑ Corresponding Required Forms (pages 83, 85, & 87, SAB)
- ❑ Corresponding Maps (pages 84, 86, & 88, SAB)
- ❑ For Review questions (page 89, SAB)

Optional for Lesson 11
- ❑ For Further Study projects (page 91, SAB)
- ❑ Additional Options for Unit (page 19, TG)

Required for Lesson 12
- ❑ Lesson 12 (page 139, SR)
- ❑ Corresponding Required Forms (pages 93 & 95, SAB)
- ❑ Corresponding Maps (pages 94 & 96, SAB)
- ❑ For Review questions (page 97, SAB)

Optional for Lesson 12
- ❑ For Further Study projects (page 98, SAB)
- ❑ Additional Options for Unit (page 19, TG)

Required for Lesson 13
- ❑ Lesson 13 (page 149, SR)
- ❑ Corresponding Required Forms (pages 99, 101, & 103, SAB)
- ❑ Corresponding Maps (pages 100, 102, & 104, SAB)
- ❑ For Review questions (page 105, SAB)

Optional for Lesson 13
- ❑ For Further Study projects (page 109, SAB)
- ❑ Additional Options for Unit (page 19, TG)

Required for Lesson 14
- ❑ Lesson 14 (page 163, SR)
- ❑ Corresponding Required Forms (pages 111, 113, & 115, SAB)
- ❑ Corresponding Maps (pages 112, 114, & 116, SAB)
- ❑ For Review questions (page 117, SAB)

Optional for Lesson 14
- ❑ For Further Study projects (page 119, SAB)
- ❑ Additional Options for Unit (page 19, TG)

Required for Lesson 15

- ❑ Lesson 15 (page 175, SR)
- ❑ Corresponding Required Form (page 121, SAB)
- ❑ Corresponding Map (page 122, SAB)
- ❑ For Review questions (page 123, SAB)

Optional for Lesson 15

- ❑ For Further Study projects (page 126, SAB)
- ❑ Additional Options for Unit (page 19, TG)

Required for Lesson 16

- ❑ Lesson 16 (page 189, SR)
- ❑ Corresponding Required Form (page 129, SAB)
- ❑ For Review questions (page 131, SAB)

Optional for Lesson 16

- ❑ For Further Study projects (page 132, SAB)
- ❑ Additional Options for Unit (page 19, TG)

Required for Unit Two

- ❑ Final Review (page 133, SAB)

Additional Options for Unit

- ❑ Project Possibilities (page 19, TG)
- ❑ Timeline Dates (page 20, TG)
- ❑ Optional Map Review (page 61, TG)
- ❑ Review Games (page 20, TG)
- ❑ Additional Reading from Book Lists (page 43, TG)
- ❑ For Further Study Younger Student Adaptations (page 78, TG)
- ❑ Family Activity Ideas (page 20, TG)

UNIT THREE
Resources

Project Possibilities

1. Have your student(s) choose a biography of one or more of these key figures from the period of revolution.

    - Abigail Adams
    - John Adams
    - Sam Adams
    - Ethan Allen
    - Benedict Arnold
    - George Rogers Clark
    - Benjamin Franklin
    - Nathanael Greene
    - Nathan Hale
    - John Hancock
    - Patrick Henry
    - Thomas Jefferson
    - John Paul Jones
    - Henry Knox
    - Marquis de Lafayette
    - Thomas Paine
    - Molly Pitcher
    - Paul Revere
    - Betsy Ross
    - Baron von Steuben
    - George Washington
    - Martha Washington

    Your student(s) should decide how the key figure's childhood and life experiences prepared that individual for the contributions that he or she made to the war effort.

2. Have your student(s) pick one or more works of historical fiction to read from the Unit Three Book List.

3. Have your student(s) select one or more creative writing projects related to the information you learn concerning the period of revolution. Projects include writing a poem about a war leader or a battle, a journal entry from a day in the life of a member of the Sons of Liberty or a soldier fighting in the field, a newspaper article or a script for a TV news report describing a battle, or a drama depicting a meeting of the Continental Congress or another significant event in the war.

    The drama could be performed for an audience or the TV news report could be performed and videotaped.

    Your student(s) can also illustrate the writing project or make a mural depicting one of the battles of the American Revolution or the various phases of fighting in the war (war in the North, war in the South, war in the West).

4. Have your student(s) compile an American Revolution Battles Notebook. There are forms in the optional forms section of the *Student Activity Book* to use to do this. If possible, plan a trip to visit a battle site. If you live in or visit a state that was one of the original thirteen colonies, go to a cemetery and see if you can find a grave dating back to the American Revolution. Also look for houses or buildings from this period in history. Take a tour if you can.

5. If you began an African American Notebook in Unit Two, add a page to the notebook about Crispus Attucks when you study Lesson 19.

Book List Reminder

See the annotated bibliography in Section Three.

Timeline Dates

As you study each important event in the period of revolution or the Steps to War, record the dates on a timeline.

- 1754 – 1763: French and Indian War (Lesson 17)
- 1763: Proclamation of 1763 and Enforcement of Navigation Acts (Lesson 18)
- 1764: Sugar Act and the Quartering Act (Lesson 18)
- 1765: Stamp Act (Lesson 18)
- 1767: Townshend Acts (Lesson 18)
- 1770: Boston Massacre (Lesson 19)
- 1772: Burning of the *Gaspee* and the Committees of Correspondence (Lesson 19)
- 1773: Tea Act and the Boston Tea Party (Lesson 19)
- 1774: Intolerable Acts and the First Continental Congress (Lesson 19)
- 1775 – 1781: Revolutionary War (Lesson 20 – 24)
- 1776: Declaration of Independence (Lesson 21)
- 1777 – 1781: Articles of Confederation (Lesson 22)
- 1783: Treaty of Paris (Lesson 24)

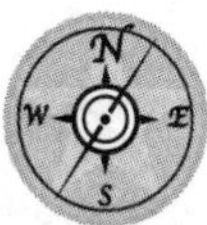

Mapmaking Reminder

Directions for completing the map forms can be found in Section Four of this *Teacher's Guide*.

Colonial Hall of Fame

The images required to complete these forms are the same images used in the *Student Reader*. For help in visual identification, I have included the lesson numbers in the squares.

Review Games

For long-term usage and durability, you may wish to either photocopy the images onto cardstock or glue them to a piece of poster board before cutting them out. All of the images, icons, and flags from the *Student Activity Book* have been included in this book for your use.

1. Cut out the twelve Steps to War. See if your student(s) can remember all the steps in chronological order, laying them out one by one.

2. Locate the descriptions of individuals from the Colonial Hall of Fame in the Unit Three Final Review. Make a copy of the descriptions. Cut out each description that has a matching picture in the Colonial Hall of Fame. Glue the descriptions to one side of an index card. Write the person's name and glue their pictures to the other and use them as flash cards for review. This review can be done during all of the lessons of Unit Three. Just keep adding pictures of individuals and descriptions to your collection of flash cards as you study them each week.

Family Activity Ideas

Lesson 17

- Build a fort with chairs, sheets, and pillows. What do you think would have been inside the forts used by the British and the French at the time of the French and Indian War?

- The French had a huge impact on North American culture. If you know someone who speaks French, ask them to teach you to count and to say a few phrases in French. You also may try listening to French language tapes from your library.

Lesson 18

- Daniel Boone was a great outdoorsman. Using your observation skills and a field guide to trees or animals in your area, try to identify at least six different types of trees or plants in your neighborhood. Next try your hand at animals or insects.

- Visit a zoo. What kinds of animals might Daniel Boone have seen in the wilderness?

Lesson 19

- Watch the movie *Johnny Tremain*, based on the book of the same title. Which part of the story do you like best? Why?

- Act out a famous scene from the Revolutionary War period or give a speech like Patrick Henry.

Lesson 20

- Many craftsmen or tradesmen were providing essential items and services during the Revolutionary War period. Blacksmiths, printers, carpenters, hatters, millers, silversmiths, wheelwrights, coopers, shoemakers, and candle and soap makers were just a few. Young people often served as apprentices to these experienced men. Where do we see craftsmen teaching others in the Bible? One example is found in Genesis 4:22, which tells us that Tubal-Cain was "an instructor of every craftsman in bronze and iron."

- Choose one or more of the occupations in question 1, find out more about them, and then try your hand at them. For example, dip candles, grind grain, make soap bars, simulate early printing techniques using cardboard or Styrofoam, or make faux silverware using modeling clay and aluminum foil. There are many books and websites with ideas and directions. It would be fun to make several crafts and set up a display table with little cards explaining each item that you made.

Lesson 21

- Spies date back even to Bible times. Read the exciting spy story found in Joshua, chapter two. There are many fascinating stories about spies during the Revolutionary War. Some of the methods that they used for sending messages included secret codes, invisible ink, and letters hidden in quills or buttons. Make a secret message to send to a friend or relative. Use this simple method for making invisible ink:

    - Squeeze a couple of lemons to obtain their juice, or use bottled lemon juice.
    - Use the juice as ink by applying it to a paintbrush or cotton swab and writing on paper.
    - Allow the paper to dry.
    - To read your invisible message, hold the paper up to a (non-halogen) light bulb. The heat will cause the writing to darken to a pale brown so the message can be seen.

- Ben Franklin had his own newspaper, the *Pennsylvania Gazette*. Make your own newspaper, using all the family's news from the day.

Lesson 22

- Does your family, school, or church fly a flag? Learn more about the protocol of raising, lowering, and storing a flag. Try making your own U.S. flag. Look at a picture of the flag to see exactly where the stars and stripes are placed.

- Learn these flag terms:

    - canton
    - field
    - fly
    - hoist
    - halyard

Lesson 23

- Watch the movie *Spy Kids* (rated PG) or *20,000 Leagues under the Sea* (rated G). Talk about the difference between their submarines and the *Turtle.*

Lesson 24

- In 1782 the Second Continental Congress officially adopted the bald eagle as the national symbol of the United States. Although many other nations used the great eagle, the bald eagle was chosen because it is the only eagle exclusive to North America and because of its size, long life, power, and spirit of freedom. However, Benjamin Franklin argued against the decision, calling the eagle a "bird of bad moral character..." Which bird did Franklin prefer? The wild turkey! Look for a picture of a bald eagle. Draw it or model one out of clay. How many different U.S. coins can you find that contain the image of the eagle?

UNIT THREE
Checklist

Please Note:
SR = *Student Reader*
SAB = *Student Activity Book*
TG = *Teacher's Guide*

Required for Lesson 17
- ❑ Lesson 17 (page 207, SR)
- ❑ Corresponding Required Form (page 139, SAB)
- ❑ Corresponding Map (page 140, SAB)
- ❑ For Review questions (page 141, SAB)

Optional for Lesson 17
- ❑ For Further Study projects (page 145, SAB)
- ❑ Additional Options for Unit (page 26, TG)

Required for Lesson 18
- ❑ Lesson 18 (page 217, SR)
- ❑ Corresponding Required Form (page 147, SAB)
- ❑ For Review questions (page 149, SAB)

Optional for Lesson 18
- ❑ For Further Study projects (page 150, SAB)
- ❑ Additional Options for Unit (page 26, TG)

Required for Lesson 19
- ❑ Lesson 19 (page 225, SR)
- ❑ Corresponding Required Form (page 153, SAB)
- ❑ For Review questions (page 155, SAB)

Optional for Lesson 19
- ❑ For Further Study projects (page 157, SAB)
- ❑ Additional Options for Unit (page 26, TG)

Required for Lesson 20
- ❑ Lesson 20 (page 237, SR)
- ❑ Corresponding Required Form (page 159, SAB)
- ❑ Corresponding Map (page 160, SAB)
- ❑ For Review questions (page 161, SAB)

Optional for Lesson 20
- ❑ For Further Study projects (page 164, SAB)
- ❑ Additional Options for Unit (page 26, TG)

Required for Lesson 21
- ❑ Lesson 21 (page 249, SR)
- ❑ Corresponding Required Form (page 165, SAB)
- ❑ Corresponding Map (page 166, SAB)
- ❑ For Review questions (page 167, SAB)

Optional for Lesson 21
- ❑ For Further Study projects (page 168, SAB)
- ❑ Additional Options for Unit (page 26, TG)

Required for Lesson 22
- ❑ Lesson 22 (page 261, SR)
- ❑ Corresponding Required Form (page 171, SAB)
- ❑ Corresponding Map (page 172, SAB)
- ❑ For Review questions (page 173, SAB)

Optional for Lesson 22
- ❑ For Further Study projects (page 175, SAB)
- ❑ Additional Options for Unit (page 26, TG)

Required for Lesson 23
- ❑ Lesson 23 (page 275, SR)
- ❑ Corresponding Required Form (page 177, SAB)
- ❑ Corresponding Map (page 178, SAB)
- ❑ For Review questions (page 179, SAB)

Optional for Lesson 23

- ❑ For Further Study projects (page 182, SAB)
- ❑ Additional Options for Unit (page 26, TG)

Required for Lesson 24

- ❑ Lesson 24 (page 287, SR)
- ❑ Corresponding Required Form (page 183, SAB)
- ❑ Corresponding Map (page 184, SAB)
- ❑ For Review questions (page 185, SAB)

Optional for Lesson 24

- ❑ For Further Study projects (page 186, SAB)
- ❑ Additional Options for Unit (page 26, TG)

Required for Unit Three

- ❑ Final Review (page 189, SAB)

Additional Options for Unit

- ❑ Project Possibilities (page 26, TG)
- ❑ Timeline Dates (page 27, TG)
- ❑ Optional Map Review (page 63, TG)
- ❑ Review Games (page 27, TG)
- ❑ Additional Reading from Book Lists (page 47, TG)
- ❑ For Further Study Younger Student Adaptations (page 92, TG)
- ❑ Family Activity Ideas (page 27, TG)

UNIT FOUR
Resources

Project Possibilities

1. Have your student(s) choose a biography of one or more of these important political and military leaders from the period of establishment and expansion.

    - George Washington
    - John Adams
    - Thomas Jefferson
    - James Madison
    - James Monroe
    - John Quincy Adams
    - Andrew Jackson
    - Martin Van Buren
    - William Henry Harrison
    - John Tyler
    - James Polk
    - Alexander Hamilton
    - John Marshall
    - Meriwether Lewis
    - William Clark
    - John C. Calhoun
    - Henry Clay
    - Daniel Webster
    - "Mad" Anthony Wayne
    - Winfield Scott
    - Zachary Taylor
    - Francis Scott Key

    Or the student(s) could conduct research online. Ask your student(s) to make a list of the leader's contributions and decide how his or her childhood and life experiences prepared this individual for the contributions that he or she made to the establishment and/or expansion of the new American nation.

2. Have your student(s) pick one or more works of historical fiction to read from the Unit Four Book List.

3. Have your student(s) select one or more creative writing projects related to the information you learn concerning the period of establishment and expansion. Projects include writing a poem about a president or a military leader, a journal entry from a day in the life of a president or a military leader, a newspaper article or a script for a TV news report describing an important event in a president's administration or a battle during the War of 1812 or the Mexican War, or a drama depicting the events of the Constitutional Convention, the War of 1812, or the Mexican War.

    The drama could be performed for an audience or the TV news report could be performed and videotaped.

    Your student(s) can also illustrate the writing project or make a mural depicting battles of the War of 1812 or the Mexican War or one of the presidents' administrations.

4. Visit online or in person some of the important historical sites in Washington, D.C. — the U.S. Capitol and Mall, the White House, and the U.S. Supreme Court. You could also visit the National Archives and see the charter documents of the United States.

5. If you have chosen to put together a Native American Notebook, pages could be added to this notebook while studying Lessons 28 and 29 of Unit Four.

6. If you have been keeping an African American Notebook, add pages to the notebook when you do the For Further Study projects on Benjamin Banneker in Lesson 26 and Jim Beckwourth in Lesson 29.

Book List Reminder

See the annotated bibliography in Section Three.

Timeline Dates

As you study the period of establishment and expansion, record the following dates on a timeline.

- 1785 – 1786: Mt. Vernon & Annapolis Conferences (Lesson 25)
- 1786 – 1787: Shays Rebellion (Lesson 25)
- 1787: Constitutional Convention (Lesson 25)
- 1789 – 1797:George Washington (Lesson 26)
- 1797 – 1801: John Adams (Lesson 26)
- 1801 – 1809: Thomas Jefferson (Lesson 26)
- 1803: Louisiana Purchase (Lesson 26)
- 1809 – 1817: James Madison (Lesson 26)
- 1812 – 1814: War of 1812 (Lesson 27)
- 1817 – 1825: James Monroe (Lesson 26)
- 1825 – 1829: John Q. Adams (Lesson 28)
- 1829 – 1837: Andrew Jackson (Lesson 28)
- 1837 – 1841: Martin Van Buren (Lesson 28)
- 1841: William Henry Harrison (Lesson 28)
- 1841 – 1845: John Tyler (Lesson 28)
- 1845 – 1849: James Polk (Lesson 28)
- 1846 – 1848: Mexican War (Lesson 29)

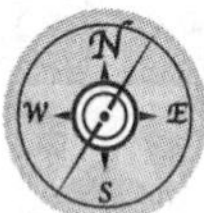

Mapmaking Reminder

Directions for completing the map forms can be found in Section Four of this *Teacher's Guide*.

Review Games

For long-term usage and durability, you may wish to either photocopy the images onto cardstock or glue them to a piece of poster board before cutting them out. All of the images, icons, and flags from the *Student Activity Book* have been included in this book for your use.

1. Cut out a picture of each of the first eleven presidents. Photocopy the list of important events that occurred during their administrations from the Unit Four Final Review and cut out each description. See if your student(s) can correctly match the events with the presidents' pictures.

2. Have your student(s) practice putting the pictures of the presidents in chronological order according to when they served their term(s) in office.

Family Activity Ideas

Lesson 25

- Read the book *George Washington's Breakfast* by Jean Fritz. Try preparing what George Washington ate for breakfast.

- Talk about how the Constitution gave a group of thirteen states a way to work together. Make your own home or family constitution with rules that might help everyone get along better. Write your constitution on a piece of poster board and hang it where everyone can see it! Example: We the students of the Rakes Homeschool, in order to have a more perfect class, promise to work together to become a united team. We will respect each other, being considerate of other people's feelings and their property. We will always be cooperative and polite, listen carefully to others and their ideas, and praise others for their accomplishments. When asked, we will work quietly and independently, thoroughly completing our work. We will actively participate in our lessons and work cooperatively with our teacher. We pledge to do whatever we can to make our year a success and will always try our hardest to be the best we can possibly be!

Lesson 26

- Plan your own expedition to explore the "unknown territories" of a local park. When Thomas Jefferson dispatched Lewis and Clark to explore the uncharted West, he believed they would encounter woolly mammoths, volcanoes, and a mountain of salt. What do you think you will discover on your expedition? Bring a journal or camera along so that you can record your discoveries — people, animals, and terrain. Pack a lunch; your journey might be long!

- Think about Sacagawea and her son. How might she have taken care of him on the long journey? Take a trip to your local bank to get one of the golden dollar coins with Sacagawea on it.

Lesson 27

- Andrew Jackson's face is a very familiar one that we might see several times a week. Where do we see it so often? On a twenty-dollar bill! Find a twenty-dollar bill, and draw a portrait of Andrew Jackson using the bill as a guide.

Lesson 28

- Think about a disagreement you've had with a friend. How did it turn out? Did one of you win, or were you both able to talk about what you wanted and come to a compromise? What does the Bible tell us about friends? Look up and discuss Proverbs 6:3, 17:9, 17:17, and 18:24

- Visit your local department of elections. Ask if you can look inside a voting booth, and see if they have educational information on the elections process.

Lesson 29

- Try one or more of these Oregon Trail activities.
    - Take a map of the U.S. and map out the Oregon Trail using pins, colored pencils, flags, and so forth.
    - Set up an area in a corner of your house that you designate to be a wagon and/or campfire. You can make a pretend fire by covering paper towel tubes with brown paper to be the logs and using orange and red crepe paper as the fire. Sit around the campfire on pillows and tell stories to each other. Or camp out!
    - Watch the movie *Seven Alone*, a fictionalized account of the true story of the Sager children's amazing journey on the Oregon Trail. Or read aloud the book on which the movie was based, *On to Oregon* by Honore Morrow.
    - Play the "Oregon Trail" computer game.

Lesson 30

- Visit a railroad station or maybe even take a train ride. Talk about what the railroad cars might have carried in the first half of the nineteenth century. What would it have been like to sleep in a passenger car?

Lesson 31

- Make a *McGuffey Reader* of your own. Write out the alphabet, and pick a word that starts with each letter of the alphabet. Illustrate each word.

- Open a dictionary at random. Have fun picking out a few interesting words on each page and reading them. Discuss how difficult it must have been to develop a dictionary! Work on your dictionary skills.

Lesson 32

- Use building blocks or clay, and make a model of a building in either the Greek Revival or Federal architectural styles.

- Read the story of Rip Van Winkle. Imagine what things might change if you fell asleep.

UNIT FOUR
Checklist

Please Note:

SR = *Student Reader*
SAB = *Student Activity Book*
TG = *Teacher's Guide*

Required for Lesson 25

- ❑ Lesson 25 (page 301, SR)
- ❑ Corresponding Required Form (page 195, SAB)
- ❑ Corresponding Map (page 196, SAB)
- ❑ For Review questions (page 197, SAB)

Optional for Lesson 25

- ❑ For Further Study projects (page 198, SAB)
- ❑ Additional Options for Unit (page 32, TG)

Required for Lesson 26

- ❑ Lesson 26 (page 311, SR)
- ❑ Corresponding Required Forms (pages 199, 201, 203, 205, & 207, SAB)
- ❑ Corresponding Maps (pages 200, 202, 204, 206, & 208, SAB)
- ❑ For Review questions (page 209, SAB)

Optional for Lesson 26

- ❑ For Further Study projects (page 211, SAB)
- ❑ Additional Options for Unit (page 32, TG)

Required for Lesson 27

- ❑ Lesson 27 (page 325, SR)
- ❑ Corresponding Required Form (page 213, SAB)
- ❑ Corresponding Map (page 214, SAB)
- ❑ For Review questions (page 215, SAB)

Optional for Lesson 27

- ❑ For Further Study projects (page 218, SAB)
- ❑ Additional Options for Unit (page 32, TG)

Required for Lesson 28

- ❑ Lesson 28 (page 337, SR)
- ❑ Corresponding Required Forms (pages 219, 221, 223, 225, 227, & 229, SAB)
- ❑ Corresponding Maps (pages 220, 222, 224, 226, 228, & 230, SAB)
- ❑ For Review questions (page 231, SAB)

Optional for Lesson 28

- ❑ For Further Study projects (page 233, SAB)
- ❑ Additional Options for Unit (page 32, TG)

Required for Lesson 29

- ❑ Lesson 29 (page 351, SR)
- ❑ Corresponding Required Form (page 235, SAB)
- ❑ Corresponding Map (page 236, SAB)
- ❑ For Review questions (page 237, SAB)

Optional for Lesson 29

- ❑ For Further Study projects (page 241, SAB)
- ❑ Additional Options for Unit (page 32, TG)

Required for Lesson 30

- ❑ Lesson 30 (page 363, SR)
- ❑ Corresponding Required Form (page 243, SAB)
- ❑ For Review questions (page 245, SAB)

Optional for Lesson 30

- ❑ For Further Study projects (page 247, SAB)
- ❑ Additional Options for Unit (page 32, TG)

Required for Lesson 31

- ❑ Lesson 31 (page 373, SR)
- ❑ Corresponding Required Form (page 249, SAB)
- ❑ Corresponding Map (page 250, SAB)
- ❑ For Review questions (page 251, SAB)

Optional for Lesson 31

- ❑ For Further Study projects (page 253, SAB)
- ❑ Additional Options for Unit (page 32, TG)

Required for Lesson 32

- ❑ Lesson 32 (page 385, SR)
- ❑ Corresponding Required Form (page 255, SAB)
- ❑ For Review questions (page 257, SAB)

Optional for Lesson 32

- ❑ For Further Study projects (page 260, SAB)
- ❑ Additional Options for Unit (page 32, TG)

Required for Unit Four

- ❑ Final Review (page 261, SAB)

Additional Options for Unit

- ❑ Project Possibilities (page 32, TG)
- ❑ Timeline Dates (page 33, TG)
- ❑ Optional Map Review (page 65, TG)
- ❑ Review Games (page 33, TG)
- ❑ Additional Reading from Book Lists (page 51, TG)
- ❑ For Further Study Younger Student Adaptations (page 105, TG)
- ❑ Family Activity Ideas (page 33, TG)

Section Three

BOOK LISTS

UNIT ONE
Book List

Primary (K–4)

Eyewitness: Viking by Susan M. Margeson and Peter Anderson. Part of the Dorling Kindersley Eyewitness series. The vivid photographs and illustrations add to the appeal of this fact-filled guide to the Viking Age.

Viking Invader by Paul Dowswell. This newspaper-style presentation is packed full of information about the Vikings, including maps, pictures, and fun facts. Part of the Newspaper Histories Series.

Around the World in a Hundred Years: From Henry the Navigator to Magellan by Jean Fritz. With her trademark humor, Jean Fritz takes us back to the age of exploration by looking at ten explorers with a thirst for adventure.

Leif the Lucky and *Columbus* by Ingri and Edgar d'Aulaire. In these two books, the stories of these legendary explorers come to life though beautiful color illustrations and intriguing text. Both are great read alouds.

Christopher Columbus (Step-Into-Reading, Step 3) by Stephen Krensky. A book for students in grades 1 – 3 to try and read on their own. Through colorful illustrations and simple text, students learn about the famous explorer.

Meet Christopher Columbus (Landmark Books) by James T. DeKay and John Edens. The story of Columbus and his voyages written in an easy-to-read format.

Christopher Columbus by Peter and Connie Roop. A Scholastic publication, this story of Columbus's life is told using excerpts from his journals.

Middle (5–8)

The Story of Rolf and the Viking Bow (Bethlehem Books) by Allen French. This tale of Iceland, told in the classic saga form, is an exciting story of Christian versus pagan values, forgiveness versus pride. Gives great insight into the Viking way of life. A great read! (Includes some witchcraft.)

The Viking Raiders by Anne Civardi. Part of the Usbourne Time Traveler series, the vivid pictures and interesting text take you back to Viking times.

The Usborne Book of Explorers by F. Everett and S. Reid. An excellent overview of the explorers starting with the early navigators of the 1400s. Suitable for students in grades 5 and up.

Exploration and Conquest: The Americas after Columbus: 1500 – 1620 by Betsy Maestro. An excellent overview of explorers to the new world after Columbus. This book not only discusses the explorers but also the effect of the exploration on the native peoples.

Marco Polo: A Journey through China by Fiona MacDonald. With detailed, colorful illustrations and small text bits, this book is packed with lifestyle and cultural details of the areas Marco Polo traveled through. It's one of the Expedition book series.

Magellan: A Voyage around the World by Fiona MacDonald. Follow Magellan on his first voyage around the world as you read this book. Another in the Expedition book series, this book introduces you to the cultures he encountered and the hardships he endured.

Explorers Who Got Lost by Diane Sansevere-Dreher. With dozens of drawings, maps, diagrams of ships, and pictures of navigational equipment, this book provides a fascinating look at the unintentional discoveries of eight explorers including Columbus, Dias, and Cabot.

Pedro's Journal: A Voyage with Christopher Columbus August 3, 1492 – February 14, 1493 by Pam Conrad. This Scholastic book is the engaging diary of a young man looking for adventure on the high seas. Hired by Columbus because he could read and write, students follow his adventures with the famous explorer.

History Pockets: Explorers of North America by Mike Graf & Kathleen McFarren, Evan-Moor Educational Publishers. This book is full of great hands-on activities. For those of you who enjoy making Lap Books™, include these activities in your lap book instead of the suggested pockets.

Discovery and Exploration. One of many games in the Learningames History Series by Educational Materials Associates, Inc. Facts, geography, and historical information is learned through fun and play. Designed for up to six players ages 8 and up. Check out www.emagame.com.

A Long and Uncertain Journey: The 27,000 Mile Voyage of Vasco Da Gama by Joan Elizabeth Goodman. Part of the Great Explorers Books series. Watercolor illustrations lead you through this exciting voyage to China. The 27,000 mile trip around the bottom of Africa was filled with danger, cruelty, and courage.

Beyond the Sea of Ice: The Voyages of Henry Hudson by Joan Elizabeth Goodman. Another in the Great Explorers Books series with a fold out map of the four voyages of Henry Hudson, this book provides interesting information about the events of each voyage.

Flint's Island by Leonard Wibberley. The adventures of Long John Silver and his search for pirate treasure.

The Swiss Family Robinson by Jonathan David Wyss. Imagine being shipwrecked on a deserted island? How would you survive? This adventurous story tells the tale of a minister and his family who draw on their resourcefulness and ingenuity to survive in paradise.

Secondary (9 and up)

Great American Statesmen and Heroes by Catherine Millard. Extremely readable, well-documented collection of short biographies from Christopher Columbus to Sam Houston. Filled with drawings and excerpts from primary source documents.

The Travels of Marco Polo by Marco Polo, translated by R. E. Latham. In this Penguin Classic book, read the incredible tales of this world traveler. Here you will read in detail about the sites and the people he meets along the way from Europe to India and China.

The Journals of Captain Cook by James Cook, selected and edited by Philip Edwards. Another Penguin Classic, this abridged version of the famous captain's journal provides detailed, first-hand accounts of three amazing adventures.

Christopher Columbus: The Four Voyages translated by J. M. Cohen and published by Penguin Classics. Using Columbus's own letters and log book, the letters of his contemporaries, and a biography of Columbus's son, Cohen has written an engaging story of Columbus's voyages and interesting insights into the man he was.

By Right of Conquest by G. A. Henty. Hernando Cortés (Cortez) led the Spanish campaign against the Aztec Empire in Mexico. Throughout these pages, students will read the adventures of Roger Hawkshaw. After being shipwrecked, Roger joins with Cortés (Cortez) in his conquest of Mexico. Please note that Henty uses vivid imagery in describing the barbarism of the Aztecs and Spaniards.

Under Drake's Flag by G. A. Henty. Sir Francis Drake was one of the most notorious seamen of his time. Ned Hearne is an Englishman who accompanies Drake's crew on many intriguing adventures, including the defeat of the Spanish Armada.

Treasure Island by Robert Louis Stevenson. If you're ready for swaschbuckling adventure, this book is for you. A classic story of pirates, sailing ships, and buried treasure that captivates the reader. There are many abridged versions of this book that would be appropriate for younger students.

Robinson Crusoe by Daniel Defoe. Shipwrecked on a Caribbean island for over thirty years, we witness struggles with nature, savages, and one's own inner darkness. Yet strength through these struggles builds admirable character.

UNIT TWO
Book List

Primary (K–4)

On the Mayflower by Kate Waters. Photographed in full color on board the *Mayflower II*, this is a dramatic portrayal of the voyage of 1620. Part of a series of books done in conjunction with Plymouth Plantation; they are very historically accurate.

Sarah Morton's Day and *Samuel Eaton's Day* by Kate Waters. These two books are perfect for your youngest students. They both provide an accurate look at a day in the life of a pilgrim girl and boy.

Three Ships Come Sailing by Gilchrist Waring. A young child's story of our country's birthplace, the settlement at Jamestown in Virginia.

Three Young Pilgrims by Cheryl Harness. When Bartholemew, Mary Allen, and Remember arrived in the New World, they never imagined life would be so hard. Beautiful illustrations add to the appeal of this book.

The If You… series for young students is published by Scholastic. These delightful books give readers an understanding of daily life for each period of history. The illustrations are colorful and often add humor to the text — *If You Sailed on the Mayflower in 1620* and *If You Lived in Colonial Times.*

Eating the Plates: A Pilgrim Book of Food and Manners by Lucille Recht Penner. From their trip on the *Mayflower* to their settlement at Plymouth, the author gives you a glimpse of what the pilgrims ate to survive. Their quest for food was ongoing and often distasteful. Here we get a picture of daily pilgrim life through food: what they ate, how they acquired it, raised it, prepared it, and served it. A "Pilgrim Menu" is included in the back.

Pocahontas and the Stranger by Clyde Robert Bulla. A re-telling of the story of the Indian princess who befriended the colonists and saved Captain John Smith's life.

Pocahontas by Ingri and Edgar d'Aulaire. Another in the series of outstanding biographies from the d'Aulaires. Full of beautiful illustrations, interesting text, and facts about this well-known Indian princess.

The Courage of Sarah Noble by Alice Dagliesh. Eight-year-old Sarah journeys into the wilderness with her father and ends up living alone with Indians. Based on a true story.

The Matchlock Gun by Walter D. Edmonds. In 1756, New York was still a British colony, and the French and Indians were constant threats to Edward and his family. When Edward's father was called away to watch for a raid from the north, only Edward was left to protect his mother and sister.

The Cabin Faced West by Jean Fritz. Anne is lonely when her family moves to the Pennsylvania frontier until a special evening when a stranger comes to dinner.

The Thanksgiving Story by Alice Dalgliesh. A Caldecott Honor book, this book tells the tale of the voyage on the *Mayflower*, the settlement at Plymouth, and the first Thanksgiving Day celebration.

Middle (5–8)

The Mayflower Secret by Dave and Neta Jackson. In this Trailblazer book, thirteen-year-old Elizabeth Tilly and her family are leaving England for the New World. Join in the adventure of their ocean crossing and settling in the new colony.

Our Strange New Land: Elizabeth's Jamestown Colony Diary by Patricia Hermes. Part of the My America series, this book is written in a diary format. The stories draw you in as Elizabeth explains her family's hardships as they settle in the first English colony in the New World, Jamestown. Students will get a vivid picture of life in the Jamestown colony.

The Starving Time: Elizabeth's Diary, Book Two, Jamestown, Virginia, 1690 by Patricia Hermes. As the title mentions, this is a continuation of Elizabeth's diary. Here we see the colony continuing to suffer through disease and lack of food. Elizabeth remains brave and hopes that her brother will arrive soon.

Squanto, Friend of the Pilgrims by Clyde Robert Bulla. This Scholastic biography tells how Squanto went across the great sea, only to return and find his family and village gone. However, he finds that new people, the Pilgrims, have come across the great sea.

The Double Life of Pocahontas by Jean Fritz. Here we read what happened after Pocahontas saved John Smith's life. Her marriage to an Englishman and her travels to England and Europe fill the pages of this well-told story.

Pilgrim Voices: Our First Year in the New World by Connie and Peter Roop. Based on the Pilgrim's own journals, this is an exciting and dramatic account of their voyage on the *Mayflower*, settling the land, meeting the Indians, enduring the hardships of illness and hunger through the winter, and more.

The Sign of the Beaver by Elizabeth Speare. This Newbery Award-winning book is about a young white boy who is lost in the Maine wilderness and finds himself rescued by an Indian chief.

The Witch of Blackbird Pond by Elizabeth Speare. A girl who was raised in luxury in the Caribbean struggles to adjust to Puritan New England.

Hostage on the Nighthawk, *Introducing William Penn* by Dave and Neta Jackson. Another exciting book in the Trailblazer series. This one finds young Theodore Story sailing to America with Governor William Penn. With yellow fever spreading around the ship, will they make it to America?

Amos Fortune: Free Man by Elizabeth Yates. This Newbery Award book tells the story of a young man born the son of a king in Africa, who is captured by slave traders and then works as a slave in colonial Massachusetts. Through all of this, his dream of freedom never dies.

Calico Captive by Elizabeth George Speare. It's 1754, and teenager Miriam Willard and her family are captured by Indians and forced to travel north to Montreal. The family is separated and sold into slavery. Miriam becomes a servant to the wealthy Du Quense family. Will she ever be reunited with her family?

Struggle for a Continent: The French and Indian Wars 1689 – 1763 by Betsy and Giulio Maestro. By the mid-1600s, England, France, Spain, and the Netherlands all had settlements in the New World, and all had hopes of acquiring more territory. Maps and illustrations throughout the book enhance your understanding of these conflicts.

The Warrior's Challenge by Dave and Neta Jackson. You'll go back to Pennsylvania in 1772, as a group of Moravian Indians are forced to move west. Along the way, they are spotted by Mohegan warriors. This is the story of two young boys making this journey.

History Pockets: Colonial America by Mike Graf & Kathleen McFarren, Evan-Moor Educational Publishers. This book is full of great hands-on activities. For those of you who enjoy making lap books, include these activities in your Lap Book™ instead of the suggested pockets.

Secondary (9 and up)

The Light and the Glory by Peter Marshall and David Manuel. This book is full of short stories that tell of God's divine plan and intervention in our nation's history. This volume begins with Columbus's voyages and takes you through American colonization, the Great Awakening, the Declaration of Independence, the Revolutionary War, and finally the signing of the U.S. Constitution.

Of Plymouth Plantation by William Bradford, published by Vision Forum. This is a firsthand account chronicled by Governor William Bradford. Learn why they left Europe and about the hardships endured in the journey to settle the New World.

Mourt's Relation: A Journal of the Pilgrims at Plymouth edited by Dwight Heath. Originally printed in 1622 under the title *A Relationship or Journal of the English Plantation settled at Plymouth*, this was the first written account of the Pilgrims' first year in the New World. Written to attract more Europeans to join them, it leaves out the difficulties faced during that first year. Despite that, it provides wonderful insight into daily pilgrim life.

With Wolfe in Canada by G. A. Henty. After a series of misfortunes, including the loss of his father, James Walsham leaves England. As a British soldier in America, he battles the French in the French and Indian War under General Wolfe.

Duel in the Wilderness by Karin Clafford Farley. Based on Washington's own journal, this book tells the true story of Major George Washington's journey in 1753 – 1754 to deliver a message from the King of England to the French commander in the Ohio wilderness.

Forgotten Founding Father: The Heroic Leadership of George Whitefield by Stephen Mansfield. After building a reputation as a fine preacher in Europe, Whitefield came to the American colonies where he preached to crowds throughout the colonies. His preaching was instrumental in the Great Awakening of the 1700s.

Jonathan Edwards: A New Biography by Iain Murray. This detailed study of Edwards's life and theological convictions is all-encompassing — from his childhood and salvation experience to his contributions in the Great Awakening and his service at Princeton University.

The Scarlett Letter by Nathaniel Hawthorne. Hester Prynne, a Puritan, was guilty of adultery, which resulted in the birth of a child. Her 1642 community spares her life, but they condemn her to wear a scarlet letter *A* on her dress for the rest of her life. How will she and the child bear the humiliation?

The Last of the Mohicans by James Fenimore Cooper. This American classic is set in upstate New York during the French and Indian War and is a rich, historical story of adventure and heroism. Please note there are graphic descriptions of the conflict, especially the attack on Fort William Henry.

UNIT THREE
Book List

Primary (K–4)

The If You... series for young students is published by Scholastic. These delightful books give readers an understanding of daily life for each period of history. The illustrations are colorful and often add humor to the text — *If You Lived at the Time of the American Revolution, If You Grew Up with George Washington,* and *If You Were There When They Signed the Constitution.*

The Fourth of July Story by Alice Dagliesh. This story takes its young readers back to the colonist's desire for freedom and the Declaration of Independence.

American History Series by Jean Fritz. These stories, written by the award-winning author Jean Fritz are entertaining, informative, and make history come alive. All are suitable for students up to grade six. *And Then What Happened, Paul Revere?* The background and story of Paul Revere's famous ride. *Can You Make Them Behave, King George?* An interesting and informative look at King George III, ruler at the time of the American Revolution. *What's the Big Idea, Ben Franklin?* An entertaining look at the intriguing life and personality of Benjamin Franklin. *George Washington's Breakfast.* Lots of fun facts are revealed as young George Washington Allen goes on a quest to find out what his namesake ate for breakfast. *Where Was Patrick Henry on the Twenty-Ninth of May?* An interesting look at the life of Patrick Henry from his days as a planter to statesman. *Why Don't You Get a Horse, Sam Adams?* A humorous look at the life of Samuel Adams. *Will You Sign Here, John Hancock?* The story of a young man who became the richest man in New England and the first signer of the Declaration of Independence. *Shh! We're Writing the Constitution.* An informative and interesting account of the Constitutional Convention of 1787.

History Maker Bios published by Barnes and Noble. This series looks at the lives of people who changed our history. These books are filled with vivid illustrations, photographs, and timelines — *John Hancock* and *George Washington* by Candice Ransom, *Benjamin Franklin* and *Thomas Jefferson* by Victoria Sherrow, *Lewis & Clark* by Candice Ransom, *Andrew Jackson* by Carol H. Behrman, *Dolley Madison* by Jean L. S. Patrick, and *Davy Crockett* by Elaine Marie Alphin.

Benjamin Franklin and *George Washington* by Ingri and Edgar d'Aulaire. The d'Aulaires have received many awards for their work, and it's easy to see why. Full of facts, these books are the perfect way to introduce your young students to the first ambassador and the first president of the United States.

The Felicity series from American Girl Books is set in Williamsburg, Virginia, around 1774. The stories are entertaining, and in the back of each book is a Looking Back section where they take a look at the historical events and customs of the times. The Looking Back section is also filled with photographs and illustrations which bring these facts to life. Suitable for ages seven and up. There are six books in the Felicity series: *Meet*

Felicity; Felicity Learns a Lesson; Felicity's Surprise; Happy Birthday, Felicity!; Felicity Saves the Day; and *Changes for Felicity.*

Middle (5–8)

Childhood of Famous Americans series published by Aladdin paperbacks. These stories are engaging and well-illustrated biographies of famous Americans from our early history. They are suitable for students ages 9 – 12. *Daniel Boone: Young Hunter and Tracker* by Augusta Stevenson; *Paul Revere: Boston Patriot* by Augusta Stevenson; *Betsy Ross: Designer of Our Flag* by Ann Weil; and *George Washington: Our First Leader* by Augusta Stevenson.

America's Paul Revere by Esther Forbes. More than just a re-telling of the famous midnight ride, this book tells you about Paul Revere's family, beginning with his parents and detailing his life. Through this you can see where he obtained the values and character that have made him an American legend.

Mr. Revere and I by Robert Lawson. This is the delightful story of the midnight ride of Paul Revere as experienced by his faithful horse.

Ben Franklin of Old Philadelphia by Margaret Cousins. This Landmark book provides an insightful look into the life of this fascinating man.

The Ben Franklin Book of Easy and Incredible Experiments by Cheryl Kirk Noll. A hands-on look at many of Franklin's scientific explorations, including electricity, weather, and musical instruments.

Ben and Me by Robert Lawson. An entertaining account of Ben Franklin's achievements told by a mouse named Amos.

Bunker Hill by Janet Tinney. An account of the life of Dr. Joseph Warren from his time at Harvard through his death at the Battle of Bunker Hill. While somewhat fictionalized, this book is loaded with actual historical facts about the pre-Revolutionary War period. A captivating read!

The American Revolution by Bruce Bliven, Jr. This Landmark Book is an exciting story of the people and events of the Revolution and the hardships endured by the troops.

Revolution Game is part of the Learningames History Series. This fun and informational game from Educational Materials Associates includes background information about the American Revolution, chronologies, statistics, study guides, activities, and more. Designed for up to six players ages 8 and up. Available at www.emagame.com.

A More Perfect Union by Betsy and Giulio Maestro. The unforgettable story of the creation of the U.S. Constitution in 1787.

Carry on, Mr. Bowditch by Jean Lee Latham. Incredible true story of young Nat Bowditch — a mathematical genius who, although denied the college education he wanted, overcame all odds and through perseverance basically rewrote the book on navigation. Inspiring read!

Secondary (9 and up)

Common Sense by Thomas Paine. In January of 1776, Thomas Paine published his pamphlet, *Common Sense*, encouraging his fellow colonists to declare independence from Britain. Within a short time, over 500,000 copies were sold. The persuasive arguments Paine offers here went on to be reflected in our Declaration of Independence.

Paul Revere's Ride by David Hackett Fischer. The title is deceiving, because this is about much more than Paul Revere's legendary ride. We are also given insight into Paul Revere himself — the family man, community leader, craftsman, social activist, and patriot. It gives us an intimate look at Boston's revolutionary movement, and the unforgettable events that followed.

True to the Old Flag by G. A. Henty. This book is particularly interesting, because it is written from the British point of view on the American Revolution. Harold Wilson is a young man from Boston who joins the British army to help put down the colonial rebellion. The story is riveting as it portrays this soldier's struggle.

Johnny Tremain by Esther Forbes. This Newbery Award-winning book is filled with adventure as it tells the story of a young silversmith apprentice who is caught up in the Boston Tea Party and the Battle of Lexington.

A Young Patriot: The American Revolution as Experienced by One Boy by Jim Murphy. Based on the diary of fifteen-year-old Joseph Plumb Martin, we get a firsthand look at events and daily life in the camps. Maps and reproductions are an added bonus to the personal account of the war.

The Real George Washington by Jay A. Parry. Part of the American Classic Series, this book gives you a personal glimpse into the life of George Washington. While the 950 pages may be intimidating, you'll come away with a deeper appreciation for the humble man who became our first president.

George Washington, Spymaster: How the Americans Outspied the British and Won the Revolutionary War by Thomas B. Allen. This is a fascinating look at the mysterious world of double agents, covert spies, and secret codes during the Revolutionary War and includes maps, a war timeline, spy talk, and of course, the secret code.

The Real Thomas Jefferson by Andrew M. Allison. Another book in the American Classic Series. Part I of this book gives you insight into Jefferson the philosopher, architect, scientist, and politician. Part II is a collection of his writings.

The Federalist Papers by Alexander Hamilton, James Madison, and John Jay. In 1787, these articles first appeared in New York newspapers anonymously. They were written to encourage voters to ratify the proposed Constitution of the United States.

The Anti-Federalist Papers and Constitutional Convention Debates by Ralph Ketcham. Not all the founding fathers were in agreement when creation of the Constitution was under consideration. This book provides papers written by Patrick Henry, John DeWitt, and others who posed dissenting opinions. Read this, and you will have a balanced view of both sides on the constitutional debate.

Give Me Liberty: The Uncompromising Statesmanship of Patrick Henry by David Vaughan. Known for the often quoted, "...give me liberty or give me death," most people know little of Henry the man or of his great faith. This book is divided into three sections. The first is about his life, the second gives insight into his views on various virtues, and the last section is a reflection on how Henry is remembered by history.

The Constitution of the United States: An Introduction, Revised by Floyd G. Cullop. This is the entire U.S. Constitution along with explanations and comments to aid the reader's understanding.

UNIT FOUR
Book List

Primary (K–4)

The Amazing Impossible Erie Canal by Cheryl Harness. At the time, it was an incredible achievement, and it revolutionized commerce in early America. In this book, students will come to understand why canals and these changes in trade and commerce were so important to our country's development.

From Sea to Shining Sea for Children by Peter Marshall and David Manuel. A Christian perspective on the growth of America from 1787 – 1837. For primary students, this is a good read aloud book. Middle school and high school students would also find this interesting reading on their own. There is also an activity book for younger students that can be purchased separately.

The Joke's on George by Michael O. Tunnell. The joke is on President George Washington when he visits the museum of Charles Wilson Peale and is fooled by a *trompe l'oeil* painting of Mr. Peale's.

The Star-Spangled Banner, illustrated by Peter Spier. Master illustrator Peter Spier sets his colorful drawings to the words of our national anthem. Included in the book are historical notes and maps about the War of 1812 and how this song came to be. Music with guitar chords is also included.

The Star-Spangled Banner by Amy Winstead. While their father is fighting in the War of 1812, two young brothers find themselves captured by the British and held prisoner along with Francis Scott Key. This is an entertaining account of the origin of our national anthem.

Trail of Tears (Step-Into-Reading, Step 5) by Joseph Bruchac. In 1838, the federal government seized the homeland of the Cherokee Nation in Georgia. This is the story of their journey to their new home in Oklahoma.

The White House Pop-Up Book by Chuck Fischer. This delightful book is full of information about the architecture and history of the White House, including its residents. The images and illustrations are captivating.

Appleseeds: Inside the White House. This little activity book gives the reader a tour of the White House, including information about pets and holidays. Appropriate for grades 2 – 4. Order directly from The White House Historical Association at www.whitehousehistory.org.

Monticello by Norman Richards. Part of the Cornerstones of Freedom series, this is a look at Thomas Jefferson and his dream home, Monticello. Vivid photographs, illustrations, and a timeline complement the text.

William Henry Harrison, Young Tippecanoe by Howard Peckham and part of the Childhood of Famous Americans series. A look at the high-spirited life of the ninth president of the United States.

Getting to Know the U.S. Presidents Series by Mike Venezia. Through vivid illustrations and interesting commentary, each book takes you through the life of each American president. Appropriate for elementary and middle school students.

Yo, Millard Fillmore! (And All Those Other Presidents You Don't Know) by Will Cleveland, Mark Alvarez, and Tate Nation. Cartoons and captions fill this book with facts about all of the presidents of the United States. Together they create a mnemonic aid to help your students memorize all of the presidents.

Our Presidents series published by the Child's World, Inc. Spirit of America. There is one volume for each of the presidents of the United States. They are easy to read biographies with interesting facts in the margins and interesting photographs and illustrations. They should be available at your local public library.

America's First Ladies Coloring Book by Leslie Franz from Dover Publications. This is a fun way of learning about the first ladies of the United States. Please note it does not include First Lady Laura Bush.

How We Crossed the West: The Adventures of Lewis and Clark by Rosalyn Schanzer. Published by the National Geographic Society, this book is full of vivid illustrations and text drawn from actual journals and letters.

The Lewis and Clark Expedition: Join the Corps of Discovery to Explore Uncharted Territory by Carol A. Johmann. This book is jam packed with fun facts and activities to do as you travel the trail with Lewis and Clark.

Susanna of the Alamo: A True Story by John Jakes Told. The story is told from the point of view of Susanna Dickinson, who along with her infant daughter were the only survivors of the Alamo fight.

California Gold Rush by Peter and Connie Roop. Part of the Scholastic History Reader series, this book traces the history of the gold rush in an easy-to-understand format.

Middle (5–8)

Growing up in Revolution and the New Nation: 1775 – 1800 by Brandon Marie Miller and published by Lerner Publications Co. in 2003. This book takes a look at life for kids during and after the American Revolution.

A Gathering of Days: A New England Girl's Journal 1830 – 1832 by Joan W. Blos. This is the journal entries of thirteen-year-old Catherine Cabot Hall of New Hampshire. Through her eyes, we witness the hardship of her mother's death, her father's remarriage, and the challenges of pioneer life.

Childhood of Famous Americans series published by Aladdin paperbacks. These stories are engaging and well-illustrated biographies of famous Americans from our early history. They are suitable for students ages 9 – 12. They have biographies on many of the American presidents including: George Washington, Thomas Jefferson, Teddy Roosevelt, Franklin Roosevelt, Harry S. Truman, Dwight D. Eisenhower, John F. Kennedy, and Ronald Reagan.

Trail of Tears by Richard Conrad Stein. Another in the Cornerstones of Freedom series, this book describes the forced migration of the Cherokee Nation to Oklahoma when the government seized their land in Georgia.

Francis Scott Key by David Collins, Sower series. An intriguing look into the life and faith of the author of the "Star-Spangled Banner."

The Ingenious Mr. Peale: Painter, Patriot, and Man of Science by Janet R. Wilson. Many of us know Charles Wilson Peale for his portraits of Franklin, Washington, and other early American leaders. In this biography, students get a complete picture of this truly American artist. It is illustrated with Peale's own drawings and paintings. Appropriate for students in grades 5 and up.

William Henry Harrison, Young Tippecanoe by Howard Peckham. Childhood of Famous Americans series. A look at the high-spirited life of the ninth president of the United States.

Presidents by James Barber. Part of the Dorling Kindersley Eyewitness Books series, this book uses vivid photographs and illustrations with intriguing text to add insight into the men who have held America's highest office.

The President's Work: A Look at the Executive Branch by Elaine Landau. Examines how presidents do their job. Lerner Publications, 2004.

President's Game. Learn the names of the presidents and biographical and historical information about each presidency while having fun. This board game is designed for up to six players, ages 8 – 15. This is part of the Learningames History Series from Educational Materials Associates, Inc. Check out www.emagame.com.

First Ladies by Amy Pastan. Another in the Dorling Kindersley Eyewitness Book series, this book is a wonderful visual history of America's first ladies.

Abigail Adams by Evelyn Witter, Sower series. An enjoyable account of the life and faith of this remarkable first lady and the mother of our sixth president.

Cobblestone: The White House, An American Symbol. This activity book is full of information about the White House. Available through The White House Historical Association at www.whitehousehistory.org.

The White House: An Illustrated History by Catherine O'Neill Grace and published by Scholastic in cooperation with the White House Historical Association. Take a behind-the-scenes look at the most famous house in America. With over two hundred photographs and clear information, you'll learn lesser-known facts about the White House. Appropriate for middle and high school students.

Monticello by Michael Burgan. Part of the We the People series, this is an overview of the history of Thomas Jefferson's famous Virginia home. Intriguing illustrations, a timeline, and a section about important people all work together to give students insight into Thomas Jefferson and the home he loved.

John Jay. Part of the Revolutionary War Leaders Series. This book is available through Christian Book Distributors. This volume takes a look at the life of John Jay, the first chief justice of the U.S. Supreme Court.

The Supreme Court by Quiri Patricia Ryon. An examination of the origins and history of the U. S. Supreme Court.

As Far As the Eye Can Reach by Elizabeth Cody Kimmel. This Landmark reprint opens the worlds of Lewis and Clark and their Corps of Discovery. Journal entries, period documents, drawings, and maps fill the pages.

Of Courage Undaunted: Across the Continent with Lewis & Clark by James Daugherty. This classic is a very readable account of the expedition and is filled with excerpts from diaries and bold drawings. Originally a Landmark Book published in 1951 and is now published by Beautiful Feet Books.

The Lewis and Clark Expedition: Join the Corps of Discovery to Explore Uncharted Territory by Carol A. Johmann. This book is jam packed with fun facts and activities to do as you travel the trail with Lewis and Clark.

Seaman: The Dog Who Explored the West with Lewis and Clark by Gail Langer Karwoski. Students will enjoy this adventure story of Lewis's brave and loyal dog, Seaman. He is the first dog known to have crossed the country. Based on primary source materials, the epic saga of the Lewis and Clark expedition told through a most unlikely and endearing hero, Seaman.

The War of 1812 by Andrew Santella and part of the Cornerstones of Freedom series. A clear presentation of the war often referred to as "The Second American Revolution."

Abandoned on the Wild Frontier by Dave and Neta Jackson and part of the Trailblazer book series. Orphaned Gilbert Hamilton meets Peter Cartwright, a Methodist circuit-rider evangelist, and moves with his family to Illinois. Once there, Gil searches for his mother who was kidnapped by Sauk Indians during the War of 1812.

Make Way for Sam Houston by Jean Fritz. Another entertaining biography by this well-known author. Here she examines the life of Sam Houston from his role in the War of 1812 to one of the founding fathers of Texas.

A Line in the Sand: The Alamo Diary of Lucinda Lawrence, Gonzales, Texas, 1836 by Sherry Garland. Part of the Dear America series, we read the diary of thirteen-year-old Lucinda and the effects of the Texas Revolution and the Alamo on her family.

Seeds of Hope: The Gold Rush Diary of Susanna Fairchild, California Territory, 1849 by Kristiana Gregory. This is part of the Dear America series, which is based on historical facts. Examine Susanna's life as her family heads west, faces hardships, and as her father risks it all to join the thousands headed to California in pursuit of fortune.

California Gold Rush: A Guide to California in 1850 by Julie Ferris. This Kingfisher Sightseers book guides you through San Francisco during the height of gold fever in 1850. The vibrant illustrations and text are very appealing. Don't be surprised if you end up with gold fever too!

The California Gold Rush by R. Conrad Stein. Another excellent Cornerstones of Freedom book. Filled with photographs and easy-to-understand text, this would be a great complement to your study.

Secondary (9 and up)

Christianity and the Constitution: The Faith of Our Founding Fathers by John Eidsmoe. This book is divided into three sections. Part one is an overview of the religious influences of the founding fathers, next he looks at the individual religious beliefs of thirteen of them, and finally he looks at the U.S. Constitution and the biblical principles contained therein.

The Religious History of America: The Heart of the American Story from Colonial Times to Today by Edwin Gaustad and Leigh Schmidt. Beginning with the colonial era, this book also examines the Revolution to the Civil War, Reconstruction to pre-WWII, then WWII to the present. An updated edition is available in paperback.

Our Sacred Honor: Words of Advice from the Founders in Stories, Letters, Poems, and Speeches by William J. Bennett. These selections provide valuable insight into the individuals who molded early American history.

The Ingenious Mr. Peale: Painter, Patriot, and Man of Science by Janet R. Wilson. Many of us know Charles Wilson Peale for his portraits of Franklin, Washington, and other early American leaders. In this biography, students get a complete picture of this truly American artist. It is illustrated with Peale's own drawings and paintings. Appropriate for students in grades 5 and up.

Adams vs. Jefferson: The Tumultuous Election of 1800 by John Ferling and published by Oxford University Press in 2004. Close elections and dirty politics are nothing new. Here we learn about a presidential campaign that resembled a bar room brawl and an election so close that the Electoral College stalemate lasted for days. Finally a secret deal was made that gave Jefferson the victory.

America Afire: Jefferson, Adams, and the Revolutionary Election of 1800 by Bernard A. Weisberger. This book is about more than just the election of 1800. It gives a clear account of political history from the signing of the Constitution through this historic election. Here we see how the founding fathers struggled with each other when interpreting the document they had authored and adopted.

Smithsonian Book of the First Ladies: Their Lives, Times, and Issues by Edith Mayo. An excellent look at the lives of these ladies who have played an important role in the history of our country. Please note, this volume does not include First Lady Laura Bush.

The Look-It-Up Book of First Ladies by Sydelle Kramer. With brief biographies of each first lady, this book is set up chronologically from Martha Washington to Laura Bush.

Abigail Adams: Witness to a Revolution by Natalie S. Bober. As wife of our second president and mother to our sixth, Abigail Adams holds a unique place in early American history. The letters she wrote to her family and friends are the heart of this book. They provide a unique look into her everyday life as well as the memorable events of her time.

The Great Little Madison by Jean Fritz. James Madison is known as the Father of the Constitution and as the fourth president of the United States. This award-winning author gives us a look not only into his political achievements, but into his early life and relationships, especially that with his wife Dolley.

The White House: An Illustrated History by Catherine O'Neill Grace, published by Scholastic in cooperation with the White House Historical Association. Take a behind-the-scenes look at the most famous house in America. With over two hundred photographs and clear information, you'll learn lesser-known facts about the White House. Appropriate for middle school and high school age students.

The Supreme Court by Quiri Patricia Ryon. An examination of the origins and history of the U.S. Supreme Court.

What's the Deal? Jefferson, Napoleon, and the Louisiana Purchase by Rhoda Blumberg. You'll get caught up in this story of the role the Louisiana territory played during the early years of our country. You'll see how people and events changed the course of our history.

Lewis and Clark on the Trail of Discovery: An Interactive History with Removable Artifacts by Rod Gragg. Don't let the small size of this book fool you. It's packed with interesting facts and copies of primary source materials including the letter from Thomas Jefferson to Lewis committing the U.S. to pay for the expedition, the secret code Lewis used for sending messages to Thomas Jefferson, and a newspaper account of the expedition's return to St. Louis.

Undaunted Courage: Meriwether Lewis, Thomas Jefferson, and the Opening of the American West by Stephen Ambrose. Well-known historian Ambrose followed the trail of Lewis and Clark and shares his experience while conveying the tale of their amazing adventure. At 528 pages, this is not for the faint of heart and can usually be found at your local library. Or you could enjoy an abridged version on CD.

The War of 1812 by Rebecca Stefoff. Takes students on a fascinating exploration of the War of 1812.

The Burning of Washington: The British Invasion of 1814 by Anthony S. Pitch. Using firsthand accounts from letters, diaries, and newspapers, the author gives an interesting viewpoint of the British invasion of Washington, D.C. in 1814.

Democracy in America and Two Essays on America by Alexis de Tocqueville, translated by Gerald E. Bevan and published by Penguin Classics. In 1831, Alexis de Tocqueville, a young French aristocrat and civil servant, made a nine-month journey through eastern America. *Democracy in America* is the result — a study of the strengths and weaknesses of the nation's evolving politics.

The Untold Story of America's First Great Invention by Andrea Sutcliffe. Students are taught that the steamboat was invented by Robert Fulton. However, seventeen years before Fulton's steamboat, John Fitch had a steamboat running across the Delaware River from Philadelphia to Trenton, New Jersey. In this interesting story, read about the the twenty-year saga of the invention of the steamboat.

Long, Bitter Trail: Andrew Jackson and the Indians by Anthony F. C. Wallace. A clear and concise account of the Indian Removal Act of 1830 and the forced migration of Native Americans that followed.

1836 Facts about the Alamo and the Texas War for Independence by Mary Deborah Petite is part of the Facts About series. It provides clear and concise information about the characters and events in a format that is interesting to the reader.

The Age of Gold: The California Gold Rush and the New American Dream by H. W. Brands. In this re-telling of the California Gold Rush, noted biographer H. W. Brands takes you on a journey to understand the excitement that drew fortune hunters and the hardships they endured. Brands does an exceptionally good job of bringing individual experiences to light.

Section Four

MAPS

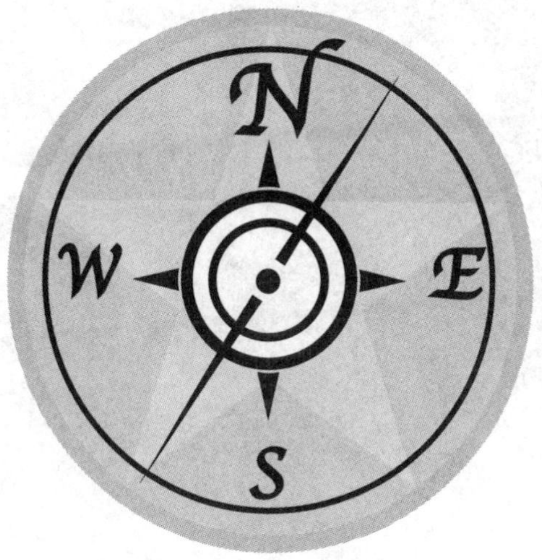

UNIT ONE
Map Work

Special Map Considerations

Unless specified below, the map portions of the *Student Activity Book* are to be completed to match the maps in the *Student Reader* and to show the paths of the explorers. I have included a legend box on each of the maps so that your students can choose colors and line patterns for multiple paths.

Lesson 2

This map should show the path of two of Prince Henry the Navigator's students — Dias and da Gama.

Lesson 3

There is no map in the Student Reader for Vespucci, as historians do not agree on the exact nature of his explorations.

Lesson 4

The Other Spanish Conquistadors map combines the explorations of Cortés and Pizarro.

Optional Map Review

Have on hand a good atlas containing a world map and a U.S. map. Be sure to use it to locate each country, city, and body of water mentioned in Unit One as you read through the lessons.

You should also have an unlabeled world map available for your students to practice finding and/or labeling all of the continents and oceans. Your students should learn to locate the principal European countries involved in the Age of European Exploration — England, France, Spain, Portugal, and the Netherlands. They should also be able to find Newfoundland, Mexico, Cuba, Panama, and other points of interest in the New World.

UNIT TWO
Map Work

Special Map Considerations

Unless specified below, the map portions of the *Student Activity Book* are to be completed to match the maps in the *Student Reader* and to show the original area of each of the colonies and label the main settlements. I have included a legend box on each of the maps, so that your students can choose colors and patterns to express different information, if so desired.

Lesson 10

As there were two distinct groups that settled the colony of Massachusetts, I thought it best to include two forms — one for Plymouth and one for the Massachusetts Bay colony.

Lesson 11

You may want to discuss the disputed area between New Hampshire and New York and show same with a different line style.

Lesson 12

You may want to discuss the disputed area between New York and New Hampshire and show same with a different line style. The New Jersey colony map should show a distinction between East and West Jersey.

Lesson 15

Your students can utilize the Proclamation of 1763 map in the *Student Reader* for help with the shading of this map.

Optional Map Review

Have on hand a good atlas containing a world map and a U.S. map. Be sure to use it to locate each country, colony, city, and body of water mentioned in Unit Two as you read through the lessons.

You could also make a large outline map of the thirteen colonies on poster board. Do not label the map. Your student(s) can use it to practice finding the location of the colonies and the important settlements in each colony.

UNIT THREE
Map Work

Special Map Considerations

These map portions of the *Student Activity Book* are to be completed to match the maps in the *Student Reader* and to show major battlesites of the French and Indian War and the American Revolution. I have included a legend box on each of the maps, so that your students can choose colors and patterns to express different information.

Optional Map Review

Have on hand a good atlas containing a world map and a U.S. map. Be sure to use it to locate each colony, city, body of water, and battle site mentioned in Unit Three as you read through the lessons.

Also have available an unlabeled map of North America. Have your student(s) practice finding all thirteen colonies/states and each of the Great Lakes and other bodies of water important in this unit.

UNIT FOUR
Map Work

Special Map Considerations

Unless specified below, the map portions of the *Student Activity Book* are to be completed to match the maps in the *Student Reader* and to show the major battlesites of the War of 1812 and the Mexican War.

Lesson 25

During this unit, the student will begin learning the location of the states and their capitals. While working on Lessons 25 – 28, the states' portion of the form on page 195 of the *Student Activity Book* should be filled in utilizing the information generated from the Impact bullets at the end of those lessons.

When the form is completed, the student will have a list of the first thirty states in the order they entered the Union. This form is designed in such a way that the student can quiz himself on the state capitals by covering the right hand column and checking state by state to see how many capitals he can remember.

On the map side of this form (page 196 of the *Student Activity Book*), the student should place numbers in the states corresponding to their numbers on page 195. For example, the number 1 should be placed in Delaware, 2 in Pennsylvania, and so on. This form is an excellent means for a student to quiz himself on the location of the thirty states on an unlabeled map.

Lessons 26 and 28

Each of the president forms in Unit Four has a U.S. map on the back. These maps are to be used to show the states that entered the Union during each president's term(s) in office and the order in which they entered. This information is found in the Impact bullets of Lessons 25 – 28. The student will need to compare the date of the state's entry with the dates of the president's term in office.

Again, the student will place numbers in the corresponding states in the order they entered the Union (1 for Delaware, 2 for Pennsylvania, and so on). Some of these maps will be blank, as some presidents had no states enter the Union during their presidencies. Please refer to the Answer Key if you have questions about this.

Lesson 31 (States and Their Capitals Review)

The form and related map for this lesson are not specifically related to the content of the lesson in the *Student Reader*, but they are, instead, a review of the states and their capitals. This form and the related map may require the use of an atlas showing each state's capital city. Please refer to the Answer Key if you have questions about this.

Optional Map Review

Have on hand a good atlas containing a world map and a U.S. map. Be sure to use it to locate each country, state, city, and body of water mentioned in the unit as you read through the lessons.

Use a United States map and the corresponding forms in the *Student Activity Book* to teach the location of states and their capitals.

Section Five

ANSWER KEY TO THE FOR FURTHER STUDY QUESTIONS

and

FOR FURTHER STUDY YOUNGER STUDENT ADAPTATIONS

Lessons 1 — 32
in the Student Activity Book

UNIT ONE
For Further Study Answers

Lesson 1: For Further Study Answers

1. Type into an Internet search engine the name of your state plus "Native Americans" or "Indians." Doing so should yield information concerning the tribes that inhabited your area of the country. When researching the culture of a particular tribe, first try typing the name of the tribe into a search engine. If you have trouble finding specific details about the tribe's clothing, tribal structure, and so forth, then type in the name of the tribe and add the cultural aspect about which you are looking for information (for example: "Cherokee clothing," "Seminole tribal structure").

2. Viking longships were known for both their seaworthiness and speed. Equipped with sails and oars, these boats were constructed using overlapping wooden planks. They ranged in size from a few dozen feet to over 150 feet in length. Because they were designed with a shallow draft (the amount of water needed for the ship to float when loaded), they were capable of maneuvering along shallow coastlines and traveling far inland by river and stream as well as traveling long distances over the open seas.

   The Vikings used their longboats to mount raids that terrorized coastal villages and monasteries in the British Isles, western Europe, Russia, and the lands around the Mediterranean Sea. Medieval Europeans were petrified of Viking warriors, who delighted in catching a settlement by surprise, attacking it, plundering it, burning it, and then disappearing. Frequently, their raids were over in just a few minutes. Most Viking warriors were well equipped with battle-axes, double-edged swords, daggers, bows, and spears. They also used round shields for defense.

   The most aggressive and fearsome of the Viking warriors were the berserkers. Before battle, berserkers worked themselves into a frenzy — painting their faces, grinding their teeth, banging their helmets, biting the edges of their shields, howling like animals, and drinking alcohol. They believed that they could work themselves into a state of ecstasy, which would make them immune to pain. Writings of medieval monks describe the ferocious behavior of these berserkers.

   Viking longships became known as "serpents of the sea" because they often had dragon or serpent figureheads at the bow. Many Viking warriors were buried in their boats. A number of Viking longships have been discovered, excavated, salvaged, and placed in museums.

3. Erik the Red was called "the Red" because of his red hair. Born in southern Norway in 950, Erik Thorvaldsson moved with his father, Thorvald, to western Iceland when Thorvald was exiled for committing manslaughter. When Erik reached manhood, he became a chieftain of his clan on Iceland. However, about 980 Erik was involved in a quarrel with his neighbors and was held responsible for the death of two men. Convicted of manslaughter, Erik was exiled from Iceland for three years.

In 982, Erik, along with his family, discovered Greenland and named the settlement that he established there Brattahild. He and his family spent three years in exile exploring Greenland and then returned to Iceland to lead a group of colonists back to Brattahild. Erik had two wives (Thorhild and Thorbjarga) and four sons (Freydis, Thorvald, Thorstein, and Leif).

4. The king of the Norse gods was Odin. His son Thor was the god of thunder, and his son Tyr was the god of war. There were many other Norse gods. Asgard, the home of the gods, was a solemn place, threatened with inevitable doom. Norse gods were not believed to be immortal. Rather, it was believed that one day they, the world, and Asgard would be destroyed because of the actions of the evil god Loki.

Lesson 1: For Further Study Younger Student Adaptations

1. Instead of requiring your younger students to research a particular tribe, look for an interesting book with general information on Native Americans that they can read or you can read to them.

2. Share illustrations of Viking ships and weapons and encourage the students to try drawing one or more of them.

3. Have them read a short biography of Erik the Red or a book with general information on the Vikings (or read one to them). You may be able to find books with hands-on activities related to the Vikings.

4. Read a Norse myth to your younger students. Show them illustrations of Norse gods and encourage your students to try drawing one or more of them.

Lesson 2: For Further Study Answers

1. The Mongols or Tartars (also known as Tatars) are an ethnic group that originated in what is now Mongolia, China, and Russia. In the middle of the thirteenth century the empire established by the Mongols encompassed more than 13 million miles and more than 100 million people. Under the leadership of Genghis Khan and then Kublai Khan, the Mongol Empire became the largest empire in world history, extending from Korea to Hungary and as far south as Vietnam and including most of the lands in between.

   The word *Khan* is a title that means ruler in Mongolian. Kublai Khan's grandfather was Genghis Khan, founder of the Mongol Empire. By 1206, Genghis Khan had united the independent nomadic tribes of Mongolia into a single fighting force that was characterized by superior military strategy and organization. From 1207 until his death in 1227, Genghis Khan led the Mongols in many bloody and destructive invasions.

   Kublai Khan conquered China and founded the Yuan dynasty of China (1271-1368), the only foreign dynasty to rule all of China. He was immortalized in Samuel Taylor Coleridge's 1816 poem "Kublai Khan." You can find a copy of this poem on the Internet.

2. You can find excerpts from *The Travels of Marco Polo* by typing that title into an Internet search engine.

3. According to some archaeological evidence, silk and silk fabric existed in China as long as 5,500 years ago. Other sources place the origin of Chinese silk-making anywhere between 2700 and 1300 BC. Regardless of the exact date, the Chinese were cultivating silkworms and weaving fibers from their cocoons at least a thousand years before the birth of Christ.

Chinese tradition credits Emperor Huang Di (also known as Huang Ti or Wu-di) and his wife, Lei-tzu, with discovering the secret of silk-making and developing methods of silk production. According to Chinese legend, one day Lei-tzu picked some cocoons from a mulberry tree in her garden and accidentally dropped one of the cocoons into her tea. Upon pulling the cocoon out, she discovered that it unwound into one long filament. Lei-tzu's husband then developed a means for domesticating silkworms and producing silk thread from the filaments.

The Chinese kept their secret for making silk from the rest of the world for many years. By the second century BC, they were exporting silk to Europe and profiting from their monopoly of silk-fabric production. The overland trade route between China and the Mediterranean became known as the Silk Road because China exported so much silk to the West. Gradually, silk-production techniques spread to other countries. According to some sources, monks who traveled from Europe to China brought back silkworm eggs about 550 AD. Other accounts credit a Chinese princess, on her way to India to be married to a prince, with smuggling out mulberry seeds and silkworm eggs in her headdress.

4. The history of the European slave trade with Africa began with the Portuguese, who were the first Europeans to explore the African coast extensively. As the Portuguese began to extend their influence down the west coast of Africa, they gained permission from local African leaders to build trading posts. Although originally built for trade in gold, ivory, and pepper, these posts were soon used for the export of slaves.

   When the Portuguese arrived on the coast of west Africa, slavery already existed on the continent. By 1445, the Portuguese had begun bringing African slaves back to their country. These Africans were captured in raids by slave traders and taken to trading posts, where they were exchanged for guns, gunpowder, knives, tools, mirrors, cloth, and beads brought from Europe. At this point in history, there was a small European market for African slaves as domestic workers in Portugal and other countries and a growing market for workers on sugar plantations on the Canary, Madeira, and Cape Verde islands. The Portuguese also made considerable amounts of gold by trading slaves to Muslim merchants.

   By 1500 the Portuguese had transported approximately 81,000 slaves to various markets. They continued to dominate the west African slave trade until the end of the seventeenth century. At that point the Dutch, who had begun capturing Portuguese trading posts along the coast, took over dominance.

Lesson 2: For Further Study Younger Student Adaptations

1. Look for illustrations of Genghis Khan and Kublai Khan and their court to share. Explain the imagery in Coleridge's poem and encourage your students to try drawing a picture of Xanadu.

2. Have them read (or read to them) a short biography of Marco Polo.

3. Explore together how silk is produced and demonstrate the difference between silk and other types of cloths.

4. Discuss how Europeans began taking Africans as slaves and explain how these slaves would eventually be brought to America. Help your students understand what it would be like to be a slave and a slave owner.

Lesson 3: For Further Study Answers

1. A nao was a merchant ship weighing between 200 and 600 tons. It had three masts (long poles rising from the bottom of the ship that support the sails and rigging) — a mainmast (center mast), a foremast (mast nearest the bow), and a mizzenmast (mast behind the mainmast).

Attached to these masts were five sails. On the mizzen was a lateen sail (triangular). On the foremast was a square foresail, and on the mainmast was a square mainsail. Above the foresail and the mainsail were topsails. In addition to these mast sails, there was a spritsail (small square sail) on the bowsprit (long pole sticking out of the bow). Most of the force used to drive a nao came from the largest mainsail.

Because a nao had a deep draft (the amount of water needed for a ship to float when loaded), it was not suited to sailing in shallow waters nor was it able to go near the coastline. Rather, it was capable of carrying a lot of cargo, and it could stand up well in heavy storms.

A caravel had a shallower draft than a nao, which allowed it to move around in the water more easily. It weighed between 150 and 300 tons, and it had little cargo space. However, it was easy to control and allowed sailors to explore shallow bays. Caravels usually had three masts and carried sails like those of a nao, except for the topsail and possibly the spritsail.

2. Dead reckoning is a method of estimating the position of a ship without astronomical observations. Before the end of the fifteenth century, this method, also known as "deduced" navigation, was the type of navigation used by European sailors. In this method, the navigator found his position by measuring the course and distance that the ship had sailed from a known point. For dead reckoning to work, the navigator had to measure his course (using a magnetic compass) and distance (multiplying the speed of the ship by the time traveled) continuously. Columbus's logbook from his first voyage contains records of continuous measurements of course and distance sailed.

   Celestial navigation makes use of observations of celestial bodies (sun, moon, stars) to measure latitude. Every star has a celestial latitude. If a navigator knows the latitude of a star directly overhead, the star's latitude is the same as the navigator's latitude on earth. If a star is not directly overhead, the navigator can measure the angle between the star and the overhead point to determine the latitude.

   Celestial navigation was not useful for sailors sailing in the Mediterranean Sea because latitude was roughly the same wherever they were. However, in the fifteenth century, when Portuguese seamen began making long voyages up and down the coast of Africa, celestial determination of latitude began to be useful.

   On Columbus's first voyage, he apparently made at least five attempts to measure his latitude using celestial navigation. None of these attempts succeeded. The most important tool that he used in his celestial navigation attempts was the astrolabe.

3. An astrolabe was an instrument used by navigators and astronomers for many centuries to measure the altitude of heavenly bodies and to determine their positions. A simple astrolabe was a disk of wood or metal with the circumference marked off in degrees. At the center of the disk was a movable pointer. By sighting with the pointer and taking readings of its position on the circle, angular distances could be determined. Astrolabes were used until the invention of the sextant in the eighteenth century.

   A quadrant was also an instrument used to measure the altitude of celestial bodies. It had a 90-degree graduated arc with a movable radius used to measure angles.

   A compass is an instrument with a magnetized metal needle that aligns itself with the earth's magnetic fields.

4. To find copies of these maps, search the Internet for "fifteenth and sixteenth century maps." One interesting aspect of these maps is that many mapmakers of this period did not want to leave gaps in their maps. Therefore, they inserted supposed coastlines (mostly erroneous), decorative embellishments, and even fancy creatures in areas where they did not have geographical information.

Lesson 3: For Further Study Student Adaptations

1. Show your students illustrations of caravels and naos. Encourage them to try drawing one or more of the ships. Discuss what it would be like to be on a ship for months at a time.

2. Explain what navigation means and provide a simple explanation of the two types of navigation. Give them the opportunity to pretend being a sea captain navigating a ship.

3. Instructions for making navigational instruments are available online. Help them try to make one.

4. Locate copies of old maps to share with them along with some modern maps. Ask your students to tell you the differences that they see between the two.

Lesson 4: For Further Study Answers

1. Sebastian Cabot was an Italian mapmaker, navigator, and explorer. Scholars think that he probably accompanied his father, John, on his 1497 and 1498 voyages for England. In 1509, Sebastian may have made another voyage in search of the Northwest Passage for England and reached Hudson Bay. In 1512 he entered Spanish service, and by 1518 he had become chief pilot of Spain.

   After Magellan's ship *Victoria* returned to Spain, Sebastian Cabot set out in 1526 on a trip for Spain to the Moluccas (Spice Islands) and China. However, he never made it farther than the mouth of the Rio de la Plata (a river between Argentina and Uruguay). After fighting with some of his crew and abandoning them, Cabot explored the Plata, Paraguay, and Parana rivers until 1529. Then lack of food and hostile natives forced him to return to Spain.

   Upon his return, Cabot was found guilty of disobeying orders and banished to Africa for a couple of years. In 1548, he re-entered English service, and five years later he became governor of a joint-stock company (eventually known as the Muscovy Company), organized to look for a Northeast Passage and open trade with China.

2. Panama is the southernmost country in Central America. In the western part of the country is a chain of mountains. There are hills in the interior, and a low range of mountains on the east coast. In the area of the country along the Caribbean Sea there are extensive forests. In 1821, Panama became part of Colombia. When Colombia rejected a U.S. proposal for canal rights in Panama, the Panamanians proclaimed their independence with U.S. backing in 1903.

   Following the Panamanian rebellion, the United States secured rights to construct and maintain a canal in Panama. The Panama Canal, completed in 1914, bisects the isthmus at its lowest and narrowest point and allows water passage from the Caribbean Sea to the Pacific Ocean. In 1977, President Carter signed a treaty providing for the return of the canal to Panama in 2000. On December 31, 1999, the U.S. government formally handed control of the Panama Canal over to Panama. The name of Panama's principal port city is Balboa.

3. You should be able to find an abundance of information on the Aztecs or Incas on the Internet.

4. Catholic priests and friars accompanied the Spanish conquistadors who came to the New World. The Franciscan and Dominican friars were the first to come to America. Their chief goal was to perform the sacraments and to introduce the Native Americans to the Catholic faith. As Spanish settlements were founded, these priests also often

established mission schools for Indian children and trained Indian adults to practice European trades and agriculture. Whether or not the Catholic Church was primarily helpful or harmful to the native populations is a matter of great debate.

Lesson 4: For Further Study Younger Student Adaptations

1. Have them read (or read to them) a short biography of the Cabots.

2. Locate photographs of Panama and of the statue of Balboa. Ask them how Panama compares to where they live.

3. Have them read another book with general information on Native Americans. You may also be able to find books with Native American crafts and other hands-on activities.

4. Explain what a Catholic priest is. Look for a drawing of a priest from this time period to show your students. Ask whether or not they think that priests should have been sent on these expeditions.

Lesson 5: For Further Study Answers

1. Peninsula — an extension of land from a larger land mass, which is surrounded by water on three sides

   Isthmus — a narrow strip of land, with water on both sides, that connects two continents or a peninsula to the mainland

   Strait — a narrow channel of water that connects two larger bodies of water (and thus lies between two land masses)

   Gulf — a relatively larger portion of a sea or ocean, which is larger than a bay and partly enclosed by land

   Bay — a small body of water, which forms an indentation in the coastline and is smaller than a gulf but larger than a cove

   Island — a land mass smaller than a continent, which is completely surrounded by water

2. Malaria is caused by protozoan parasites transmitted by mosquitoes. Its symptoms include a headache, fever, vomiting, and other flu-like symptoms. Malaria can kill if it progresses to the point of destroying red blood cells and clogging capillaries carrying blood to the brain.

   Dysentery is caused by the bacterium shigella and is transmitted by food or water contaminated with feces from an infected person. These bacteria produce inflammation of the lining of the large intestines, which causes symptoms that include fever, abdominal pains, diarrhea, vomiting, and dehydration. Dysentery can be fatal if dehydration becomes too severe.

   Scurvy is caused by a diet insufficient in vitamin C, which affects the synthesis of collagen in the body. A lack of collagen causes the body's capillary walls to break down, leading to hemorrhaging in cells throughout the body. As a result of this internal hemorrhaging, a person with scurvy will exhibit black-and-blue spots on the skin, joint pain, gum disease, anemia, and weakness. Severe cases of scurvy can be life threatening.

   Typhus or typhoid fever is caused by the bacterium salmonella typhi and is transmitted by food or water contaminated with feces from an infected person. Its symptoms include high fever; headache; lack of appetite; abdominal pains; severe diarrhea; a rash of flat, rose-colored spots; and even extreme confusion and delusions. Typhus can be fatal.

3. Following Ponce de Leon's exploration of Florida in 1513, the Spanish government sent six expeditions to settle the area. However, all of these attempts failed. Then in 1565, Admiral Don Pedro Menendez de Aviles was named governor of Florida. He and a group of six hundred Spanish soldiers and settlers arrived in Florida on August 28, 1565, the Feast Day of St. Augustine.

   Menendez and his men hastily fortified the area and named it St. Augustine. As a result of the governor's brilliant military maneuvers, the Spanish were able to destroy a French fort established nearby on the St. John's River. The Spanish settlement at St. Augustine succeeded, making it the oldest continuously occupied settlement of European origin in the United States.

   Today in St. Augustine there are thirty-six buildings of colonial origin (1565 – 1764) and another forty reconstructed colonial buildings. Some of the historical sites that can be visited there include the Castillo de San Marcos, the Mission of Nombre de Dios, the Fountain of Youth, the Museum of Weapons, and the Spanish Quarter Village.

4. Search the Internet for information on the Wampanoag.

Lesson 5: For Further Study Younger Student Adaptations

1. Explain these geographical terms: *peninsula, isthmus, strait, gulf, bay,* and *island.* Encourage your students to draw pictures of them. Give them an opportunity to point out examples of these on a map.

2. Discuss one or more of these diseases: malaria, dysentery, scurvy, and typhus. Also discuss the dietary limitations that came from being on a ship. Look for a recipe for hard tack and help them try to make it.

3. Locate photographs of the city of St. Augustine to show them.

4. Have the students read (or read to them) another book with general information on Native Americans or encourage them to do more Native American hands-on activities.

Lesson 6: For Further Study Answers

1. St. Lawrence was an archdeacon of Rome during a period of time when Christianity was forbidden there. At the beginning of August, in the year 258, Emperor Valerian issued an edict calling for the immediate execution of all bishops, priests, and deacons in Rome. On August 6, Pope Sixtus II was apprehended in one of the catacombs and beheaded.

   Four days later, Lawrence was commanded to appear for his execution and to bring with him the treasure that Pope Sixtus had entrusted to him. Lawrence obeyed the order and brought with him many of Rome's crippled, blind, and poor people, announcing that these were the true treasures of the church. The archdeacon was then cooked to death on a gridiron. Since the fourth century, Lawrence has been one of the most honored martyrs of the Catholic Church.

2. Cabeza de Vaca was part of a royal expedition of 250-300 men, who left Spain in 1527 to travel to the North American mainland. After surviving a hurricane near Cuba, the group secured a new boat, reached Tampa Bay in the spring of 1528, and claimed the land for Spain. However, the expedition soon faced numerous diseases as well as hostility from Native Americans in the area. The group of survivors ended up hiding in a coastal swamp and living off the flesh of their horses. Finally, later in 1528, they built five crude rafts and set sail, hoping to return to Cuba. Three of the rafts sank, but the two surviving rafts, carrying eighty men, landed at Galveston Island.

By the following spring, only fifteen men had survived. These fifteen crossed Texas from east to west, following the Colorado River and hoping to reach the Spanish outpost in Mexico. By 1533 there were only four survivors, one of whom was de Vaca. Although their precise route is not clear, these four appear to have traveled into New Mexico and Arizona and through Mexico's northern provinces and to have been the first Europeans to see American buffalo. For a time they were enslaved by an Indian tribe, but they were also helped by other tribes. Finally, in 1536, eight years after arriving in Florida, de Vaca and his three fellow travelers reached Mexico City, where they were welcomed by Viceroy Mendoza.

3. Use the Internet to research the *De Soto Chronicles* and to read portions of it.

4. The Grand Canyon is an enormous, steep-sided gorge created by the Colorado River in northern Arizona. One of the seven natural wonders of the world, the Grand Canyon measures 277 miles long and ranges in width from 4 to 18 miles with a depth of more than a mile.

   The Painted Desert is a plateau region located in north central Arizona, east of the Colorado and Little Colorado rivers. It is known for its irregularly eroded layers of colorful yellow and red sediment and clay.

   The Continental Divide is a series of mountain ridges extending from Alaska southward through the United States into Mexico and Central America. It is the watershed of North America, dividing the continent's principal water drainage into that flowing eastward to the Atlantic Ocean and that flowing westward to the Pacific Ocean.

Lesson 6: For Further Study Younger Student Adaptations

1. Discuss what a martyr is. Share the story of St. Lawrence.

2. Using a map, point out all of the places that de Vaca visited and explain why de Vaca went there.

3. Have your students read (or read to them) a short biography of DeSoto.

4. Share photographs of the Grand Canyon, Continental Divide, and Painted Desert.

Lesson 7: For Further Study Answers

1. Sir Humphrey Gilbert, half-brother of Sir Walter Raleigh, was an English soldier, navigator, and explorer. Convinced of the existence of a Northwest Passage, Gilbert expounded on his beliefs in *A Discourcs of a Discoveries for a new Passage to Cataia*, which he presented to Queen Elizabeth I in 1566. This famous paper inspired Martin Frobisher, John Davis, and others to lead explorations in the North Atlantic regions. Gilbert himself received a patent from Queen Elizabeth I to found colonies in America and reached Newfoundland on his second westward voyage in 1583, taking possession of the region in the name of the queen. On his way home to England in September 1583, Gilbert was lost at sea in a storm.

2. Martin Frobisher was an English navigator who sailed westward in search of the Northwest Passage. During his first expedition, Frobisher reached Labrador and Baffin Island and sailed through the bay that today bears his name. When he returned to England, he brought some black ore that he believed contained gold and an Eskimo to prove that he had actually reached Cathay (China).

   Frobisher returned to Baffin Island on two more journeys and explored Frobisher Bay and a short distance up the Hudson Strait. Since no gold was found in any of his cargoes of ore, Frobisher was discredited in England for a period of time. Eventually, his good name was restored when he won glory as commander of a ship in

Sir Francis Drake's expedition to the West Indies in 1585. Frobisher was also knighted for his services in the defeat of the Spanish Armada in 1588. Six years later, he was wounded in a battle with a Spanish treasure ship and died at sea.

3. The story of the Lost Colony has fascinated historians for a long time. Many scholars believe that Native Americans killed the colonists. Other scholars speculate that the Roanoke settlers were killed by Spanish troops who had come to the region from Florida or that the English colonists just moved farther inland and married into Native American tribes.

4. Well-known English "sea dogs" of the Elizabethan era include Francis Drake, John Hawkins, Martin Frobisher, and Walter Raleigh. These swashbuckling sea captains were known for their military and maritime skills and their appetite for Spanish gold. In the 1530s these and other English seamen began to prey upon Spanish ships sailing between Europe, Africa, and America. The notorious exploits of these sea dogs, who especially targeted Spanish galleons loaded with silver and gold returning from the New World, helped provoke the eventual naval showdown between England and Spain in 1588. They also provided Elizabeth and other investors with unbelievable profits (as high as 4000 percent).

Lesson 7: For Further Study Younger Student Adaptations

1. Show them a picture of Sir Humphrey Gilbert. Using a map, point out where Gilbert explored.

2. Show them a picture of Martin Frobisher. Using a map, point out where Frobisher explored.

3. Have your students read (or read to them) a book about the Lost Colony.

4. Locate pictures of one or more of the "sea dogs" to share and encourage them to think about what a battle at sea would be like.

Lesson 8: For Further Study Answers

1. The Muscovy Company, also called the Russia Company, was formed in 1555 by Sebastian Cabot and a group of London merchants to continue the search for a Northeast Passage to China and the East Indies. It was granted a monopoly of the newly opened Russian trade and was the first English joint-stock company in which the capital remained regularly in use (instead of being repaid after each voyage). In 1698, the company lost its monopoly due to political opposition. However, the company continued in existence until 1917.

2. A replica of Henry Hudson's *Half Moon* was constructed at the Snow Dock in Albany, New York, and launched in June 1989. It was built to be a living history exhibit, operated by the New Netherland Museum as a means of providing historic interpretation of the Dutch role in exploring America. A full-scale reproduction of the original *Half Moon*, the ship has cabins and decks authentically furnished with navigational instruments, weapons, tools, trading goods, and sea chests true to the era. However, although the ship is authentic in appearance, it was constructed using modern materials and techniques.

3. Use the Internet to find information on the Iroquois.

4. The Northwest Passage is a water route from the Atlantic Ocean to the Pacific Ocean through northern Canada and the northern coast of Alaska. Sought by European navigators since the sixteenth century, the existence of the Northwest Passage was not proven until the early nineteenth century by the British explorer Sir John Franklin. No expedition made it entirely through the Northwest Passage until the Norwegian explorer Roald Amundsen led a group across it from 1903 to 1906.

Lesson 8: For Further Study Younger Student Adaptations

1. Explain what a monopoly is. Using a map, point out the area over which the Muscovy Company was given a monopoly.

2. Show them photographs of the replica of Hudson's ship, as well as other photographs from this living history exhibit.

3. Have your students read (or read to them) another book with general information on Native Americans or do more Native American hands-on activities.

4. Using a map, point out where the Northwest Passage was discovered and explain when that happened.

UNIT TWO
For Further Study Answers

Lesson 9: For Further Study Answers

1. The London Company, also called the Virginia Company of London, was a joint-stock company established by royal charter (James I) on April 10, 1606. A joint-stock company is a business organization that pools its members' capital in a common fund. This type of company first appeared during the Renaissance. During the seventeenth century, joint-stock companies became a popular way to raise large amounts of capital for trading expeditions and establishing colonies

   The pooled capital of a joint-stock company is called the company's stock. The company's partners are known as shareholders, because they receive shares for their contribution to the stock. Shares represent decision-making power in the company as well as how much of the profit each shareholder receives. Shareholders are free to transfer their shares to someone else, even without consent of the other shareholders. However, they are also legally liable for all of the company's debts; and their shares determine how much of the company's losses for which they are liable. A 10 percent share in a company would mean 10 percent of the company's profits, as well as liability for 10 percent of any company debt.

   The difficult early years of the Jamestown colony were catastrophic for the London Company. New subscribers to the company reneged on payment for their shares, and the company was forced to deal with dozens of court cases. To send more colonists to Jamestown, the company incurred further debt. Because no gold and few trading commodities were found in Virginia, there was really nothing to offset the company's losses.

   These financial difficulties, complicated by political infighting and bad publicity, led the London Company to organize an advertising campaign for its colonial venture. The company published articles promoting the Jamestown colony, persuaded clergymen to preach on the importance of supporting colonization, and placed broadsheets promoting Virginia on street corners. Potential investors were told that their purchase of shares would help England become a stronger nation, heathen natives receive the opportunity to be converted to Christianity, and the unemployed to find work overseas. Over time, the London Company would publish more than twenty-five promotional books and pamphlets.

   Eventually, a new charter permitted the company to run a lottery as a fundraiser. John Rolfe's success with tobacco as a cash crop also helped the company financially. However, by 1621 the London Company was in financial trouble again; the company's debt was over 9,000 pounds. In 1624, King James I revoked the company's charter, and Virginia became a royal colony.

2. Chief Wahunsonacock, (or Powhatan, as the English called him) was the leader of the Algonquian confederacy, made up of approximately thirty Algonquian tribes in eastern Virginia at the time of the establishment of Jamestown. Today Powhatan is primarily known as the father of Pocahontas, but in the early seventeenth century Powhatan was known as the powerful ruler of the Powhatan nation. To find out more, research Powhatan and the Algonquian on the Internet.

3. John Smith began life as the son of an English farmer. At age thirteen he begged his father to allow him to go to sea with Sir Francis Drake. Smith left England at about age sixteen when his father died and joined French volunteers fighting for Dutch independence from Spain. He then worked on a merchant ship in the Mediterranean. In 1600, he went to Hungary to help Austrian forces fight the Turks. Two years later, he was wounded in battle in Transylvania and captured and sold as a slave to the Turks. Eventually, Smith escaped and returned to England in the winter of 1604 – 1605.

   Smith was a red-bearded man, short but scrappy. A strong, confident leader, he was considered by many to be arrogant and boastful. After leaving Jamestown to return to England, Smith published a number of works about Virginia, including *True Relation of Virginia, Map of Virginia, Generall Historie of Virginia,* and *True Travels.*

   In 1614, Smith mounted an expedition to "northern Virginia," which he called New England, and mapped the coastline there from Penobscot Bay to Cape Cod. These maps were later used by the Pilgrims when they came to America. In 1615, Smith again sailed for New England but was forced to return home because of stormy weather. A year later, he published a volume entitled *A Description of New England.*

4. Before serving as English colonial governor of Virginia, Thomas De La Warr was involved in fighting in the Netherlands and was knighted when serving in Ireland. When De La Warr returned to England from Jamestown, he published *Relations. . . of the Colonies Planted in Virginia (1611).* Receiving reports of Samuel Argall's (his successor) tyrannical leadership at Jamestown, De La Warr decided to return to America. However, he never made it. He died at sea on June 17, 1618. Most scholars believe that the state of Delaware, the Delaware River, and the Delaware Bay all received their name from Thomas De La Warr.

Lesson 9: For Further Study Younger Student Adaptations

1. Discuss the financial hardships faced by the Virginia colonists and how they were overcome.

2. Have your students read (or read to them) a short biography of Pocahontas.

3. Have your students read (or read to them) a short biography of John Smith.

4. Explain how Delaware got its name. Using a map, point out where Delaware is located.

Lesson 10: For Further Study Answers

1. The *Speedwell* was a companion ship to the *Mayflower*. The Leyden Separatists bought the *Speedwell* while still in Holland. They boarded it at Delftshaven and sailed to Southampton, England. There they met the *Mayflower*, which had been chartered by the merchant investors. In Southampton they were joined by other Separatists as well as colonists hired by the investors.

   The *Speedwell* and the *Mayflower* began the voyage together. However, the *Speedwell* was leaky, forcing the expedition to return to England — first to Dartmouth and then to Plymouth. Finally, the Pilgrims decided to sell the *Speedwell*, and all of its passengers had to be wedged into the *Mayflower*. These difficulties prevented the group from leaving in April, which they hoped to do in order to reach the New World in time to plant crops.

2. The Mayflower Compact is a short document that can be easily found on the Internet. There are also a variety of excerpts from *Of Plimoth Plantation* available online. You can also use the Internet to find the words of Longfellow's poem "The Courtship of Miles Standish."

3. Mary White was probably born in England and then migrated with her parents to Massachusetts in 1639. In 1656 she married Joseph Rowlandson, who was ordained as a Puritan minister in 1660, and together they had four children (one of whom died in infancy). Near the end of King Philip's War in 1676, Narragansett and Nipmunk Indians burned down the town of Lancaster, Massachusetts, and captured many of its settlers. Among the captives taken were Mary and her three children. Joseph had been on his way to Boston to find military help for the people of Lancaster. Mary and the children lived with their captors in the forest for three months until they were finally ransomed and reunited with Joseph. However, Sarah, age six, had died in captivity from her wounds; and their home had been destroyed in the attack.

The Rowlandsons lived in Boston until Joseph accepted a call to a congregation in Wethersfield, Connecticut, in 1677. A year later he preached a sermon about his family's captivity entitled "A Sermon of the Possibility of God's Forsaking a People that have been near and dear to him." Just three days later, Joseph died very suddenly. In 1679, Mary married Captain Samuel Talcott. Little is known about her life from this point on until her death around 1710.

In 1682, an autobiographical narrative of Mary Rowlandson's captivity was published. Some believe that its anonymous preface was written by Increase Mather, a prominent clergyman of the time. Rowlandson's book was originally entitled *The Soveraignty and Goodness of God, Together with the Faithfulness of His Promises Displayed; Being a Narrative of the Captivity and Restauration of Mrs. Mary Rowlandson, Commended by her to all that Desire to Know the Lord's Doings to, and Dealings with her. Especially to her Dear Children and Relations.* This narrative offered a vivid account of her experiences in the context of her Calvinist beliefs, portraying the natives as instruments of God. Rowlandson's writings were also notable for their attempt to depict an understanding of her captors as individuals who suffered themselves and showed some compassion to their captives. An immediate best-seller, Mary Rowlandson's narratives went through many editions.

John Eliot was born in England and decided to migrate to New England in 1631 because of his Puritan beliefs. Soon after he arrived in Boston, he married Hannah Mulford, who had been betrothed to him in England. Hannah would become his faithful helper, and together they would have one daughter and five sons (only one of whom would survive him). In December 1632, Eliot became the pastor of a church near Boston (Roxbury), where he would serve for the rest of his life.

Soon, Eliot began to take a strong interest in the spiritual and physical well-being of the native population in the area. He studied their dialects, translated the Ten Commandments and the Lord's Prayer, and by 1646 had begun to preach to them in their own language. In 1649, Parliament set up the Society for the Propagation of the Gospel in New England to support John Eliot's work. With the society's financial assistance, Eliot established a number of native settlements, providing housing, clothing, churches, and schools for the Indians.

Perhaps Eliot's most significant and lasting achievement was his translation of the Bible into the Algonquian language. The complete Bible, which first appeared in 1663, was the first Bible to be published in America. English and European language Bibles would not be printed in America until a century later because they could be so easily and inexpensively imported from England. Eliot also published a number of literary works on religious subjects.

4. In January 1692, a group of young girls in the Salem community began to act strangely — displaying trance-like states and convulsions and speaking oddly. The people of the village prayed and fasted concerning the reason for the girls' behavior. Doctors called in to examine them could find no physical reason for their behavior. Thus, the village people reasoned that their behavior was being caused by Satan.

In February the girls were pressured to reveal who in the community was influencing their behavior. They identified three women, who were examined and imprisoned. One of the women, a slave named Tituba, confessed to seeing the devil and to the existence of a group of witches in the village. A month later the girls also accused a woman who was an upstanding member of the Puritan church.

From this point on until the fall, many in Salem were accused of witchcraft, charged, tried, and condemned to death. Those accused were required to either confess they were witches or be condemned to death. From June through September nineteen people were hanged, one was crushed to death under the weight of rocks, and at least four died in prison. By October, the hysteria had stopped. The governor intervened to dismiss the court trying the accused, and those in jail were acquitted or given reprieves. Eventually, the court cleared the names of those who had died.

Cotton Mather, pastor of Boston's North Church, was a fervent believer in the existence of witchcraft. In 1689, Mather published a book entitled *Memorable Providences*, which described a case of alleged witchcraft occurring in Boston in 1688. Children of a Boston mason had exhibited strange behavior following a disagreement they had had with an Irish washerwoman named Mary Glover. After examining the children, Mather decided that they had come under the spell of Glover's witchcraft. *Memorable Providences* was widely read throughout the New England colonies.

Three of the five judges appointed to the court that heard the Salem witchcraft trials were friends of Mather and members of his church. Mather wrote a letter to one of these judges, suggesting how they might approach issues of evidence at the upcoming trials. In August, Mather preached a sermon proclaiming that the Last Judgment was coming soon. He also witnessed the execution of ex-minister George Burroughs for witchcraft. When Burroughs was able to recite the Lord's Prayer perfectly (something witches were thought incapable of doing), some in the crowd called for his execution to be stopped. However, Mather reminded them that Burroughs had been duly convicted by a jury.

After the witch trials had ended, the judges agreed to turn over the court records to Mather. They seemed to hope that Mather would portray their role in the trials favorably. Mather's book, *Wonders of the Invisible World*, provided very interesting insights into the witch trials and Mather's thinking. Later in his life, Mather seemed to minimize his significant role in the Salem trials. Following this incident, orthodox Puritans never regained their previous hold on the Massachusetts government, and Puritan church membership continued to decline.

Lesson 10: For Further Study Younger Student Adaptations

1. Locate a photograph of Plymouth Rock to show your students and explain its significance.
2. Have your students read (or read to them) the Longfellow poem "The Courtship of Miles Standish" or a short biography of William Bradford.
3. Share the stories of Mary Rowlandson and John Eliot.
4. Have your students read (or read to them) a short book on the Salem witch trials or explore some of the interesting information that can be found online.

Lesson 11: For Further Study Answers

1. Adriaen Block was a Dutch navigator, fur trader, and explorer, sent by Amsterdam merchants to explore the regions discovered by Henry Hudson. During his four voyages between 1611 and 1614, Block explored the coastal and river valley areas between present-day New Jersey and Massachusetts. He discovered the Connecticut River, explored Narragansett Bay, and sailed past and named Block Island. Block also may have been the first European to enter Long Island Sound and has been credited with being the first person to determine that Long Island and Manhattan were islands.

In addition to exploring the region, Block worked to establish early trade with the Native Americans in the area. When he returned from his last voyage, he compiled a map of his explorations. On this 1614 figurative map, many features of the mid-Atlantic region appeared for the first time. Block's map was also the first to apply the name "New Netherlands" to the area between English Virginia and French Canada. You should be able to find a copy of Block's 1614 map online.

2. Anne Hutchinson was born in England and emigrated with her husband and family to Massachusetts Bay in 1634. Apparently an intelligent and articulate woman, Hutchinson began to share her theological beliefs within the Puritan community and to hold weekly discussion group meetings in her home. According to Hutchinson, true godliness came from an inner experience of the Holy Spirit, not from conforming to religious rules. She insisted that establishing a government that required people to follow Biblical law demonstrated a belief in the covenant of works. Hutchinson's emphasis upon the covenant of grace, as opposed to the covenant of works, caused Puritan leaders in the community (such as John Cotton and John Winthrop) to call her an antinomian heretic.

   Antinomianism is the belief that Christians are not bound by moral law. Hutchinson's opponents had her tried for this heresy by the General Court in 1637. She was found guilty, excommunicated, and banished from the colony. Anne, her husband, her children, and a group of her followers moved to Rhode Island, a colony known as a refuge for religious dissenters. They established a settlement on the island of Aquidneck in 1638. After Anne's husband died, she moved her family to Long Island, New York. There in 1643 she and all of her children except one were killed by Native Americans.

   You will probably find conflicting opinions about whether or not Anne Hutchinson was an antinomian heretic. Because there are no written records of her beliefs, historians have had to interpret the records of her trial and the writings of her contemporaries in an attempt to understand her thoughts and deeds. As a result, there are varying interpretations of Hutchinson's actions and theology.

3. John Wheelwright emigrated to Massachusetts Bay in 1636 to escape religious persecution in England after he became a Puritan. He accepted a pastorate at a Puritan church in Mount Wollaston, Massachusetts. Because he publicly defended the views of his sister-in-law, Anne Hutchinson, Wheelwright became alienated from Puritan leaders in Boston.

   In January 1637, he preached a sermon on the day of a fast that had been called by the General Court. Although the majority of the congregation approved his preaching of the sermon, Wheelwright was tried by the General Court and pronounced guilty of sedition and contempt. He was banished from Massachusetts Bay in 1637. A year later, Wheelwright and a group of his friends established a settlement at Exeter, New Hampshire. In later years Wheelwright served other churches in New Hampshire, Maine, and Massachusetts. (His sentence of banishment from Massachusetts was withdrawn when he acknowledged some error on his part.)

   Thomas Hooker was born into a Puritan family in England. After graduating from Cambridge, he developed into a powerful preacher. However, Hooker eventually ran into trouble with English religious authorities over matters of theology and fled to Holland. In 1633, Hooker and several dozen of his followers emigrated to Massachusetts. There Hooker again ran into trouble for his views. One of Massachusetts's most influential preachers, John Cotton, held the position that only church members who owned property should be allowed to vote. Hooker, on the other hand, believed that all men should have the right to vote, regardless of religious or property qualifications.

   In 1636, Hooker moved on to Connecticut, where he continued to voice his democratic viewpoints. In the spring of 1638, Hooker preached a powerful sermon at the opening session of the General Court of Connecticut on the text that "the foundation of authority is laid in the free consent of the people." A year later, he played an instrumental role in securing the adoption of the Fundamental Orders of Connecticut.

4. The Fundamental Orders recognized that the settlements of Windsor, Hartford, and Wethersfield existed along the Connecticut River because it had pleased Almighty God by the "wise disposition of his divine providence so to order and dispose of things" in such a way to make it possible. This document also maintained that a people gathered around the word of God needed an orderly and decent government established according to God. It stated that the people of these three settlements entered into a confederation together in order to maintain and preserve the liberty and purity of the Gospel of the Lord Jesus Christ and the discipline of the churches.

Lesson 11: For Further Study Younger Student Adaptations

1. Show your students a picture of Adriaen Block. Using a map, point out where Block explored.

2. Provide a simple explanation of the theological debate surrounding Anne Hutchinson. Ask your students their opinion about this.

3. Using simple terms, explain the theological issues surrounding John Wheelwright and Thomas Hooker. Discuss whether or not these issues are important today.

4. Read to your students the sentences in the Fundamental Orders of Connecticut that refer to God and the role of religion in the founding of the colony. Remind them of the faith of many of the early American settlers.

Lesson 12: For Further Study Answers

1. The Dutch West India Company was a trading and colonizing company, chartered by the Dutch Republic in 1621 and organized in 1623. The amazing success of the Dutch East India Company was an important factor that led to its establishment. The Dutch West India Company was given a trade monopoly over the African coast between the Tropic of Cancer and the Cape of Good Hope and over the American coast between Newfoundland and the Strait of Magellan.

   Initially, the company was interested in taking Brazil away from Portugal, but it was unsuccessful in its attempts to do so. In the 1620s and 1630s the company was successful in establishing a number of trading posts in North America, including Fort Orange on the site of Albany, New York; Fort Nassau on the Delaware River; Fort Good Hope on the site of Hartford on the Connecticut River; and Fort Amsterdam on the southern tip of Manhattan Island. This area became known as New Netherlands.

   At first England did not contest this Dutch settlement on lands claimed by the English because it was involved in wars with France and Spain. When the warfare ended, the English took over New Netherlands from the Dutch West India Company in 1664. After this point, the company engaged primarily in the African slave trade, although it still had colonies in Guiana.

2. The Pennsylvania Dutch country is an area in southeastern Pennsylvania, centered around Lancaster and the surrounding countryside. The term *Pennsylvania Dutch* should really be "Pennsylvania German," since the so-called Pennsylvania Dutch have nothing to do with the Netherlands. Rather, the descendants of this group of people originally emigrated from German-speaking areas of Europe, and they referred to the German dialect they spoke as "Deutsch," which eventually became corrupted into "Dutch." Although not all Pennsylvania Dutch are Amish, they are the best-known group. The Amish have retained their German dialect and eighteenth century traditional way of life.

3. James II was the son of Charles I and the brother of Charles II. As early as 1672, he converted to Catholicism. In 1673, he opposed the Test Act, which prohibited Catholics and Dissenters from holding positions of power in the government. When James assumed the throne in 1685, English Protestants rallied around his nephew, whom they believed should be king. James easily put down the rebellion and then had Catholics promoted to high-status positions.

   James's second wife gave birth to a male heir in 1688, and this interfered with Parliament's desire for James's Protestant daughter Mary to succeed him to the throne. Faced with the possibility of a Catholic dynasty, a group of powerful English leaders invited Mary and her husband, William of Orange, to take the throne. Although James II's army was two times the size of William's, James was not able to do battle because so many of his officers had deserted to the Protestant side.

   On December 18, 1688, William of Orange was welcomed into London, while James II fled down the river in disguise and spent the rest of his life in exile in France. The "Glorious Revolution" had succeeded without a shot being fired; and on February 8, 1669, William and Mary were declared king and queen of England. The College of William and Mary in Williamsburg, Virginia, is named for these co-monarchs.

4. George Fox, founder of the Society of Friends, underwent a mystical experience in 1646, in which he came to believe that true Christianity was not an outward profession of faith but rather an inner light granted by Christ to the believing soul. Fox believed that revelation was not confined to the Bible and that a direct experience with God was available to all people without the mediation of a priest and the sacraments. He taught that worship services did not need to be planned and led by a paid minister. Instead, those attending should sit in silence and speak when moved by the Spirit to do so. In 1647, Fox began preaching his beliefs publicly. Although he attracted many followers, he also encountered physically violent crowd reactions and was imprisoned eight times between 1649 and 1654.

   Members of the Society of Friends were called Quakers by outsiders. This term referred to the fact that the group admonished people to "quake in the presence of the Lord." Quakers were often ridiculed or persecuted for refusing to serve in the military, swear oaths of allegiance to anyone but God, and to pay taxes. Those belonging to the Society of Friends believed that all people were equal before God and that all people should be treated the same. They were generally frugal and hardworking people, who dressed and lived simply and considered spiritual values to be more important than material possessions. However, they also were often shrewd businessmen, who did well financially as merchants and traders.

Lesson 12: For Further Study Younger Student Adaptations

1. Review what a monopoly is and point out on a map the places over which the Dutch West India company held a monopoly.

2. Explain the meaning of "Pennsylvania Dutch." Show your students photographs of the Pennsylvania Dutch country today.

3. Tell the story of James II and William and Mary.

4. Show them illustrations of Quakers and Quaker worship services from the colonial period. Have your students compare Quaker services to the worship services with which they are familiar.

Lesson 13: For Further Study Answers

1. Use the Internet to research the Lenni-Lenape tribe.

2. In his letter to the Indians, William Penn told the natives that God had written his law in the hearts of all people, teaching and commanding them to love, help, and do good to one another. He insisted that he wanted the English and Native Americans to live together as neighbors and friends. God did not create them to harm and destroy one another but to live kindly together. Penn mentioned that he was well aware of the cruel and unjust manner in which the natives had been treated by many other European settlers. However, he maintained that he and the people whom he would send wanted to gain their love and friendship.

3. In 1751, the Pennsylvania Assembly ordered the purchase of a bell for the State House steeple (today Independence Hall) as a means of commemorating the fiftieth anniversary of William Penn's 1701 Charter of Privileges. To be inscribed on the bell was Leviticus 25:10 — "Proclaim liberty throughout all the land unto all the inhabitants thereof." The bell's inscription also said, "and ye shall hallow the fiftieth year."

   The word *Pennsylvania* is spelled "Pensylvania" on the Liberty Bell. The spelling of Pennsylvania had not been universally adopted at that time. In fact, the state's name was also spelled Pensylvania in the original U.S. Constitution.

   The bell arrived in Philadelphia in September 1752, but it was not hung until March 1753. There is widespread disagreement concerning when and why the bell became cracked. According to some sources, the bell was cracked by a stroke of the clapper as it was first hung up due to flaws in the casting.

   The Liberty Bell was rung frequently to call the state assembly together and to gather people for special events and announcements. During the American Revolution it was tolled for meetings of the Continental Congress, the early battles of the war, and the public reading of the Declaration of Independence. When the British occupied Philadelphia in 1777, the bell was removed from the city and hidden in the floorboards of Zion Reformed Church in Allentown, Pennsylvania.

4. The original charters granted by the English to the Penn and Calvert families in North America did not clearly state the boundaries between the Pennsylvania and Maryland colonies. This led to friction over the years between the two colonies, and the dispute was finally submitted to an English court.

   In 1760, the Penn and Calvert families compromised and selected Charles Mason, an English mathematician and astronomer, and Jeremiah Dixon, an English mathematician and land surveyor, to survey the border between the two colonies. Mason and Dixon worked from 1763 to 1767 to settle this century-old boundary dispute. They ran a line west from the Delaware border for 244 miles, with every fifth milestone bearing a replica of the Penn and Calvert coats of arms.

   This Mason-Dixon line was later extended to delineate the border between Pennsylvania and Virginia. In the years leading up to the Civil War, the line was considered to be the division between slave and free states.

Lesson 13: For Further Study Younger Student Adaptations

1. Have your students read (or read to them) another book with general information on Native Americans or do more Native American hands-on activities.

2. Have your students read (or read to them) a short biography of William Penn.

3. Share the story of the Liberty Bell.

4. Explain what the Mason-Dixon line is and point it out to them on a map.

Lesson 14: For Further Study Answers

1. The Stono Rebellion was a slave revolt that occurred near Charleston, South Carolina, in 1739. The rebellion was named after the Stono River, because it began on the bridge crossing that river. Before dawn on Sunday, September 9, twenty African-American slaves gathered near the Stono River. At the bridge they seized some guns and ammunition from a store and then killed the two storekeepers.

   From there the group walked to the Godfrey home, burned the house down, and killed Mr. Godfrey and his son and daughter. Heading south, they came to Wallace's Tavern, where they spared the life of the innkeeper because he was kind to his slaves. However, the white settlers of the next six houses all were killed.

   By late morning other slaves had joined the revolt, and any whites they encountered were chased and killed. In the late afternoon the slaves stopped at a large field to rest, having traveled over ten miles. About 4:00 P.M. a group of white planters with guns approached the slaves. Some of the slaves fled, but others fought back. By dark about thirty slaves were dead, and at least thirty had escaped. Over the next month, the planters tracked down almost all the rest of the slaves involved in the rebellion and shot or hanged them.

   Eventually, thirty whites and as many as sixty slaves were killed as a result of the Stono Rebellion, one of the deadliest slave revolts in the colonial period. No one knows exactly what caused this rebellion; it probably was due to a combination of factors. An epidemic in the area that fall had disrupted the local government. Also, the news that England and Spain were at war had just arrived. This report raised the hopes of the Carolina slaves that the Spanish in St. Augustine might be friendly to them if they decided to run away to Florida. An already tense atmosphere was further strained by the passage of the Security Act in August, which required that all white men carry firearms to church on Sundays (due to fears concerning the possibility of a slave revolt). Following the Stono Rebellion, South Carolina passed stricter slave laws, prohibiting African-American slaves from growing their own food, earning their own money, assembling in groups, or learning to read.

2. Use the Internet to research the Cherokee.

3. Edward Teach, known as Blackbeard, was one of the most feared pirates of the colonial era. His nickname came from his long black beard that he braided and tied with black ribbons. From 1716 to 1718, Blackbeard and his pirate crew terrorized sailors on the Caribbean Sea and the Atlantic Ocean. Using the Outer Banks as his home base, Blackbeard robbed many merchant ships along the Carolina, Virginia, and Delaware coasts. Local townspeople tolerated Blackbeard's presence because they wanted to buy the goods he had stolen (which were usually cheaper than imported English goods). Ship owners, merchants, and planters, however, were all hurt by the pirates' activities.

   The governor of Virginia, Alexander Spotswood, finally decided that the time had come to stop Blackbeard. Spotswood sent two ships commanded by Lieutenant Robert Maynard of the Royal Navy to capture the pirate. During the fight between the pirates and the British sailors, Blackbeard was killed. As a warning to other pirates, Blackbeard's head was cut off and suspended from the bow of Maynard's ship.

   Stede Bonnet, known as the "gentleman pirate" because of his good manners, was a retired army officer who owned a sugar plantation in Barbados. According to legend, he purchased his own sloop, which he named the *Revenge*, to escape his nagging wife and recruited a crew of seventy men. Although he lacked experience in piracy, Bonnet and his crew successfully plundered several ships off the Carolina and Virginia coasts.

In March 1718, Bonnet met Blackbeard, and the two of them decided to sail together. Within a few days, Blackbeard realized Bonnet's lack of experience and decided to use that to his advantage. Blackbeard convinced Bonnet to let one of his lieutenants take command of the *Revenge*, while Bonnet sailed as a guest aboard Blackbeard's ship. During his stay on Blackbeard's ship, Bonnet participated in the siege of Charleston (Charles Town).

After the siege was over, Blackbeard told Bonnet that he was going to disband his fleet and accept a pardon from the governor of North Carolina. He suggested that Bonnet do the same. Bonnet agreed and left immediately in a small boat for Bath, North Carolina, to receive his pardon. When he returned, Blackbeard was gone, along with all of Bonnet's booty. Although Bonnet swore to get revenge, he never met up with Blackbeard again.

In September 1718, Bonnet anchored his ship at Cape Fear, North Carolina. Colonel William Rhett, commissioned by the Carolina colony to track down the pirates who had humiliated Charleston, came upon Bonnet while he was still at Cape Fear. After a bloody battle, Bonnet was captured and taken to Charleston. There in November he and approximately thirty other crew members were found guilty of piracy and sentenced to hang. While in prison, Bonnet wrote a letter to the governor, pleading for his life. However, the letter did not succeed in changing the governor's mind, and Bonnet was hung on December 10, 1718. His body was left hanging for four days as a warning against piracy.

4. The War of Jenkins' Ear began in October 1739, when England declared war on Spain. The English were angry over stories of the mistreatment of their merchant seamen, whom the Spanish accused of smuggling. The unsettled border of Florida was also an issue. The war took its name from an English sea captain, named Robert Jenkins, who had been arrested by the Spanish in 1731 on a smuggling charge. During Jenkins's imprisonment, the Spanish had cut off one of his ears and told him to give it to the English king. When Jenkins brought his pickled ear to the House of Commons, public opinion was so enraged that the English soon declared war on Spain.

   During the War of Jenkins' Ear, General James Oglethorpe in Georgia was granted reinforcements and ordered to capture the Spanish fort at St. Augustine. Although the American forces besieged St. Augustine for thirty-eight days, they finally had to abandon the effort to capture it. However, in 1742 at the Battle of Bloody Marsh, Oglethorpe and his men were more successful. They ambushed the Spanish on St. Simon's Island, killing several hundred of them with only one American casualty. Although the War of Jenkins' Ear ended as a standoff in 1742, the Spanish no longer presented a threat to Georgia and the Carolinas. Georgia had fulfilled its original purpose of serving as a buffer for the British colonies from the Spanish.

Lesson 14: For Further Study Younger Student Adaptations

1. Continue your discussion of slavery by explaining what happened during the Stono Rebellion.

2. Have your students read (or read to them) another book with general information on Native Americans or do more Native American hands-on activities.

3. Share the stories of Blackbeard and Stede Bonnet as well as drawings of pirates and their activities.

4. Explain how the War of Jenkins' Ear got its name and encourage them to try drawing the event that led to war.

Lesson 15: For Further Study Answers

1. Use the Internet to research colonial hornbooks, *New England Primer*, and Anne Bradstreet's poetry.

2. Use the Internet to find pictures of colonial clothing. Use "seventeenth century American clothing," and "eighteenth century American clothing" as search terms.

3. Cholera is caused by the bacterium vibro cholerae and is spread by eating food or drinking water contaminated with the bacteria. These bacteria cause an acute infection of the small intestines. Symptoms of cholera include severe vomiting and diarrhea, which can quickly lead to dehydration. Today, modern sanitation and treatment of drinking water have virtually eliminated cholera in developed counties.

   Smallpox is caused by a virus. It is spread from saliva droplets and is highly contagious, especially during the first week. Symptoms of smallpox include fever, vomiting, backache, weakness, and a skin eruption with pimples that form scabs. When these scabs slough off, they usually leave permanent pitted scars or pocks. A program by the World Health Organization eradicated all smallpox viruses from the world in 1977, except for samples saved by governments for research purposes.

   Scarlet fever is caused by streptococcal bacteria. The bacteria produce an infection of the throat and a toxin that creates a rash one to two days after the onset of the disease. Other symptoms may include chills, abdominal pain, vomiting, and general malaise. Once a very serious childhood disease, scarlet fever is now easily treated.

   Rickets is a childhood disorder caused by a vitamin D deficiency (due to a poor diet or lack of sunlight). When the body is deficient in vitamin D, it is not able to regulate calcium and phosphate levels properly. Progressive softening and weakening of the bone structure can occur, and one of the results can be bowlegs. Today, rickets is rare in developed countries.

   Tuberculosis is caused by the mycobacterium tuberculosis and is spread through the breathing in of infectious droplets expelled from the respiratory tract of an infected person. The disease typically affects and damages the lungs. However, the tuberculosis bacteria may spread to other organs. Symptoms of the disease include coughing up mucus and sputum, fever, chest pain, and weight loss. Treatment with antibiotics must be administered over many months for remission of the disease to occur. If left untreated, the disease is progressive and death may result.

4. Use the search terms, "colonial cookbooks" and "The Frugal Housewife by Susannah Carter" to research these items on the Internet.

Lesson 15: For Further Study Younger Student Adaptations

1. Locate illustrations of colonial hornbooks as well as online instructions for the students to make their own hornbooks.

2. Encourage the students to use the Colonial Family Life form (in the optional section) to draw pictures of colonial clothing.

3. Share the symptoms of one or more of the illnesses prevalent during the colonial period and compare medical treatments today with those in colonial times.

4. Find online directions for colonial recipes and help the students prepare one or more of them. Give them the opportunity to try churning butter (again, you can find directions online).

Lesson 16: For Further Study Answers

1. John Peter Zenger emigrated to New York from Germany in 1710 and apprenticed as a printer to William Bradford, printer of the *New York Gazette*. In 1733 the New York governor, William Cosby, quarreled with the colony's council over his salary and removed the chief justice from the state's Supreme Court when he found himself unable to control the judiciary. An opposition group arose to fight Cosby politically, and these wealthy, powerful men established an opposition newspaper, the *New York Weekly Journal*. They hired John Peter Zenger to be the printer and editor of this paper.

   The *New York Weekly Journal* published articles critical of Governor Cosby. By November 1734, Cosby had had Zenger arrested and charged with seditious libel. After spending more than eight months in prison, Zenger finally went to trial, defended by the prominent Philadelphia attorney Alexander Hamilton. Through his successful defense of Zenger, Hamilton established the precedent that a statement is not libelous, even if it is defamatory, if it can be proven to be true. Zenger's trial was significant in establishing the right of a free press in the American colonies.

   If Zenger had been found guilty, he might have suffered a variety of punishments. Many of the American colonies punished criminals and troublemakers in the center of town so that everyone could see. Two common methods of punishment were the stocks (a wooden framework with holes in it in which the feet or the feet and hands of the convicted would be locked) and the pillory (a wooden and iron framework with a hole in which the head of the convicted was held in a tight grip). Those subjected to being locked in the stocks or the pillory served out their punishment regardless of the weather and might have rotting fruit and other objects thrown at them. Other forms of punishment included the whipping post (where the convicted would be whipped with the public watching), brandings (often of the tongue), and maiming (one's ears and/or his nostrils cut off).

2. As early as the 1670s, colonists and Native Americans in New York and the New England colonies were hunting whales from small sailing ships along the coast. When the whales were captured, killed, and towed ashore, their blubber would be removed and boiled in large iron pots. The oil extracted from this whale blubber was used primarily for lamp fuel. Whalebone or baleen from the whale's upper mouth would also be removed and used to make products such as fishing rods, corsets, umbrellas, and hair brushes. Whale teeth were saved and later carved with decorations and inscriptions, creating a novelty called scrimshaw popular among the upper class.

   Systematic deepwater hunting of sperm whales began from Nantucket, Massachusetts, after 1712. At this point American commercial whaling became very important economically to the New England region. Sperm whale oil burned more cleanly and brightly than other whale oil and was a superior lubricant. Also, the spermaceti from the head of the sperm whale was used to produce the finest grade of candles, a profitable New England export to the mother country.

   Triangular trade referred to the profitable trade routes that connected the New England colonies, England or Africa, and the West Indies during the eighteenth century. The most famous of the triangular trade routes involved shipping molasses and sugar from the West Indies to New England, where it was used to make rum. New England rum was then shipped to west Africa, where it was traded for slaves. The African slaves were shipped from west Africa to the West Indies, where they were auctioned off to plantation owners in the Southern colonies.

   Another triangular trade route began with the shipping of flour and meat from New England to the West Indies. Sugar was then shipped from the West Indies to England, where it was exchanged for manufactured goods that were brought back to the colonies.

   You will be able to find examples of colonial furniture and metalwork by searching the Internet.

3. Jonathan Edwards was born in East Windsor, Connecticut, into a family with a long tradition in the pastoral ministry. Considered to be one of the greatest preachers in American history, Edwards succeeded his maternal grandfather to the pulpit of the Congregationalist church in Northampton, Massachusetts, in 1729. Beginning in 1734, six conversions in Edwards's church turned into thirty conversions a week, drawing people from as far as a hundred miles away.

   Edwards's preaching and writings have been credited with bringing about the first Great Awakening in American history. The power of his preaching was not due to the sensational or theatrical. Observers commented that Edwards did not use big gestures or move much and did not try to impress with an elegant style. Rather, he convinced with the weight of his arguments and the intensity of his spiritual feeling. As his congregation listened to Edwards preach God's Word, many of them cried, screamed, and fainted; repented of their sin; and turned to the Lord. On July 8, 1741, Edwards preached his famous sermon, "Sinners in the Hands of an Angry God." The congregation's emotional response to this sermon was so overwhelming that Edwards was not able to finish the sermon because so many wanted to know how to be saved. Because Edwards considered personal conversion to be critical, he insisted that only those who had made a profession of faith (which included a description of their conversion experience) be able to receive communion. This reversed his grandfather's policy, alienating his congregation and leading to his dismissal in 1750. For the next several years, Edwards served as a missionary pastor to Native Americans in Stockbridge, Massachusetts. He also wrote a number of theological treatises and published many of his sermons. In the fall of 1757, Edwards assumed the presidency of the College of New Jersey (later renamed Princeton University). However, he held this position for less than a year, because he died in March 1758, from smallpox.

   David Brainerd was born in Connecticut and orphaned at the age of fourteen. Licensed to preach in 1742, he decided to devote himself to missionary work among the Native Americans in 1743. In this mission work he was supported by the Scottish Society for Promoting Christian Knowledge. Brainerd worked first at a native settlement near Stockbridge, Massachusetts. Later he ministered among the Delaware Indians in Pennsylvania and New Jersey.

   At this period in American history, many church leaders in the colonies argued about whether Native Americans even possessed souls to be saved. Brainerd was deeply burdened for the spiritual and physical welfare of the Indians and sacrificially labored on their behalf. Suffering from tuberculosis, Brainerd refused to put his health needs above the needs of the natives and ended up cutting his life short. Although he fell in love with Jerusha Edwards, daughter of Jonathan Edwards, his ill health prevented their marriage. On October 19, 1747, Brainerd at the age of thirty-nine died at the Edwards's home.

   In 1746, the Scottish Society for Promoting Christian Knowledge published Brainerd's *Journal* in two parts. In 1749 Jonathan Edwards edited Brainerd's diary and other writings into a book entitled *An Account of the Life of the Late Reverend David Brainerd.* This book became a missionary classic, used by God to challenge Christians worldwide to greater service for Christ.

4. Use the Internet to research colonial games, toys, quilts, music, and dances. You should find a wealth of information. You can find instructions online to play cat's cradle and other games.

Lesson 16: For Further Study Younger Student Adaptations

1. Have your students read (or read to them) a short biography of John Peter Zenger. Explain the meaning of libel and discuss the significance of freedom of the press. You could also show the students pictures of the stocks and the pillory and explain how these and other forms of colonial punishment were used in a very public fashion.

2. Locate illustrations of whaling and colonial furniture and metal work to show him. Compare colonial furniture to today's furniture. Encourage the students to use the Colonial Culture form (in the optional section) to draw a picture of colonial transportation.

3. Read a short excerpt from Edwards's sermon "Sinners in the Hands of an Angry God" and ask your students how it compares to sermons they have heard in church. Share the story of David Brainerd's missionary work and have them compare Brainerd's ministry to that of present-day missionaries whom they may know.

4. Demonstrate how to do cat's cradle and show them pictures of colonial toys and crafts. Have them learn one or more songs from the colonial period.

UNIT THREE
For Further Study Answers

Lesson 17: For Further Study Answers

1. Jeffrey Amherst became a soldier at about age fourteen and served in the War of the Austrian Succession and in the European theater during the Seven Years' War. Amherst became a primary contributor to the British victory in the French and Indian War. In 1758, Amherst was chosen by William Pitt to lead the British siege on Louisbourg. Amherst's success at Louisbourg opened the St. Lawrence River to the British and led to his being named British commander-in-chief in North America. Amherst was involved in the Battle of Quebec in 1759; and in 1760 he captured Montreal, ending French rule in North America.

   From 1760 until 1763 Amherst held the position of military governor of Canada. Because he was unable to suppress Pontiac's Rebellion, he was recalled to London. A letter still exists in which Amherst seriously discussed the idea of spreading smallpox to hostile Native American forces by means of gift blankets exposed to smallpox. This idea had already been tried in June 1763, with the Delaware Indians by the commander of Fort Pitt. It is disputed whether Amherst actually followed through on this idea, but tribes in western Pennsylvania were struck with a devastating smallpox outbreak at that time.

   Amherst was knighted in 1761 and made a baron in 1776. Because of his close ties with many Americans, Amherst refused to take a field position in the American Revolution. However, he did serve in an advisory role for the British during that war. Both the town of Amherst, Massachusetts, and Amherst College were named for Jeffrey Amherst.

2. Use the Internet to research the fort you are interested in studying.

3. General James Wolfe entered the British army at the age of fourteen and served in the War of the Austrian Succession. In 1757, William Pitt made Wolfe second in command under General Jeffrey Amherst in North America. Wolfe's capture of the French fortress of Louisbourg earned him command of the British military and naval expedition against Quebec.

   When Wolfe and his troops launched a frontal attack on the French at Quebec, the attack was unsuccessful. Wolfe's aides then counseled him to consider landing downstream, southwest of Quebec. Wolfe decided to move five thousand of his men to the suggested area. Then he and his troops climbed a cliff to the Plains of Abraham above Quebec and forced the French into an open battle there on September 13, 1759. Although Wolfe was mortally wounded, the British won a decisive victory. Wolfe was shot in the wrist and died a few days later from an infection.

   The fact that General Wolfe died at the moment of victory inspired many painters, sculptors, poets, and songwriters to immortalize this tragic hero. Benjamin West painted *The Death of General Wolfe* in 1770 and exhibited it a year later at the annual Royal Academy Exhibition. In 1772, King George III appointed West historical painter to the court. West also served as the second president of the Royal Academy of Arts and became well known for his large-scale history paintings.

In *The Death of General Wolfe*, West depicted Wolfe and the other British officers and soldiers in modern uniform, instead of traditional attire. The figure at Wolfe's left has been identified as a surgeon in the British army. West also included an American Indian in the painting. Sir Joshua Reynolds, president of the Royal Academy, tried to convince West not to depart from the neoclassical painting tradition, and King George III proclaimed that he would not buy a painting with British heroes shown in modern clothing. However, when West's painting was finally displayed, it was received with great critical acclaim. Reynolds apologized for his error in judgment, and King George ordered a copy for the royal collection. Wolfe actually painted at least four replicas of the original and earned royalties from hundreds of engravings based upon the painting.

4. George Washington served as a volunteer aide to British Major General Edward Braddock in 1755. The British had sent a large army to capture Fort Duquesne from the French. Even though Braddock's expedition suffered a terrible defeat, Washington demonstrated great courage and tactical skills in battle. Governor Dinwiddie of Virginia then placed Washington in charge of that colony's frontier defenses. At times Washington struggled to maintain discipline over his men and argued with his superiors over battle tactics.

   From his experiences in the field during the French and Indian War, Washington came to a firm understanding of the role that discipline played in an army. He learned the importance of a military leader's attention to administrative details and to the welfare of his soldiers. Washington also gained experience in making do with limited resources and in adapting formations and tactics to the terrain. These lessons would serve him well as commander of the Continental army during the American Revolution.

Lesson 17: For Further Study Younger Student Adaptations

1. Share the story of Jeffrey Amherst's life and military career. Show them illustrations of weapons used during the French and Indian War.

2. Find pictures of one or more of the forts used during the French and Indian War. Discuss what fighting was like in this war.

3. Show your students the Benjamin West painting and explore what they can learn about the Battle of Quebec by looking at it. Share the lyrics to the song about General Wolfe's death.

4. Have your students read (or read to them) a short biography of George Washington. Focus on his life before the American Revolution.

Lesson 18: For Further Study Answers

1. George III was the first king in the Hanoverian line to be born in England. He ruled for sixty years (1760 – 1820), the longest reign of any British king. The years of his reign encompassed the American Revolution, the French Revolution, and the beginnings of the Industrial Revolution. When George III assumed the throne at the age of twenty-two, he took steps to recover royal power that had been lost by his predecessors. The most notable of those steps was the dismissal of the powerful William Pitt the Elder.

   As early as 1765, George's performance as king was impacted by the fact that he suffered from porphyria, a blood disease that has plagued several British monarchs. Porphyria affects the skin or central nervous system and can cause seizures, hallucinations, depression, senility, and blindness. Eventually, George III's illness would lead to his eldest son ruling as Prince Regent from 1811 until his father died in 1820.

George III was a strong supporter of the war against America. The collaboration of George III with Lord North, who became prime minister in 1770, resulted in a series of policies that led inevitably to the American Revolution. When the American colonies were finally given their independence, George considered abdicating the throne. As king, George laboriously read every line of every document that he received, strongly supported educational causes, maintained an interest in agriculture and science, and developed a royal library.

2. Daniel Boone, American soldier and explorer, was born near Reading, Pennsylvania. He spent his youth hunting and trapping and came to know friendly Native Americans in the forests. When he was fifteen, his family moved to the Yadkin Valley in North Carolina. Several years later, Boone left home to join a military expedition in the French and Indian War. After the war was over, he returned to his family home for a while.

   Following the French and Indian War, the British government prohibited exploration and settlement of the Kentucky wilderness. However, Boone was among the many colonial settlers who ignored the Proclamation of 1763, which prohibited colonial expansion west of the Appalachian Mountains. In 1767, Boone traveled to the edge of Kentucky and camped there for a while. Two years later, Boone and five other men set out to explore lands even farther west, beyond the Cumberland Mountains. They passed through the Cumberland Gap and explored large areas of Kentucky for almost two years.

   In 1775 Boone worked with the Transylvania Company to establish a trail through the Cumberland Gap. By the end of the year, Boone and twenty-eight other men had finished blazing this trail, which eventually became known as the Wilderness Road. They also had established Boonesborough on the Kentucky River, the first U.S. settlement west of the Appalachian Mountains.

   During the American Revolution, Kentucky was organized as a Virginia county, and Boone served as a captain in the local militia. In 1778, Boone was captured by Shawnee Indians and given up for dead. However, Boone was able to escape in time to warn the settlers at Boonesborough of an impending British and Indian attack. Following the Revolution until his death in 1820, Boone continued moving and lived in Ohio, West Virginia, and Missouri. In 1784, he published a book called *Adventures*, which received much public acclaim.

3. Samuel Adams, born in Boston, came from a Puritan background and graduated from Harvard University. Although he was a poor businessman, he was an excellent politician. His true genius lay in his ability to educate and motivate people. Sam Adams was a passionate advocate of republicanism and a good friend of Thomas Paine. He also was one of the first and most vocal colonial supporters of independence and was one of the leaders of the Boston Sons of Liberty. The British considered Sam Adams to be an agitator and a public enemy.

   In 1765, Adams was elected to the Massachusetts Assembly, and he served as a delegate to the First and Second Continental Congresses. He also signed the Declaration of Independence, worked as a member of the Massachusetts convention to form a state constitution, and served as governor of the state.

4. First known as the Loyal Nine, the Sons of Liberty originated in Boston in the summer of 1765 to agitate against the Stamp Act. It was a group composed primarily of small businessmen, artisans, and laborers (like the silversmith Paul Revere), as well as radical intellectuals (like Sam Adams). A New York chapter apparently was also organized in early 1765. According to tradition, the Boston chapter gathered beneath the Liberty Tree for meetings and the New York chapter met beneath the Liberty Pole. For reasons of secrecy and safety, these groups usually met late at night.

   Eventually, these two original Sons of Liberty organizations established correspondence and communication with emerging Sons of Liberty groups in other colonies. Although begun as a secret society, the Sons of Liberty quickly built a broad public base of political support. The Sons of Liberty planned and directed colonial protests to the Townshend Acts and Boston Tea Party, as well as the propaganda following the Boston Massacre.

At times the Sons of Liberty engaged in violent activities. They tarred and feathered leading Loyalists and royal tax collectors or hung them in effigy. Mobs smashed windows and broke into homes and offices of royal officials to vandalize them or burn them to the ground. There were also opportunists who used the name of the Sons of Liberty to commit violent acts not related to the cause. By far the most effective tool of the Sons of Liberty was their use of newspaper articles to publicize their activities. A great many in the group were printers and publishers, and their use of newspaper propaganda served to embolden patriots in every colony.

Lesson 18: For Further Study Younger Student Adaptations

1. Have your students read (or read to them) a short biography of King George III. Discuss how the king's mental and physical health impacted his reign.

2. Have your students read (or read to them) a short biography of Daniel Boone. Look for drawings of Boonesborough. Have them locate on a map the areas of the country that Boone explored.

3. Have your students read (or read to them) a short biography of Sam Adams.

4. Share drawings of the "Liberty Tree" and the "Liberty Pole" and talk with them about the activities that took place there.

Lesson 19: For Further Study Answers

1. John Hancock was a wealthy Bostonian merchant, who gained much of his wealth smuggling in goods in defiance of the Navigation Acts. In June 1768, British customs officials seized Hancock's sloop, because they believed that he had smuggled goods on board. An angry crowd of Bostonians mobbed the customs officials during the seizure.

   Although John Hancock was a generous supporter of the Sons of Liberty, Sam Adams considered him to be too flamboyant and financially motivated. In the years immediately preceding the American Revolution, Hancock headed Boston's Committee of Public Safety, which had begun preparing minutemen for hostilities with the British. Serving as president of the Continental Congress, Hancock was the first to sign the Declaration of Independence. From 1780 until 1793, Hancock served as the governor of Massachusetts.

2. Crispus Attucks has been traditionally considered the first casualty of the America Revolution. Attucks was probably a runaway slave with both African American (his father) and Native American (his mother) ancestry. Historians know very little about Attucks and have constructed accounts of his life more from speculation than facts. In 1770, Attucks was shot and killed in the Boston Massacre. Although Attucks has been traditionally depicted as one of the leaders of the crowd defying the British, there has been much debate over whether he was a rabble-rouser or a hero. Martin Luther King, Jr., referred to Attucks in the introduction of his book *Why We Can't Wait* as an example of someone whose contribution to history has been overlooked.

3. John Adams emerged as Boston's foremost attorney in the years preceding the American Revolution. He often stood alone, taking on controversial causes and defending his moral convictions, regardless of the cost to him personally. For example, Adams defended the eight British soldiers involved in the Boston Massacre because he believed that they had the right to be defended. Perhaps the deepest thinker of his generation, Adams's lonely integrity was rooted in his Puritan heritage.

Following the Boston Tea Party, Adams wrote, "The die is cast. Swim or sink, live or die, survive or perish with my country was my unalterable determination." One of the earliest advocates of revolution, John Adams represented Massachusetts in the First and Second Continental Congresses and eventually served on some fifty committees, including the committee that drafted the Declaration of Independence. Although Adams became known for his brilliance and strong work ethic, he also gained a reputation for being stubborn and unwilling to work for a compromise.

4. Patrick Henry gave a famous speech at Virginia's Revolutionary Convention in March 1775, in which he said, "I know not what course others may take, but as for me, give me liberty or give me death." Henry had a reputation as a passionate and fiery orator, probably the most celebrated orator of the American Revolution. Born north of Richmond, Virginia, Henry failed in early attempts at shopkeeping and farming. However, in 1760 he began a career as a lawyer and quickly made a name for himself.

   In 1765, Henry was elected to the Virginia House of Burgesses, where he furthered his radical reputation in the debate over the Stamp Act. Henry, along with Thomas Jefferson and Richard Henry Lee, also helped to organize the committees of correspondence in Virginia. In 1774, he was selected as a delegate to the First Continental Congress. Although Henry commanded militiamen at the beginning of the Revolution, he served most notably in state government during this period. He was elected the first governor of Virginia when it became an independent commonwealth in 1776. Following the war, he opposed ratification of the U.S. Constitution because he was concerned that it impaired states' rights. Later he worked on behalf of the Bill of Rights.

Lesson 19: For Further Study Younger Student Adaptations

1. Have your students read (or read to them) a short biography of John Hancock. Show them John Hancock's famous signature on the Declaration of Independence and discuss how "John Hancock" became a synonym for any signature.

2. Share what is known about Crispus Attucks's life. Explain the difference between the lifestyles of a free African American and a slave.

3. Have your students read (or read to them) a short biography of John Adams.

4. Read a short excerpt from Patrick Henry's famous speech. Have your students read (or read to them) a short biography of Patrick Henry.

Lesson 20: For Further Study Answers

1. Use the Internet to research the poems and poets.

2. Ethan Allen, born in Connecticut, was the oldest of eight children. When his father died at an early age, Ethan was left to care for the family. After his brothers and sisters grew older, Ethan moved to a region known as New Hampshire Land Grants (now Vermont). Settling in Bennington, he became involved in the struggle between New York and New Hampshire over control of the region.

   Between 1770 and 1775, Allen commanded a volunteer militia, known as the Green Mountain Boys. The group was named "Green Mountain" in defiance of the New York threat to drive the New Hampshire settlers off the fields and "into the Green Mountains." This group operated liked vigilantes; they used intimidation and violence to keep their land grants from becoming property of New York. Allen was declared an outlaw by the royal governor of New York, and at one point a bounty of sixty pounds was put on his head.

The Green Mountain Boys were involved in the American victory at Fort Ticonderoga in May 1775 and in the American military expedition against Canada. Allen was taken prisoner by the British near Montreal in September 1775. He was held in confinement until he was exchanged for another prisoner in 1778. Allen returned home and received a commission as a lieutenant colonel in the Continental army.

The same year Allen appeared before the Continental Congress in support of Vermont's claim for recognition as an independent state. Between 1780 and 1783, he negotiated with the governor of Canada, supposedly to establish Vermont as a British province. He was charged with treason, but the charge was never substantiated. His actions seemed to be intended to force the Continental Congress to take action on the Vermont case. Allen died in 1789. When New York relinquished its claim to the land, Vermont applied for statehood and became the fourteenth state in the Union in 1791.

3. Joseph Warren was an influential doctor and surgeon in Boston as well as a leading colonial champion of the cause of liberty. The Stamp Act agitation had aroused his interest in politics, and he soon became associated with Sam and John Adams. He contributed articles to the *Boston Gazette* over the signature "True Patriot." Joseph Warren and Sam Adams were two leaders in the first Boston committee of correspondence, and Warren was also an active member of the committee of public safety. In 1772, he was selected to deliver the commemorative oration on the anniversary of the Boston Massacre.

   When Sam Adams left Massachusetts to attend the First Continental Congress in 1774, Warren assumed leadership of the radicals in Boston. He authored the Suffolk Resolves, a strongly worded statement urging forcible opposition to England if it should prove to be necessary. The resolves also pledged support to measures recommended by the Continental Congress.

   On April 18, 1775, Warren made the decision to dispatch Paul Revere and William Dawes to warn the people of Lexington and Concord that British troops were approaching. During the British return march the following day, the doctor exposed himself continually to enemy fire to take care of the wounded.

   Three days before the battle of Breed's Hill, Warren was appointed major-general of the Massachusetts troops by the provincial congress. During this battle Warren was shot in the back of his head and his body was thrown into a ditch by a British officer. Months later Warren's body was identified by Paul Revere, who recognized a false tooth that he had made for Warren. Warren's tragic death strengthened the zeal of Massachusetts Whigs for the cause of independence.

4. The main weapons of the American Revolution were the muzzle-loading flintlock musket, its attached bayonet, and the cannon. Secondary weapons included rifles, pistols, and swords. A rifle took a long time to load compared to a musket. Muskets could be fired every fifteen seconds. Rifles, much more accurate than muskets, took at least thirty seconds to load and sometimes as long as a minute. By the time a soldier could force his rifle ball down the barrel, he might be killed with a bayonet.

   Early in the war, the Americans had a shortage of bayonets, which were needed for fighting at close range or in damp weather when wet gunpowder and flints made firearms useless. When France joined the war, they helped to alleviate the American shortage of bayonets and arms, providing a hundred thousand muskets and bayonets.

   Firearms during the time of the American Revolution used black powder. Black powder was discovered in the ninth century and was the only known practical explosive widely used until the twentieth century. Today, black powder is primarily used for fireworks and in reproduction weapons. Smokeless powder replaced black powder as a propellant at the end of the nineteenth century and is used in all modern guns.

Cannon were exceedingly important on the battlefield during the American Revolution. Infantry that was not supported by cannon usually lost if the enemy had cannon. Revolutionary War cannon fired solid balls, small shot, and sometimes shells and had a range of several hundred yards.

Lesson 20: For Further Study Younger Student Adaptations

1. Read Longfellow's poem "The Midnight Ride of Paul Revere" or excerpts from it.

2. Have your students read (or read to them) a short biography of Ethan Allen. Ask your students to discuss whether or not they would have enjoyed being a member of the Green Mountain Boys.

3. Share the story of Dr. Warren's activities as a Patriot before his death. Review what a martyr is and discuss why Warren became known as the "martyr of Bunker Hill."

4. Show your students some illustrations of weapons used during the American Revolution. Encourage them to try drawing one or more of the weapons.

Lesson 21: For Further Study Answers

1. Henry Knox served with distinction as an artillery officer during the American Revolution and as George Washington's first secretary of war. He participated in almost every important military engagement during the war. A witness to the Boston Massacre, Knox was one of the volunteers at the Battle of Breed's Hill. Impressed with Knox's knowledge of artillery, Washington commissioned him colonel of artillery and sent him on the Ticonderoga mission in 1775. Knox succeeded in hauling back to Boston the badly needed artillery that had been captured from the British as this fort.

   Knox became Washington's trusted advisor and loyal friend. He continued to work organizing the American artillery and fought in the battles around New York in 1776. Under Knox's supervision, Washington and his troops crossed the Delaware on Christmas night, 1776, to attack the Hessians at Trenton. For this achievement, Knox was given a commission as brigadier-general. Under Knox's direction, American artillery was effective in the Battles of Princeton, Brandywine, Germantown, and Monmouth. His masterful placement of the siege cannons at Yorktown was an important factor in the American victory there.

   At the end of the war, Knox was made a major general and placed in command at West Point. His friendship with Washington continued after the war. Knox served as secretary of war under the Articles of Confederation and in Washington's first administration. Then Knox retired from public service and moved to Maine with his family. There his home was frequently full of important guests from all over the world. Knox loved good food and ended up weighing nearly three hundred pounds. He died unexpectedly when a chicken bone lodged in his intestines.

2. You can find interesting information and pictures by using the Internet to research Thomas Jefferson's and Benjamin Franklin's inventions.

3. The official signed copy of the Declaration of Independence, issued by the members of the Second Continental Congress in 1776, was kept at the Library of Congress until 1952. Then it was moved to the National Archives. However, the Library of Congress retains Jefferson's original rough draft. In the days immediately following July 4, 1776, Jefferson made six annotated longhand copies of the official congressional draft, in which he underlined the passages that the Continental Congress had changed. Four of these six survive and can be

found at the Library of Congress, the New York Public Library, the Massachusetts Historical Society, and the American Philosophical Society

On July 5, 1776, about two hundred broadsides of the text of the Declaration of Independence were printed at John Dunlap's shop and rushed to the thirteen colonies and the army. A broadside was a sheet of paper printed on one or both sides, much like a newspaper page today. There are twenty-five known surviving Dunlap broadsides — twenty-one copies belong to public libraries, historical societies, universities, and city halls, and the remaining four are owned by private owners and foundations.

John Trumbull's painting in the Rotunda does not depict the actual signing of the Declaration of Independence. It does feature the committee that drafted the Declaration of Independence — John Adams, Robert Sherman, Thomas Jefferson, and Benjamin Franklin — standing before John Hancock and portraits of forty-two of the fifty-six signers and five other patriots. If you look closely, you can see that John Adams is standing on Thomas Jefferson's foot. An engraving of this painting can be found on the back of the two-dollar bill. (In the engraving, Adams's foot was moved off of Jefferson's foot.)

4. Nathan Hale was a young schoolteacher in Connecticut when the American Revolution broke out. Commissioned as an officer in the Connecticut militia, he was involved in the siege of Boston and then moved to New York to take place in the military operations there. In September 1775, Hale volunteered to cross British lines and gather information about British forces on Long Island. He went on his mission disguised as a schoolmaster.

   Unfortunately, Hale was captured by the British and taken to General Howe's headquarters, where he was interrogated and ordered executed the following morning. During the evening before his execution, Captain Hale asked for a clergyman to attend him, but his jailer refused. He then requested a Bible and again received a refusal. On the morning of his execution, Hale wrote two letters — one to his mother and one to a fellow officer. Shortly before his death, he uttered these words on the gallows, "I only regret that I have but one life to lose for my country."

Lesson 21: For Further Study Younger Student Adaptations

1. Discuss what artillery means and explain Henry Knox's role with the nation's artillery during the American Revolution.

2. Share pictures of Jefferson's and Franklin's inventions and explain how they work.

3. Find a copy of the Declaration of Independence to show to your students. Have them examine Trumbull's painting and tell you what they have learned from it.

4. Explain why spies are used during times of war. Tell your students the story of Nathan Hale and the famous saying attributed to him.

Lesson 22: For Further Study Answers

1. The Marquis de Lafayette was a French aristocrat famous for his participation in the American Revolution. Lafayette entered the French army at the age of fourteen. When the British colonies proclaimed their independence, he was nineteen years old.

   Lafayette believed in the political ideals of the American Revolution and shared the French hatred of Great Britain. In fact, Lafayette's father had died fighting the British.

In 1777, Lafayette signed an agreement with the colonies to serve as a volunteer in their military without compensation. He invested his own funds to outfit a ship, persuaded several other French officers to join him, and sailed for America that April. Landing in South Carolina, Lafayette headed north to Philadelphia to join Washington and his troops. The Frenchman formed a friendship with Washington that would last until Washington's death. (He even named his son after Washington.)

Lafayette's first military engagement was at the Battle of Brandywine in September 1777. Although he was wounded, he fought courageously, which endeared him to the American troops. In early 1778, Lafayette commanded troops for a projected expedition to Canada, and he fought at the Battle of Monmouth in August 1778. In 1779, Lafayette returned to France, where he consulted with the French king concerning the further direction of his services and French aid for the colonists.

When he returned to America later in 1779, Lafayette landed in Boston and then reported to Washington. From April until October of 1781, he was charged with the defense of Virginia. He led American forces in Virginia against both Benedict Arnold and Lord Cornwallis and fought at the Battle of Yorktown. Immediately following the British surrender, Lafayette returned to France and served as a diplomatic aid to Benjamin Franklin during the peace negotiations in Paris.

In 1824, Lafayette came back to the United States for a year-long tour.

2. On June 14, 1777, the Continental Congress passed the first Flag Act to establish an official flag for the new American nation. The act proclaimed that "the flag of the United States be made of thirteen stripes, alternate red and white, that the union be thirteen stars, white in a blue field, representing a new Constellation."

   The first flag used by the colonies, called the Grand Union, was first flown in late 1775 or early 1776. This flag featured thirteen alternating red and white stripes to represent the thirteen colonies and a field of blue in the upper corner of the flag that included the British Union Jack (which consisted of the red cross of St. George of England and the white cross of St. Andrew of Scotland). This flag was flying on July 4, 1776, when the colonies proclaimed their independence.

   No one knows with absolute certainty who designed or sewed the flag called for by the Flag Act of 1777. The journals of the Continental Congress indicate that Francis Hopkinson, a congressman from New Jersey, was to design it. According to legend, the Philadelphia seamstress Betsy Ross sewed the first flag. George Washington supposedly paid a visit to the widow's upholstery shop in 1776. Betsy's grandson recalled hearing the family story about this visit when he was five years old — the account of Washington and Ross sitting in the parlor, drawing sketches, and talking about what the flag should look like. The Ross family also has old letters that describe this visit. However, historians do not know for certain who actually sewed the first flag.

3. Benedict Arnold was probably the most notorious traitor in American history. During the early years of the American Revolution, he served as a general in the Continental army and became well known for leading successful campaigns and winning battles. He joined Ethan Allen in securing Fort Ticonderoga and participated in the Battle of Quebec, where he was shot in the leg. In 1776 he oversaw the construction of America's first gunships on Lake Champlain, and in 1777 he played an important role in the American victory at Saratoga. However, during this period, Arnold was passed over by the Continental Congress for a promotion to major general, despite Washington's protests.

   In 1778, Arnold became commander of Philadelphia after the British evacuation. There he met Peggy Shippen, who belonged to a family known for its Loyalist sympathies. In April 1779, Arnold married this young woman. The same year he was court-martialed because of disputes that he had with civil authorities, but he was cleared of all charges except a few minor ones. Historians later discovered that Arnold's financial dealings in Philadelphia were more corrupt than suspected at the time. Apparently, Arnold was heavily in debt and entered into real estate speculation schemes and authorized government supplies for personal use. However, even though Arnold was reprimanded by Washington, he was given command of West Point in 1780.

By this point Arnold had already begun bargaining with the British. He engaged in correspondence with Sir Henry Clinton in New York City and arranged to hand over West Point to the British for a sum in excess of 10,000 pounds and a commission in the British army. On September 23, 1780, three American soldiers in New York captured a young British officer, Major John Andre. In his boots they found papers revealing Arnold's plans, which would have opened up the entire Hudson River valley to the British and cut the United States in two.

When Arnold learned of Andre's capture, he escaped to a British warship in the Hudson and joined the British forces. His wife feigned innocence, and two of Arnold's aides-de-camp were cleared of any complicity. Arnold was appointed brigadier general in the British army and led two savage raids against the Americans — one in Virginia and one in New London, Connecticut. After the war Arnold moved with his wife and children to London. However, he was never fully trusted there. When Arnold died, he was buried in the uniform of a Continental soldier.

4. The Articles of Confederation had twelve articles. Article I stated that the name of the Confederacy would be the United States of America. Article II stated that each state retained "its sovereignty, freedom and independence, and every power, jurisdiction and right" which was not delegated to the United States in Congress assembled. Article III stated that the states entered into a "firm league of friendship with each other" for their "common defense, the security of their liberties, and their mutual and general welfare."

Lesson 22: For Further Study Younger Student Adaptations

1. Have your students read (or read to them) a short biography of the Marquis de Lafayette.

2. Show them pictures of early American flags. Encourage your students to try drawing one or more of them.

3. Discuss what it means to be a traitor. Explain the story of Benedict Arnold and his betrayal of the Patriot cause.

4. Find a copy of the Articles of Confederation and show it to your students. Explain that this document established a framework for the way our nation's government would be run. In simple terms, explain why it was soon replaced by a new document.

Lesson 23: For Further Study Answers

1. Baron von Steuben was a Prussian army officer who served with George Washington in the American Revolution. At the age of seventeen, he entered the Prussian army, and he served with distinction during the Seven Years' War. An avid student of military strategy, von Steuben mastered the skills of a drillmaster and eventually served as an aide-de-camp to King Frederick II. When peace came in 1763, he was discharged. For the next fourteen years he was unable to find military employment, although he did become part of the royal court and received the title of Baron. During this time Von Steuben, suffering from financial difficulties, tried unsuccessfully to sell his military services to several European countries.

   During the summer of 1777, he traveled to France to visit with the American envoy there, Benjamin Franklin. He hoped to convince Franklin that his military skills could help the American colonial army. Although Franklin was impressed with von Steuben, he decided to introduce the Prussian to General Washington as a lieutenant general in the King of Prussia's services (instead of as a captain).

By December 1777, von Steuben was in Portsmouth, New Hampshire. On February 23, 1778, the Prussian drillmaster arrived at Valley Forge to help train the Continental army. In March von Steuben began drilling the soldiers, and by May Washington had obtained for him the appointment of inspector general, with the rank of major general. The following winter von Steuben prepared his Regulations for the Order and Discipline of the Troops of the United States, which became the American army's standard drill manual.

The results of von Steuben's work were clear at the Battle of Monmouth, where he rallied the disordered and retreating troops of General Charles Lee. In 1781, he served under the Marquis de Lafayette in Virginia, and at the siege of Yorktown he commanded one of the three divisions of Washington's army.

After the war von Steuben became a citizen of the United States and resided in New York City, where he became a very popular figure. Congress passed a vote of thanks for his service, gave him a gold-hilted sword in 1784, and later granted him a pension of $2,400. Von Steuben also received land grants from New York, New Jersey, Virginia, and Pennsylvania.

The American painter Charles Wilson Peale was a frequent visitor to the Continental army's encampment at Valley Forge. Peale admired von Steuben's work with the soldiers there. In late 1779 or early 1780, Baron von Steuben commissioned Peale to paint his portrait.

2. Count Casimir Pulaski, a Polish soldier, was forced to flee his native land when the Poles failed to defeat their Russian invaders. By 1777 Pulaski had ended up in Paris. There he met Benjamin Franklin, who was recruiting volunteers to fight with the American Patriots against the British. Pulaski enthusiastically responded to Franklin's plea for help, since Britain had recommended that Poland be partitioned by hostile surrounding nations in 1772.

   While awaiting a formal appointment by Congress, Pulaski was invited by Washington to serve on his staff at the Battle of Brandywine. Pulaski's performance at Brandywine earned him a commission as brigadier general of the entire U.S. cavalry. He spent the winter of 1777-1778 at Trenton training and outfitting the cavalry units and often used his own money to secure equipment for his troops when congressional funding was lacking. However, in 1778 Pulaski asked to be relieved of his position because he wanted to be able to form an independent cavalry legion that would have the ability to act on its own.

   With the support of George Washington, Pulaski received congressional permission in March 1778 to develop this special cavalry unit. For the next several months he recruited Americans, Poles, Irishmen, Frenchmen, and Germans from his headquarters in Baltimore. In 1779, Pulaski and his cavalry unit were ordered south to join General Lincoln. During the siege of Savannah, Pulaski was shot in the leg and fell from his horse. Within days, gangrene had killed him. Pulaski has been referred to as the "Father of American cavalry," and most states in America have some county, town, street, school, or highway named for Pulaski.

3. The *Turtle* was designed by David Bushnell, a graduate of Yale University. Just over seven feet long and made of wood, the *Turtle* was propelled underwater by a system of levers and pedals. Bushnell wanted the *Turtle* to be able to steal up alongside a warship at anchor, attach a cask of gunpowder to its hull, and slip away before a timing device made the powder cask explode. When the *Turtle* attempted to blow up the *HMS Eagle* in New York Harbor in September 1776, it failed.

4. The origin of the words and music of "Yankee Doodle" are not known exactly. However, some historians believe that the music and words go back to a fifteenth century Dutch harvesting song that began "Yanker dudel doodle down." The British may have also used the tune for a nursery rhyme known as Lucy Locket.

   However, the words with which we are familiar today were written by Dr. Richard Schuckburg in 1758. Schuckburg, a British army doctor serving in the American colonies during the French and Indian War, looked down on the Americans and made fun of them in his lyrics. The word *yankee* was of Dutch origin; *janke* meant foolish fellow or country bumpkin. "Macaroni" was used to refer to a fancy ("dandy") style of Italian dress widely imitated in England at the time. The Americans, however, liked "Yankee Doodle" and added verses to the song.

Lesson 23: For Further Study Younger Student Adaptations

1. Explain what a drillmaster does. Discuss in more detail Baron von Steuben's training techniques and why they were successful.

2. Explain what the cavalry is and ask whether your students would prefer to serve in the cavalry or infantry.

3. Explain what a submarine is and describe the world's first submarine attack.

4. Encourage your students to sing as many verses of "Yankee Doodle" as you can locate. Explain the origin and meaning of the song.

Lesson 24: For Further Study Answers

1. The Continental Congress had no power to tax the American people. Distrust of centralized power lay at the heart of the American Revolution; the colonists had revolted against the British because of their taxes. To raise money to fight the war, Congress flooded the colonies with paper money, creating hugely inflationary prices that in effect "taxed" the American people. American continental dollars became so worthless that they were sometimes used to light fires. By the end of the Revolution, it took six hundred Continentals to equal one Spanish silver dollar — thus, the phrase "not worth a Continental." Militiamen and soldiers sometimes mutinied for lack of pay. Congress received some money from the colonies for war expenses. However, gifts and loans from other nations, especially France, the Netherlands, and Spain, were what enabled the Americans to keep fighting. Even then, the United States ended the war deeply in debt.

2. In many respects the American Revolution was also a civil war — American Patriots versus American Loyalists. Loyalists, colonials who supported the British cause, were called Tories by the Patriots. Historians estimate that as many as 20 percent of the white American population (about half a million) were Tories.

   The Loyalists were strongest in the far Southern colonies (Georgia and the Carolinas) and in the Middle colonies (especially New York and Pennsylvania). Loyalists belonged to all social classes and occupations. Wealthy merchants tended to remain loyal, as did officeholders under the crown. Loyalists also included small farmers, craftsmen, and shopkeepers, as well as some African Americans, Indians, indentured servants, and German immigrants. Only about 19,000 Loyalists actually fought in the conflict.

   Revolutionary leaders deeply resented the leaders of Loyalist armed bands. The property of many Loyalists was confiscated by the Patriots during the war, and the matter of restoring these properties to their owners was discussed in negotiations for the Treaty of Paris. The treaty stipulated that Congress should urge the states to make restitution to the Loyalists. However, little was done, and for many years there were lawsuits concerning various properties. After the war, many Loyalists settled in the Bahamas and other parts of the West Indies, the maritime provinces of Canada, and in England.

3. Use the Internet to research Gilbert Stuart, Charles Wilson Peale, and John Singleton Copley You should also go to the website of the National Gallery of Art. Gilbert Stuart painted the portrait of Washington on the one-dollar bill.

4. Use the Internet to research Revolutionary War songs.

Lesson 24: For Further Study Younger Student Adaptations

1. Show your students pictures of Continental paper dollars and Continental coins. Compare the two.

2. Review the difference between a Loyalist and a Patriot. Encourage your students to think about what it would be like for Loyalists and Patriots to live in the same community.

3. Look for works painted by artists during the American Revolution to share with your students.

4. Find lyrics of songs from the American Revolution and sing them together.

UNIT FOUR
For Further Study Answers

Lesson 25: For Further Study Answers

1. Mount Vernon has a website where you can take a virtual tour.

2. The U.S. Constitution has seven articles: Article I — Legislative Branch; Article II — Executive Branch; Article III — Judicial Branch; Article IV —Relation between the States; Article V — The Amendment Process; Article VI — General Provision and Supremacy of the Constitution; and Article VII — Ratification Process.
   The Great Compromise and the Three-Fifths Compromise are found in Article I.
   The Constitution has been amended twenty-six times.

3. Use the Internet for your research on delegates to the Constitutional Convention. The National Archives website has a short biography of each delegate.

4. Each of these historic sites has its own website.

Lesson 25: For Further Study Younger Student Adaptations

1. Share pictures of Mount Vernon.

2. Have your students refer to the copy of the U.S. Constitution in the appendix of the *Student Reader*. Remind them of the copy of the Articles of Confederation that you examined earlier. Explain that the main sections of the Constitution are called articles, and show them the articles. Explain what an amendment is, and show them the amendments.

3. Have your students read (or read to them) a short book about the Constitutional Convention.

4. Show your students photographs from the historic district of Philadelphia.

Lesson 26: For Further Study Answers

1. Alexander Hamilton and Aaron Burr clashed repeatedly on the political stage. In 1791, Burr successfully captured a U.S. Senate seat from Hamilton's father-in-law. In 1800, Burr obtained a private document written by Hamilton that was highly critical of John Adams, the Federalist president. Burr had the document published, which was embarrassing to Hamilton and furthered the rifts developing in the Federalist party. That same

year, when Thomas Jefferson and Aaron Burr tied in balloting for the presidency, Hamilton lobbied Congress to choose Jefferson. Jefferson was selected president, and Burr served as vice president.

In the New York governor's race of 1804, Burr ran as an independent. Hamilton tried to convince New York Federalists not to support Burr, who was soundly defeated by the Republican candidate. At a political dinner for the Federalist Party in New York in February 1804, Hamilton voiced a "particularly despicable" slur regarding Aaron Burr. Rumors and newspaper reports about this reached Burr, who wrote Hamilton and demanded an apology. When Hamilton waffled in his response and did not respond satisfactorily to a second letter, Burr challenged him to a duel.

Although Hamilton wanted to avoid the duel, his political career would be over if he did so. Thus, on July 11, 1804, Hamilton and Burr met on the dueling grounds at Weehawken, New Jersey. Each fired a shot from a .56 caliber pistol. Burr shot Hamilton, who fired into the air either to avoid shooting Burr or as a reflex after being shot. Hamilton was rowed across the river to New York City, where he died the next day. Burr was indicted on two counts of murder but never prosecuted.

After completing his vice-presidential duties in 1805, Burr apparently entered into a conspiracy to take lands west of the Mississippi River away from Spain. When news of Burr's activities reached President Jefferson, he ordered Burr's arrest. Burr was taken to Richmond to stand trial on charges of treason. Chief Justice Marshall presided over Burr's trial and he insisted on the narrowest possible interpretation of treason (requiring an overt act and not just a conspiracy to do so). The prosecution's case was not handled well, and Burr was acquitted.

2. Jefferson commissioned Meriwether Lewis to head an expedition to explore the newly purchased Louisiana Territory. His main instructions to Lewis were to follow the Missouri River west and to find out if this river connected with an all-water route to the Pacific Ocean. Jefferson also told Lewis to map the area and to learn as much as possible about the native peoples, animals, plants, minerals, soil, and climate of the area. He wanted observations and records of everything that would be of interest to the U.S. commercially and scientifically.

   Meriwether Lewis was a Virginia neighbor of Jefferson's and his personal secretary. An experienced woodsman and a respected military leader, Lewis had studied botany, navigation, medicine, and natural history. William Clark was Lewis's longtime friend and a veteran of the Indian wars. Lewis chose Clark to serve as co-leader of the expedition. The two men got along well and respected each other. Lewis was better educated than Clark but could be moody and withdrawn. Clark was outgoing and warm and had a practical nature. The strong, disciplined leadership of Lewis and Clark was the primary reason for the success of the expedition.

   Lewis and Clark explored from the Mississippi River to the Pacific Ocean and back. They returned from their expedition with careful notes, maps, and samples of plants and animals. In present-day North Dakota they met a sixteen-year-old Native American named Sacajawea. A member of the Shoshone Tribe, Sacajawea was married to a French fur trader and pregnant. Lewis and Clark hired Sacajawea's husband to serve as a translator of the Indian languages for them, but Sacajawea was actually more help than he was. She served as an interpreter and negotiator for Lewis and Clark and traveled with them from North Dakota to the Oregon coast and back.

3. Benjamin Banneker was a self-taught African-American astronomer, mathematician, surveyor, and publisher. In 1789, he correctly predicted a solar eclipse, and from 1791 to 1802 he published the *Pennsylvania, Delaware, Maryland, and Virginia Almanac and Ephemeris*. Banneker was appointed by President Washington to the District of Columbia Commission, which was responsible for the survey work that established the original boundaries of the city. The architect in charge of the project, Pierre L'Enfant, suddenly resigned and left, taking the plans with him. However, Banneker was able to reproduce the plans from memory, which saved the U.S. government much effort and expense.

4. The XYZ Affair is the name given to an incident in French-American relations that occurred in 1797 – 1798. When Adams became president in March 1797, the French had seized nearly three hundred U.S. ships going to British ports. The French had ordered retaliatory action against the United States in response to the Jay Treaty of 1795, which partially violated American agreements with France. Some of the anti-French Federalists in Congress were demanding war with France, because the French continued to seize American ships and refused to recognize America's minister to France.

   In 1797, President Adams sent three diplomats (Charles Cotesworth Pinckney, John Marshall, and Elbridge Gerry) to France in an attempt to avoid war. These three men met with three French agents, known only as X, Y, and Z. The agents demanded $250,000, a $12 million loan from the United States, and an apology for comments made by Adams in order for the negotiations to occur. The three American diplomats found this bribery unacceptable and are often cited as saying, "Millions for defense, sir, but not one cent for tribute." President Adams released a report about this affair, and many Americans were furious. A declaration of war almost came, but Adams appointed new diplomats who eventually were able to avert war.

   The Citizen Genet Affair began in 1793, when Edmond-Charles Genet was sent to the United States from France to ask for American support in the wars with Britain and Spain. When Genet was dropped off in Charleston, South Carolina, he stayed there instead of traveling to the U.S. capital in Philadelphia to see President Washington. The people of Charleston greeted his arrival with enthusiasm and threw parties in his honor. However, his goal in South Carolina was to recruit and arm American privateers to join French expeditions against British trade. He also organized American volunteers to fight Spanish allies of Britain in Florida. Finally, Genet set sail for Philadelphia, stopping along the way to continue to raise support for the French cause.

   When Genet met with Washington, he asked for suspension of American neutrality in the war between France and Britain. When he was turned down and informed that his actions were not acceptable, Genet continued to defy American wishes. Washington sent Genet a long letter of complaint. When a new government took power in France in early 1794, Genet was recalled to France. Genet knew that he would likely be sent to the guillotine, so he asked Washington for asylum. Ironically, Alexander Hamilton, Genet's greatest opponent in the cabinet, convinced Washington to grant him safe haven.

Lesson 26: For Further Study Younger Student Adaptations

1. Explain the reason for duels during the early years of our nation. Tell them the story of the Hamilton-Burr duel.

2. Have your students read (or read to them) a short book about the Lewis and Clark expedition.

3. Tell the story of Benjamin Banneker and the role that he played in the early days of the nation's capital. Remind your students again of the difference between living as a free African American and living as a slave.

4. Share how tense American relations were with France in the early years of our nation's history and the role that the Citizen Genet and XYZ Affairs played in that tension.

Lesson 27: For Further Study Answers

1. During the War of 1812, Francis Scott Key was a thirty-five-year old lawyer living in Georgetown, Virginia. After the burning of Washington, D.C., Key found out that his friend, Dr. William Beanes, had been taken captive by the British soon after they left the capital. Key secured the services of Colonel John Skinner, the government's prisoner of war exchange agent. On September 13, Key and Skinner set sail on a truce ship and

met the British fleet in the Chesapeake Bay. Although they succeeded in negotiating Dr. Beanes's release, the men were detained by the British overnight during the bombardment of Fort McHenry, one of the forts defending Baltimore. From this vantage point, Key witnessed the British attack on Fort McHenry, after which he wrote the words to "The Star-Spangled Banner."

Key's poem was first published under the title "Defense of Fort McHenry." The poem soon gained widespread popularity sung to the British tune "To Anacreon in Heaven." In 1939, the U.S. Congress enacted a law that made "The Star-Spangled Banner" the official national anthem. It had already been adopted as such by the U.S. Army and Navy. Some people feel that "The Star-Spangled Banner" is too difficult to sing.

2. Andrew Jackson began his military career at the age of thirteen when he joined friends and neighbors to fight off the British at Hanging Rock, North Carolina, during the last year of the American Revolution. Later, after becoming a lawyer and moving to Tennessee, he became a major general in the Tennessee militia. In 1812, the governor of Tennessee gave Jackson the rank of major general of U.S. forces.

The War of 1812 made Andrew Jackson a national military hero, which paved the way for his election as president. During the winter and spring of 1813, he and the troops that he commanded fought two devastating campaigns against the pro-British faction of the Creek Indians. Assisted by pro-American Indian allies, Jackson succeeded in crushing Creek resistance at the Battle of Horseshoe Bend. Following this victory, Jackson forced all the Native Americans in the region (even those who were friendly to the Americans) to surrender enormous amounts of land in Georgia and Alabama.

Impressed by Jackson's leadership abilities and military resourcefulness, the federal government placed him in command of the defense of New Orleans. During this battle the determined and talented Jackson improvised with a combination of Tennessee sharpshooters, Creole Louisiana militiamen, pirates, and free African Americans to defeat the British in forty-five minutes. Jackson's victory made him a legend and symbol of virtue to the American public, who had seen too many humiliating defeats and too much military ineptitude during the War of 1812. General Jackson emerged as a national hero and became known as Old Hickory. Because of his strict discipline and exceptional robustness, Jackson's men began to say that he was "as tough as hickory" and the nickname stuck.

In 1817, Jackson fought Native Americans in Spanish Florida in the First Seminole War. He apparently exceeded his orders by deposing the Spanish authorities and executing two British subjects. Efforts to get Jackson censured by the U.S. Congress failed, and his military activities in Florida led to U.S. acquisition of that territory from Spain in 1819. Jackson's rugged individualism and courage made him larger than life on the national scene. However, his military actions were devastating to millions of Native Americans.

William Henry Harrison served as an aide-de-camp to General "Mad Anthony" Wayne in the Northwest Territories during the 1790s and earned a reputation for his leadership in the American campaigns against Native Americans in the region. In 1798, he was appointed governor of the Northwest Territory and two years later governor of the Indiana Territory. In this position he continued to defeat Native American tribes and afterwards to negotiate treaties with them that deprived them of their lands for little money.

In 1811, Harrison won a victory over Tecumseh's confederation forces at Tippecanoe, a creek in northwestern Indiana. This battle led to the breakup of the confederation, established Harrison's military reputation nationally, and brought about his nickname "Tippecanoe" or "Old Tip." Just like Jackson, Harrison's military actions were tragic for millions of Native Americans.

During the War of 1812 Harrison was a general in the U.S. Army and defeated combined British and Indian forces at the Battle of the Thames. Because Tecumseh was killed in this battle, Harrison became a national hero. After the war Harrison served in the U.S. House of Representatives until 1819. He joined with others in Congress in trying to censure Andrew Jackson for his actions in the Seminole War. This led to great animosity between Jackson and Harrison.

3. Tecumseh was a Shawnee leader who fought against U.S. expansion into the Midwest in the early 1800s. He was present at the Battle of Fallen Timbers in 1794, when U.S. General Anthony Wayne defeated a coalition of Native Americans. Although many of the Indian leaders signed the Treaty of Greenville, which forced the natives into northwest Ohio, Tecumseh did not sign it. He believed that the land belonged to all of the Indians and that he and the other Indians had a responsibility to keep white settlers from moving onto the land. He held that a cession of land by any one tribe was illegal without the consent of all of the others.

In 1808 Tecumseh and his brother, Tenskwatawa, a religious visionary known as the Prophet, were forced out of Ohio and established a village in Indiana Territory. The camp became known as Prophetstown and sat at the junction of the Tippecanoe and Wabash rivers. Native Americans from different tribes who had the same beliefs as Tecumseh and the Prophet came to live at their village, and Tecumseh traveled as far as Iowa and the Gulf of Mexico to gain the support of other tribes. His goal was to make the Ohio River the permanent boundary between the United States and the Indian lands.

The Prophet claimed to have a vision concerning the reason for the misery of the Native Americans. He proclaimed that the Master of Life was displeased that so many native people had turned away from their old ways and adopted the ways of the white man. Tenskwatawa called for a total rejection of white culture by the Indians — its clothing, technology, alcohol, and religion. If the Native Americans did so, the Master of Life would give them back their land.

White settlers in the area became concerned as Prophetstown grew. They feared that an Indian uprising was being planned and wanted Governor Harrison to act. In the fall of 1811, Harrison received permission to launch military action. While Tecumseh was away on a trip, Harrison stationed his troops close to the Indians in Prophetstown. Tecumseh had warned the Prophet not to fight the Americans while he was away, but his brother did not listen. The Prophet believed that his powers would protect the native warriors, so he led the Indians into battle against Harrison's troops. When the natives realized that the Prophet's powers were not protecting them, they retreated into the woods. Harrison's forces then easily took over Prophetstown and burned it to the ground.

Tecumseh was killed on October 5, 1813, at the Battle of the Thames near Thamesville, Ontario. The Prophet remained in Canada for ten years following the War of 1812 and never succeeded in regaining a position of leadership. In 1825, at the invitation of the governor of the Michigan territory, the Prophet returned to the United States and used his influence to promote Indian removal. A year later he accompanied a Shawnee party from Ohio traveling to Kansas. The Prophet settled at the site of present-day Kansas City, Kansas, and in the fall of 1832 he posed for the artist George Catlin there. He died in November 1836.

4. The Hartford Convention of 1815 was a secret meeting of New England Federalists held in Hartford, Connecticut, from December 15, 1814 until January 5, 1815. Of the twenty-six delegates attending the meeting, twelve were from Massachusetts, seven from Connecticut, four from Rhode Island, two from New Hampshire, and one from Vermont.

Prior to the beginning of the War of 1812, New England Federalists had opposed the Embargo Act of 1807. When fighting began, they called the war "Mr. Madison's War" and detested the expenses required to fight it (even though contraband trade and manufacturing fostered by American isolation was bringing wealth to New England). The New England states refused to surrender their militia to national service, and the federal loan of 1814 got almost no support in New England. Some Federalist extremists even contemplated a separate peace between New England and Great Britain.

At the Hartford Convention a proposal to secede from the Union was discussed and rejected. The grievances of New England were reviewed, and a final report proposed several constitutional amendments that would redress what the New Englanders believed to be unfair advantages for the southern states under the Constitution. By the time the Hartford delegation arrived in Washington, D.C., to make their recommendations, the War of 1812 had ended. In fact, the Treaty of Ghent had already been signed by President Madison, making the Hartford report awkward and embarrassing. The delegation quickly withdrew their recommendations. The Federalist Party never regained the prestige that it lost because of the Hartford Convention and fared so poorly in the 1816 election that it did not even field a candidate in 1820.

Lesson 27: For Further Study Younger Student Adaptations

1. Have your students read (or read to them) all four stanzas of "The Star-Spangled Banner." Encourage them to memorize the first stanza and have them practice singing it.

2. Have your students read (or read to them) a short biography of Andrew Jackson.

3. Have your students read (or read to them) a short biography of Tecumseh.

4. Explain what secession means. Discuss whether or not your students believe that states should be allowed to secede if they want to do so.

Lesson 28: For Further Study Answers

1. Henry Clay was an American statesman and orator who represented Kentucky in the U.S. House of Representatives and U.S. Senate, served as secretary of state under John Quincy Adams, and made four failed bids for the U.S. presidency. Known for his keen abilities as a compromiser and his passionate devotion to the Union, Clay was an extremely influential American political figure in the first half of the nineteenth century. He belonged to the short-lived National Republican Party and then to the Whig Party.

   At the age of twenty, Clay moved from Virginia to Kentucky, where he quickly established himself as a successful lawyer. His friendliness, charm, and oratorical skills made him an immensely popular figure. As Speaker of the House, Clay was a prominent War Hawk, who pushed for expansion and war with the British. He served as a peace commissioner in the negotiations that ended the War of 1812.

   Although Clay himself was a slave owner, he favored the emancipation of slaves and their resettlement in Africa. He negotiated the Compromise of 1820, which dealt with expansion and the spread of slavery. The "Great Compromiser" also negotiated the Compromise Tariff of 1833 and the Compromise of 1850, which brought about a temporary subsiding of sectional passions regarding slavery.

   Clay gained widespread support in his home state of Kentucky and throughout the West for his American System, a plan to strengthen the U.S. economy by tying the North, South, and West together. By the 1830s he had emerged as a national leader of the National Republican Party, which later became known as the Whig Party.

2. Daniel Webster was a U.S. representative, U.S. senator, and U.S. secretary of state, who was famed for his ability as an orator. Along with Henry Clay and John C. Calhoun, Webster was one of the most important political figures in the first half of the nineteenth century. Like Clay, he had a passionate devotion to the Union and a willingness to compromise.

   In 1812, Daniel Webster was elected to the U.S. House of Representatives because of his opposition to the War of 1812. A lawyer and Federalist Party leader, Webster represented Massachusetts for two terms in Congress and then returned to Boston in 1816. During the next six years, he won several major constitutional cases before the Supreme Court, including *Dartmouth College v. Woodward*, *Gibbons v. Ogden*, and *McCulloch v. Maryland*. This success established Webster as the nation's leading lawyer and orator.

With the death of the Federalist Party, Webster joined the National Republican Party and allied himself with Henry Clay. In 1828, he backed high tariff legislation because Massachusetts's dominant economic interests had shifted from shipping to manufacturing. When John C. Calhoun argued that South Carolina had the right to nullify this tariff, Webster defended the Union and cried "Liberty and Union, now and forever, one and inseparable."

As secretary of state, Webster negotiated an important treaty with Britain but left the cabinet in 1843 due to Whig pressure (all the other cabinet members had already resigned after Tyler replaced Harrison as president). Webster opposed the 1845 annexation of Texas and the Mexican War. In March 1850, he gave a powerful speech before the Senate in support of the Compromise of 1850, denouncing Southern threats of secession and urging Northern support for a stronger fugitive slave law. In 1850, Webster was again made secretary of state and supervised the strict enforcement of the Fugitive Slave Act. Webster's position had divided the Whigs and alienated antislavery factions but preserved the Union for another ten years.

3. John C. Calhoun was a prominent American politician during the first half of the nineteenth century. He represented South Carolina in the U.S. House of Representatives and U.S. Senate and served as secretary of state, secretary of war, and vice president of the United States. Calhoun was a War Hawk who quickly gained recognition for his powerful support for war against Britain. He belonged to the Democratic-Republican Party and then to the Democratic Party.

   Calhoun was a staunchly determined and serious man with a powerful mind and tongue who became known as the "cast-iron." Afraid that the Southern way of life was in danger, he defended slavery as necessary and good. He also fought the tariffs wanted by the North and maintained that individual states had the authority to nullify laws that they considered to be unconstitutional (based on the fact that individual states had ratified the constitution).

   In December 1832, Calhoun became the first vice president to resign from office. He and President Jackson had developed a rift because Jackson opposed nullification. Jackson, in a famous toast said, "Our federal Union —it must and shall be preserved." Calhoun's toast was "Our Union, next to our liberties most dear." When South Carolina refused to collect the required tariffs, Jackson threatened to send troops to the state. Robert Hayne gave up his Senate seat to become the governor of South Carolina, and Calhoun resigned as vice president and took Hayne's seat. Calhoun remained a powerful figure in Washington until his death and the perpetual opponent of Whig politicians Clay and Webster.

4. The Election of 1840 was the first election won by the Whig Party and the first campaign with songs, slogans, and an emphasis on personalities and not issues. It also experienced the biggest jump in voter turnout of any presidential election in American history — about 60 percent (900,000 new voters were mobilized).

   This huge increase in voter turnout has usually been attributed to the nature of the campaign.

   In the 1840 presidential campaign, the Whigs depicted Harrison as a military hero and used the famous campaign slogan "Tippecanoe and Tyler, Too." They portrayed Harrison as a man of the people and slammed Van Buren as a pampered dandy. The Democrats mocked Harrison as an old has-been, content to retire to a log cabin with a barrel of hard cider. The Whigs turned around and gave voters free whiskey and hard cider and slogans like "Van, Van, Van — Van's a Used Up Man." This type of demagoguery seemed to be successful in bringing massive numbers of new voters to the polls.

Lesson 28: For Further Study Younger Student Adaptations

1. Have your students read (or read to them) a short biography of Henry Clay. Explain to them what a compromiser is.

2. Have your students read (or read to them) a short biography of Daniel Webster. Look for one of his speeches and read a short excerpt from it.

3. Have your students read (or read to them) a short biography of John C. Calhoun. Explain why Calhoun and Jackson became such bitter enemies.

4. Look for political cartoons and song lyrics from the 1840 election to share.

Lesson 29: For Further Study Answers

1. The mountain men were fur-clad, grizzled adventurers who were the first to explore the American West. Jedediah Smith was perhaps the most famous of all the mountain men. While still a young man, Smith joined a fur-trading expedition to the Rocky Mountains led by General William Ashley. As one of the original "Ashley Men," Smith and his party of trappers rediscovered the South Pass — a passage to the Northwest through present-day Wyoming and the key to the settlement of Oregon and California. Eventually, Ashley took Smith as a partner.

   In his lifetime, Smith would travel more extensively through unknown western territory than any other man. He was the first American to cross west over the Continental Divide, to travel through California's Sierra Nevada Mountains, to enter California lowland across the Mojave Dessert, and to cross the Great Basin Desert and return east overland. Although Smith was undoubtedly an accomplished outdoorsman, he did not fit the stereotype of the typical mountain man — he didn't smoke or drink alcohol, and he often prayed and meditated.

   In 1830, Smith, mourning the death of his mother, decided to give up mountain exploration. He and his two current partners sold their shares in the Rocky Mountain Fur Company, and he purchased a home in St. Louis. However, Smith had agreed to make one more trip to the Southwest to procure supplies for the new owners of the Rocky Mountain Fur Company. While looking for water on the Santa Fe Trail, he was killed by Comanche warriors. Smith had planned to edit and publish his journals and construct a master map of his explorations. Of course, his death prevented that from happening.

   Pikes Peak in Colorado is named for Zebulon Pike, an American solder and mountain man. In 1805, General James Wilkinson, a political ally of Aaron Burr and governor of the Upper Louisiana Territory, ordered Pike (an army officer) to discover the headwaters of the Mississippi River. Pike was also ordered to negotiate peace treaties with the tribes that he encountered. The two-man exploring party commanded by Pike traveled two thousand miles by boat and on foot from St. Louis up to northern Minnesota. Pike wrongly thought that he had discovered the source of the Mississippi River at Leech Lake, Minnesota.

   In 1806, Pike led another army expedition, this time to the southwestern borders of the Louisiana Purchase. He was ordered to explore the Arkansas and Red rivers and to obtain information about nearby Spanish territory. It was on this trip that he unsuccessfully tried to climb the peak later named for him. From Colorado his party headed south and ended up in northern New Mexico, where they were charged with illegal entry into Spanish territory. All of Pike's maps, notes, and papers were seized by the Spanish, and he and his men were escorted across Texas and released on the Spanish-American border in Louisiana. Pike's published account of this expedition stirred American businessmen and politicians with thoughts of expanding into Texas. Pike was later killed in battle during the War of 1812.

   Jim Beckwourth was an African-American mountain man and scout. Born in Virginia, Beckwourth escaped from the South and headed for the freedom of the West. He was adopted by the Crow Indians and lived with them for a while along the Bighorn and Yellowstone rivers. During the gold rush, Beckwourth came to California and did some prospecting. He knew that one of the biggest challenges facing forty-niners was making it through the Sierra Nevada.

In 1851, Beckwourth discovered a pass through the northern Sierra that now bears his name. Three years later he began dictating his autobiography to an itinerant justice of the peace in the California gold fields. The judge polished Beckwourth's narrative, and it was published by Harper and Brothers in 1856. Later historians have discovered that much of what Beckwourth related in his autobiography actually occurred.

Davy Crocket was a celebrated backwoods hunter, warrior, and statesman. Born in northeastern Tennessee, Crockett died a hero's death at age forty-nine at the Alamo. From 1813 -1814 he commanded a battalion in the Creek Indian War. Then Crockett served two terms in the Tennessee legislature and three terms in the U.S. Congress, even though he had almost no formal education. Between 1822 and 1823 he also supposedly killed 105 bears.

The Whigs latched onto Crockett as a genuine man of the people and appeared to be grooming him for the White House. In addition to his image as a strong and heroic frontiersman, Crocket was a natural story-teller, whose common sense and sense of humor made him a charismatic personality. When pro-Jackson forces cost Crockett re-election to the House in 1835, he headed for Texas with a group of fellow adventurers. In March 1836, Crocket and 139 others were massacred by the Spanish at the Alamo.

2. Marcus and Narcissa Whitman were part of a small group of brave Presbyterian missionaries who played an important role in opening the Oregon Trail. Both of the Whitmans were from upstate New York. Narcissa pledged her life to missionary work at the age of sixteen. Marcus studied medicine, became an elder in a Presbyterian church, and was approved by a missions board to go west to establish a base for missionary work. At the same time, Narcissa was denied her opportunity to serve by the same board, because the board believed that missionary work was not suitable for an unmarried woman. When Marcus returned from his reconnaissance mission of potential mission sites, he and Narcissa quickly decided to marry and minister together. Such a marriage of convenience was not uncommon for missionary couples during this period.

   In the spring of 1836, the Whitmans traveled west with another missionary couple, Henry and Eliza Spaulding. Narcissa and Eliza were the first white women to cross the Rocky Mountains. After reaching the Walla Walla valley in September, the Spaldings continued westward; the Whitmans stayed to minister to the local Cayuse. However, Narcissa's health declined, their baby daughter drowned, and the Cayuse did not seem open to Christianity. Differences in culture led to growing tensions between the Cayuse people and the Whitmans. The Walla Walla mission became an increasingly important stop along the Oregon Trail, but passing immigrants added to the tension.

   In 1847, a measles outbreak killed half the local Cayuse. Some of the Cayuse blamed these deaths on Dr. Whitman. Even though the Whitmans provided medical attention to everyone, it seemed as if only the white people recovered because the natives had no natural immunity to the white man's diseases. The Cayuse were also very alarmed about the growing migration of white settlers into their territory. On November 29, 1847, a band of Cayuse killed the Whitmans and a dozen others.

3. The California gold rush started at Sutter's Mill in the Sacramento Valley in January 1848. James Marshall, one of Sutter's employees, found a gold nugget. Word of the discovery soon got out. In fact, by late 1848, the news had spread across the country and as many as five thousand miners were already at work. At this point, gold was relatively easy to find and new strikes were made almost every day. Gold fever spread to the eastern United States and many foreign countries over the next several years. Prospectors journeyed overland and by boat to California, with their numbers peaking in 1851.

   Although all of these prospectors were intent on making an easy fortune, most did well to find enough gold to barely pay for their living expenses. Sutter's property was ruined as squatters invaded his land, and his workers left in search of gold. By 1852, most of the surface gold had been mined and panning for gold was no longer profitable. At this point, successful mining required the blasting of hard rock, diversion of streams, and hydraulic destruction of hillsides.

One out of five of the miners who came to California died as a result of disease, malnutrition, accidents, and suicide. Those who survived lived in tents and cooked their food over open fires. The price of food and other supplies was very inflated. Heavy snow and rain in the winter made for difficult living and working conditions, and many mining camps were destroyed by fire. Sanitation was poor, and miners were not able to bathe or wash their clothes very often. Card games and gambling were popular ways to pass the time when not mining.

Levi Strauss was born in Bavaria and came to San Francisco during the California gold rush. Trained as a tailor, he hoped to make wagon covers and tents for forty-niners. However, he found no market for those products. Instead, he used his canvas to make durable pants, which were perfect for miners to wear in their work. Eventually, Strauss opened a factory to make these pants and began using copper rivets at the stress points. He also changed from canvas material to blue denim; in France such material was called genes. The company founded by Strauss still makes apparel, and the garments he designed are known as levis.

Henry Wells worked as a freight agent on the Erie Canal in the 1830s. By the 1840s, he owned an express service that brought valuable items from Albany to St. Louis. In 1841, Wells met William Fargo, who worked as the freight agent in Auburn, New York. Fargo's business abilities impressed Wells, and eventually the two men formed the American Express Company. Wells was president of this company from its founding in 1850 until 1868, and Fargo was president from 1868 until his death.

After the California gold rush began, Wells and Fargo recognized the need that westerners had for expanded express and banking services. They were unable to convince American Express to head west, so in 1851 they founded Wells, Fargo, and Company. This company held a near monopoly on express and banking services in California for several years.

Bret Harte was an American author and poet, remembered for his writings about pioneer life in California. Born in Albany, New York, Harte moved to California with his widowed mother in 1854 and worked there in a number of jobs — teacher, miner, journalist, and messenger. While living in San Francisco, he contributed prose and poetry to a literary journal called *The Californian.*

Then in 1868 Harte became editor of *The Overland Monthly*, another literary magazine. His story, "The Luck of Roaring Camp," appeared in the second edition of this magazine and brought Harte instant nationwide fame. His stories of the American West became much in demand in the eastern United States. Eventually, Harte moved back east, to New York and then Boston, where he continued to produce literary works that captured life in California in the years following the gold rush.

4. Sequoyah was born to a Native American mother and white father. He saw fighting in the War of 1812 and the Creek War. For more than a dozen years, he also devoted much time to working on a written language for the Cherokee. Using a phonetic system, Sequoyah created eighty-five letters, or characters, that make up the Cherokee syllabary. These characters represented all the combinations of vowel and consonant sounds that formed the spoken language of the Cherokee. Word soon spread about Sequoyah's invention, and within months thousands of Cherokee were able to read and write.

   Worcester v. Georgia was a case in which the Supreme Court held that the Cherokee Indians were entitled to federal protection from the actions of state governments. When this decision was handed down, John Marshall was still chief justice of the Supreme Court. In this decision the court ruled that the Cherokee nation was a distinct community with self-government and that the laws of Georgia had no force with this community. Samuel Worcester was a Congregational minister and missionary, who had come to preach and teach Native Americans in Georgia. The state of Georgia wanted to get rid of ministers like Worcester, so they passed a law saying that all whites living in the Indian portion of Georgia had to be licensed. Worcester was not given a license, and he was arrested two times. Eventually, he was sentenced to four years of prison at hard labor. Worcester appealed to the Supreme Court, and the Marshall court ruled that the laws of Georgia could not be applied to the Cherokee. President Jackson, however, ignored this Supreme Court ruling.

Lesson 29: For Further Study Younger Student Adaptations

1. Share the 1955 "Davy Crockett" song and pictures of coonskin caps. Show photographs of Pike's Peak.
2. Tell the story of Dr. Marcus and Narcissa Whitman and discuss the difficulties of traveling the Oregon Trail.
3. Sing the song "Oh, My Darling, Clementine" together. Tell them about the successes of Levi Strauss, Henry Wells, and William Fargo.
4. Have your students read (or read to them) a final book with general information on Native Americans or do more Native American hands-on activities.

Lesson 30: For Further Study Answers

1. Samuel Slater's Rhode Island System of factory management employed families, including children, who not only worked but also lived at the mill site. In 1803, Slater built a mill village, which he called Slatersville. The town included the large, modern mill; tenement houses for the workers; and company stores, schools, and churches. A family division of labor emerged under Slater's system. The adult men were employed as farm hands and artisans in the village, the adult women stayed at home, and the children and teens worked in the mill.

   When Slater's mill opened in December 1790, seven boys and two girls between the ages of seven and twelve operated the seventy-two spindles. Under the supervision of an adult, these youths were capable of producing three times as much as families working in their home. To keep his youthful workers from becoming sleepy or lethargic, Slater would whip them or sprinkle them with water. On Sundays they attended a school established for them by Slater. Child labor proved to be an inexpensive and fairly reliable labor force for Slater and other early factor owners. During the nineteenth century in many mechanized industries anywhere from one-quarter to one-half of the labor force was young women and men under the age of twenty.

   The Lowell System of factory management employed young farm girls (ages twelve to twenty-five) from the surrounding countryside as its labor force. These female workers were housed in well-run boarding-houses and were strictly supervised at work and home (the company even required that they have religious devotions). Their rent was deducted from their pay, but they were paid good wages (higher than wages in any other mill towns and six times the wages of a teacher). They enjoyed many opportunities for self-improvement — access to a circulating library and literary magazines, lectures at the Lowell Lyceum, and opportunities to go by rail into Boston. Lowell's system drew international attention for its combination of efficient production and humane treatment of its workers. However, by 1834 an economic downturn led to wage cuts at the Lowell mill and conditions for its workers began to gradually deteriorate.

2. The Erie Canal is a canal in New York State that runs from the Hudson River to Lake Erie, connecting the Great Lakes with the Atlantic Ocean. Construction of the canal was proposed as early as 1699. However, it was not until 1798 that the Niagara Canal Company began preparations for building it. The first section of the

canal was finished in 1819, and the entire canal was opened in 1825. The canal was 363 miles long, forty feet wide, and four feet deep with eighty-three locks.

When New York politicians began proposing a canal, even President Jefferson thought it was a crazy idea. Dewitt Clinton, mayor of New York City and then governor of the state, supported the idea; and his opponents began calling the proposal "Clinton's Folly" or "Clinton's Big Ditch." However, when the canal opened, it was hailed as the greatest engineering feat in the world and referred to as "Clinton's Wonder" or the "Grand Canal." Towns quickly grew up around the canal, and it paid for itself in tolls in less than ten years. The Erie Canal made New York the largest city in the colonies and caused Albany and Buffalo also to grow in importance and size.

3. In the years following the War of 1812, large eastern cities were very interested in cultivating trade with the expanding West. Before the coming of the railroads in the 1830s, the nation experienced the continuation of a turnpike era and a canal-building stage. John Stevens is considered to be the father of American railroads. In 1826, he was able to demonstrate the feasibility of steam locomotion on a circular track constructed on his New Jersey estate. The first railroad charter in North America was granted to Stevens, and work soon began on the first operational U.S. railroads.

   The Baltimore and Ohio Railroad (B & O), the first common carrier railroad in the United States, was chartered in 1827. Surveying and construction on the B & O began in 1830, and fourteen miles of track had been laid by the end of the year. The roadbed of the B & O was extended to Frederick, Maryland, in 1831 and to Point of Rocks in 1832. The B & O relied on horsepower until a locomotive was placed in its service in 1831.

   Soon, other operating lines joined the B & O. Acceptance of railroads by the American public came quickly in the 1830s. However, there was some opposition to them. Some ministers preached against the "iron horse," some physicians warned of the dangers of excessive speed, and stagecoach companies also voiced their opposition. However, construction of railroads in the U.S. progressed rapidly, and railroads became big business. Although most of the early investment in U.S. railroads was private, some state and city governments did help finance some early railroads. By 1840 the nation had almost three thousand miles of railway, whereas all of Europe had only eighteen hundred miles.

4. Samuel F. B. Morse was an American inventor and painter. Known for his portraits and historic scenes, Morse was founder of the National Academy of Design. However, Morse is most famous for inventing the electric telegraph and Morse code. In 1832, while on a ship returning from Europe, Morse conceived the idea of an electromagnetic telegraph.

   By 1836 Morse had constructed a working telegraph set and introduced a circuit relay, which made transmission possible for any distance. He also developed a dot-and-dash transmission code system, which was named for him. The following year, Morse applied for a patent application, and in 1843 the U.S. Congress voted $30,000 for an experimental line between Baltimore and Washington. This line was completed with additional financial help from Alfred Vail and Ezra Cornell. On May 24, 1844, the historic message "What hath God wrought?" flashed from Washington to Baltimore. Morse's system gained quick acceptance worldwide.

Lesson 30: For Further Study Younger Student Adaptations

1. Show pictures of the Rhode Island System and the Lowell System of factory management. Have your students think about whether they would have liked to have worked or lived under these conditions.

2. Share the "Erie Canal" song. Make certain that they understand how a canal operates.

3. Look for pictures of early American railroad cars and tracks. If any of the students have traveled on a train, ask them to discuss their experiences.

4. Have your students read (or read to them) a short biography of Samuel F. B. Morse. Demonstrate Morse code and encourage them to try sending a message in code.

Lesson 31: For Further Study Answers

1. Elizabeth Cady Stanton and Lucretia Mott met at the World Anti-Slavery Convention in London in 1840. This conference refused to allow the female delegates from America to participate in the debates because of their gender. The women were also required to sit together behind a partition away from the men. Stanton was the young wife of an antislavery agent, and Mott was a Quaker preacher and reform veteran. The two of them talked about the possibility of calling a convention to discuss the status of women.

   In the summer of 1848, Mott was visiting her sister in Waterloo, New York. Stanton lived in nearby Seneca Falls. The two of them met together with some other women in the community. All except Stanton were Quakers, a group that allowed women some measure of equality. Before their meeting was over, the women had decided to call a convention to discus the conditions and rights of women.

   The Declaration of Sentiments was written by Stanton and modeled after the Declaration of Independence. It asserted that all men and women had been created equal, and it listed eighteen grievances of the women concerning their treatment by men (the same number of grievances leveled against the King of England). The declaration also contained a number of resolutions, the most radical of which was that it was the duty of women to gain for themselves the right to vote. Even Lucretia believed that such a resolution would make the women look ridiculous, and Mr. Stanton was not pleased.

   The Seneca Falls Convention took place on July 19 – 20, 1848. The only publicity for the convention was a small, unsigned notice in the *Seneca County Courier*. However, about three hundred people (including forty men) attended. The famous abolitionist and former slave Frederick Douglass was in attendance. James Mott, Lucretia's husband, presided over the meeting; and all of the resolutions, except for women's suffrage, passed unanimously. A hundred men and women signed the Declaration, but subsequent criticism caused some to remove their names. Many newspaper writers and preachers ridiculed the proceedings in Seneca Falls. However, Frederick Douglass printed a positive report in his newspaper, the *North Star*.

2. The *McGuffey's Eclectic Readers* are still considered to be one of America's most famous teaching tools. The word *eclectic* means that the reading selections were taken from a wide range of literature and covered a wide range of subject matter.

3. Noah Webster was an American journalist and textbook author. During the American Revolution, he attended Yale. After graduation, he taught school in order to earn a living, and later he studied law and was admitted to the bar. Webster believed that American children should learn from American textbooks, not textbooks that came from England. Therefore, he wrote and published his own textbook, *A Grammatical Institute of the English Language*, which was in three parts — reader, grammar, and speller. Most people called this the "Blue-backed Speller" because of its blue cover. This pioneer American textbook was soon widely used in schools throughout the country. Before 1861, more than a million copies of it were sold each year.

   When he was forty-three, Webster started writing the first American dictionary. He published his dictionary of the English language in 1806. Then in 1828 he published the first edition of his *An American Dictionary of the English Language* in two volumes. Webster believed that words should be spelled and pronounced the same way throughout the country (Americans in different parts of the country spelled and pronounced words differently) and that Americans should not speak or spell just like the English. He added American words to his dictionary that were not in English dictionaries, such as *squash, chowder, hickory,* and *skunk.* He also used American spellings — "music" instead of "musick" and "color" instead of "colour." His dictionary soon became the best-selling book in America. In fact, Webster's dictionary was so popular that "Webster's" became synonymous with dictionary to many Americans.

Webster also released his own modern English translation of the Bible in 1833. He used the King James Version as the foundation, consulted the Hebrew and Greek, and looked at other versions and commentaries. Then he replaced words that were no longer used, changed grammar, and eliminated words that could be seen as offensive. Although Webster's translation was not widely accepted, it was the most significant English language translation of the Bible to be done since the King James two centuries earlier. Recently, the Webster translation has enjoyed popularity in online formats, because it may be used without paying any royalties (its age makes it public domain material).

4. Use the search term "nineteenth century recipes" to research American recipes from 1800 to 1850.

Lesson 31: For Further Study Younger Student Adaptations

1. Explain why the Seneca Falls convention happened and read an excerpt from the Declaration of Sentiments.

2. Look for excerpts from the *McGuffey Eclectic Readers* and have your students look them over and compare them to their reading books.

3. Look for excerpts from Noah Webster's books and share them.

4. Find online directions for American recipes from the first half of the nineteenth century and help them prepare one or more of them. Encourage them to work on the Nineteenth Century Family Life form (in the optional section).

Lesson 32: For Further Study Answers

1. Among Stephen Foster's most popular songs were "Oh! Susanna," "De Campton Races," "Old Folks at Home," "Jeanie with the Light Brown Hair," "Beautiful Dreamer," and "My Old Kentucky Home."

2. Use the Internet to research Washington Irving's short stories and poems by Henry Wadsworth Longfellow.

3. Use the Internet to research Thomas Cole, George Caleb Bingham, and George Catlin and other early nineteenth century painters.

4. Use the Internet to research American Federal architecture and American Greek Revival architecture. To find photographs of plantation exteriors and interior, use the search terms "southern plantation" or "antebellum architecture."

Lesson 32: For Further Study Younger Student Adaptations

1. Find some of Stephen Foster's songs to share. Discuss how the America of Foster's songs compares with the America of today.

2. Share the story of Rip Van Winkle.

3. Look for paintings by American artists of this time period and show them to the students.

4. Show your students photographs of American buildings and homes built in the Federal and Greek Revival architectural styles. Encourage them to work on the Nineteenth Century Culture form (in the optional section).

Section Six

ANSWER KEY TO THE FORMS, MAPS, AND FOR REVIEW QUESTIONS

Lessons 1 — 32

Name ____________ Date ____________

LESSON I: LEIF ERIKSSON

Flag of the country where he was born	Flag of country for which he did exploration	Picture of the explorer
Iceland	Greenland	

Year born **980? or 970?** Year died **1020?**

How many voyages of exploration did he take? **1**

During what years did he participate in exploration? **1000 or 1001**

What area(s) of the world did he explore? **Baffin Island, Newfoundland, Labrador, Nova Scotia, and Cape Cod (all or some of these locations – there are several historical theories)**

List the achievement(s) for which he should be remembered

The first European known to have discovered land in North America and to have attempted to plant a colony there

Lesson 1: The First Americans and Leif Eriksson 1

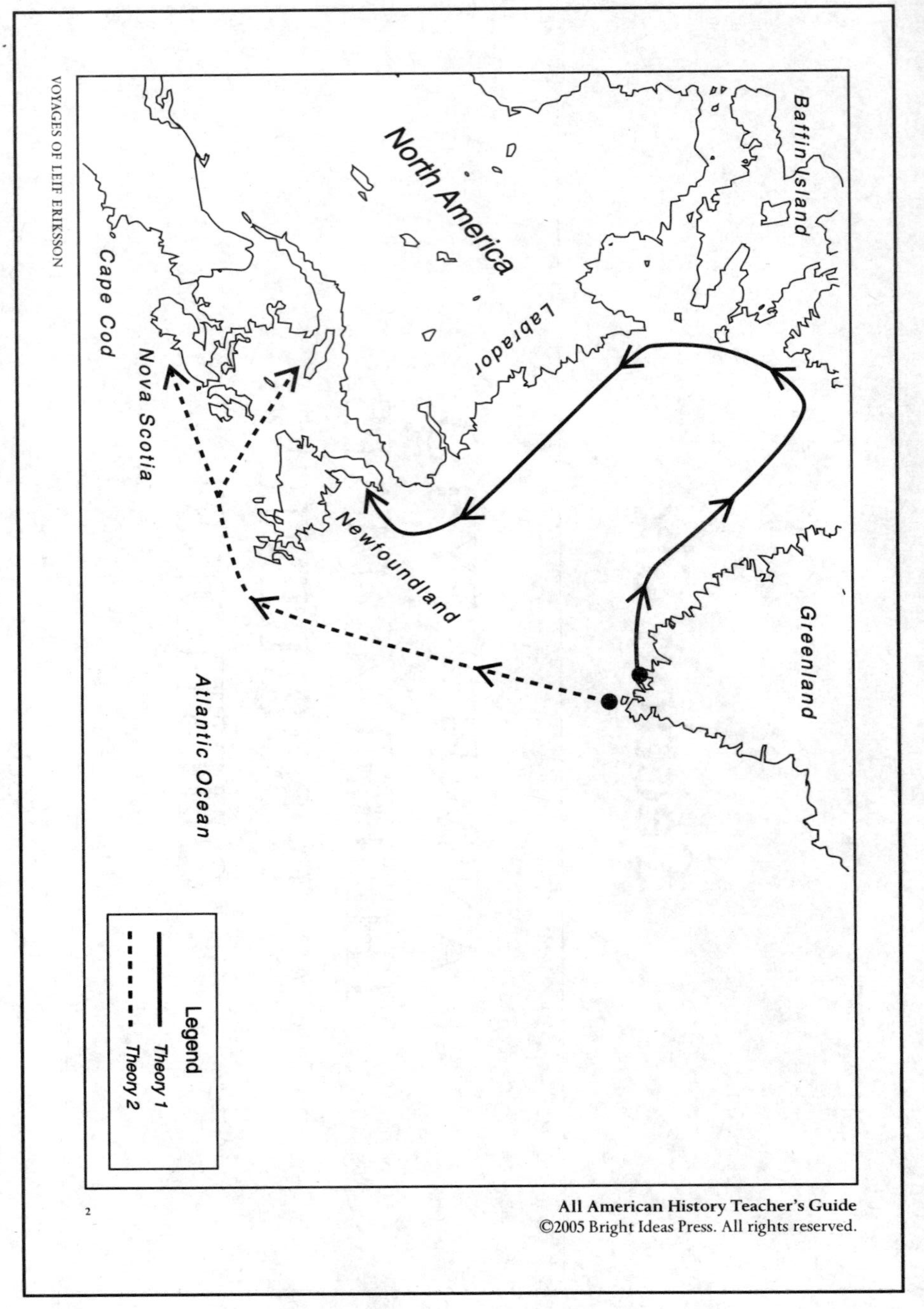

VOYAGES OF LEIF ERIKSSON

2 All American History Teacher's Guide

LESSON 1: FOR REVIEW

Write the letter of the correct answer in the space provided.

__C__ 1. The country that was NOT involved in the Age of European Exploration was
- A. Spain
- B. Portugal
- C. Greenland
- D. England

__A__ 2. Most people living in Europe during the late fifteenth century
- A. stayed near their own villages most of their lives
- B. realized that the world had seven continents
- C. had church maps showing the world to be round
- D. believed that ocean travel was a relatively safe undertaking

__B__ 3. The Age of European Exploration was sparked by all of the following EXCEPT
- A. development of new navigational instruments
- B. revival of Chinese scientific learning
- C. construction of sea vessels capable of transoceanic voyages
- D. better mapmaking skills

__C__ 4. One of the most important reasons why Europeans wanted to sail westward in the sixteenth century was to
- A. find a western trade route to South America
- B. destroy sea monsters
- C. conquer land for one's country
- D. prove that the world was flat

__B__ 5. European explorers during the sixteenth century
- A. had no desire to spread their religion to other areas of the world
- B. brought about an expansion of the world's economy
- C. did little to change existing civilizations in the land that they explored
- D. were generally unwilling to take big risks

__C__ 6. The first Americans probably
- A. did not arrive until the fifteenth century
- B. migrated from various European countries
- C. traveled across the Bering Sea from Siberia to Alaska
- D. crossed the Atlantic from the continent of Africa

__D__ 7. By the beginning of the sixteenth century, Native Americans
- A. had grown to no more than 500,000
- B. had failed to organize into tribal groups
- C. had developed only very primitive civilizations
- D. had scattered from Alaska to Chile

__D__ 8. The first recorded European explorer of America was
- A. Erik the Red
- B. King Olav
- C. Bjarni Herjolfsson
- D. Leif the Lucky

__B__ 9. Erik the Red discovered and colonized
- A. Iceland
- B. Greenland
- C. Great Britain
- D. Newfoundland

__C__ 10. When Leif Eriksson returned from King Olav's court, he brought with him
- A. gold
- B. tobacco
- C. Christianity
- D. potatoes

__A__ 11. Native Americans
- A. helped to save several European settlements from starvation
- B. were disgusted by European materials and skills
- C. refused to give up any of their land in return for European goods
- D. were already immune to the diseases brought from Europe

B 12. Most European explorers and colonists in America during the sixteenth and seventeenth centuries
- A. paid a fair price for tracts of land belonging to Native Americans
- B. tried to increase the natives' dependence upon European manufactured goods
- C. improved the health and quality of life of many native tribes
- D. did not seem interested in establishing their supremacy over Native Americans

D 13. When Leif Eriksson sailed west in 1000 – 1001 A.D., he was seeking to retrace the route of another Norseman
- A. Erik the Red
- B. King Olav
- C. Thorfinn Karlsefni
- D. Bjarni Herjolfsson

D 14. Leif and his men explored and named all of the following except
- A. Markland
- B. Vinland
- C. Helluland
- D. Thorvaldland

B 15. During their explorations, Leif and his men
- A. found nothing of interest to bring back with them to Greenland
- B. succeeded in rescuing sailors found shipwrecked on a reef
- C. never stayed in one location long enough to put up housing or hunt for food
- D. were captured by native Skraelings

D 16. After Leif returned to Greenland,
- A. he immediately made plans for another voyage of exploration
- B. the Vikings showed no interest in colonizing the land explored by Leif and his men
- C. Erik the Red continued to encourage his son to venture forth to new lands
- D. Leif's brother and sister and other Vikings sought to colonize the area Leif had explored

A 17. Viking settlements in America
- A. did not last long
- B. received much assistance from the Skraelings
- C. never provided any usable crops or products
- D. have not been documented by any reliable evidence

B 18. In the years immediately following Eriksson's explorations,
- A. many Europeans sought to sail west to the land he discovered
- B. many stories about his adventures were told among the Vikings and eventually were written down in sagas
- C. Europeans looked at the world in a different way
- D. Europeans read the Viking sagas and became consumed with interest in Vinland

LESSON 1: FOR FURTHER STUDY

1. Research which tribe(s) of Native Americans lived in your area of the country. Pick one to study in more detail, and record your information on the Native American tribe form. What happened to them over the years? Do they still have a presence in the region? Is there a museum or an annual powwow that you can visit?

2. Look for descriptions and drawings of the longboats used by the Vikings. Why were they referred to as "serpents of the seas"? Research Viking warfare. Why were other Europeans so afraid of Viking warriors?

3. Find out more about Erik the Red. Why was he known as "the Red"? Where was he born and why did he have to leave there? Describe his family life and his character. Read some excerpts from *The Saga of Erik the Red.*

4. Read about the gods and goddesses of Norse mythology (the Viking religion). Who was the chief Norse god? Where was the home of the gods? Were the Norse gods believed to be immortal? If you are interested, go to the library and check out a book of Norse myths and read several. Some scholars believe that J.R.R. Tolkien's *Lord of the Rings* was influenced by Norse mythology.

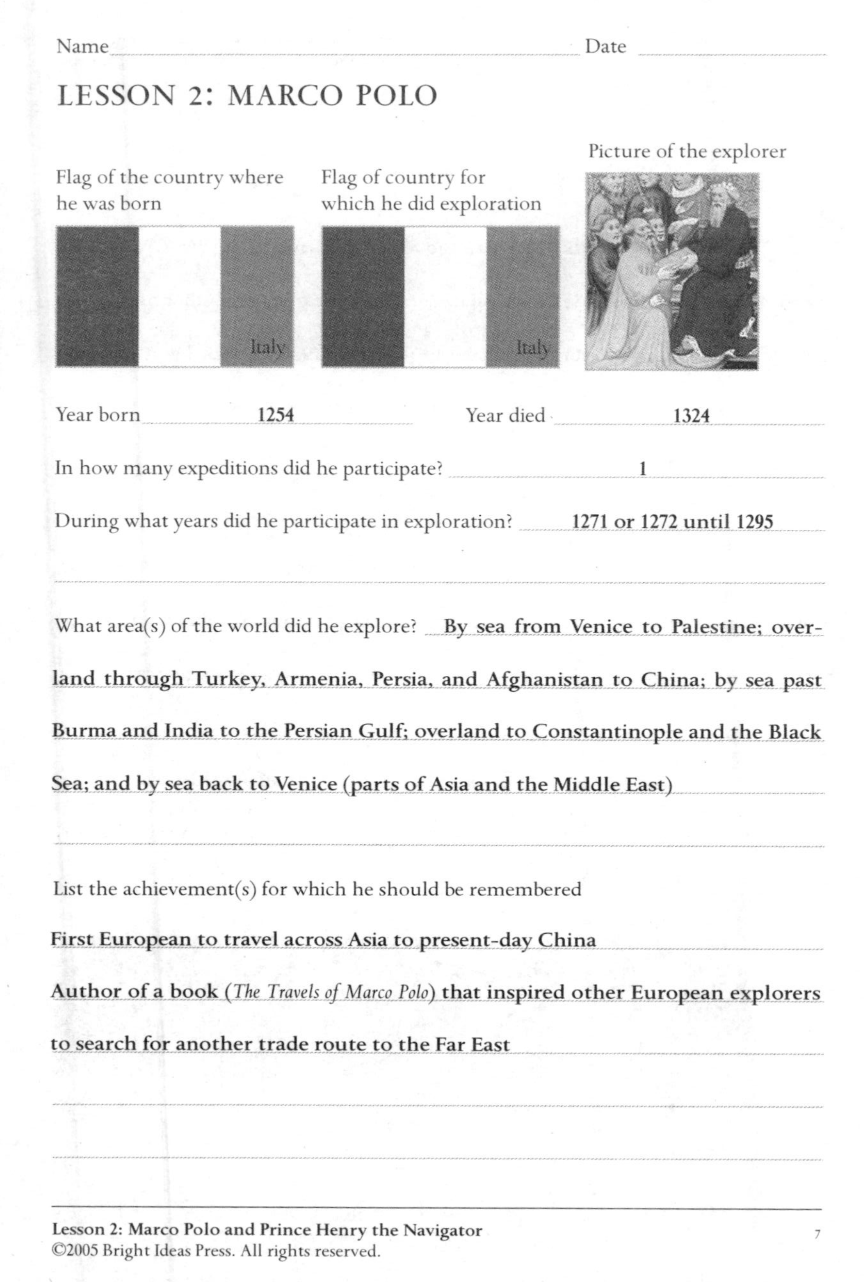

Name ______________ Date ______________

LESSON 2: MARCO POLO

Flag of the country where he was born — Italy

Flag of country for which he did exploration — Italy

Picture of the explorer

Year born **1254** Year died **1324**

In how many expeditions did he participate? **1**

During what years did he participate in exploration? **1271 or 1272 until 1295**

What area(s) of the world did he explore? **By sea from Venice to Palestine; overland through Turkey, Armenia, Persia, and Afghanistan to China; by sea past Burma and India to the Persian Gulf; overland to Constantinople and the Black Sea; and by sea back to Venice (parts of Asia and the Middle East)**

List the achievement(s) for which he should be remembered

First European to travel across Asia to present-day China

Author of a book (*The Travels of Marco Polo*) that inspired other European explorers to search for another trade route to the Far East

Lesson 2: Marco Polo and Prince Henry the Navigator 7

VOYAGES OF MARCO POLO

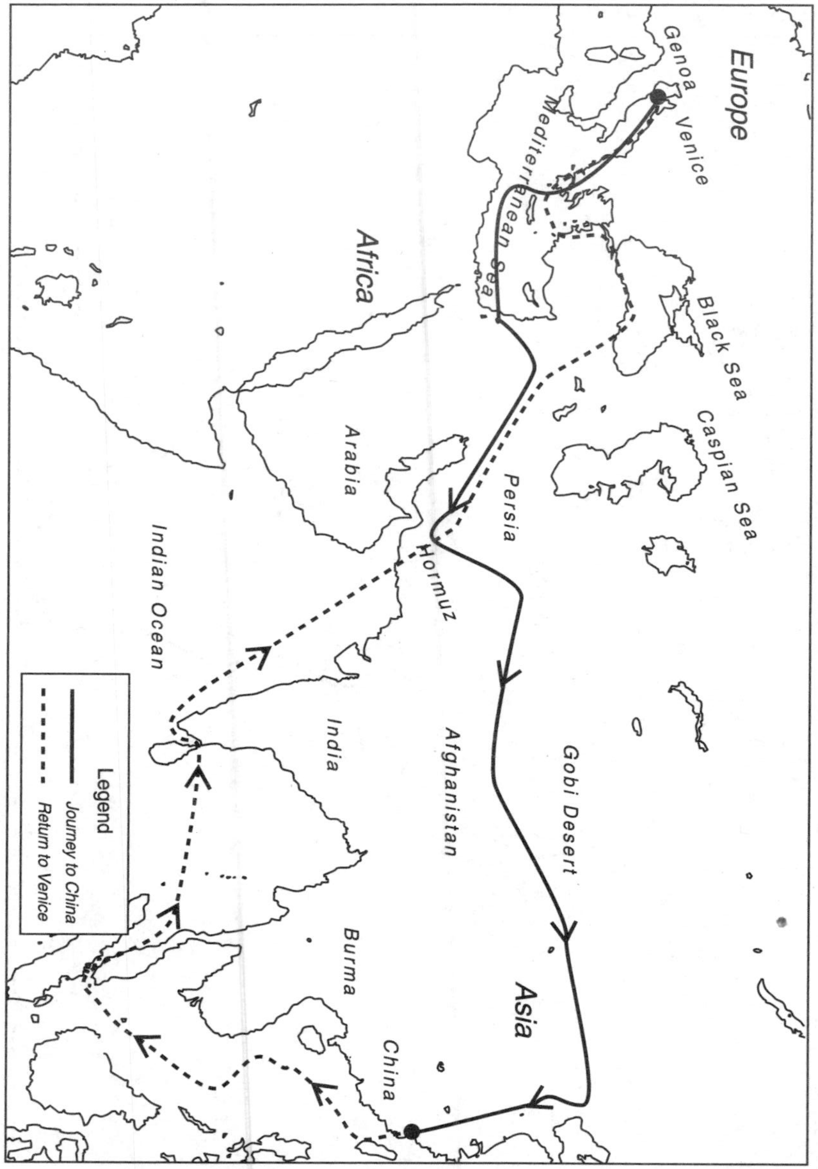

Europe
Genoa
Venice
Black Sea
Caspian Sea
Mediterranean Sea
Persia
Gobi Desert
Asia
Hormuz
Afghanistan
Africa
Arabia
India
China
Burma
Indian Ocean

Legend
Journey to China
Return to Venice

8

All American History Teacher's Guide

Name __________ Date __________

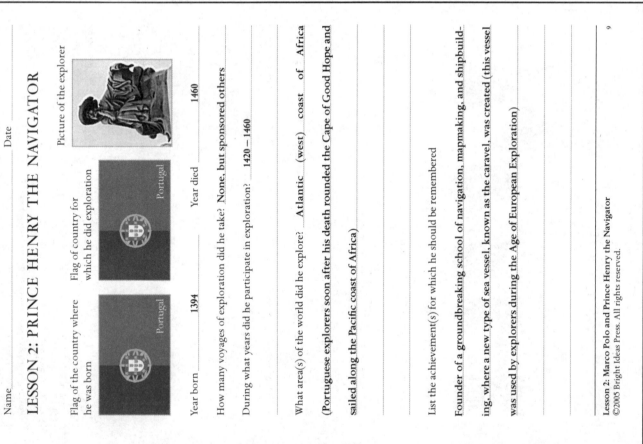

LESSON 2: PRINCE HENRY THE NAVIGATOR

Flag of the country where he was born — Portugal

Flag of country for which he did exploration — Portugal

Picture of the explorer

Year born **1394** Year died **1460**

How many voyages of exploration did he take? **None, but sponsored others**

During what years did he participate in exploration? **1420 – 1460**

What area(s) of the world did he explore? **Atlantic (west) coast of Africa (Portuguese explorers soon after his death rounded the Cape of Good Hope and sailed along the Pacific coast of Africa)**

List the achievement(s) for which he should be remembered

Founder of a groundbreaking school of navigation, mapmaking, and shipbuilding, where a new type of sea vessel, known as the caravel, was created (this vessel was used by explorers during the Age of European Exploration)

Lesson 2: Marco Polo and Prince Henry the Navigator 9

VOYAGES OF PRINCE HENRY THE NAVIGATOR'S SAILORS

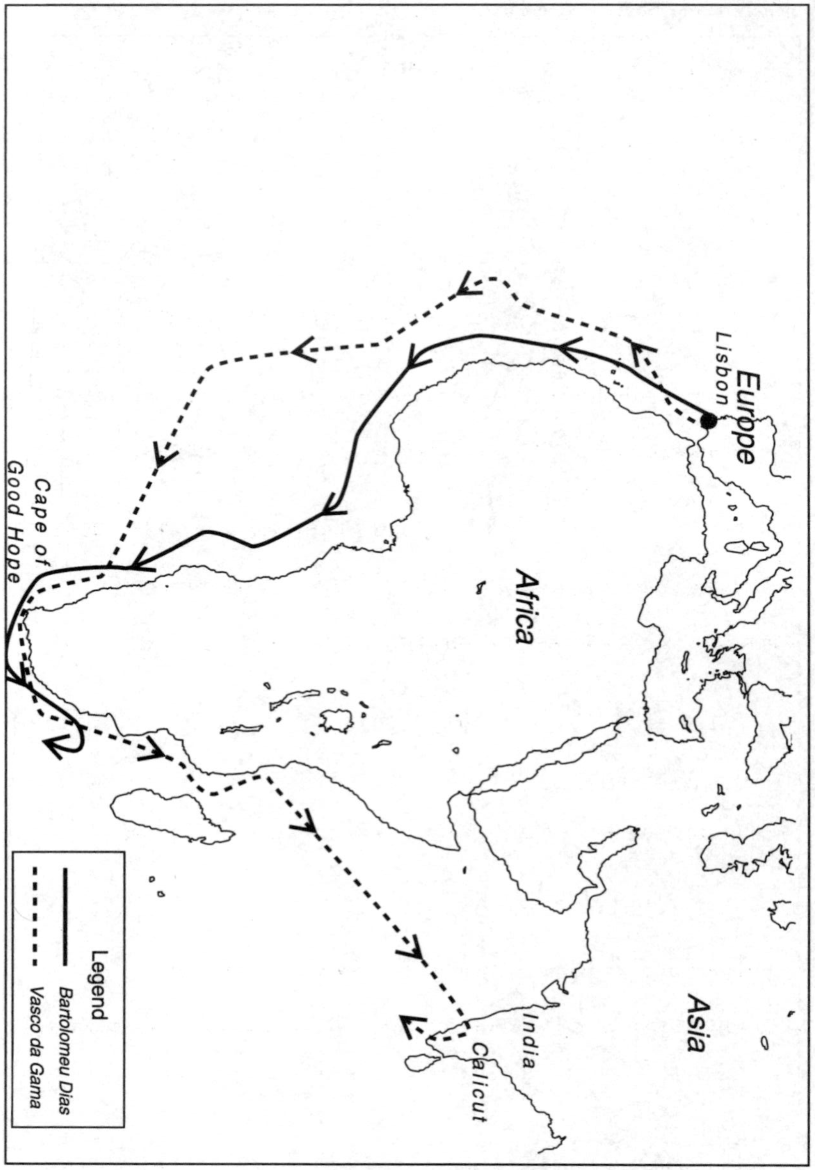

10 All American History Teacher's Guide

LESSON 2: FOR REVIEW

Write the missing word or words in the spaces provided.

1. About the time of Marco Polo's birth, Nicolo and Maffeo Polo traveled to the city of **Constantinople**, a major trade link between the Mediterranean and Black seas.

2. As a result of Christian military expeditions to the Holy Land, known as **the Crusades**, many Europeans were introduced to the riches of eastern Asia for the first time.

3. European trade in Asian luxury items was monopolized by **Asian** middlemen and **Italian** middlemen.

4. The Portuguese royal prince and patron of explorers was known as **Prince Henry the Navigator**.

5. The location of the Portuguese school of navigation, mapmaking, and ship-building was **St. Vincent Promontory at Sagres**.

6. A new type of sea vessel, the Portuguese **caravel**, was developed at Prince Henry's school.

7. Marco Polo was about **17** years old when he traveled with his father and uncle to Cathay. The trip to Cathay took almost **4** years.

8. By the time that he left the court of the Khan, Marco Polo was about **40** years old. During his years in Cathay, he went on many special missions for the emperor.

9. When the Polos returned to Venice, the Italian city-state was engaged in a naval war with **Genoa**. Marco was captured during this conflict and thrown into prison.

10. Because he constantly talked of Asia and the incredible profits to be earned by trading there, Marco Polo became known in Venice as **Marco Millions**.

11 *The Travels of Marco Polo* inspired a number of European explorers, including **Christopher Columbus**, who took the book with him on his first voyage across the Atlantic in 1492.

12. In 1453, the Muslims took over the trade city of **Constantinople**, shutting down the land route to Asia for European merchants and explorers.

13. For forty years Prince Henry financed and sent out Portuguese sea captains in caravels to explore the western coast of **Africa**.

Write the corresponding letter of the correct answer in the space provided.

A. Vasco da Gama
B. Bartolomeu Dias
C. Gil Eannes
D. Kublai Khan
E. Rustichello

__C__ 1. First Portuguese sea captain to round Cape Bojador

__D__ 2. Mongol ruler of Cambulac (present-day Peking)

__A__ 3. First Portuguese sea captain to sail around the southern tip of Africa to India and back

__E__ 4. Italian Romance writer who served as a scribe for Marco Polo

__B__ 5. First Portuguese sea captain to round the Cape of Good Hope

LESSON 2: FOR FURTHER STUDY

1. Find out when the Mongol (Tartar) Empire was at its height. From what area did the Mongols originate? What does the word *Khan* mean? Who was Kublai Khan's grandfather? For what was he known? Which dynasty was founded by Kublai Khan? What famous 1816 poem immortalized Kublai Khan? See if you can find a copy of this poem and read it.

2. Read some short excerpts from *The Travels of Marco Polo*. Do any of his statements seem to be exaggerations to you?

3. The Chinese carefully guarded their secret of silk making for years. When did they first begin making silk? Who is traditionally given credit for inventing the Chinese methods of raising silkworms and spinning silk thread? How did Europeans finally learn this Chinese secret?

4. Find out how the Portuguese became involved in the West African slave trade. Who had replaced them as the dominant country in this slave trade by the end of the seventeenth century?

Name________________________ Date ____________

LESSON 3: CHRISTOPHER COLUMBUS

Flag of the country where he was born — Italy

Flag of country for which he did exploration — Spain

Picture of the explorer

Year born **1451** Year died **1506**

How many voyages of exploration did he take? **4**

During what years did he participate in exploration? **1492 – 1504**

What area(s) of the world did he explore? **Bahamas, Cuba, Haiti, Dominican Republic, Puerto Rico, Jamaica, Martinique, Guadeloupe, Trinidad, coast of Venezuela, eastern coast of Central America from Honduras to Panama (islands in the Carribean, eastern coast of Central America, and northern coast of Venezuela)**

List the achievement(s) for which he should be remembered

First European to discover the islands of the Caribbean, Central America, and the northern coast of South America. (Gave Spain a huge advantage over European countries in empire building.) Discoverer of a trade route across the Atlantic using trade winds (still used today by sea captains)

Lesson 3: Christopher Columbus and Amerigo Vespucci 15

VOYAGES OF CHRISTOPHER COLUMBUS

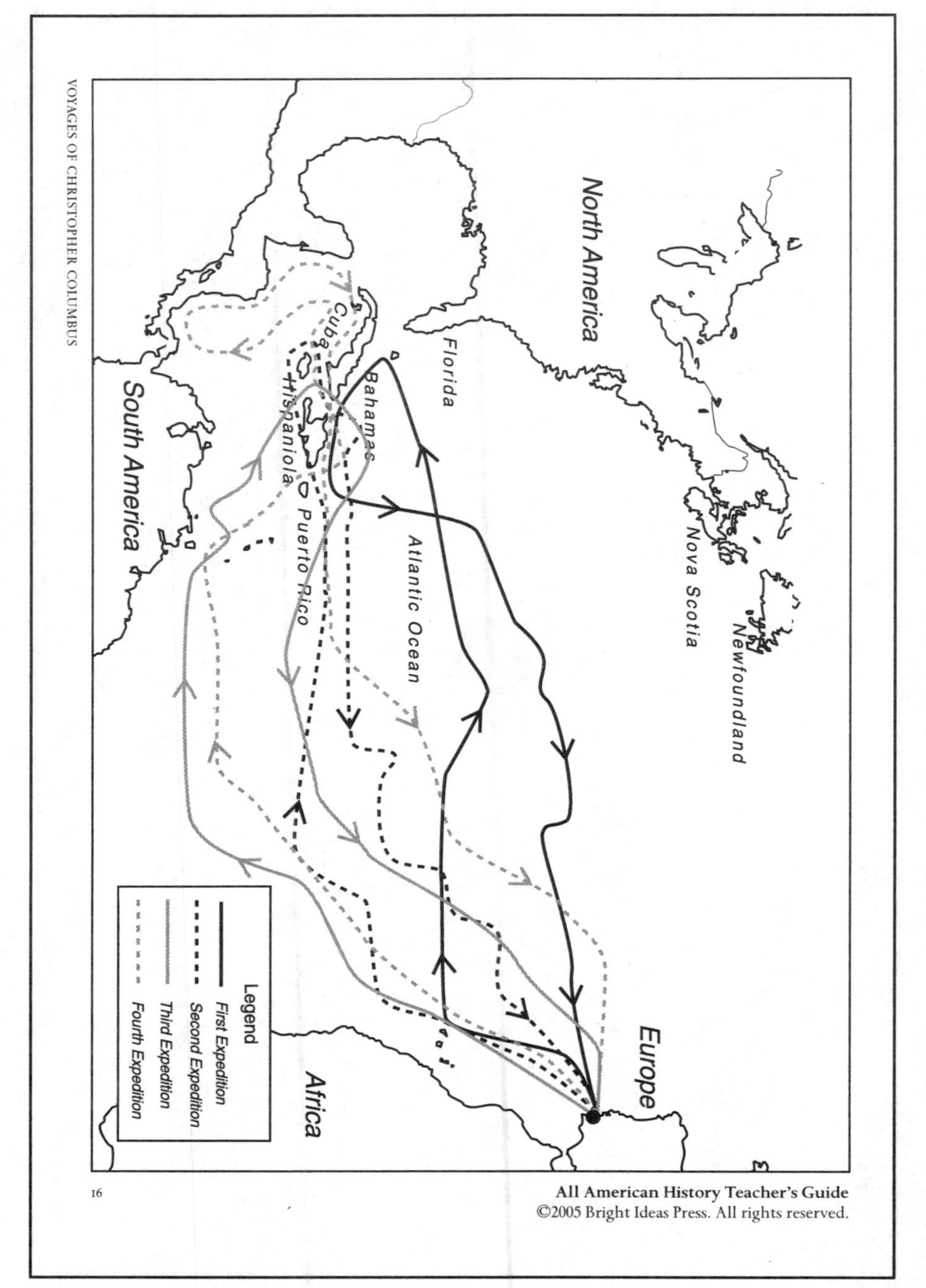

16

All American History Teacher's Guide

Name ______ Date ______

LESSON 3: AMERIGO VESPUCCI

Year born **1454 or 1451?**

Year died **1512**

How many voyages of exploration did he take?

claimed to have made 4

Picture of the explorer

Flag of the country where he was born	Flag of country for which he did exploration	Flag of country for which he did exploration
Italy	Spain	Portugal

During what years did he participate in exploration? **1497 – 1504**

What area(s) of the world did he explore? **parts of South America, including Venezuela and Brazil**

List the achievement(s) for which he should be remembered

One of the first believers in the discovery of a "New World"

Latin form of his given name (Amerigo) used as the name for the new continent

LESSON 3: FOR REVIEW

Write T for True and F for False in the space provided.

T 1. Although Columbus learned the family trade of wool weaving, his true ambition was to be a sailor.

T 2. When his life was spared in a pirate attack at sea, Columbus believed that God had saved him so that he might accomplish great things.

F 3. Columbus's estimate of the distance between the Canary Islands and Japan was amazingly accurate.

F 4. After only one meeting with the Spanish king and queen, Columbus persuaded them to finance his westward expedition.

T 5. Ferdinand and Isabella promised Columbus one-tenth of the riches that he brought back from his expedition, governorship of all the lands that he visited, and the title "Admiral of the Ocean Sea."

T 6. Amerigo Vespucci supposedly met Christopher Columbus and may have helped that explorer prepare for his third expedition.

T 7. On his first westward expedition, Columbus set sail westward with three small wooden ships — two caravels and one nao.

F 8. The expedition captained by Columbus was stalled at sea and traveled more than one hundred days without sight of land.

T 9. Columbus first landed on an island, which he named San Salvador (probably Watling Island in the Bahamas).

T 10. Because Columbus believed that he had reached the East Indies, he called the dark-skinned people on the islands Indians.

F 11. The first Spanish colony established in the New World, La Navidad on Hispaniola, flourished from the very beginning.

F 12. Columbus, with all three ships, returned to Spain a hero.

T 13. After returning from his first journey, Columbus made three more westward expeditions.

T 14. During his trips to the New World, Columbus never set foot on the continent of North America.

T 15. When Columbus died, his reputation was greatly diminished and his health was poor.

F 16. No documents still exist from Columbus's voyages of discovery.

T 17. There has been great confusion concerning the details of the voyages made by Amerigo Vespucci to the New World.

T 18. Vespucci sailed with both Spanish and Portuguese sea captains.

T 19. As a result of the publication of Vespucci's letters to Lorenzo de Medici, Vespucci became established as the first person known to write about the belief that a new continent had been discovered.

F 20. Vespucci named the new continent America after himself.

LESSON 3: FOR FURTHER STUDY

1. Look for descriptions and sketches of caravels and naos used during the Age of European Exploration. Find out about the different parts of a caravel (the *Nina* and *Pinta* were caravels) and a nao (the *Santa Maria* was a nao).
2. What does it mean to navigate by dead reckoning? This was the method used by Columbus and most sailors of his day. Who developed celestial navigation and when? How does celestial navigation work?
3. Learn more about navigational instruments used during the Age of European Exploration, such as the astrolabe, quadrant, and compass. See if you can find drawings or pictures of these instruments.
4. See if you can locate copies of maps produced during the fifteenth and sixteenth centuries. How do they compare to modern maps?

Name ______ Date ______

LESSON 4: JOHN CABOT (GIOVANNI CABOTO)

Flag of the country where he was born — Italy

Flag of country for which he did exploration — England

Picture of the explorer

Year born **1451** Year died **1498**

How many voyages of exploration did he take? **2**

During what years did he participate in exploration? **1496 – 1498**

What area(s) of the world did he explore? **Newfoundland, Labrador, and Nova Scotia (historians aren't sure exactly which) and the nearby Canadian coastline (lands in northwest Atlantic)**

List the achievement(s) for which he should be remembered

First explorer to establish English claims to land in the New World

Name used for many islands, straits, and lakes in North Atlantic

Lesson 4: Cabot, Balboa, and Other Spanish Conquistadors 21

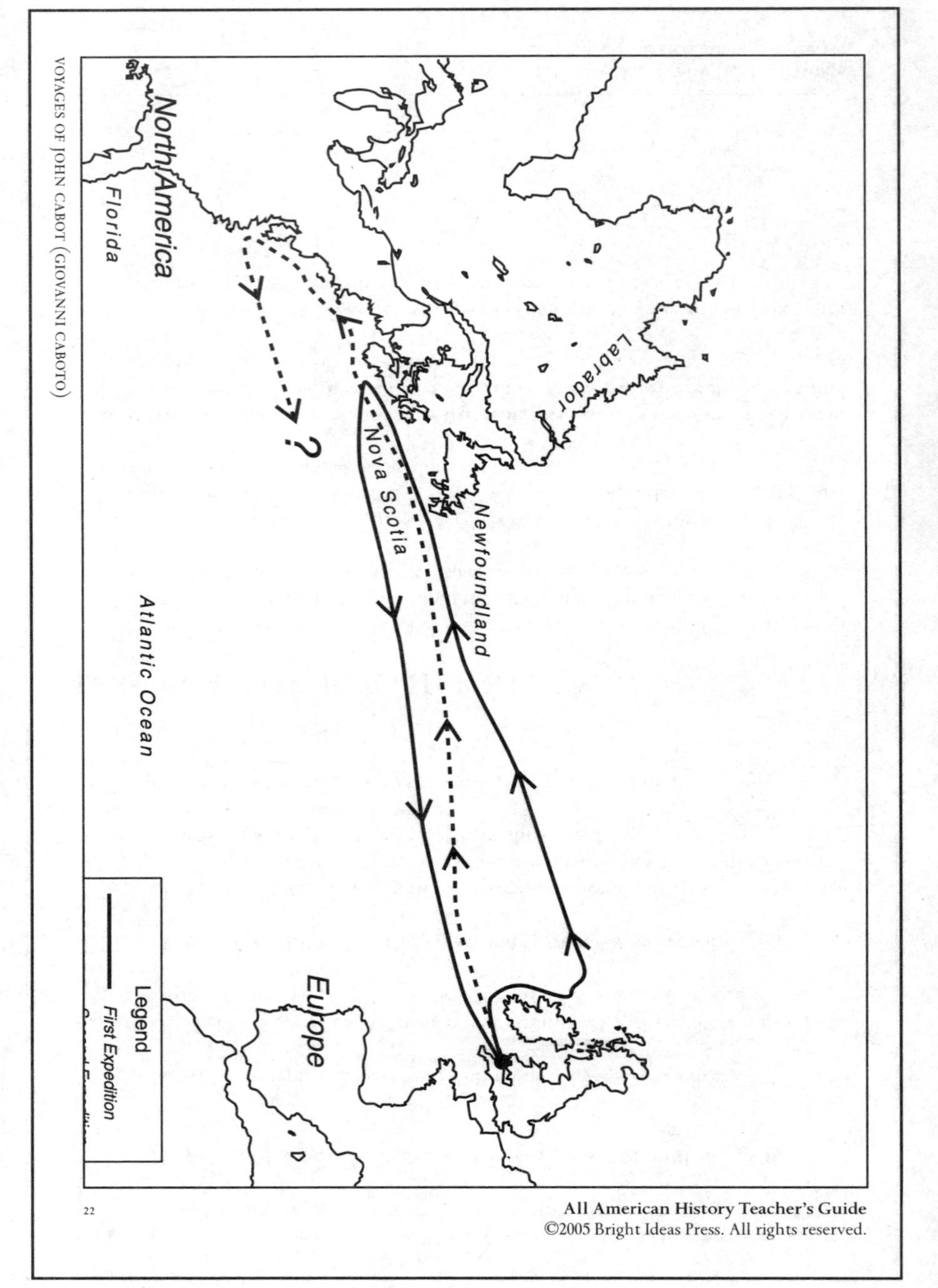

VOYAGES OF JOHN CABOT (GIOVANNI CABOTO)

22

All American History Teacher's Guide

Name ______________ Date ______________

LESSON 4: VASCO NUNEZ DE BALBOA

Flag of the country where he was born: Spain

Flag of country for which he did exploration: Spain

Picture of the explorer

Year born **1475** Year died **1519**

In how many expeditions did he participate? **at least 4**

During what years did he participate in exploration? **1500 or 1501 until 1513**

What area(s) of the world did he explore? **primarily the area around Panama**

List the achievement(s) for which he should be remembered

First European to sight the Pacific Ocean from an American shore

Inspiration for Spanish exploration and conquest along the western coast of South America

Lesson 4: Cabot, Balboa, and Other Spanish Conquistadors 23

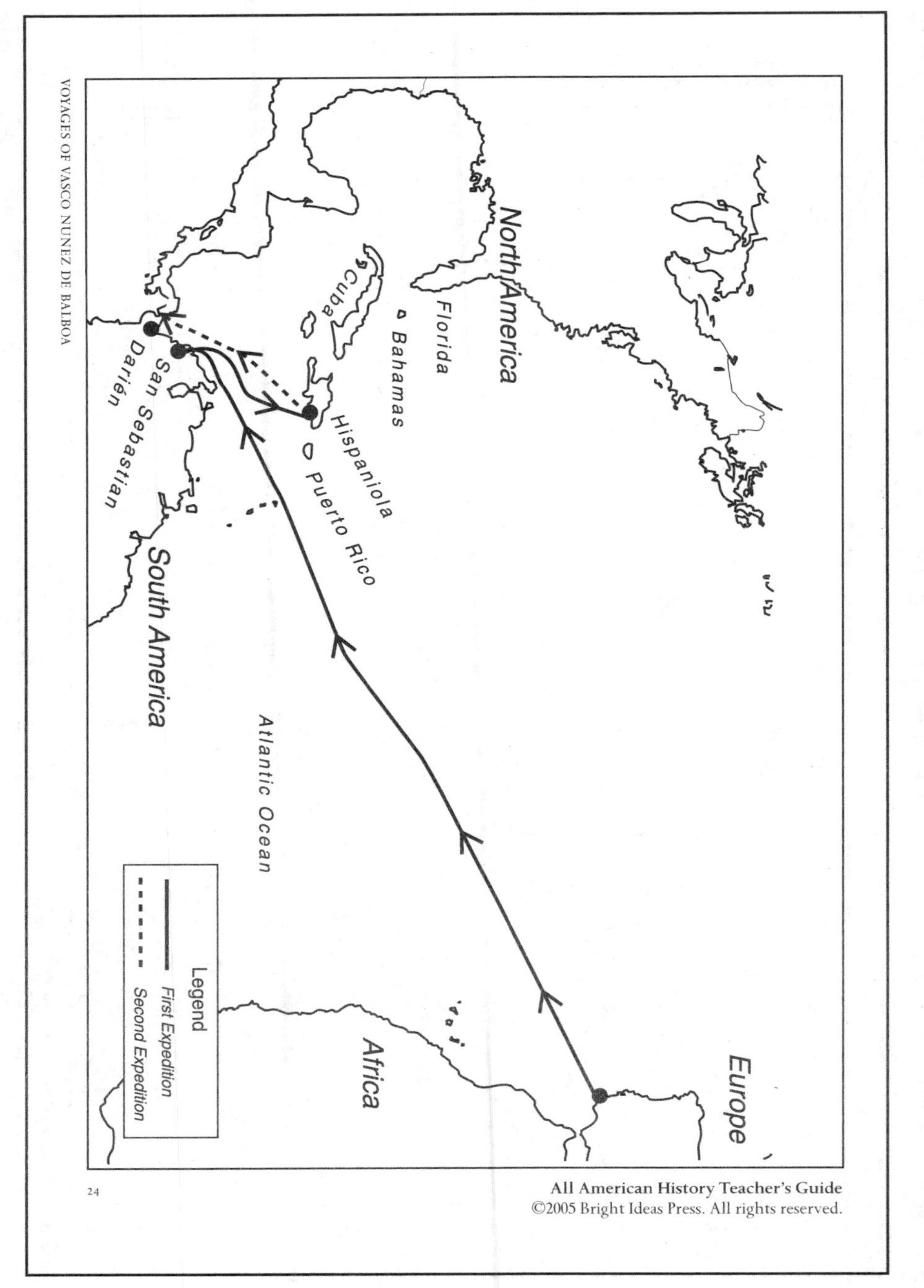

VOYAGES OF VASCO NUNEZ DE BALBOA

24

All American History Teacher's Guide

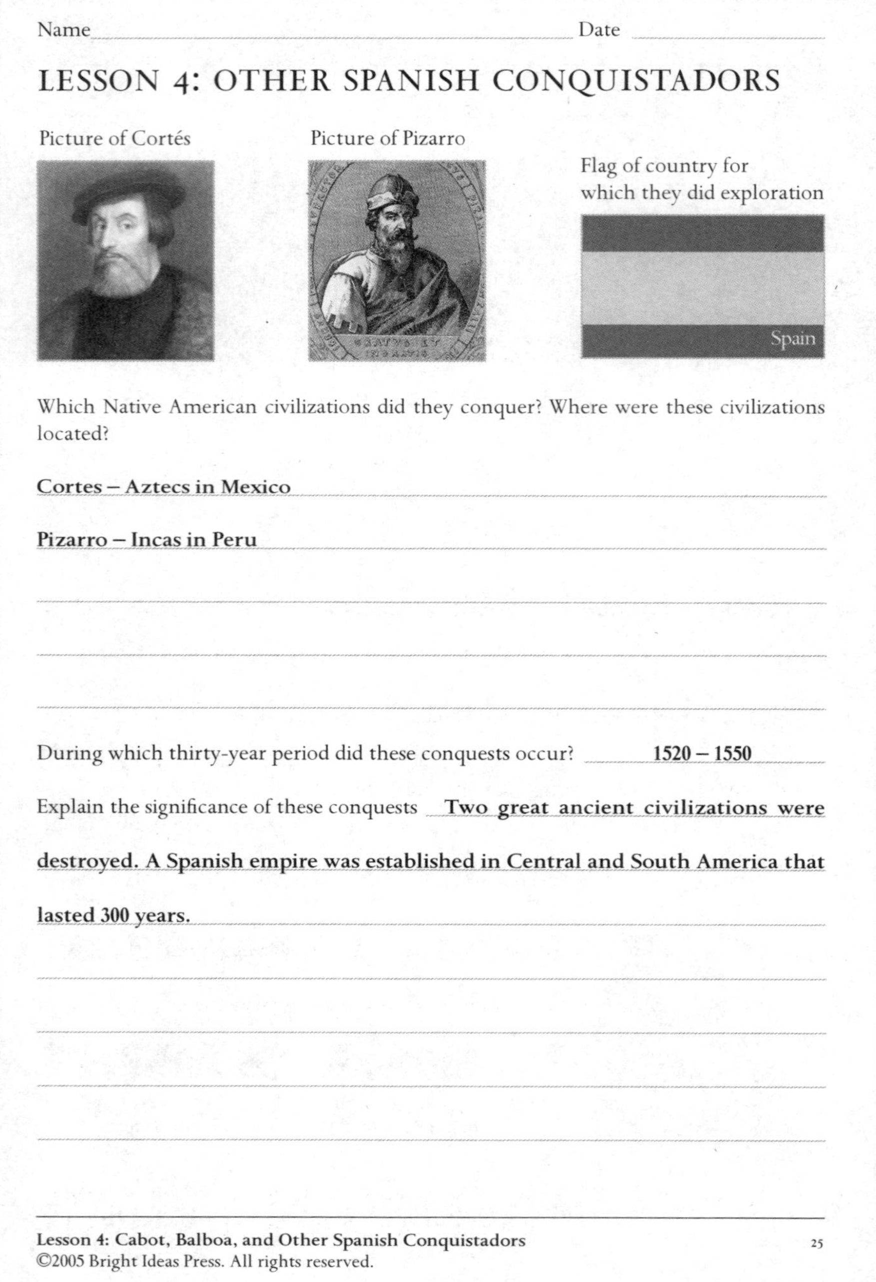

Name_______________ Date_______

LESSON 4: OTHER SPANISH CONQUISTADORS

Picture of Cortés

Picture of Pizarro

Flag of country for which they did exploration

Spain

Which Native American civilizations did they conquer? Where were these civilizations located?

Cortes – Aztecs in Mexico

Pizarro – Incas in Peru

During which thirty-year period did these conquests occur? **1520 – 1550**

Explain the significance of these conquests **Two great ancient civilizations were destroyed. A Spanish empire was established in Central and South America that lasted 300 years.**

Lesson 4: Cabot, Balboa, and Other Spanish Conquistadors 25

North America
Florida
Bahamas
Cuba
Tenochtitlan
Veracruz
Hispaniola
Puerto Rico
Atlantic Ocean
Africa
South America
San Mateo
Tumbes
San Miguel
Cajamarc
Sechura Desert
Lima
Cusco
Legend
Cortés's Expedition
Pizarro's Expedition

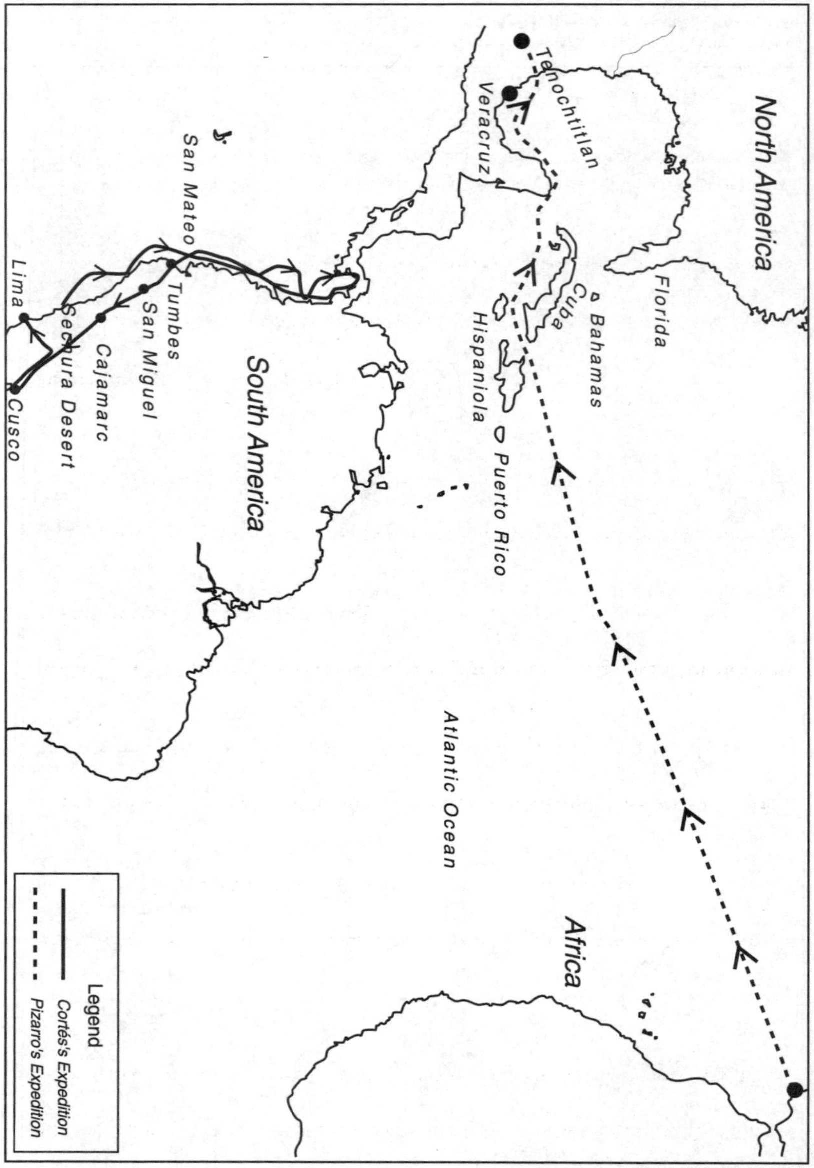

VOYAGES OF SPANISH CONQUISTADORS

26

All American History Teacher's Guide

LESSON 4: FOR REVIEW

Write the corresponding letter of the correct answer in the space provided.

A. John Cabot
B. Vasco Nuñez de Balboa
C. Hernando Cortés
D. Francisco Pizarro

A 1. Italian navigator who sailed for England

C 2. Spanish adventurer believed to be a legendary Aztec god

B 3. First European known to sight the waters of the Pacific Ocean from an American shore

B 4. Spanish explorer who made Pedrarias jealous and faced execution on false charges of treason

A 5. Captain of the *Matthew*, who claimed land along the Canadian coast for England

A 6. Explorer believed to have found "new lands" on the bottom of the ocean

D 7. Spanish adventurer who served on expeditions with Balboa and Cortés

C 8. Governor of Mexico for seven years before being ordered back to Spain

D 9. Conquistador who ravaged the Inca Empire in Peru

B 10. Explorer who amassed a fortune in Darien and made friends with many of the surrounding native tribes

Write the missing word or words in the spaces provided.

1. The land west of the Line of Demarcation was decreed by the pope to belong to **Spain** and the land east of the line to **Portugal**.

2. Because of the Treaty of Tordesillas, Portugal was able to claim **Brazil**.

3. The country that was not involved in the negotiations concerning the Line of Demarcation but was eager to sponsor its own western expedition was **England**.

4. The main thrust of early Spanish exploration in the New World was in **Central America** and **South America**.

5. From 1520 – 1550, the Spanish carved out a New World Empire that lasted **300** years.

6. The Spanish noblemen/adventurers who led the wave of conquest in America were known as **conquistadors**.

7. The two great civilizations conquered and plundered by the Spanish were the **Aztec** and **Inca** civilizations.

LESSON 4: FOR FURTHER STUDY

1. Research the life of John Cabot's son, Sebastian. (1474 – 1557). For which country did he explore in 1526? Where was he supposed to go and why? Where did he go instead and why? How did this expedition end? What invitation did Sebastian receive around 1548?

2. Learn about the geography of Panama. What role has Panama played in American history? What is the name of Panama's principal port city? Look for a photograph of the statue of Balboa overlooking Panama Bay.

3. Read about the Aztecs or the Incas. Record your information on a Native American Tribe form.

4. What role did Roman Catholic priests play in expeditions led by the Spanish in America and in early Spanish-American settlements? Look especially for information concerning their relationships with Native Americans.

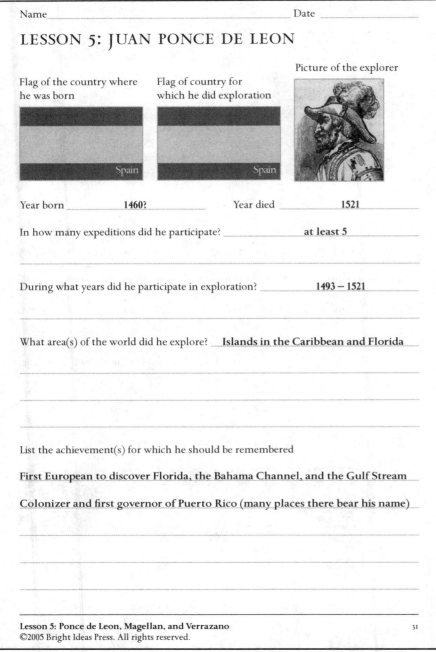

Name __________ Date __________

LESSON 5: JUAN PONCE DE LEON

Flag of the country where he was born	Flag of country for which he did exploration	Picture of the explorer
Spain	Spain	

Year born **1460?** Year died **1521**

In how many expeditions did he participate? **at least 5**

During what years did he participate in exploration? **1493 – 1521**

What area(s) of the world did he explore? **Islands in the Caribbean and Florida**

List the achievement(s) for which he should be remembered

First European to discover Florida, the Bahama Channel, and the Gulf Stream

Colonizer and first governor of Puerto Rico (many places there bear his name)

Lesson 5: Ponce de Leon, Magellan, and Verrazano 31

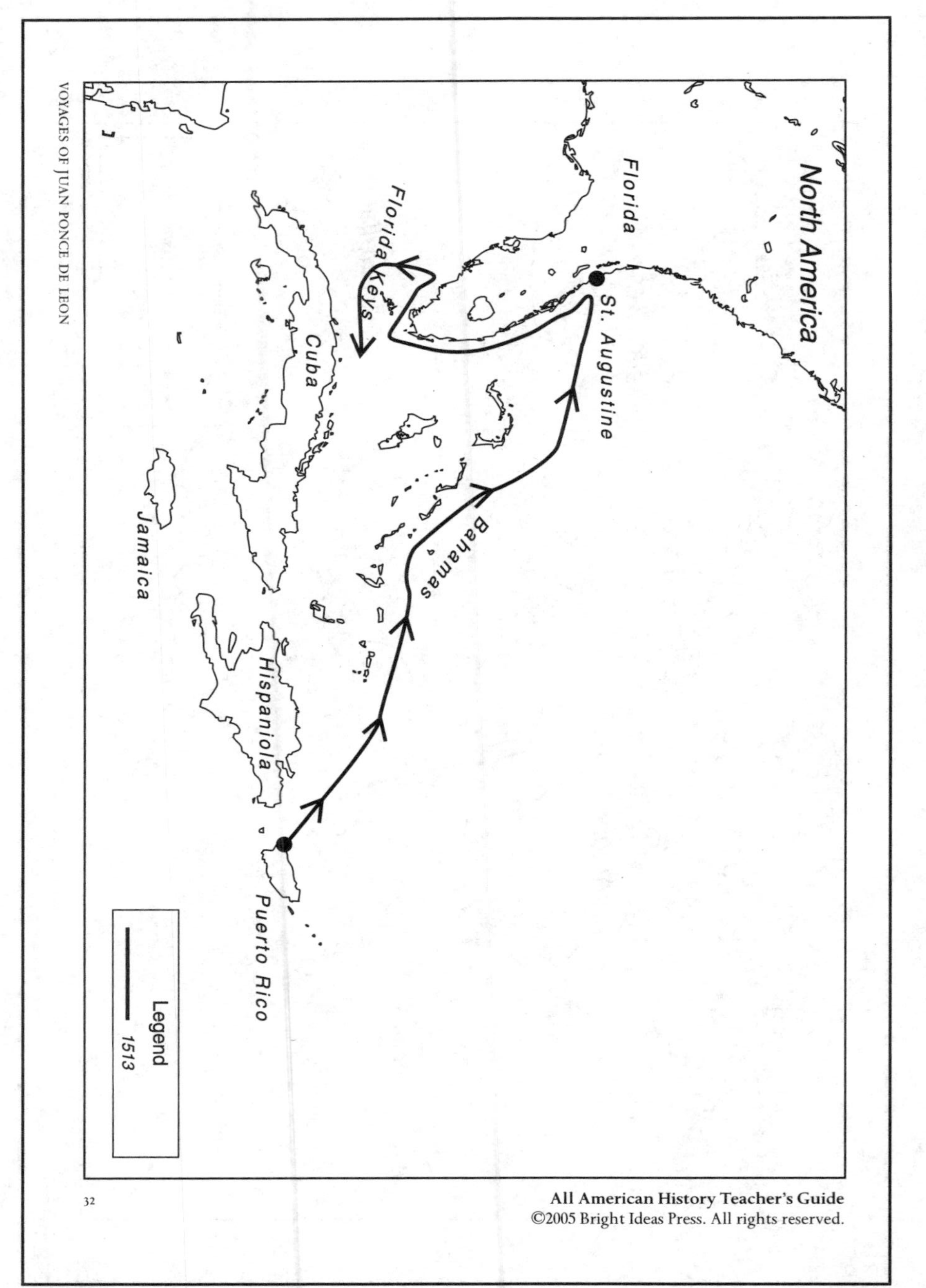

VOYAGES OF JUAN PONCE DE LEON

32 All American History Teacher's Guide

Name ____________ Date ____________

LESSON 5: FERDINAND MAGELLAN

Flag of the country where he was born — Portugal

Flag of country for which he did exploration — Spain

Picture of the explorer

Year born **1480** Year died **1521**

How many voyages of exploration did he take? **1**

During what years did he participate in exploration? **1519 – 1521**

What area(s) of the world did he explore? **East coast of South America, Pacific Ocean (Philippines and the Moluccas), Indian Ocean, around Africa, and back to Spain (Magellan himself died in the Philippines); circumnavigated the Earth**

List the achievement(s) for which he should be remembered

First to prove that the world is round and that the Far East could be reached by sailing west from Europe

VOYAGES OF FERDINAND MAGELLAN

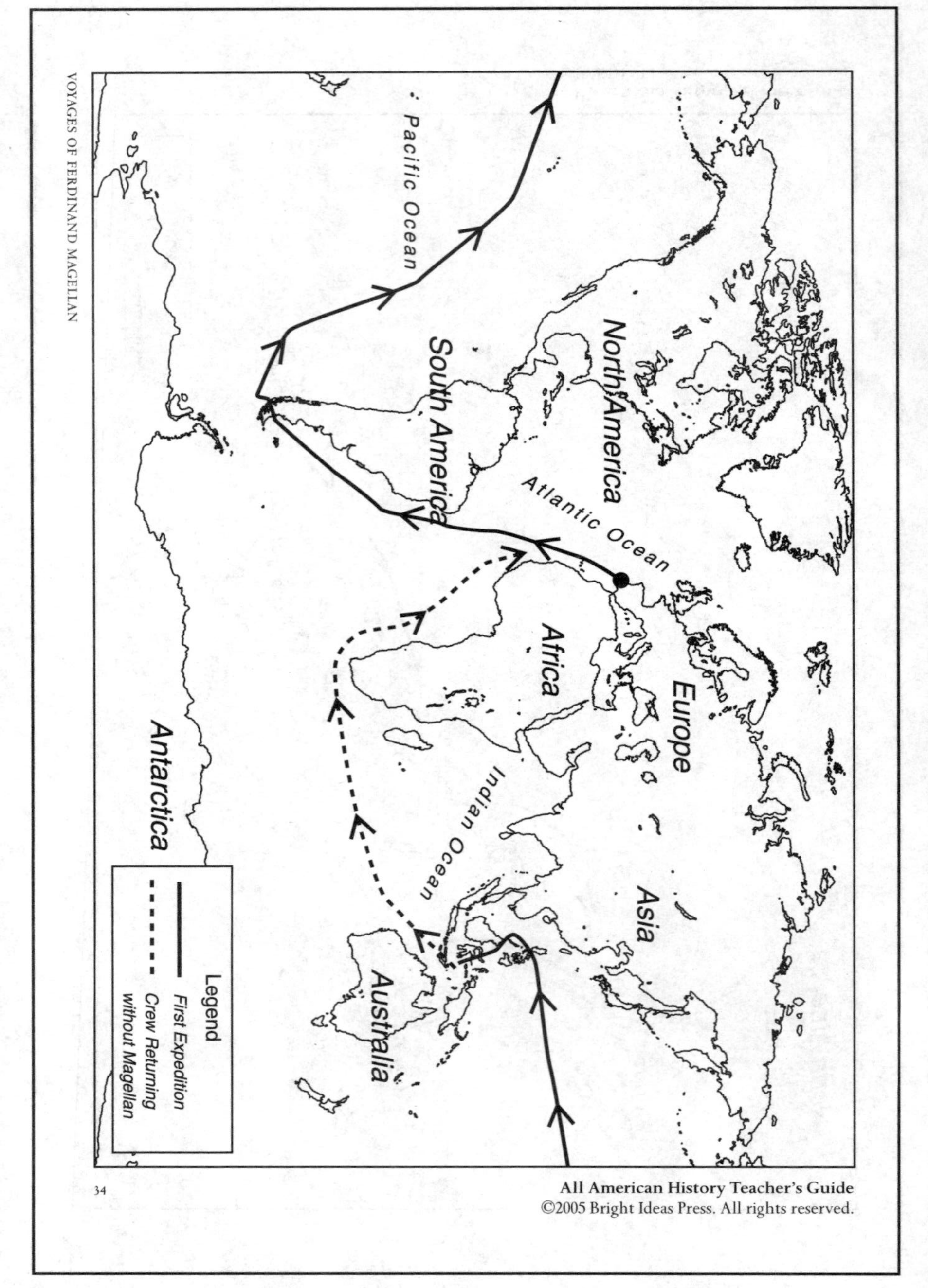

Name________________ Date ________

LESSON 5: GIOVANNI DA VERRAZANO

Flag of the country where he was born — Italy

Flag of country for which he did exploration — France

Picture of the explorer

Year born **1485? or 1480?** Year died **1528?**

How many voyages of exploration did he take? **3**

During what years did he participate in exploration? **1525 – 1528**

What area(s) of the world did he explore? **East coast of North America from the Carolinas to Maine and Newfoundland, Brazil, and Florida**

List the achievement(s) for which he should be remembered

First European to discover New York Bay and Narragansett Bay

Establisher of French right to claim territory in North America

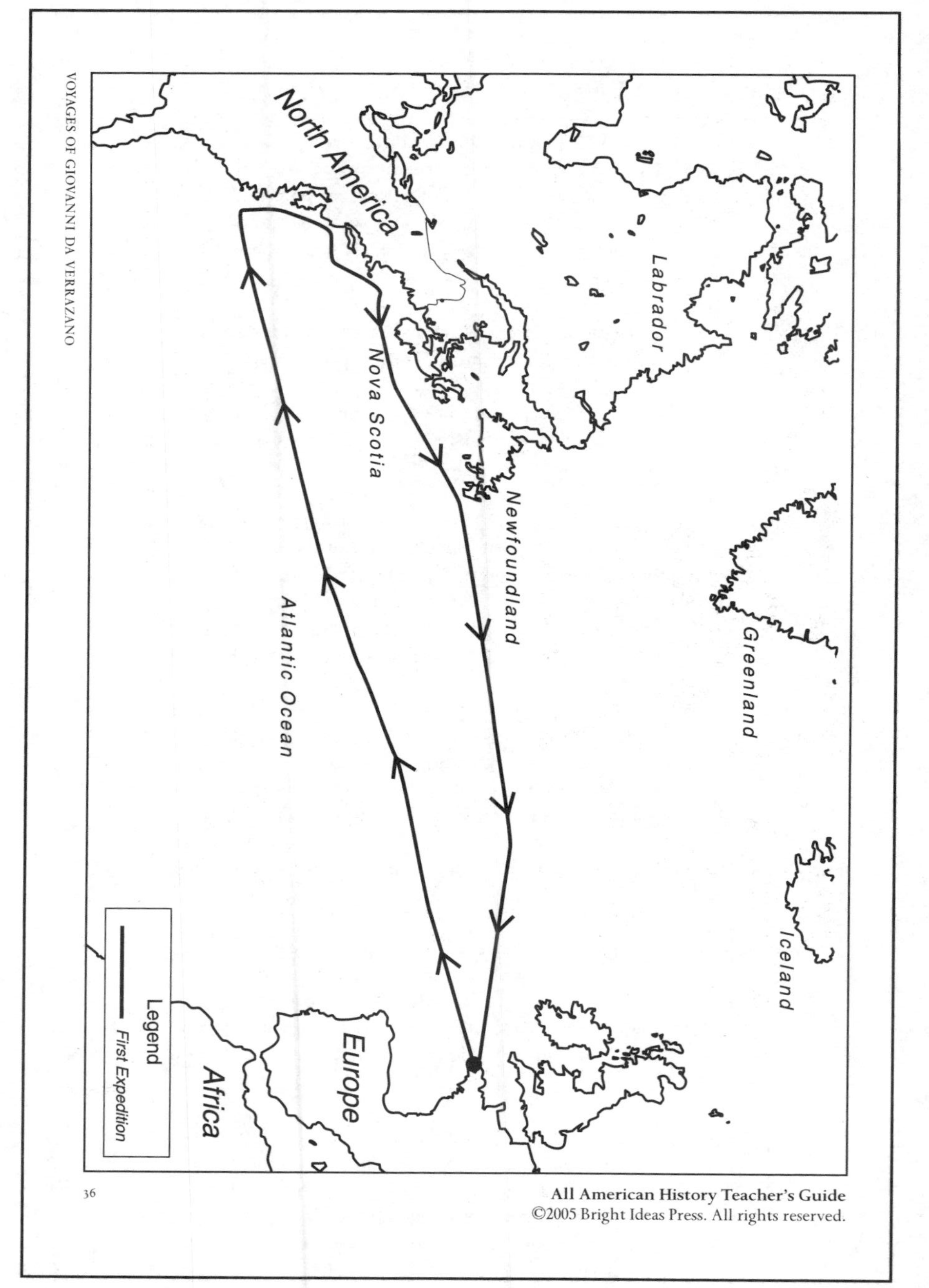

VOYAGES OF GIOVANNI DA VERRAZANO

LESSON 5: FOR REVIEW

Write the letter of the correct answer in the space provided.

__A__ 1. The Spanish soldier and explorer Ponce de Leon
- A. served as the first governor of Borinquen
- B. accompanied Balboa on his trek across Panama
- C. found himself imprisoned by Nicolas de Ovando on Hispaniola
- D. negotiated impressive peace treaties with Native Americans

__B__ 2. In his early years of adulthood, Ferdinand Magellan
- A. worked for a library
- B. traveled as far east as Malacca and the Moluccas
- C. enlisted as a soldier but never fought in any military campaigns
- D. moved to Africa to live

__A__ 3. When Magellan decided to search for a westward route to the Far East,
- A. he believed that he could find a strait in the southern part of America
- B. he found a sponsor in the English king Henry VIII
- C. he consulted with Columbus about his plans
- D. he insisted on using only Portuguese sea captains as commanders of his ships

__D__ 4. Italian navigator Giovanni da Verrazano
- A. was born into a poor Florentine family
- B. lived all of his life in Florence
- C. sailed for the Portuguese down the west coast of Africa
- D. captured two of Cortés's Spanish galleons

__B__ 5. Ponce de Leon's expedition to search for Bimini
- A. never left Borinquen
- B. probably landed just north of present-day St. Augustine
- C. encountered very friendly Native Americans
- D. succeeded in its goal of locating a fountain of youth

__D__ 6. Ponce de Leon accomplished all of the following EXCEPT
- A. the discovery of the Bahama Channel
- B. the first observations of the Gulf Stream
- C. naming the land that he discovered Florida
- D. establishment of a permanent Spanish settlement at St. Augustine

__C__ 7. When Magellan departed from Spain in the fall of 1519,
- A. he sailed with one ship and a small band of men
- B. he headed west to Hispaniola
- C. he planned to sail south toward Brazil
- D. he had no qualms concerning the loyalty of his crew and commanders

__D__ 8. Which of the following did NOT happen to Magellan between March and late September 1520?
- A. he put down the first of several mutinies of his crew
- B. he wintered near the harbor of San Julian
- C. he lost one of his ships in a reconnaissance expedition
- D. he discovered good sources of fresh food supplies

__C__ 9. During October and November 1520, Magellan
- A. failed to discover the strait for which he was looking
- B. decided to return to Spain
- C. faced the desertion of the captain of the San Antonio, which meant the loss of most of their provisions
- D. reached Japan

__B__ 10. As Magellan and his men crossed the Pacific, they
- A. found the water to be very turbulent
- B. almost starved to death
- C. found many beautiful islands to stop to explore
- D. reached the East Indies in less than a month's time

__B__ 11. When Magellan's expedition reached the Philippines, he
- A. found no natives to greet him and his men
- B. preached the Gospel to the natives and witnessed many conversions
- C. quickly gathered provisions and immediately sailed for Spain
- D. received a miraculous healing from a terrible disease

__C__ 12. As Magellan's men left the Philippines, they
   A. were ready to mutiny against his leadership again
   B. decided not to try to reach the Moluccas
   C. burned one of their ships because they did not have enough crew for three ships
   D. headed east back across the Pacific

__A__ 13. In 1522, the expedition that had left Spain with Magellan
   A. returned with eighteen men in one ship
   B. did not return with a profit for its investors
   C. carried no crewmen willing to write about their voyage
   D. headed back to Brazil under the leadership of Sebastian del Cano

Write the missing word or words in the spaces provided.

1. Verrazano was commissioned by the king of **France** to lead an expedition to the New World.

2. As he planned his voyage, Verrazano decided to follow a route somewhat north of the route used by **Columbus** on his first journey.

3. When he first touched land in America, Verrazano was probably at a point south of present-day **Cape Fear, North Carolina**.

4. After sailing south, Verrazano eventually turned back to the north because he did not want to encounter **the Spanish in Florida**.

5. Verrazano decided that the area behind the Outer Banks was **the Pacific Ocean**.

6. The Frenchmen in Verrazano's expedition were the first Europeans known to have seen the **New York** Bay and **Narragansett** Bay.

7. In present-day New England Verrazano encountered the **Wampanoag** tribe, whose descendants would befriend the Pilgrims.

LESSON 5: FOR FURTHER STUDY

1. Make sure that you know the meaning of the following geographical terms: *peninsula*, *isthmus*, *strait*, *gulf*, *bay*, and *island*. Can you draw a picture of each of these?

2. Sailors during the Age of European Exploration faced a number of diseases, such as malaria, dysentery, scurvy, and typhus. Pick several of these diseases and find out their causes and symptoms.

3. Read more about the city of St. Augustine. When was it founded as a permanent Spanish colony in the New World? What historical sites can you visit today in St. Augustine?

4. Research the Wampanoag tribe. How were they helpful to the Europeans who arrived in America? Record the information on a Native American Tribe form.

Name ____________________ Date ____________

LESSON 6: JACQUES CARTIER

Flag of the country where he was born: France

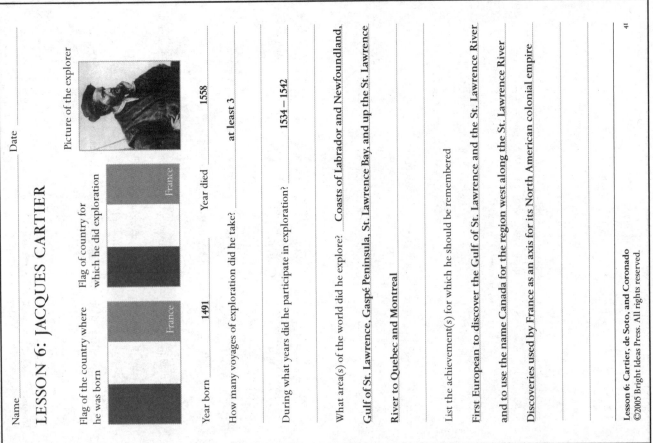

Flag of country for which he did exploration: France

Picture of the explorer

Year born **1491** Year died **1558**

How many voyages of exploration did he take? **at least 3**

During what years did he participate in exploration? **1534 – 1542**

What area(s) of the world did he explore? **Coasts of Labrador and Newfoundland, Gulf of St. Lawrence, Gaspé Peninsula, St. Lawrence Bay, and up the St. Lawrence River to Quebec and Montreal**

List the achievement(s) for which he should be remembered

First European to discover the Gulf of St. Lawrence and the St. Lawrence River and to use the name Canada for the region west along the St. Lawrence River

Discoveries used by France as an axis for its North American colonial empire

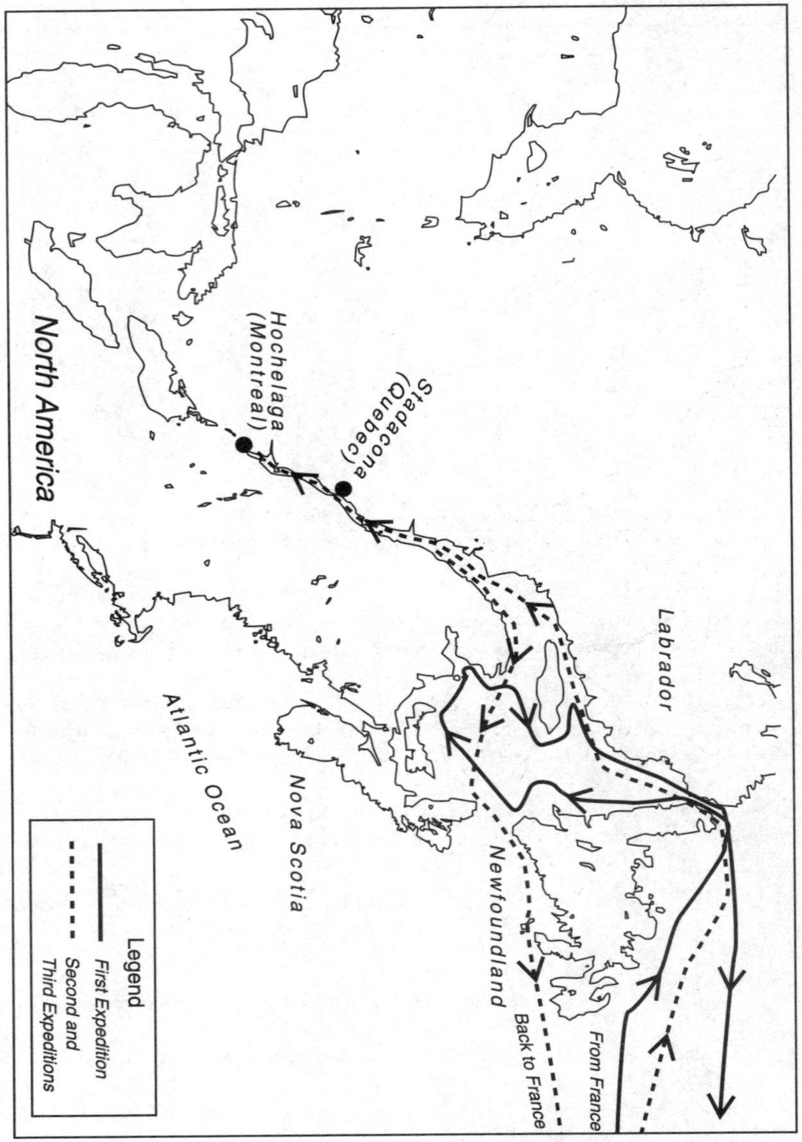

VOYAGES OF JACQUES CARTER

North America
Hochelaga (Montreal)
Stadacona (Quebec)
Labrador
Newfoundland
Nova Scotia
Atlantic Ocean
From France
Back to France
Legend
First Expedition
Second and Third Expeditions

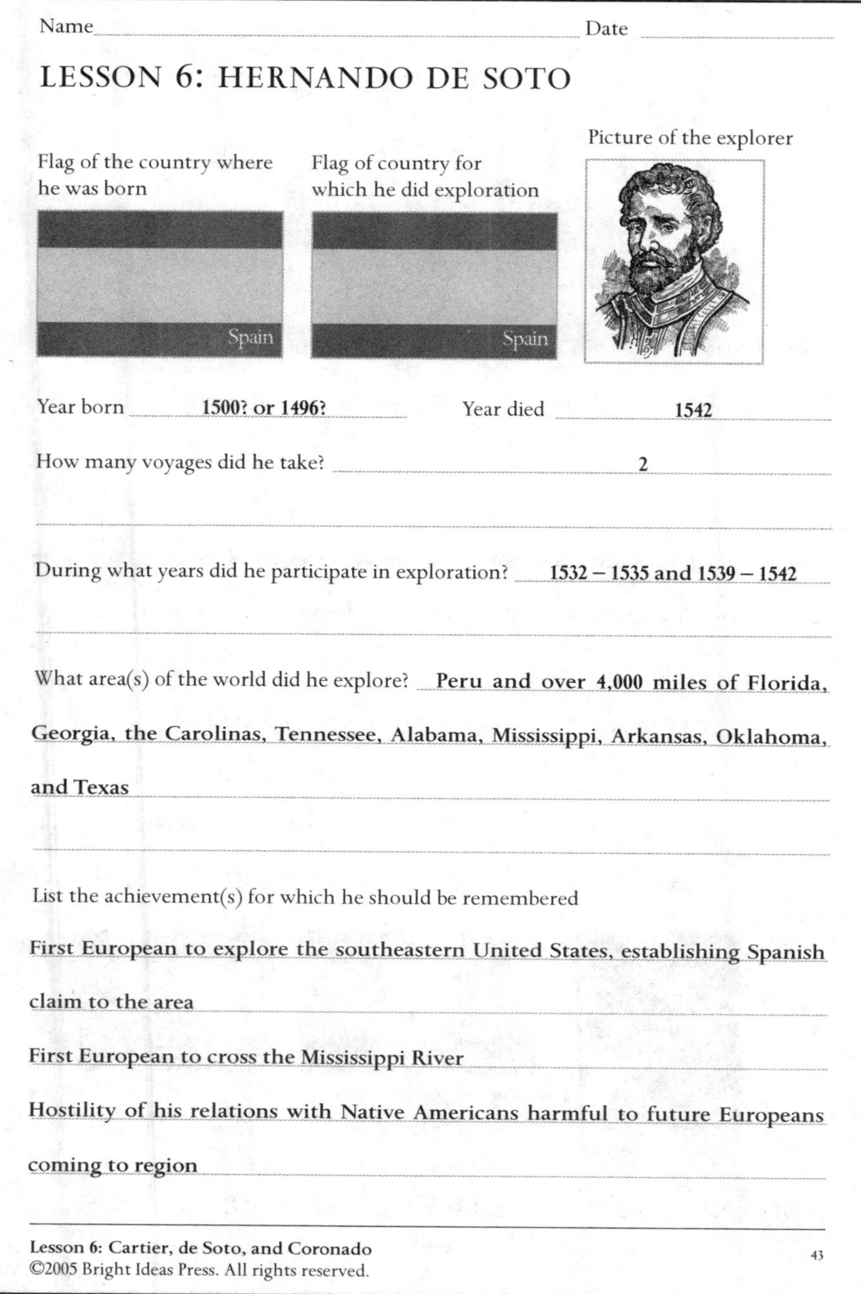

Name ________________ Date ________

LESSON 6: HERNANDO DE SOTO

Flag of the country where he was born — Spain

Flag of country for which he did exploration — Spain

Picture of the explorer

Year born **1500? or 1496?** Year died **1542**

How many voyages did he take? **2**

During what years did he participate in exploration? **1532 – 1535 and 1539 – 1542**

What area(s) of the world did he explore? **Peru and over 4,000 miles of Florida, Georgia, the Carolinas, Tennessee, Alabama, Mississippi, Arkansas, Oklahoma, and Texas**

List the achievement(s) for which he should be remembered

First European to explore the southeastern United States, establishing Spanish claim to the area

First European to cross the Mississippi River

Hostility of his relations with Native Americans harmful to future Europeans coming to region

Mexico
Gulf of Mexico
Natchez
Tallahassee
Havana
Cuba
Atlantic Ocean
North America
Legend
First Expedition

VOYAGES OF HERNANDO DE SOTO

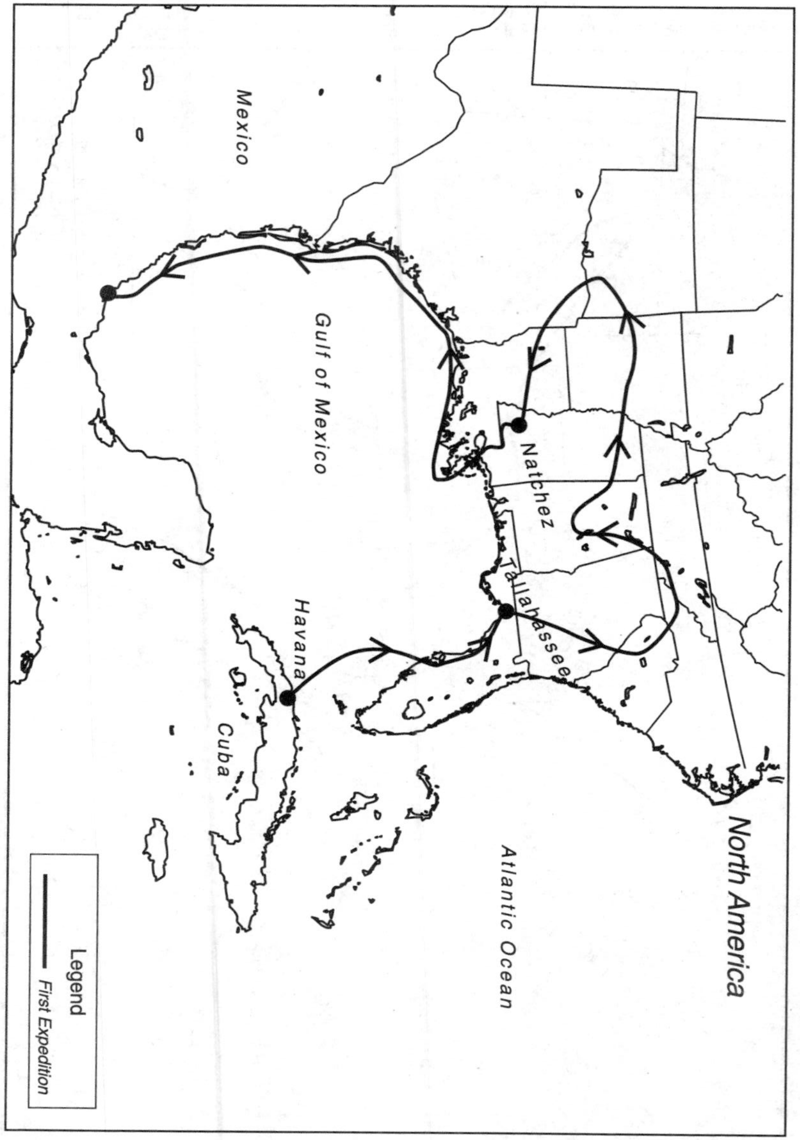

Name ____________ Date ____________

LESSON 6: FRANCISCO VASQUEZ DE CORONADO

Flag of the country where he was born: Spain

Flag of country for which he did exploration: Spain

Picture of the explorer

Year born **1510** Year died **1554**

How many voyages did he take? **1**

During what years did he participate in exploration? **1540 – 1542**

What area(s) of the world did he explore? **Most of the southwestern United States, including Arizona, New Mexico, Texas, Oklahoma, and Kansas**

List the achievement(s) for which he should be remembered

First European to explore the southwestern region of the United States, establishing Spanish claim to this vast territory

Lesson 6: Cartier, de Soto, and Coronado 45

VOYAGES OF FRANCISCO VASQUEZ DE CORONADO

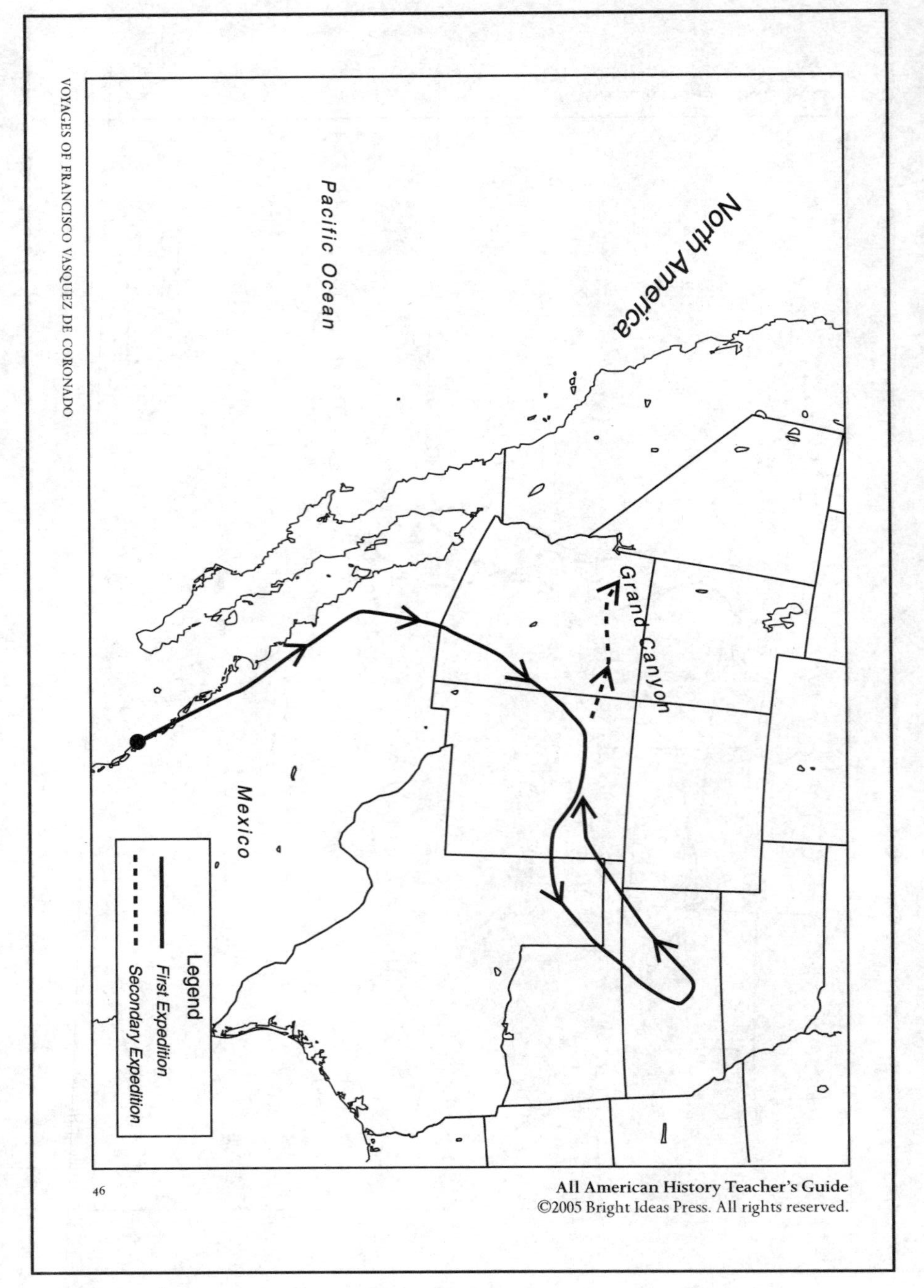

46 All American History Teacher's Guide

LESSON 6: FOR REVIEW

Write the missing word or words in the spaces provided.

1. French navigator Jacques Cartier possibly accompanied **Verrazano** on his expedition to the Atlantic coast of North America.

2. The French king Francis I persuaded the pope in 1533 to amend the **Treaty of Tordesillas** to pertain only to land that had already been discovered.

3. Cartier and his men claimed the Gaspé Peninsula for France and established a friendship there with **the iroquois**.

4. Cartier was the first European known to sail on the **St. Lawrence** River, which he named for a French saint.

5. During his expeditions to eastern Canada, Cartier sailed as far inland as the Indian village of Stadacona, which is present-day **Quebec**.

6. From Stadacona, Cartier and his men used smaller boats to go further up river to the village of Hochelaga, located by a mountain which Cartier named **Mont Real**.

7. A number of Frenchmen who came to the New World with Cartier died from **scurvy**.

8. As a result of Cartier's detailed documentation of his North American expeditions, **maps** were produced that would be quite useful to French explorers, traders, and missionaries.

Write T for True and F for False in the space provided.

T 1. At the age of nineteen, Hernando de Soto traveled to Darien with Pedradrias and there witnessed the execution of Balboa.

T 2. De Soto took part in the Spanish conquest of Nicaragua and Peru.

F 3. When De Soto returned to Spain from America in 1535 – 1536, he was impoverished and disillusioned.

T 4. Emperor Charles V gave Hernando de Soto rights to conquer and settle Florida.

F 5. During his trek through the present-day southeastern United States, de Soto was careful to treat the Native Americans there with respect and dignity.

T 6. Native Americans continually told de Soto and his men that great wealth existed in some faraway location.

T 7. The men on de Soto's expedition were the first Europeans known to see and cross the Mississippi River.

F 8. De Soto eventually returned to Spain a national hero.

T 9. Coronado was commissioned by the viceroy of New Spain to search for the Seven Cities of Cibola.

T 10. Men on Coronado's expedition were the first Europeans known to see the Grand Canyon and Painted Desert.

F 11. Coronado was praised by Mendoza for the success of his expedition.

T 12. De Soto and Coronado established Spanish claims to the southeastern and southwestern regions of North America.

LESSON 6: FOR FURTHER STUDY

1. Research the life of St. Lawrence. Why was he one of the most honored martyrs of the Catholic Church?

2. Read about Alvar Nunez Cabeza de Vaca (1490 – 1560). What happened to his expedition that was sent to explore the Florida coast?

3. The *De Soto Chronicles* were personal journals written by three officers of Hernando de Soto's expedition — Luis Fernandez de Biedma (a factor of the Spanish crown), the Gentleman of Elvas (a Portuguese officer), and Rodrigo Rangel (de Soto's private secretary). Find an excerpt from the chronicles and read it. Look particularly for information concerning the Spaniards' relationship with the Native Americans whom they encountered on their expedition.

4. Coronado and his men saw the Grand Canyon, the Continental Divide, and the Painted Desert. Find out more about these natural phenomena and look for photographs of them.

Name________________ Date ________

LESSON 7: SIR FRANCIS DRAKE

Flag of the country where he was born — England

Flag of country for which he did exploration — England

Picture of the explorer

Year born **1540** Year died **1596**

In how many expeditions did he participate? **led 3; participated in many**

During what years did he participate in exploration? **1577 – 1580, 1585,1587**

What area(s) of the world did he explore? **Circumnavigation of globe – east coast of South American, west coast of South and North America (possibly as far north as Vancouver), Philippines and Spice Islands, Indian Ocean, and both coasts of Africa**

List the achievement(s) for which he should be remembered

First Englishman to visit the west coast of North America and leader of second expedition to sail around the world

English commander in defeat of Spanish Armada, which lead to Spain's decline as a world colonial power

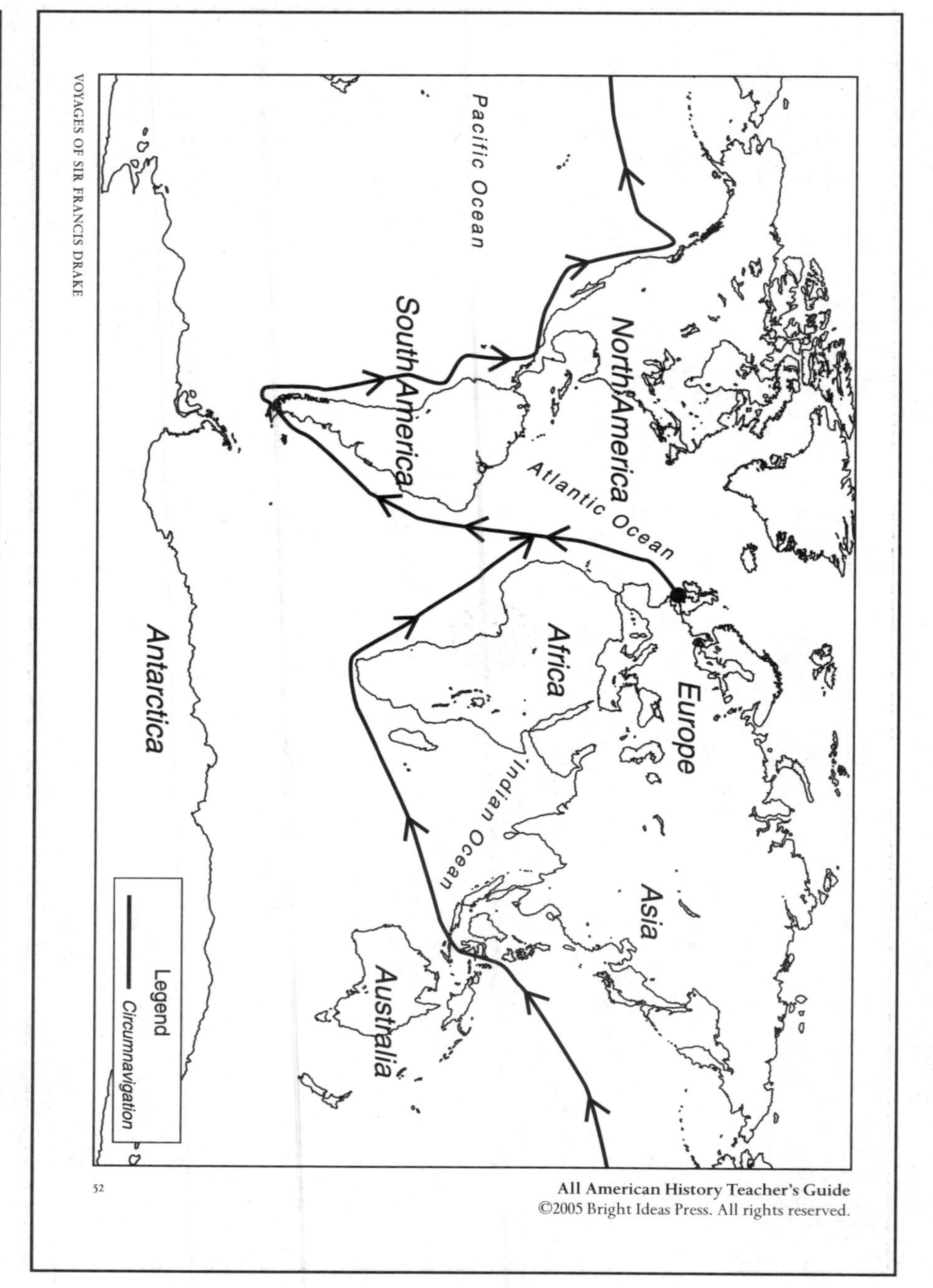

VOYAGES OF SIR FRANCIS DRAKE

Name__________ Date __________

LESSON 7: SIR WALTER RALEIGH (RALEGH)

Flag of the country where he was born: England

Flag of country for which he did exploration: England

Picture of the explorer

Year born **1552? or 1554?** Year died **1618**

In how many expeditions did he participate? **1; sponsored at least 2**

During what years did he participate in exploration? **1583 – 1590**

What area(s) of the world did he explore? **North Carolina coast (attempt to plant the colony on Roanoke Island); Raleigh himself traveled to Lisbon to the Canary Islands, Trinidad, and Venezuela**

List the achievement(s) for which he should be remembered

First individual known to attempt establishment of an English colony in North America

Lesson 7: Sir Francis Drake and Sir Walter (Ralegh) Raleigh 53

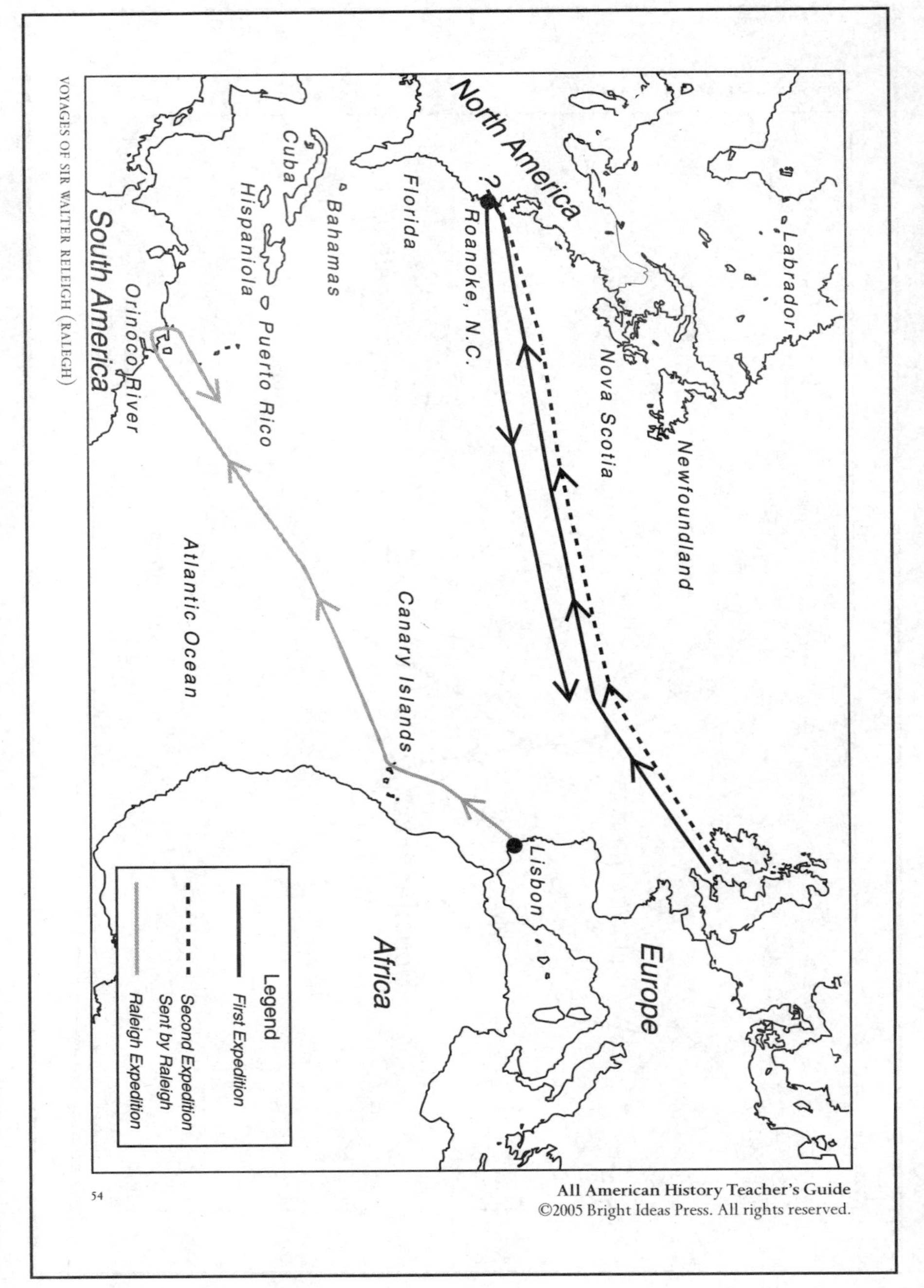

VOYAGES OF SIR WALTER RELEIGH (RALEGH)

54

All American History Teacher's Guide

LESSON 7: FOR REVIEW

Write the missing word or words in the spaces provided.

1. Sir Francis Drake was an English sea captain who was fearless in his raids of Spanish and Portuguese ships. He was known as the **Dragon**, and he and his fellow English sea captains came to be called **sea dogs**.

2. In 1567, Drake participated in an expedition against the Spanish in the West Indies and Central America with his distant relative, the British admiral **Sir John Hawkins**.

3. Sir Walter Raleigh, a favorite of the British monarch **Queen Elizabeth I**, benefited greatly from his royal connection.

4. Drake's only ship that completed the circumnavigation of the globe was named **the** *Golden Hind*.

5. Scholars think Drake stopped to repair his leaking ship near present-day **San Francisco**, which he named Nova Albion.

6. After returning to England, Drake served as mayor of Plymouth and in the House of Commons before resuming his daring raids for the queen. In 1588, Drake played a major role in the defeat of **the Spanish Armada**.

7. Raleigh did not lead his colonizing expedition personally because **the queen insisted that he stay home**.

8. The two sea captains sent out by Raleigh reported finding an island named **Roanoke**, which seemed to be suitable for colonization.

9. In his royal charter, Raleigh was given a region in America named **Virginia**, in honor of Elizabeth I, Virgin Queen of England.

10. The first group of English colonists sent out by Raleigh were led by **Sir Richard Grenville**.

11. A year after going to Roanoke, Raleigh's first group of colonists returned to England with **Sir Francis Drake**, who had stopped by to visit with them.

12. Raleigh's confidante, **Thomas Harriott**, published *A Briefe and True Report of the New Found Land of Virginia* after returning with the first group of colonists.

13. The first English child known to be born in the New World was **Virginia Dare**, granddaughter of the Roanoke colony's governor, John White.

14. Governor White could not return to Roanoke from England with supplies for three years because **all English ships were commissioned to fight the Spanish Armada**.

15. A Roanoke product popularized in England by Raleigh was **tobacco**.

16. After imprisoning Raleigh, Queen Elizabeth finally released him to go on an expedition to search for **the Lost City of Gold (El Dorado)**.

17. King James accused Raleigh of **treason** and sentenced him to die.

18. After spending more than a decade in the Tower of London, Raleigh was released to go on another expedition. In 1618 Raleigh died as a result of **being beheaded**.

LESSON 7: FOR FURTHER STUDY

1. Read about Sir Humphrey Gilbert. Where did he explore? What important paper did he write in 1566?
2. Who was Martin Frobisher? Where did he explore? What did he find?
3. Do further research on the Lost Colony. Do you have a theory about what happened to it?
4. Sir Francis Drake was the best known of the English sea dogs during the Elizabethan era. Find out the names of other sea dogs. How successful were their exploits?

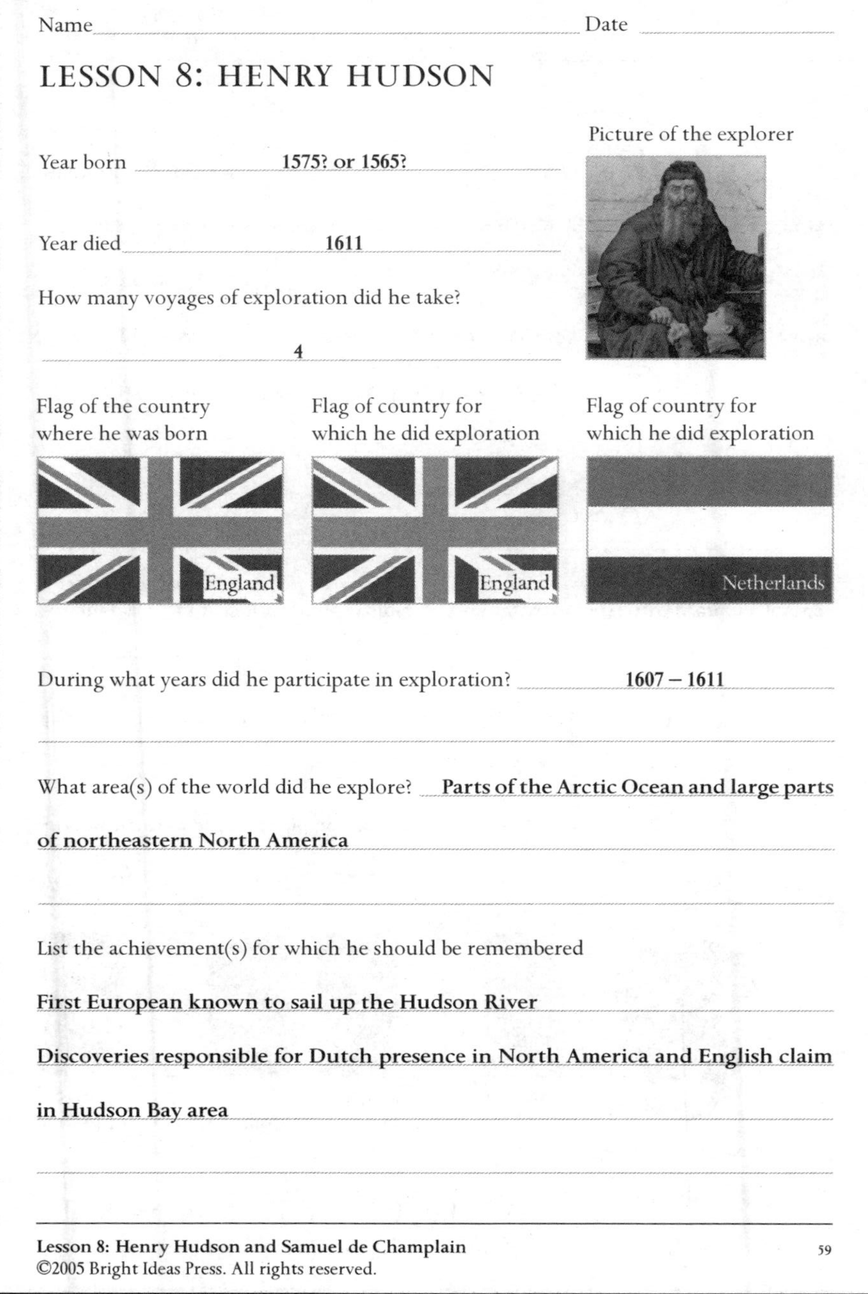

Name ________ Date ________

LESSON 8: HENRY HUDSON

Year born **1575? or 1565?**

Year died **1611**

How many voyages of exploration did he take?

4

Picture of the explorer

Flag of the country where he was born	Flag of country for which he did exploration	Flag of country for which he did exploration
England	England	Netherlands

During what years did he participate in exploration? **1607 – 1611**

What area(s) of the world did he explore? **Parts of the Arctic Ocean and large parts of northeastern North America**

List the achievement(s) for which he should be remembered

First European known to sail up the Hudson River

Discoveries responsible for Dutch presence in North America and English claim in Hudson Bay area

Lesson 8: Henry Hudson and Samuel de Champlain 59

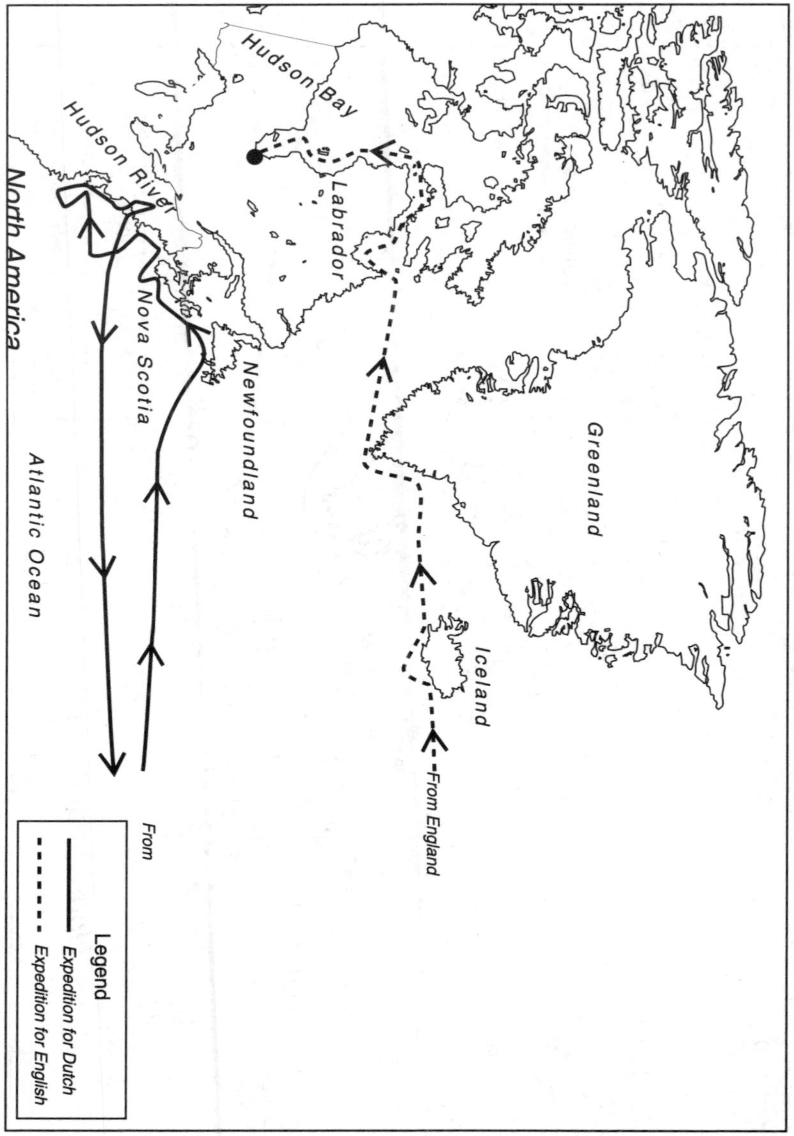

VOYAGES OF HENRY HUDSON

Hudson Bay
Hudson River
North America
Labrador
Nova Scotia
Newfoundland
Atlantic Ocean
Greenland
Iceland
From England
From
Legend
Expedition for Dutch
Expedition for English

60 All American History Teacher's Guide

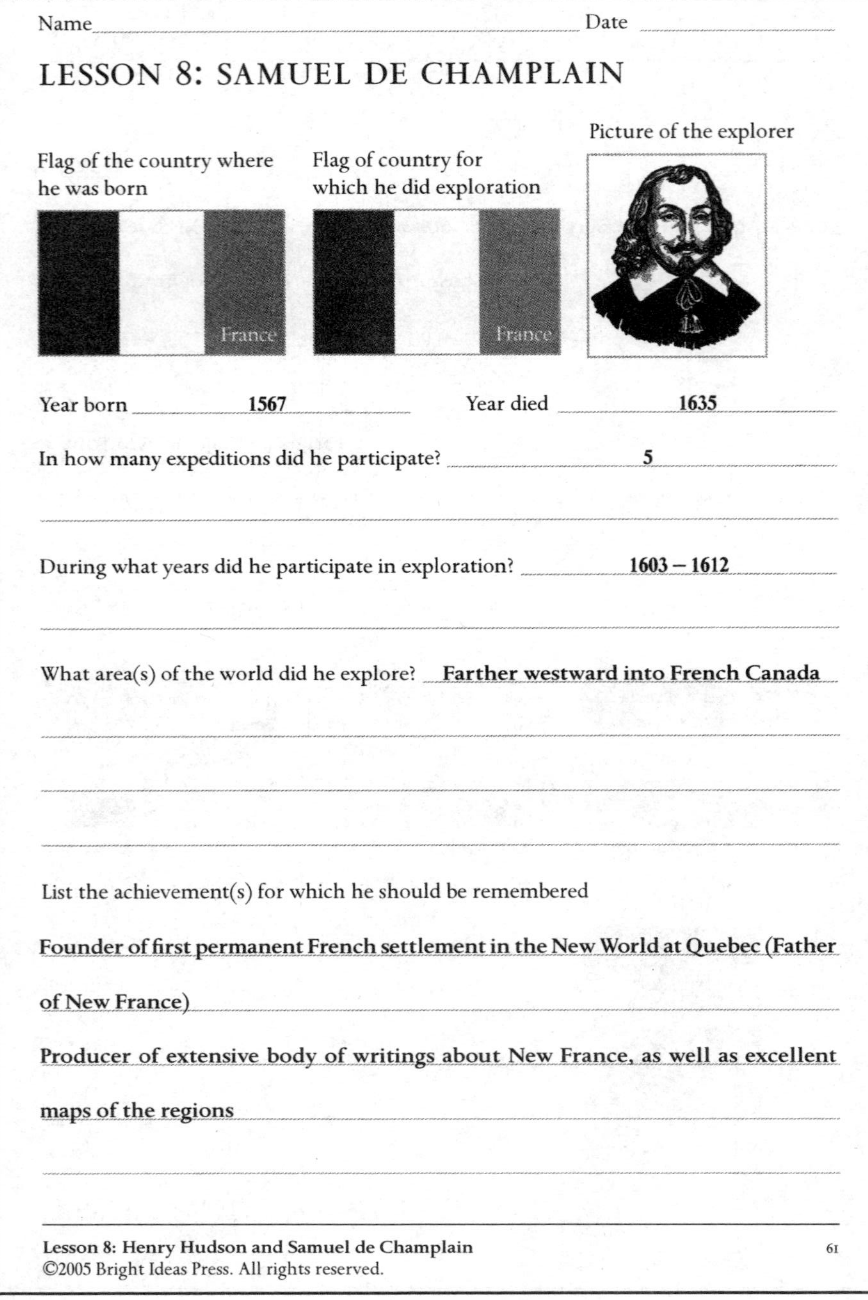

Name__________ Date __________

LESSON 8: SAMUEL DE CHAMPLAIN

Flag of the country where he was born — France

Flag of country for which he did exploration — France

Picture of the explorer

Year born **1567** Year died **1635**

In how many expeditions did he participate? **5**

During what years did he participate in exploration? **1603 – 1612**

What area(s) of the world did he explore? **Farther westward into French Canada**

List the achievement(s) for which he should be remembered

Founder of first permanent French settlement in the New World at Quebec (Father of New France)

Producer of extensive body of writings about New France, as well as excellent maps of the regions

Lesson 8: Henry Hudson and Samuel de Champlain 61

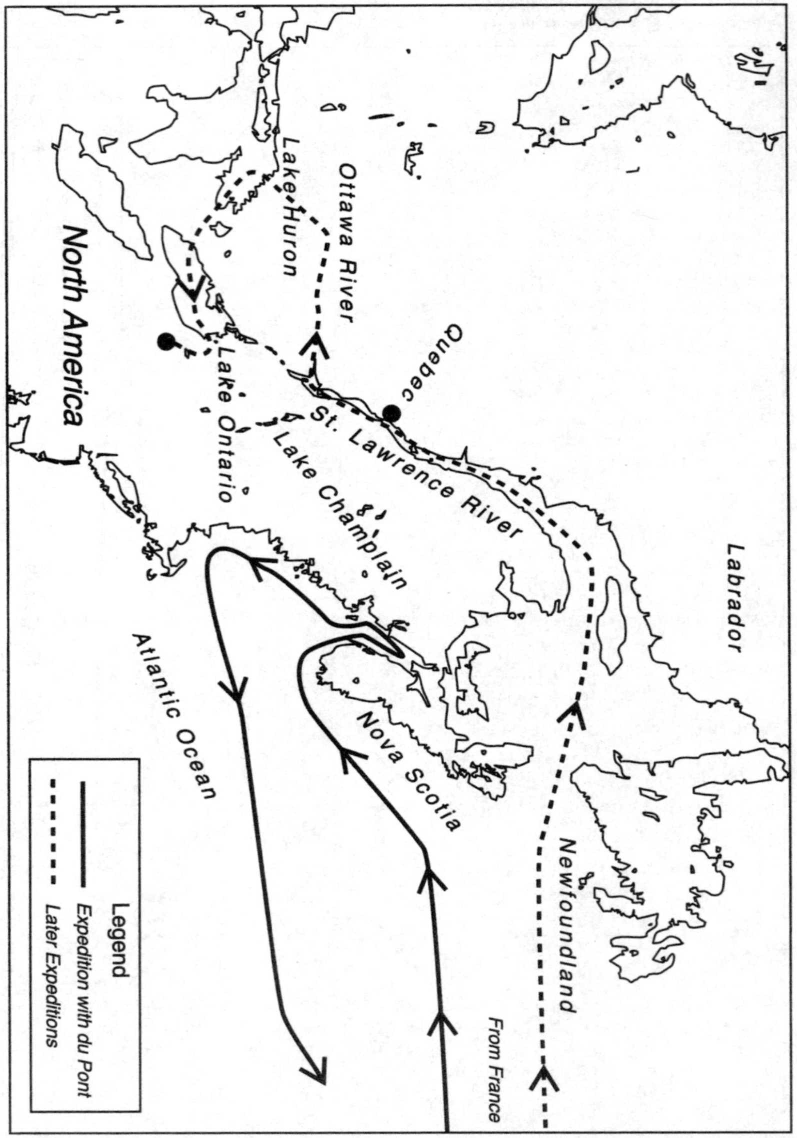

VOYAGES OF SAMUEL DE CHAMPLAIN

All American History Teacher's Guide 62

LESSON 8: FOR REVIEW

Write T for True and F for False in the space provided.

T 1. Little is known about the personal life of Henry Hudson.

F 2. Samuel de Champlain had little navigational experience before sailing to the New World.

T 3. Henry Hudson made four voyages to America.

F 4. Hudson made three voyages for the Dutch and one for the English.

T 5. Although Hudson was a competent and courageous leader, he could be stubborn and often mismanaged his crews.

F 6. Hudson had no connection to the English Muscovy Company before it sponsored two of his expeditions.

T 7. Hudson's son John accompanied him on at least two of his voyages.

T 8. The goal of Hudson's first voyage was to find a passage to the Far East by going across the North Pole.

T 9. Hudson sailed farther north than any known previous European explorer.

F 10. Hudson sailed as far south as Florida.

F 11. There are no geographical features in the United States named for Henry Hudson.

T 12. As a result of Hudson's third voyage, the Dutch laid claim to land in North America.

F 13. Hudson returned to England after his expeditions and died a wealthy man.

T 14. Champlain, known as the Father of New France, visited America on at least five different occasions.

T 15. Champlain founded the first permanent French settlement in the New World at Quebec.

F 16. The maps produced by Champlain of the regions he explored were inaccurate due to his inabilities as a surveyor and cartographer.

T 17. During his excursions, Champlain explored Lake Huron and Lake Champlain and established a fur-trading post at Montreal.

F 18. Champlain's relationships with Native Americans created one hundred fifty years of friendship between the French and the Iroquois.

LESSON 8: FOR FURTHER STUDY

1. Learn more about the Muscovy Company, the first major English joint-stock trading company. What was its other name? Which English explorer was instrumental in its founding? When it was chartered in 1555, what monopoly was it given?

2. A replica of Hudson's Dutch ship, the *Half Moon*, was built in Albany, New York, and launched in 1989 to celebrate the Dutch role in exploring and colonizing America. Find out more about this living history exhibit.

3. Research the Iroquois tribe. Record the information on a Native American tribe form.

4. Was a Northwest Passage to the Far East ever discovered? Explain the reason(s) why or why not.

UNIT I: FINAL REVIEW

Write the corresponding letter of the explorer in the space provided.

A. Balboa	J. Prince Henry
B. Cabot	K. Hudson
C. Cartier	L. Magellan
D. Champlain	M. Marco Polo
E. Columbus	N. Ponce de Leon
F. Coronado	O. Raleigh
G. De Soto	P. Verrazano
H. Drake	Q. Vespucci
I. Leif Eriksson	

__Q__ 1. Origin of the name applied to the new continents discovered during the Age of European Exploration

__C__ 2. First European to discover and explore the St. Lawrence River

__O__ 3. English gentleman who sponsored the expedition that established the Lost Colony

__D__ 4. Father of New France and the first cartographer of New England

__I__ 5. First European known to have discovered and to have sought to colonize in North America (around 1000 A.D.)

__N__ 6. Important colonizer in Puerto Rico and Hispaniola and first European to discover Florida, the Bahama Channel, and the Gulf Stream.

__G__ 7. Explorer of the present-day southeastern United States and first European to cross the Mississippi River

__M__ 8. Author of an influential book that inspired other European explorers to search for another trade route to the Far East

__E__ 9. Discoverer of a trade route across the Atlantic still used by sea captains today and the first European to explore the Bahamas, Cuba, and Hispaniola.

__B__ 10. Explorer who established England's claim to an American empire

__L__ 11. Mariner whose expedition was the first to circumnavigate the globe

A. Balboa	J. Prince Henry
B. Cabot	K. Hudson
C. Cartier	L. Magellan
D. Champlain	M. Marco Polo
E. Columbus	N. Ponce de Leon
F. Coronado	O. Raleigh
G. De Soto	P. Verrazano
H. Drake	Q. Vespucci
I. Leif Eriksson	

__P__ 12. First European to discover New York Bay and Narragansett Bay and the establisher of the French claim to American territory

__J__ 13. Founder of a groundbreaking school of navigation and shipbuilding

__F__ 14. Explorer of the present-day southwestern United States in search of the Seven Cities of Cibola

__H__ 15. Leader of the second expedition to sail around the world

__K__ 16. Reason for the establishment of a Dutch presence in North America

__A__ 17. First European to sight the Pacific Ocean from an American shore

Name ______________________ Date ______________

LESSON 9: THE VIRGINIA COLONY

Picture of key figure

Flag of country that played a role in its founding

England

Motivation for founding

$

Year of the first permanent colony settlement **1607**

Founded by a company or proprietor(s); if a company, write its name

London Company

Name of this colony's key figure **John Smith**

List some other individuals who were instrumental in the early years of this colony

Powhatan, Pochahontas, John Rolfe, Lora De La Warr

Key settlements **Jamestown**

List any other important facts about this colony or significant events in its development

First permanent English settlement in North America

Cash crop – tobacco – instrumental to its survival

1619: "tobacco brides," African slaves, and House of Burgesses

Bacon's Rebellion

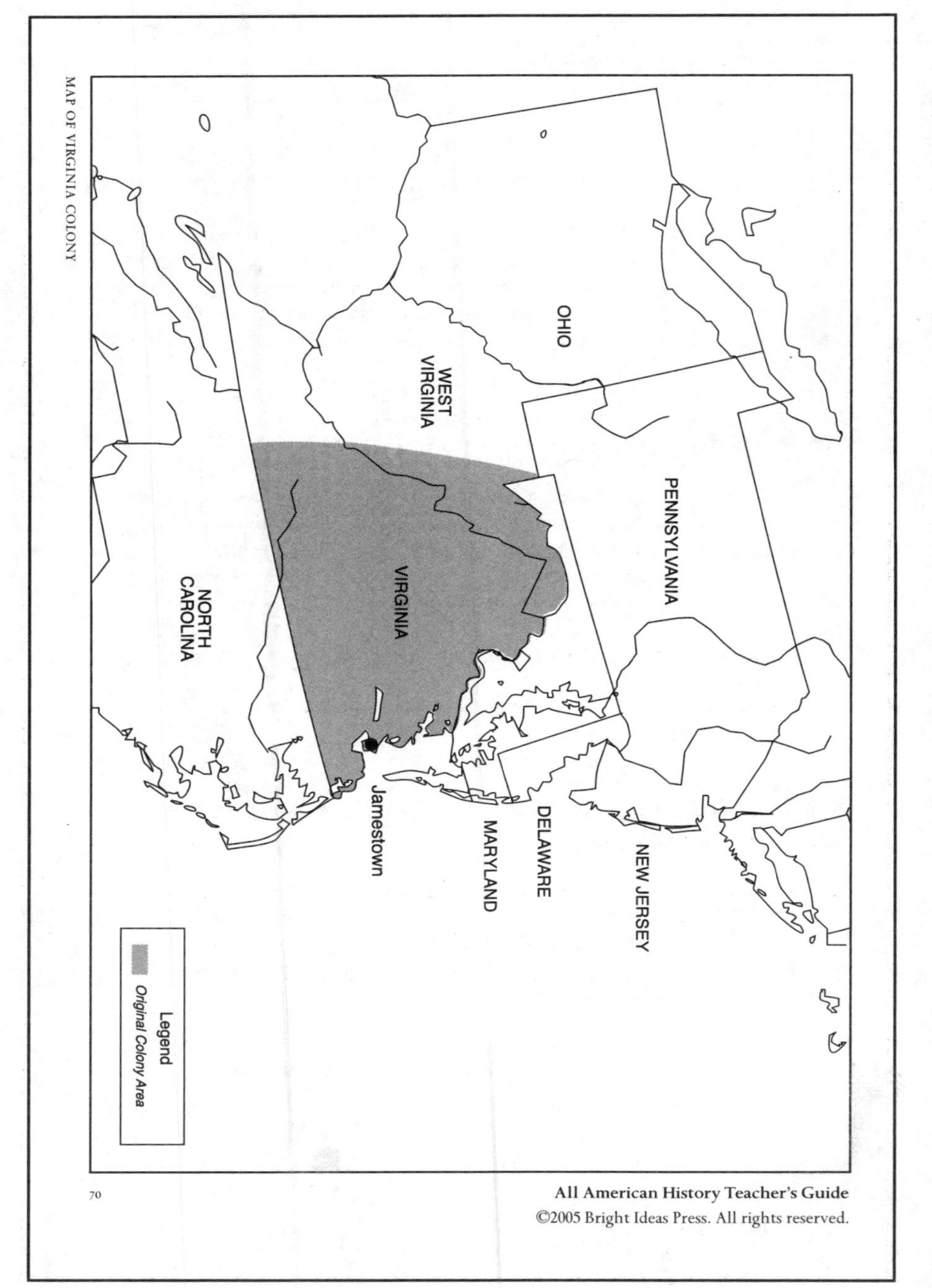

MAP OF VIRGINIA COLONY

LESSON 9: FOR REVIEW

Write T for True and F for False in the space provided.

F 1. At the beginning of the seventeenth century only the countries of Spain and England claimed land in North America.

T 2. English colonies in North America developed along the Atlantic coast from present-day Georgia to Maine.

T 3. By 1750, the English had established thirteen colonies divided into three distinct regions: New England, Middle, and Southern.

F 4. There was one primary motive behind the establishment of English colonies in America—economic gain.

T 5. Until the early seventeenth century, England was not in a strong position to establish colonies in America.

F 6. In December 1606, the London Company sent three ships to Virginia under the command of Captain John Smith.

F 7. The English decided to plant their new colony at Cape Henry, an elbow of beach in the Chesapeake Bay.

F 8. The settlers named their colony James Towne after their governor.

F 9. Native Americans in Virginia were quite friendly to the English colonists, welcoming them with gifts.

T 10. Many of the first colonists at Jamestown were not well equipped to survive in the wilderness and were preoccupied with looking for gold.

T 11. The location chosen for Jamestown was not a favorable one for colonization.

T 12. Captain John Smith was elected president of the Jamestown council in the fall of 1608 and worked hard to motivate and organize the colonists.

F 13. After Smith left Virginia to return to England, the Native Americans in the area continued to cooperate and work well with the colonists.

T 14. Indentured servants were given free passage to America in exchange for seven years of unpaid labor.

T 15. The winter of 1609 – 1610 was known as the "starving time" in Jamestown history; only 10 percent of the colonists survived.

F 16. Under the easygoing leadership of Lord De La Warr, the colonists at Jamestown failed to do what needed to be done to rebuild their community.

F 17. The marriage of Pocahontas and John Smith resulted in a spirit of peace and goodwill between the colonists and the Native Americans for a time.

T 18. John Rolfe's discovery of a way to grow a mild, high-quality tobacco ensured the economic survival of Jamestown.

T 19. In 1619, ninety tobacco brides arrived in Jamestown, the London Company traded for their first African slaves, and the Virginia governor established the House of Burgesses.

T 20. Nathaniel Bacon led a rebellion against Governor Berkeley because the governor refused to support Virginia frontiersmen against the attacks of Native Americans.

LESSON 9: FOR FURTHER STUDY

1. The London Company, a joint-stock company, was used to establish Jamestown. Define *joint-stock company* and learn about how such a company works. How did the London Company seek to deal with the financial hardships it faced during the early years of the Virginia Colony? When and why was the company's charter revoked and what happened to the Virginia Colony afterwards?

2. Research the life of Chief Powhatan (1547 – 1618), head of the Algonquian confederacy. Learn about the Algonquian tribe. Record the information on a Native American tribe form.

3. Read more about Captain John Smith, especially his early life. At what age did he begin his adventures? Look for a painting of John Smith. What did he look like? Why do you think some people considered him to be arrogant? What areas of North America did John Smith explore and map after leaving Jamestown? What writings did Smith leave behind?

4. Find out more about Lord De La Warr (Sir Thomas West). To what do most scholars believe that his name was given?

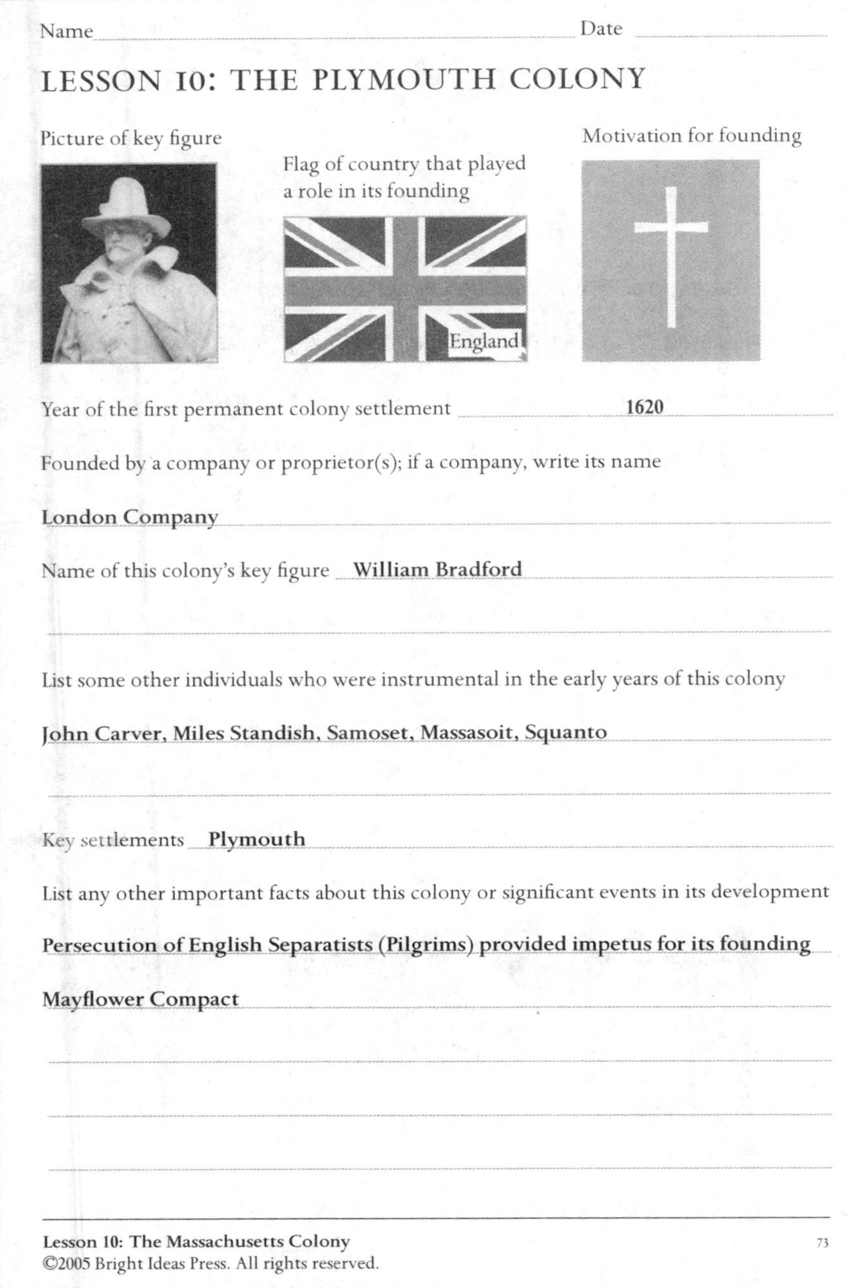

Name ______ Date ______

LESSON 10: THE PLYMOUTH COLONY

Picture of key figure

Flag of country that played a role in its founding

England

Motivation for founding

Year of the first permanent colony settlement **1620**

Founded by a company or proprietor(s); if a company, write its name

London Company

Name of this colony's key figure **William Bradford**

List some other individuals who were instrumental in the early years of this colony

John Carver, Miles Standish, Samoset, Massasoit, Squanto

Key settlements **Plymouth**

List any other important facts about this colony or significant events in its development

Persecution of English Separatists (Pilgrims) provided impetus for its founding

Mayflower Compact

Lesson 10: The Massachusetts Colony 73

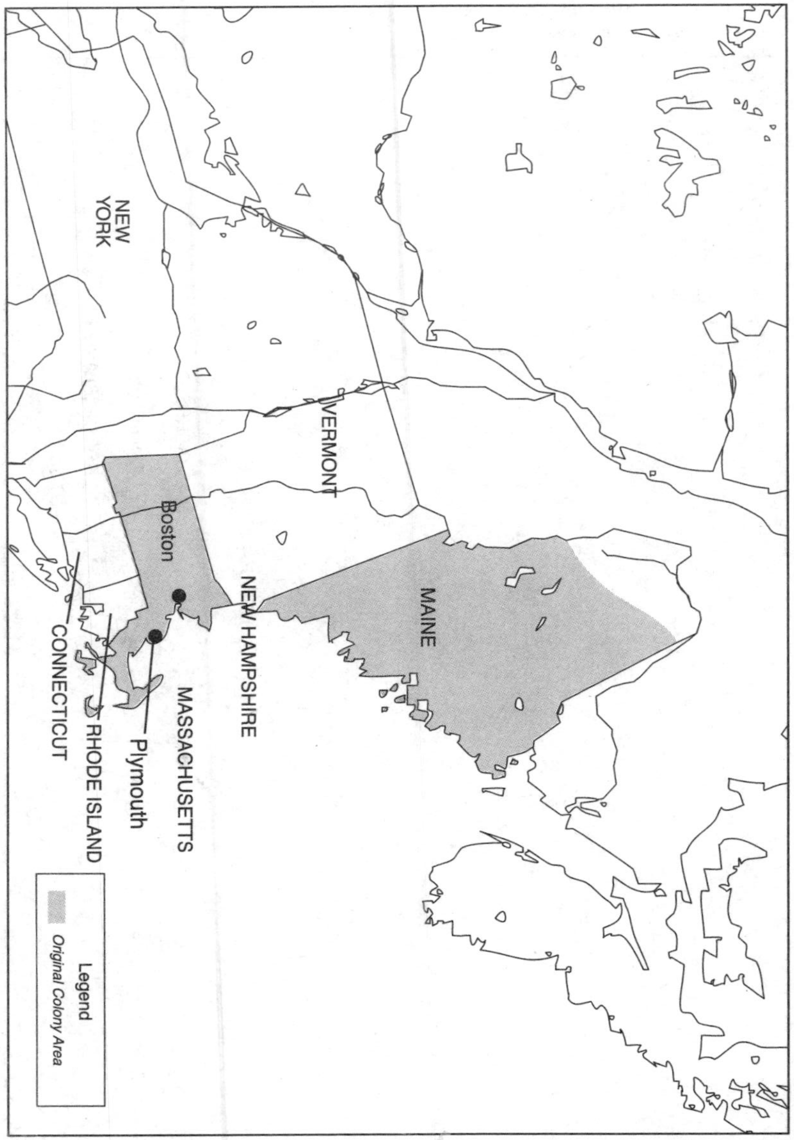

MAP OF PLYMOUTH COLONY

NEW YORK

VERMONT

Boston

NEW HAMPSHIRE

MAINE

MASSACHUSETTS

Plymouth

RHODE ISLAND

CONNECTICUT

Legend

Original Colony Area

74

All American History Teacher's Guide

Name__________ Date __________

LESSON 10: THE MASSACHUSETTS BAY COLONY

Picture of key figure

Flag of country that played a role in its founding

England

Motivation for founding

Year of the first permanent colony settlement **1630**

Founded by a company or proprietor(s); if a company, write its name

Massachusetts Bay Company

Name of this colony's key figure **John Winthrop**

List some other individuals who were instrumental in the early years of this colony

Puritans

Key settlements **Boston, Watertown, Charlestown, Dorchester, Salem**

List any other important facts about this colony or significant events in its development

Religious persecution of English Puritans provided impetus for its founding

Ongoing influence/importance of Puritan church in early years (known as "city upon a hill")

Lesson 10: The Massachusetts Colony 75

MAP OF MASSACHUSETTS BAY COLONY

NEW YORK
VERMONT
NEW HAMPSHIRE
MAINE
MASSACHUSETTS
Boston
Plymouth
RHODE ISLAND
CONNECTICUT
Legend
Original Colony Area

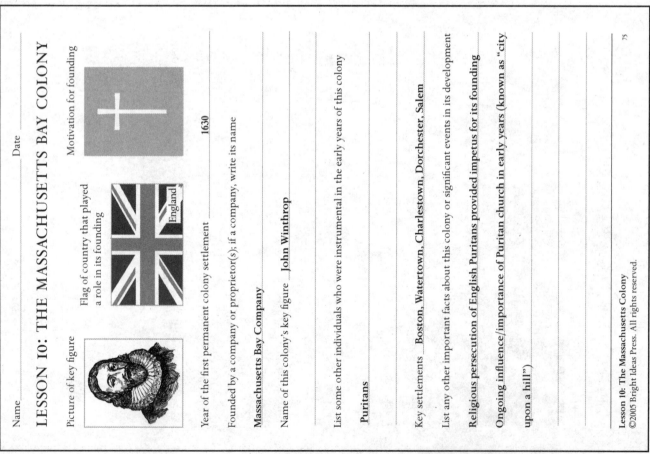

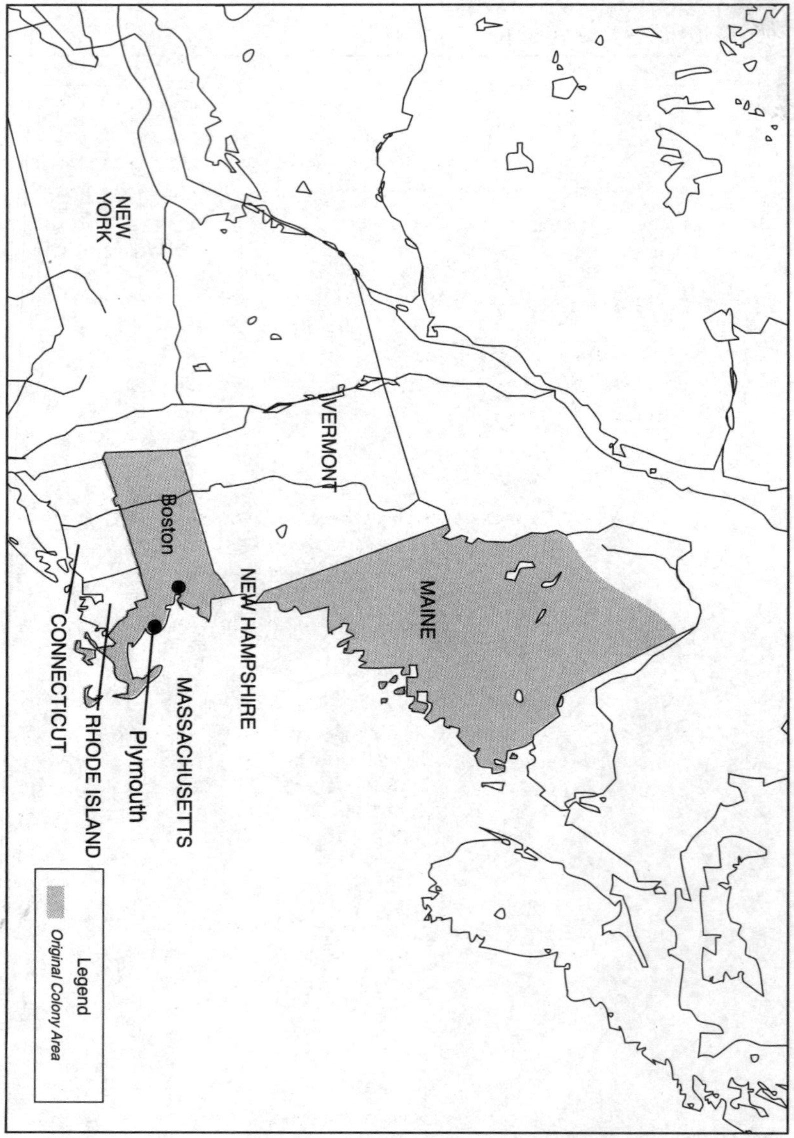

76 All American History Teacher's Guide

LESSON 10: FOR REVIEW

Write the letter of the correct answer in the space provided.

__A__ 1. The English Puritans who called themselves Saints wanted to
- A. separate from the Church of England and form a completely new church
- B. establish the Catholic church as the state church
- C. add new rituals to the established church
- D. make the king head of their church

__C__ 2. Which of the following is NOT true about the Separatists who moved from Scrooby to Leiden?
- A. they fled Scrooby because King James I was persecuting them
- B. they were allowed to worship as they pleased in Leiden
- C. they enjoyed city life
- D. they were concerned that their children were forgetting their English language and heritage

__B__ 3. During the 1620s a group of Puritans remaining in England
- A. rebelled against King Charles and deposed him
- B. began planning to sail to America to establish a holy community
- C. were unable to persuade King Charles to grant them a royal charter for a colony
- D. decided that they no longer cared if they had religious freedom

__B__ 4. The Puritan lawyer elected to serve as the first governor of the Massachusetts Bay Colony was
- A. John Alden
- B. John Winthrop
- C. William Bradford
- D. John Wesley

__D__ 5. The group sailing on the *Mayflower* in 1620
- A. were all Separatists
- B. were all gentleman unaccustomed to hard work
- C. were motivated by the expectation of finding gold
- D. included Separatists and Strangers

__B__ 6. On the *Mayflower*, the Pilgrims
- A. developed many cases of scurvy and suffered a large number of deaths
- B. included a baby named Oceanus, who was born at sea
- C. had quarters that were spacious and full of sunlight
- D. sighted land at Jamestown

__B__ 7. Before disembarking from the *Mayflower*, the Pilgrims
- A. decided to sail further south down the coast toward Virginia
- B. drew up and signed an agreement known as the Mayflower Compact
- C. voted to sever their ties with England and King James I
- D. elected Miles Standish to be their governor

__C__ 8. During their first months at Plymouth, the Pilgrims
- A. planted crops
- B. enjoyed the balmy weather
- C. worked in the cold to build houses and a church
- D. decided to give up and go back to England

__A__ 9. By spring of 1621,
- A. only half of the original Plymouth colonists were still alive
- B. the Plymouth colonists had decided not to plant any crops
- C. most of the Plymouth colonists had decided to return to the homeland on the *Mayflower*
- D. a majority of the Plymouth colonists had been killed by members of the Wampanoag tribe

__D__ 10. The chief of the Wampanoag tribe, with whom Governor Carver signed a treaty of peace that lasted 50 years, was
- A. Samoset
- B. Squanto
- C. Patuxet
- D. Massasoit

C 11. Which of the following was NOT true of Squanto, a Native American known by the Pilgrims?
- A. he had been kidnapped by sailors from an English ship and taken to Europe as a slave
- B. he taught the Pilgrims to plant corn, catch fish, trap beavers, and tap maple trees
- C. his people, the Patuxet, resented his kindnesses to the Pilgrims
- D. the Pilgrims believed that he was sent by God to help them

D 12. By the end of the first year of the Plymouth colony, the Pilgrims
- A. had seen their first crops ruined by drought
- B. had engaged in warfare with the Wampanoag tribe
- C. had received adequate food and other supplies from England
- D. had shared a three-day feast of thanksgiving with the Wampanoag

D 13. The man who served as Plymouth's governor for more than thirty years and wrote *Of Plimoth Plantation* was
- A. John Carver
- B. Miles Standish
- C. William Brewster
- D. William Bradford

D 14. The colony at Plymouth
- A. was unable to buy out the London merchants of the Virginia Company
- B. obtained its own charter
- C. grew into a large, enonomically diverse settlement
- D. was eventually taken over by the Massachusetts Bay Colony and ceased being a separate colony

D 15. The Puritans selected which site for their colony in New England?
- A. Salem
- B. Charlestown
- C. Providence
- D. Boston

A 16. The colonists at Massachusetts Bay
- A. represented all levels of English society
- B. suffered very few deaths in their first winter
- C. were lazy and unwilling to do what needed to be done to make their settlement a success
- D. grew very slowly in number

C 17. During the early development of Massachusetts Bay,
- A. the colony had no governor
- B. the colony had no representative body
- C. only members of the Puritan Church could vote
- D. there was complete religious freedom for everyone

C 18. King Philip was
- A. the father of Massasoit
- B. a courageous leader who encouraged his tribe and others to cooperate with the English
- C. the leader of an Indian coalition that attacked more than fifty English colonial villages
- D. captured and sold into slavery

B 19. In establishing the Dominion of New England, James II
- A. made provision for a representative assembly
- B. appointed Sir Edmund Andros royal governor with dictatorial powers
- C. eliminated the Navigation Acts
- D. divided New England into separate regions

B 20. After the overthrow of James II,
- A. Governor Andros was re-elected governor of the Dominion of New England
- B. Massachusetts was made a royal colony
- C. Massachusetts was not allowed to keep the lower house of the General Court
- D. voting rights were extended to all men and women in the colony

LESSON 10: FOR FURTHER STUDY

1. Research the role that the ship the *Speedwell* played in the history of Plymouth Colony. Discover the significance of Plymouth Rock.

2. Look for copies of original source documents, such as the Mayflower Compact and William Bradford's *Of Plimoth Plantation*. Try reading them. Look up words that you don't understand. Read *The Courtship of Miles Standish* by Henry Wadsworth Longfellow.

3. Discover what happened to a pastor's wife named Mary Rowlandson during King Philip's War. Look for excerpts from her *Narrative* and read about her experiences with the Nipmuc tribe. Find out about John Eliot, the Puritan missionary who was known as the Apostle to the Indians.

4. Perhaps one of the most infamous events in the history of Massachusetts Bay was the 1692 – 1693 Salem witch trials. Determine what caused the outbreak of this witch hunt in Salem and the role that the Reverend Cotton Mather and other ministers played in it. Read about the results of the court trials and the ways in which this incident impacted life in the Massachusetts colony.

Name __________ Date __________

LESSON II: THE NEW HAMPSHIRE COLONY

Picture of key figure

Flag of country that played a role in its founding

England

Motivation for founding

Year of the first permanent colony settlement **1622**

Founded by a company or proprietor(s); if a company, write its name

Laconia Company

Name of this colony's key figure **John Wheelwright**

List some other individuals who were instrumental in the early years of this colony

David Thomson, Sir Fernando Gorges and John Mason

Key settlements **Exeter, Hampton**

List any other important facts about this colony or significant events in its development

Originally known as the "main;" eventually divided into two parts

Many problems – religious conflicts, economic troubles, boundary disputes with

Massachusetts, and frontier wars with Native Americans

Lesson 11: The New Hampshire, Rhode Island, and Connecticut Colonies 83

MAP OF NEW HAMPSHIRE COLONY

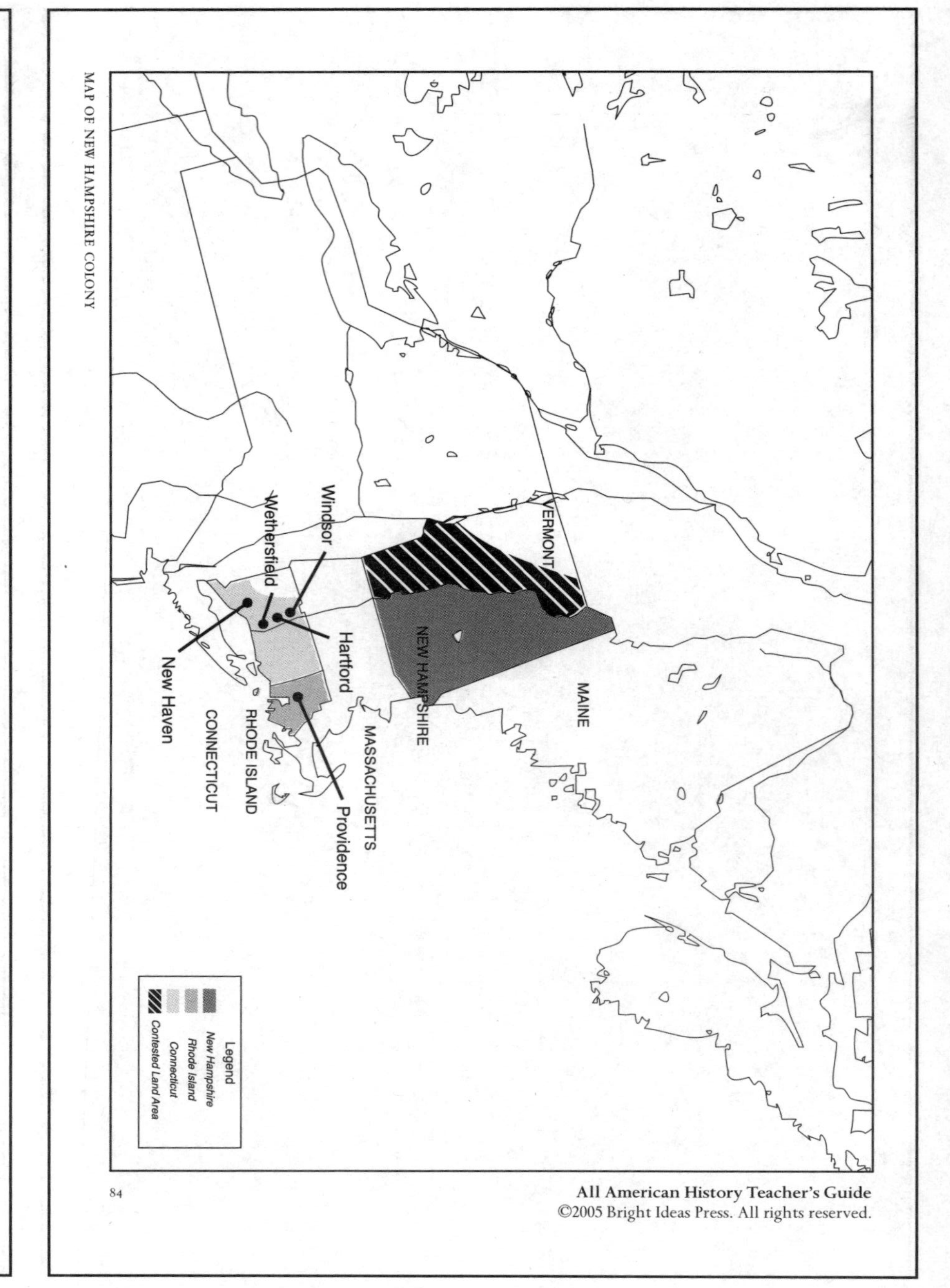

84

All American History Teacher's Guide

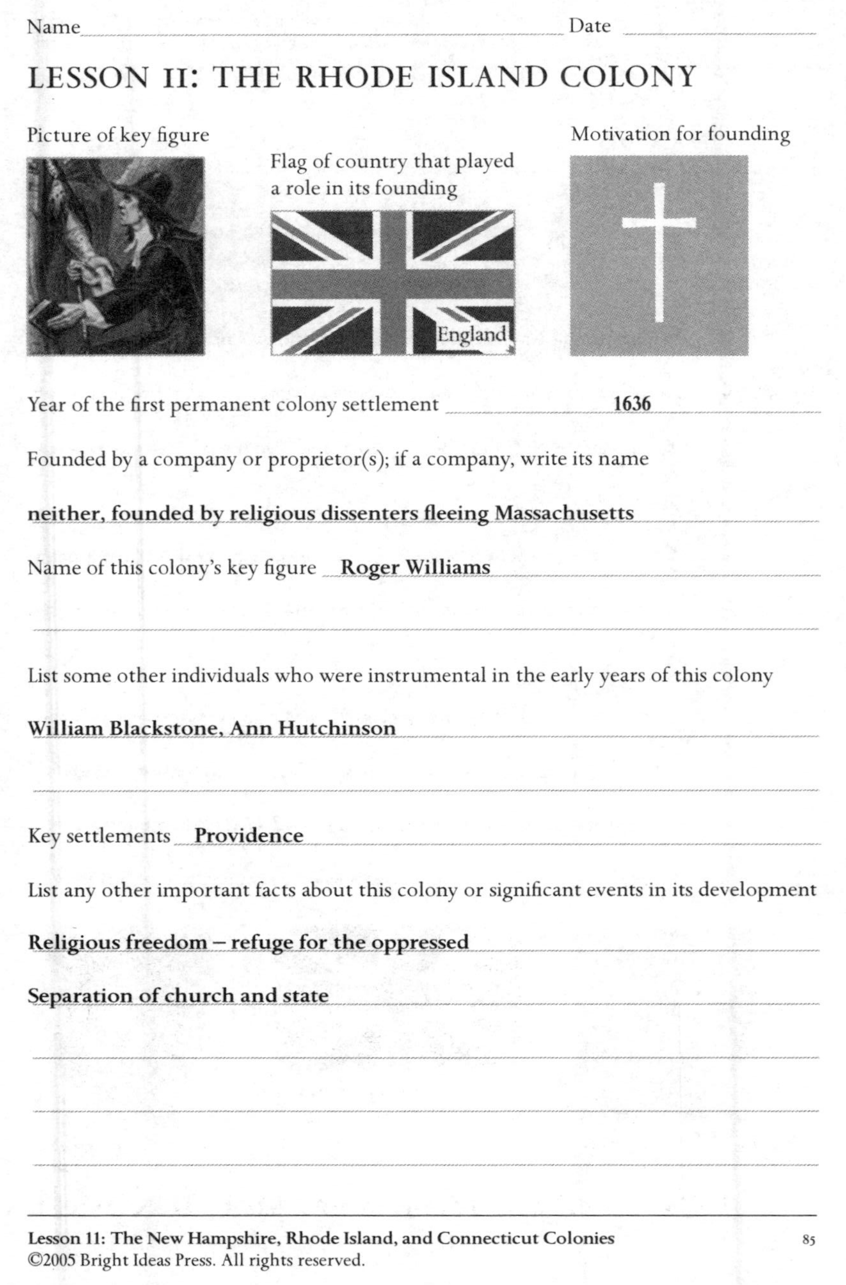

Name ____________ Date ____________

LESSON 11: THE RHODE ISLAND COLONY

Picture of key figure

Flag of country that played a role in its founding

Motivation for founding

Year of the first permanent colony settlement **1636**

Founded by a company or proprietor(s); if a company, write its name

neither, founded by religious dissenters fleeing Massachusetts

Name of this colony's key figure **Roger Williams**

List some other individuals who were instrumental in the early years of this colony

William Blackstone, Ann Hutchinson

Key settlements **Providence**

List any other important facts about this colony or significant events in its development

Religious freedom – refuge for the oppressed

Separation of church and state

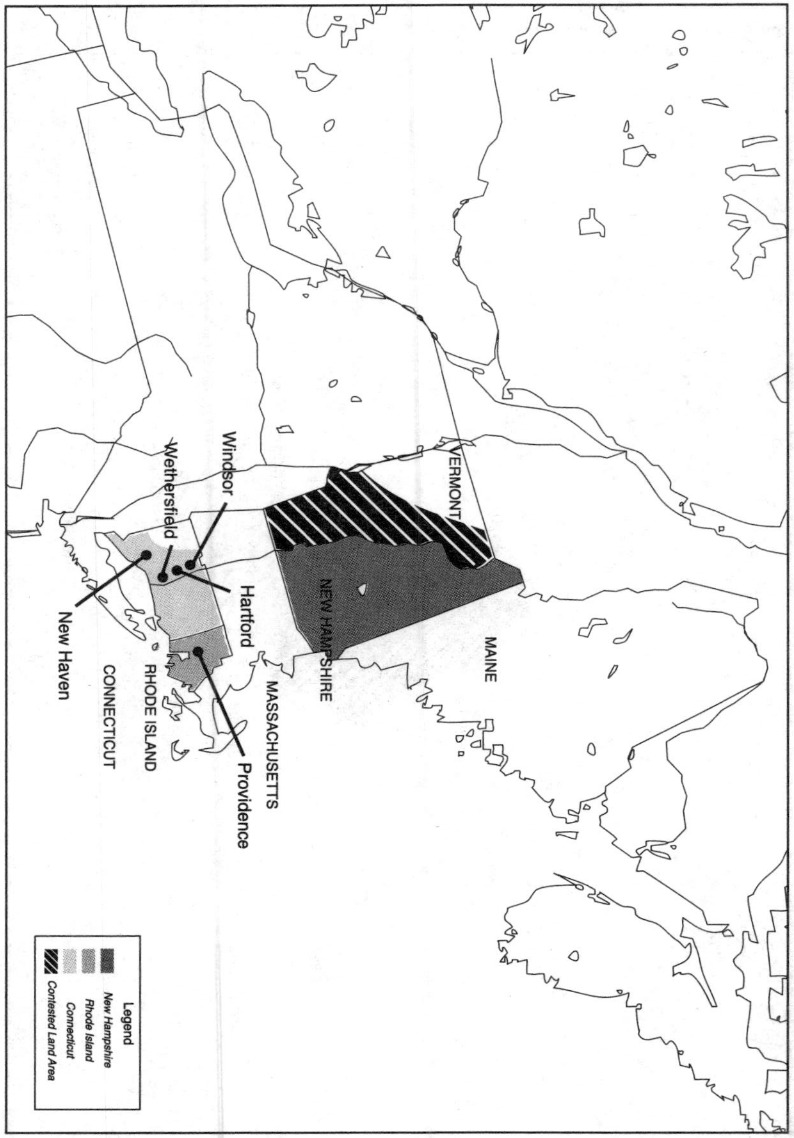

MAP OF RHODE ISLAND COLONY

Name ______________________ Date ______________

LESSON II: THE CONNECTICUT COLONY

Picture of key figure

Flag of country that played a role in its founding

England

Motivation for founding

Year of the first permanent colony settlement **1636**

Founded by a company or proprietor(s); if a company, write its name

neither, founded by fur trappers and religious dissenters

Name of this colony's key figure **Thomas Hooker**

List some other individuals who were instrumental in the early years of this colony

John Oldham, John Davenport

Key settlements **Hartford, Windsor, Wethersfield, New Haven**

List any other important facts about this colony or significant events in its development

New Haven theocracy (unsuccessful in remaining independent)

Pequot Massacre; New England Confederation

Fundamental Orders of Connecticut

Lesson 11: The New Hampshire, Rhode Island, and Connecticut Colonies 87

MAP OF CONNECTICUT COLONY

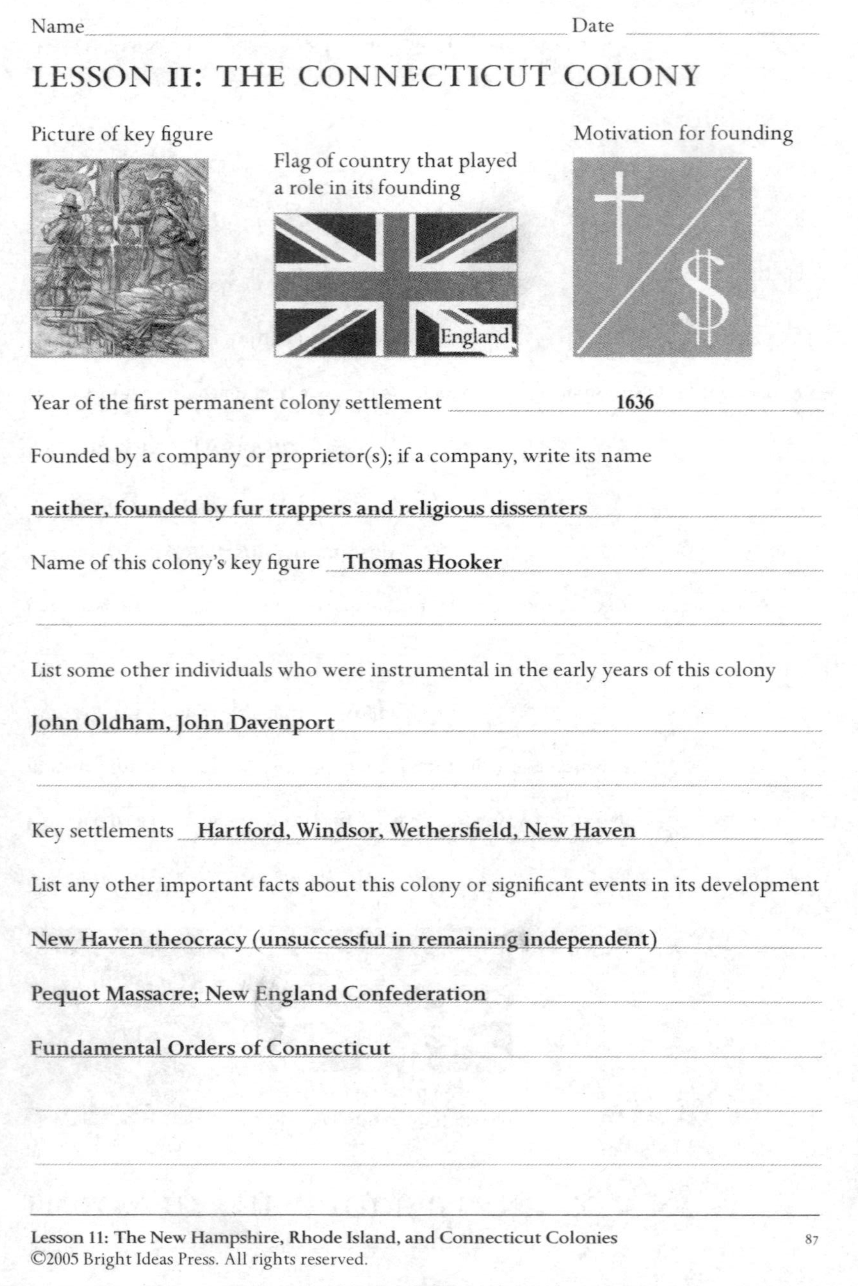

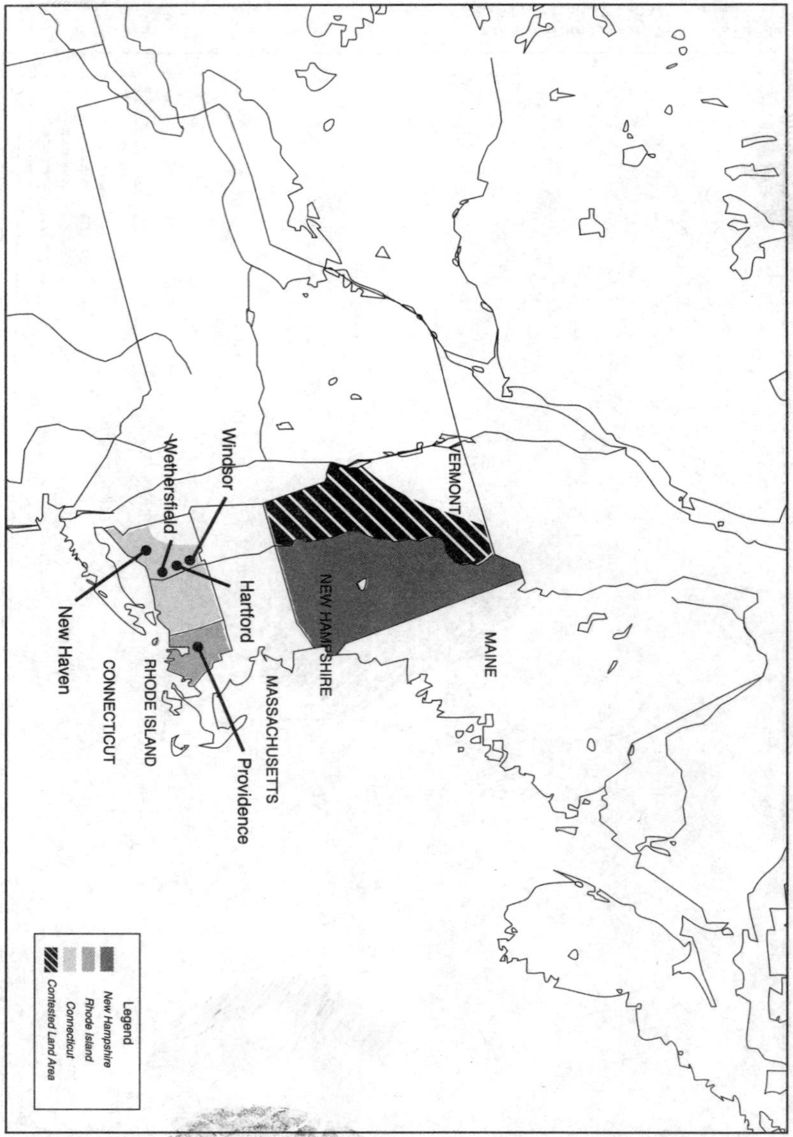

88 All American History Teacher's Guide

LESSON 11: FOR REVIEW

Write the corresponding letter of the correct answer in the space provided.

A. Adriaen Block
B. William Blackstone
C. Fernando Gorges
D. Thomas Hooker
E. Anne Hutchinson
F. John Oldham
G. David Thomson
H. John Wheelwright
I. Roger Williams

H 1. Puritan minister who was banished from Massachusetts Bay due to his religious beliefs and moved on to Exeter, New Hampshire

A 2. Dutch explorer who may have named Rhode Island

E 3. Massachusetts outcast who came to Rhode Island and received Roger Williams's help in forming a settlement at Portsmouth

D 4. Puritan minister who sought authorization from the Massachusetts General Court to settle in Connecticut and established a settlement eventually known as Hartford

F 5. Massachusetts fur trader who came to Connecticut in 1633 and established a small outpost at Wethersfield

B 6. Hermit minister from the Church of England who was the first settler of what became Boston and the first settler of Rhode Island

I 7. Puritan minister who was exiled from Massachusetts Bay and received help from the Wampanoag tribe to survive and then establish Providence Plantations

C 8. English merchant who founded the Laconia Company with John Mason and received a land grant that included New Hampshire and part of Maine

G 9. Leader of the first group of English settlers to arrive in New Hampshire on the *Jonathan* in 1623

Write the missing word or words in the spaces provided.

1. The land grant that King James I gave to John Mason and Ferdinand Gorges was called the **main** because it was located on the mainland of a coast that was dotted by islands.

2. There are **two** theories regarding the origin of the name Rhode Island.

3. **Three** different groups arrived in Connecticut in 1633.

4. New Hampshire settlers, realizing that they were not strong enough to stand alone against outside attacks, appealed to **Massachusetts** for help and remained under its authority for almost fifty years.

5. Roger Williams preached that there should be separation of **church and state** and believed that the Puritans had no legal title to their land because they had not paid the natives for it.

6. Plymouth, Massachusetts Bay, Connecticut, and New Haven united to form the **New England Confederation** in 1638 as a means of common protection against Native American attacks. They excluded Rhode Island from this group.

7. The colony formed by John Davenport at the mouth of the Quinnipiac River, which was stricter than the other Puritan colonies, was **New Haven**. It was eventually ordered to unite with the colony of Connecticut.

8. The **Pequot** tribe in the Mystic River valley, resentful of the movement of English settlers into the New England region, was eventually massacred.

9. With the creation of the **Fundamental Orders** in 1639, Connecticut became the first English colony in America with a written plan of government, a constitution with ideas that foreshadowed those in the U.S. Constitution.

10. When the Dominion of New England was formed in 1686, Connecticut refused to surrender its charter to Governor Andros and supposedly hid it **in the Charter Oak**.

LESSON II: FOR FURTHER STUDY

1. Read more about the Dutch explorer Adriaen Block, who became a famous personality during his lifetime. Where did he venture and what did he find?

2. Ann Hutchinson was accused by Puritan leaders of being an antinomian heretic. Define *antinomianism* and research exactly what Hutchinson taught. Decide if you believe that she was a heretic.

3. Read more about the beliefs of John Wheelwright and Thomas Hooker. Why were these Puritan ministers banished from the Massachusetts Bay Colony? How did their beliefs compare to Anne Hutchinson's?

4. Look for a copy of the Fundamental Orders of Connecticut. You should be able to find it easily online. What does the opening statement of this document have to say about the role of God and Christianity in the founding of this colony?

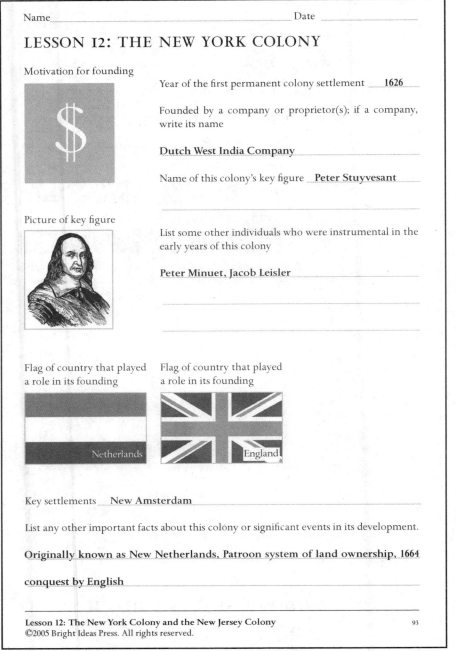

Name ______________________ Date ________

LESSON 12: THE NEW YORK COLONY

Motivation for founding

$

Year of the first permanent colony settlement **1626**

Founded by a company or proprietor(s); if a company, write its name

Dutch West India Company

Name of this colony's key figure **Peter Stuyvesant**

Picture of key figure

List some other individuals who were instrumental in the early years of this colony

Peter Minuet, Jacob Leisler

Flag of country that played a role in its founding

Netherlands

Flag of country that played a role in its founding

England

Key settlements **New Amsterdam**

List any other important facts about this colony or significant events in its development.

Originally known as New Netherlands, Patroon system of land ownership, 1664 conquest by English

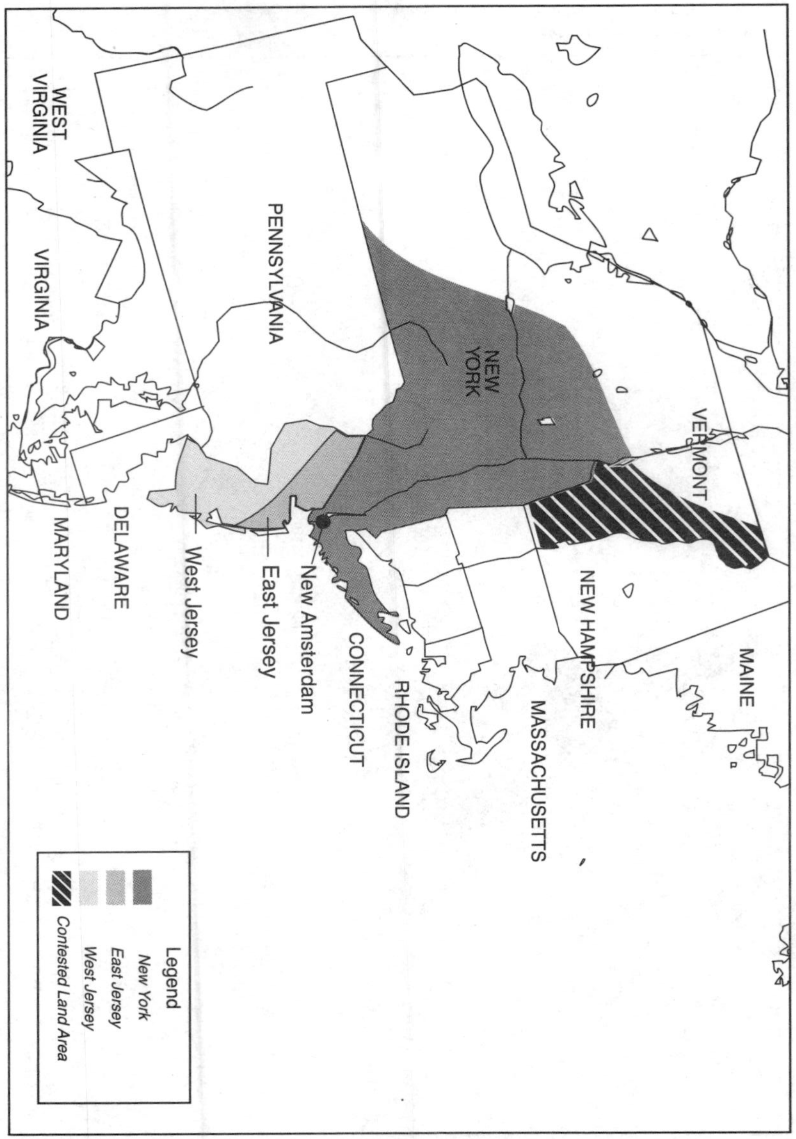

MAP OF NEW YORK COLONY

WEST VIRGINIA
VIRGINIA
PENNSYLVANIA
NEW YORK
VERMONT
MAINE
NEW HAMPSHIRE
MASSACHUSETTS
RHODE ISLAND
CONNECTICUT
New Amsterdam
East Jersey
West Jersey
DELAWARE
MARYLAND

Legend
New York
East Jersey
West Jersey
Contested Land Area

Name ________________ Date ________

LESSON 12: THE NEW JERSEY COLONY

Motivation for founding

Year of the first permanent colony settlement **1664**

Founded by a company or proprietor(s); if a company, write its name

proprietor

Name of this colony's key figure **Sir George Carteret, Sir John Berkeley**

Picture of key figure

List some other individuals who were instrumental in the early years of this colony

Philip Carteret

Flag of country that played a role in its founding

Netherlands

Flag of country that played a role in its founding

England

Key settlements **Elizabethtown**

List any other important facts about this colony or significant events in its development

Gift by Duke of York to two friends, Quit rent system for land use, Division into East and West – both eventually owned by mostly Quaker proprietors

MAP OF NEW JERSEY COLONY

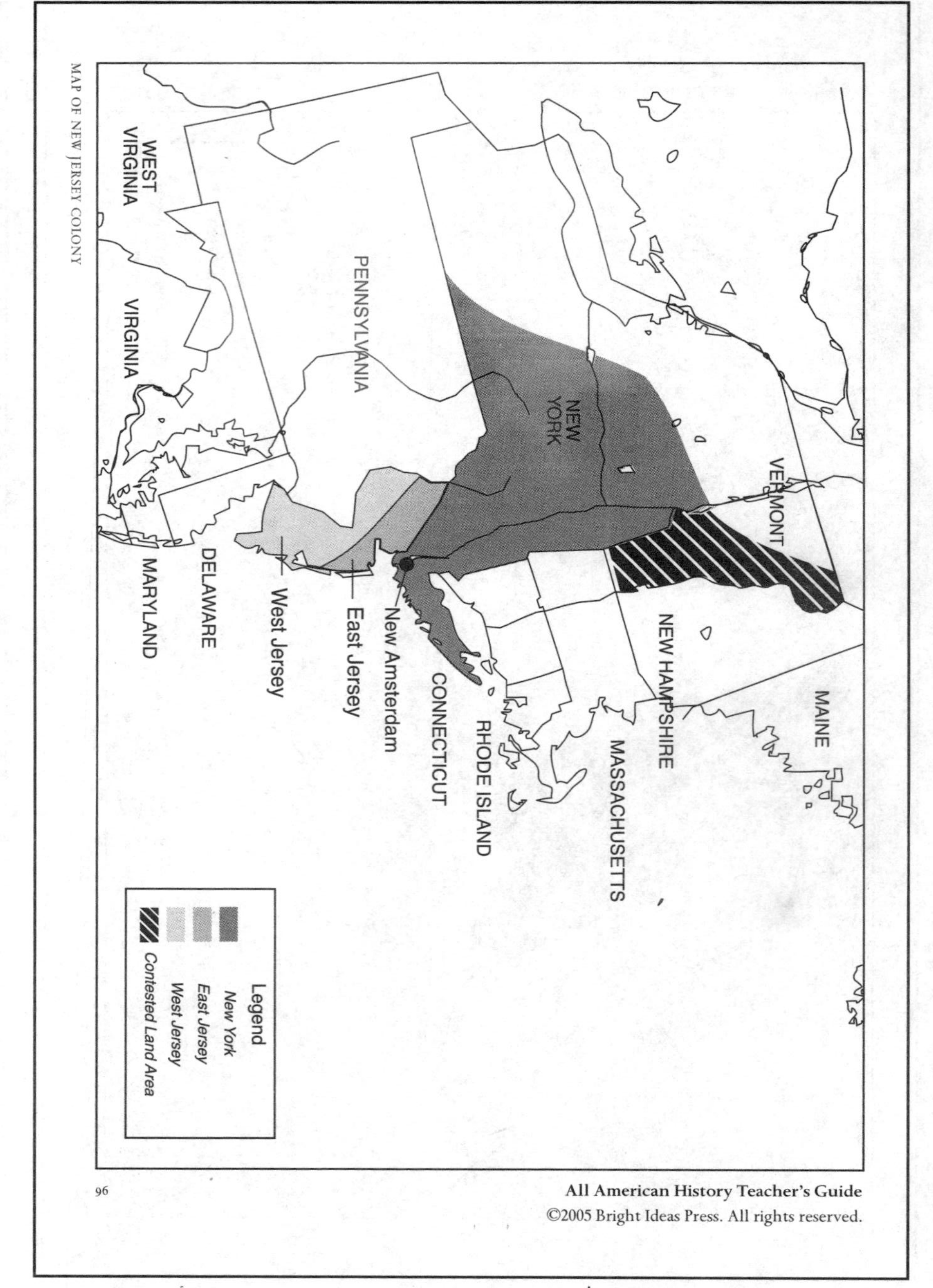

LESSON 12: FOR REVIEW

Write T for True and F for False in the space provided.

__T__ 1. Based upon the explorations of Adriaen Block and Henry Hudson, the Netherlands claimed a large area in North America, which included parts of present-day New York, New Jersey, Delaware, and Connecticut.

__F__ 2. The Dutch West India Company was primarily interested in looking for gold in New Netherlands.

__F__ 3. It was quite easy for the Dutch West India Company to find colonists willing to come to New Netherlands.

__F__ 4. There were no European settlers in New Jersey until 1664.

__T__ 5. The director-general of New Netherlands, Peter Minuit, supervised the building of the city of New Amsterdam.

__T__ 6. During its early years, New Amsterdam was a cosmopolitan seaport.

__T__ 7. The Dutch West India Company established a patroon system of land ownership in New Netherlands.

__F__ 8. The last director-general of New Netherlands, Peter Stuyvesant, was an easy-going, fun-loving leader.

__T__ 9. Stuyvesant was responsible for repairing the buildings and roads in New Amsterdam, as well as for re-establishing order in the city.

__T__ 10. In 1664, Englishmen sent by James, the Duke of York, took over New Netherlands with no shots fired.

__T__ 11. New York was named for its new owner, James, Duke of York.

__F__ 12. When the English took over New Netherlands, they treated the Dutch people there with contempt and forced many of them to return to Holland.

__T__ 13. Between 1660 and 1684, King Charles II created five new English colonies in North America as a way to repay people to whom he was in debt.

__F__ 14. Jacob Leisler was a wealthy Dutchman who championed the cause of New York merchants and large landowners.

__T__ 15. After the English takeover of New Netherlands, the Duke of York gave the area west of New York to two of his friends — Sir George Carteret and Sir John Berkeley.

__F__ 16. Carteret supposedly named the land grant New Jersey after his favorite cow.

__F__ 17. Carteret and Berkeley refused to give the people of New Jersey a representative assembly or freedom of religion.

__T__ 18. The people of New Jersey were forced to pay an annual rental fee to the proprietors called a quit rent. The fee was waived for the first seven years but eventually this deferment ended.

__T__ 19. In the 1670s, New Jersey was divided into East New Jersey and West New Jersey, with Quakers eventually becoming proprietors in both.

__T__ 20. During the early 1700s, the governor of New York also served as the governor of New Jersey.

LESSON 12: FOR FURTHER STUDY

1. Research the Dutch West India Company. When was it established and by whom? How long was it in existence? What monopoly was it given? What business ventures did it sponsor?

2. Who were the Pennsylvania Dutch and where is the Pennsylvania Dutch country? Why is the term *Pennsylvania Dutch* misleading?

3. Look for drawings and engravings of James II (Duke of York before he ascended the throne). Who were James II's father and brother? Why was the birth of James's son in 1688 such a pivotal event? What was the Glorious Revolution and what role did William and Mary play in it? To what in the New World did William and Mary give their name?

4. Read about the Quaker faith during the colonial period. What were their worship services like? Explain their views about the government and war. How did their views affect their lives?

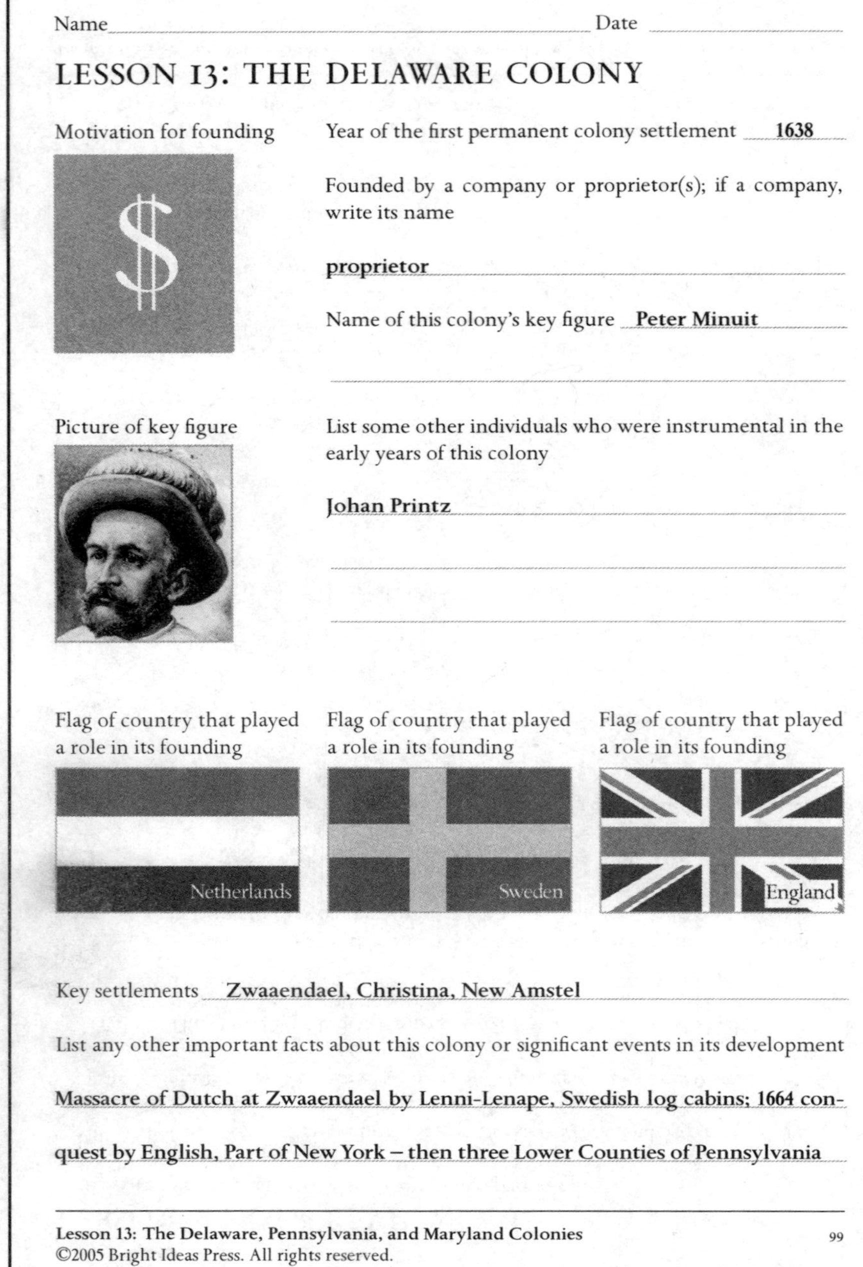

Name________________ Date________

LESSON 13: THE DELAWARE COLONY

Motivation for founding

Year of the first permanent colony settlement **1638**

Founded by a company or proprietor(s); if a company, write its name

proprietor

Name of this colony's key figure **Peter Minuit**

Picture of key figure

List some other individuals who were instrumental in the early years of this colony

Johan Printz

Flag of country that played a role in its founding

Netherlands

Flag of country that played a role in its founding

Sweden

Flag of country that played a role in its founding

England

Key settlements **Zwaaendael, Christina, New Amstel**

List any other important facts about this colony or significant events in its development

Massacre of Dutch at Zwaaendael by Lenni-Lenape, Swedish log cabins; 1664 conquest by English, Part of New York – then three Lower Counties of Pennsylvania

Lesson 13: The Delaware, Pennsylvania, and Maryland Colonies 99

MAP OF DELAWARE COLONY

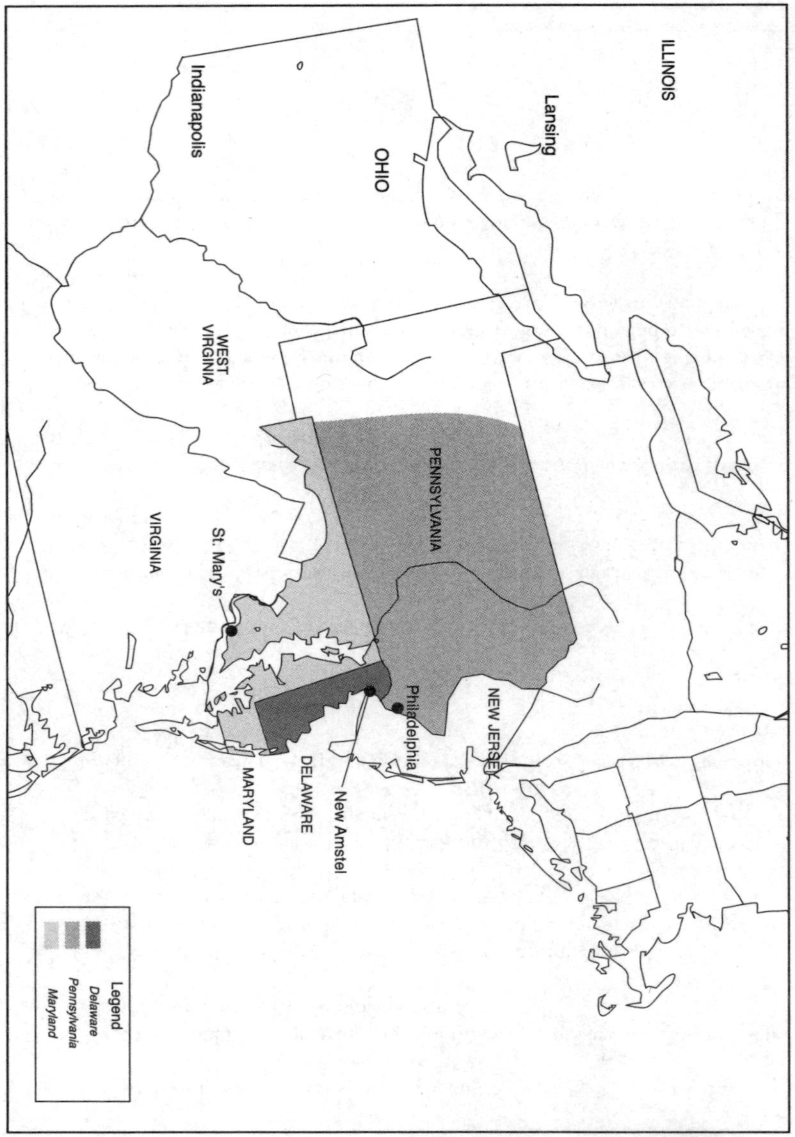

ILLINOIS
Lansing
OHIO
Indianapolis
WEST VIRGINIA
VIRGINIA
St. Mary's
PENNSYLVANIA
Philadelphia
NEW JERSEY
New Amstel
DELAWARE
MARYLAND
Legend
Delaware
Pennsylvania
Maryland

100
All American History Teacher's Guide

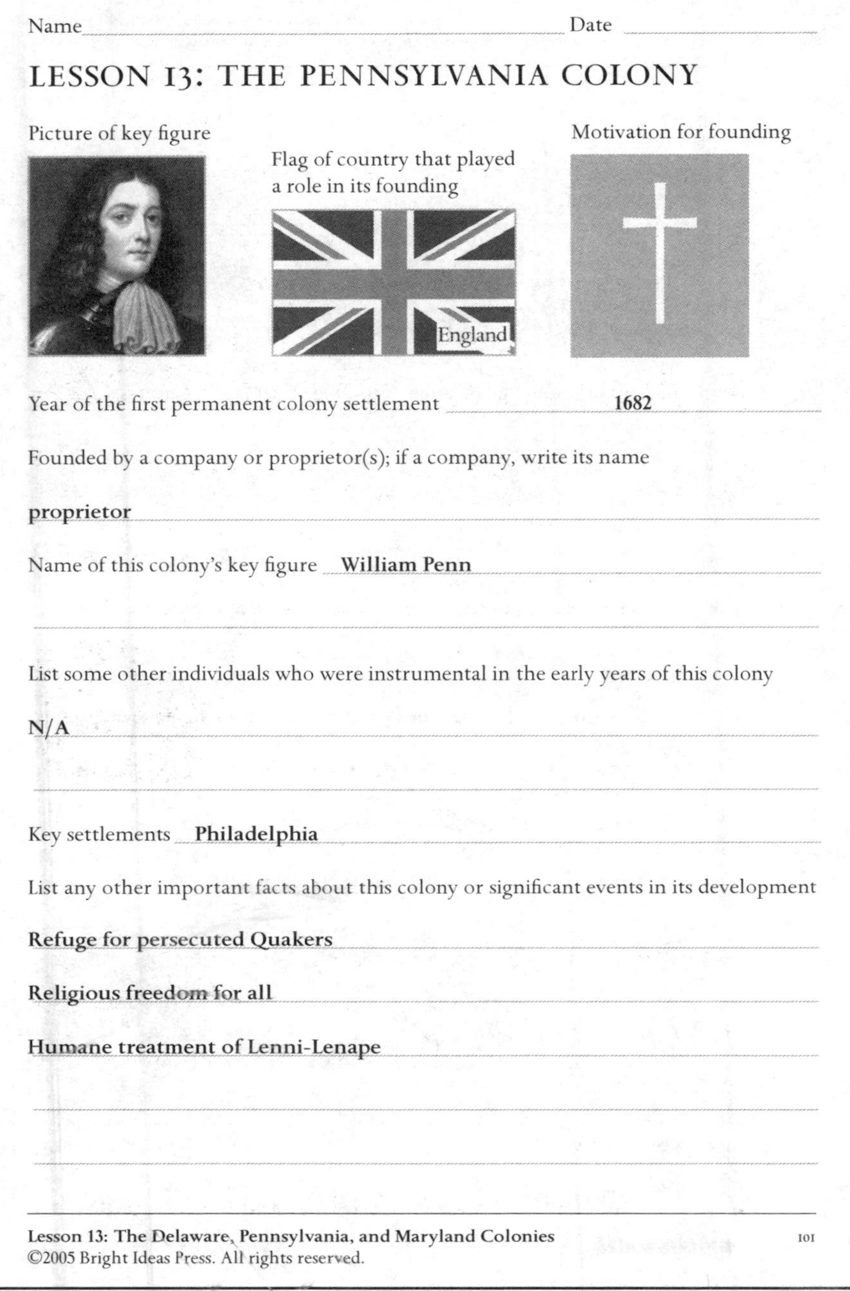

Name ______________________ Date ______________

LESSON 13: THE PENNSYLVANIA COLONY

Picture of key figure

Flag of country that played a role in its founding

Motivation for founding

Year of the first permanent colony settlement **1682**

Founded by a company or proprietor(s); if a company, write its name

proprietor

Name of this colony's key figure **William Penn**

List some other individuals who were instrumental in the early years of this colony

N/A

Key settlements **Philadelphia**

List any other important facts about this colony or significant events in its development

Refuge for persecuted Quakers

Religious freedom for all

Humane treatment of Lenni-Lenape

MAP OF PENNSYLVANIA COLONY

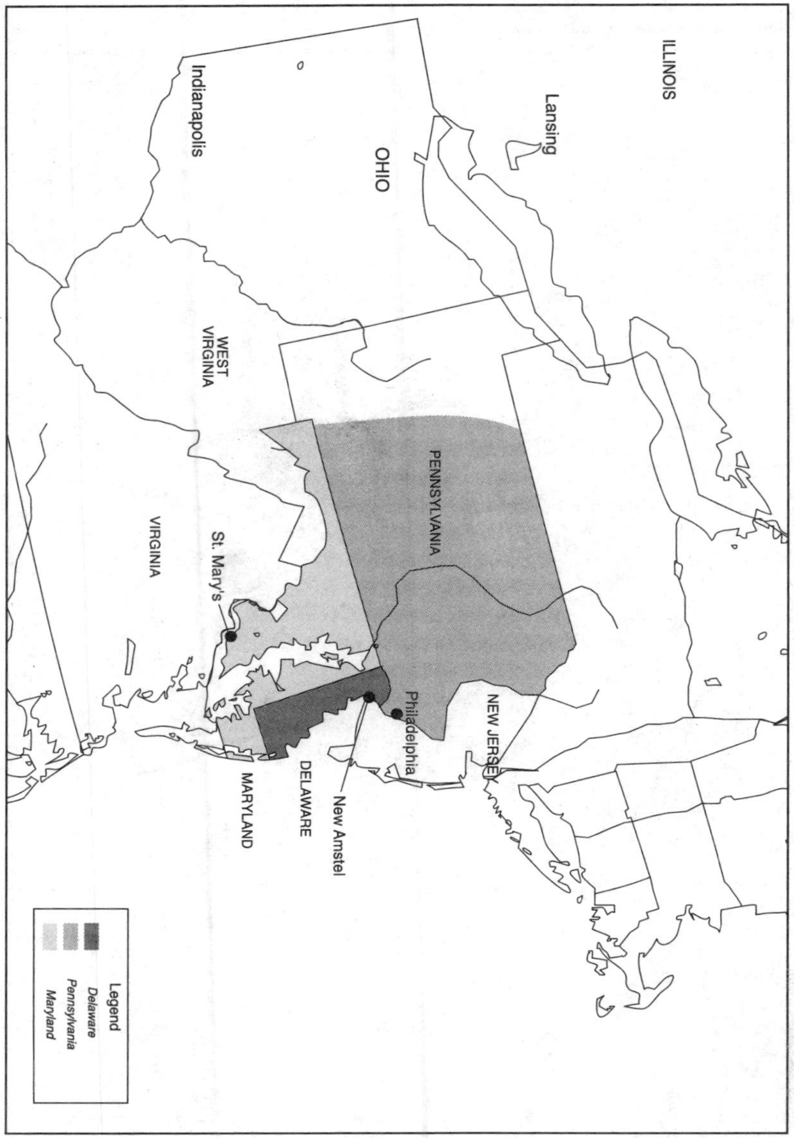

ILLINOIS
Lansing
OHIO
Indianapolis
WEST VIRGINIA
VIRGINIA
PENNSYLVANIA
NEW JERSEY
Philadelphia
New Amstel
DELAWARE
MARYLAND
St. Mary's
Legend
Delaware
Pennsylvania
Maryland

Name________________ Date ________

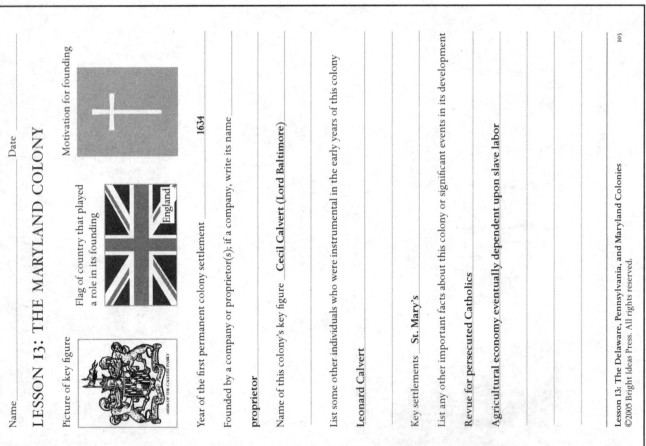

LESSON 13: THE MARYLAND COLONY

Picture of key figure

ARMS OF THE CALVERT FAMILY

Flag of country that played a role in its founding

England

Motivation for founding

Year of the first permanent colony settlement **1634**

Founded by a company or proprietor(s); if a company, write its name

proprietor

Name of this colony's key figure **Cecil Calvert (Lord Baltimore)**

List some other individuals who were instrumental in the early years of this colony

Leonard Calvert

Key settlements **St. Mary's**

List any other important facts about this colony or significant events in its development

Revue for persecuted Catholics

Agricultural economy eventually dependent upon slave labor

Lesson 13: The Delaware, Pennsylvania, and Maryland Colonies 103

MAP OF MARYLAND COLONY

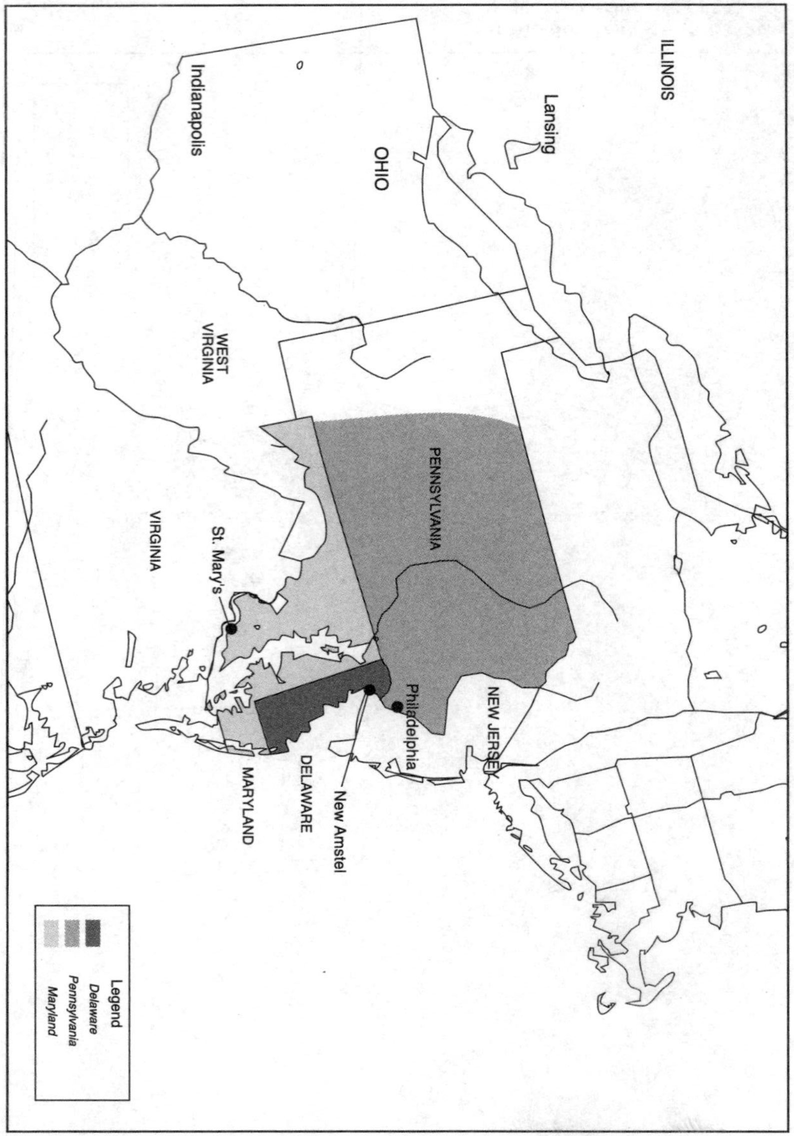

104 All American History Teacher's Guide

LESSON 13: FOR REVIEW

Write the letter of the correct answer in the space provided.

__B__ 1. A sea captain from Virginia named Samuel Argall discovered a bay in 1610, which he named for the governor of Virginia. The bay that Argall found was the
- A. Chesapeake Bay
- B. Delaware Bay
- C. Narragansett Bay
- D. New York Bay

__C__ 2. By 1631, the Dutch had organized a colony near present-day Cape Henlopen as a base for whaling and for trade with the Lenni-Lenape. This settlement was called
- A. Christina
- B. New Amstel
- C. Zwaanendael
- D. Casimir

__D__ 3. The Dutch and Lenni-Lenape had problems concerning the suspected stealing of
- A. a Dutch child
- B. an Indian tomahawk
- C. gunpowder
- D. a metallic Dutch coat of arms

__C__ 4. The principal figure in the establishment of Pennsylvania as an English colony was
- A. Lord Baltimore
- B. King Charles II
- C. William Penn
- D. King James II

__D__ 5. Which of the following was NOT true about the colony of Pennsylvania?
- A. it was given to Penn by King Charles to repay a debt owed to Penn's father
- B. its name means Penn's Woods
- C. it consisted of land west of the Delaware River between present-day New York and Maryland
- D. it was established as a royal colony

__C__ 6. George Calvert managed to remain a favorite of King James I, even though he
- A. lost all of his money
- B. betrayed him several times
- C. converted to Catholicism
- D. moved to America

__D__ 7. King Charles I granted Lord Baltimore a charter to start a colony north of the Potomac River. This colony became known as
- A. Georgia
- B. Charles Town
- C. Delaware
- D. Maryland

__A__ 8. Baltimore's colony was a proprietary colony, which he saw as a refuge for persecuted
- A. Catholics
- B. Puritans
- C. Quakers
- D. Jews

__B__ 9. The man hired to be the first governor of New Sweden was
- A. Samuel Argall
- B. Peter Minuet
- C. Peter Stuyvesant
- D. John Amstel

__A__ 10. The first Swedish settlement in the New World was located in a village named
- A. Christina
- B. Wilhemina
- C. Wilmington
- D. New Amstel

__A__ 11. The Swedes are known for being the first Europeans in America to
- A. build log cabins
- B. pay the Native Americans for their land
- C. build a fort to protect their settlement
- D. have their own governor

__C__ 12. New Sweden grew and prospered under the leadership of a man the natives called Big Tub. This man's name was
- A. Peter Minuet
- B. Peter Stuyvesant
- C. Johan Printz
- D. William Usselinx

__D__ 13. By 1655, New Sweden had been conquered by another European nation, and a new town named New Amstel had been laid out. The nation that took over New Sweden was
- A. England
- B. France
- C. Spain
- D. the Netherlands

__A__ 14. In 1664, the Dutch/Swedish settlement in Delaware had been taken over by another European nation. The new conquering nation was
- A. England
- B. France
- C. Spain
- D. the Netherlands

__B__ 15. From 1682 until 1704, the three lower counties of Delaware were part of the colony of
- A. Maryland
- B. Pennsylvania
- C. New Jersey
- D. Virginia

__A__ 16. Penn's advance party of colonists
- A. was instructed to choose a site with care on a dry spot near the Delaware River
- B. was told to scare away all the Native Americans in the area
- C. was given plans for building walls and fortifications
- D. was not successful in laying out the city of Philadelphia

__C__ 17. Penn's "holy experiment"
- A. did not offer generous land grants to its colonists
- B. did not give the right to vote to all male landowners
- C. was noteworthy in its treatment of the Lenni-Lenape
- D. was known for its intolerance and persecution of religions other than the religion of the Quakers

__B__ 18. The Pennsylvania Colony
- A. had few problems with its government
- B. attracted settlers from all over Europe
- C. was plagued by landowners who oppressed their tenants
- D. never grew to be very big

__B__ 19. Cecil Calvert planned that the distribution of land in his colony
- A. would be very fair and equal
- B. would be based on the English feudal system
- C. would not create social and class systems
- D. would make him quite wealthy

C 20. The settlers in Baltimore's colony

A. never used slaves
B. suffered during several grim "starving times"
C. developed an agricultural economy, with tobacco as its most profitable export
D. were unable to establish good relations with the Native Americans in the area

LESSON 13: FOR FURTHER STUDY

1. Research the Lenni-Lenapi tribe of Delaware and Pennsylvania. Record the information on a Native American Tribe form.

2. Look for William Penn's letter to the Indians and examine it carefully. How was this a remarkable document? See if you can find other writings by William Penn.

3. Read the story of the Liberty Bell. Why did the Pennsylvania Assembly order the bell in 1751? What Bible verse is inscribed on the bell? Why was this verse appropriate? Why is *Pennsylvania* misspelled on the bell?

4. Research Charles Mason and Jeremiah Dixon and the role that they played in the colonial history of Maryland. What is named for them today?

Name__________ Date__________

LESSON 14: THE NORTH CAROLINA COLONY

Picture of key figure

Flag of country that played a role in its founding

England

Motivation for founding

$

Year of the first permanent colony settlement **1653**

Founded by a company or proprietor(s); if a company, write its name

proprietors

Name of this colony's key figure **The Eight Lords Proprietor**

List some other individuals who were instrumental in the early years of this colony

Sir Robert Heath, John Culpeper

Key settlements **New Bern**

List any other important facts about this colony or significant events in its development

Slower economic growth than South Carolina due to geography

Independent-minded tobacco farmers

Tuscarora raids

Lesson 14: The North Carolina, South Carolina, and Georgia Colonies 111

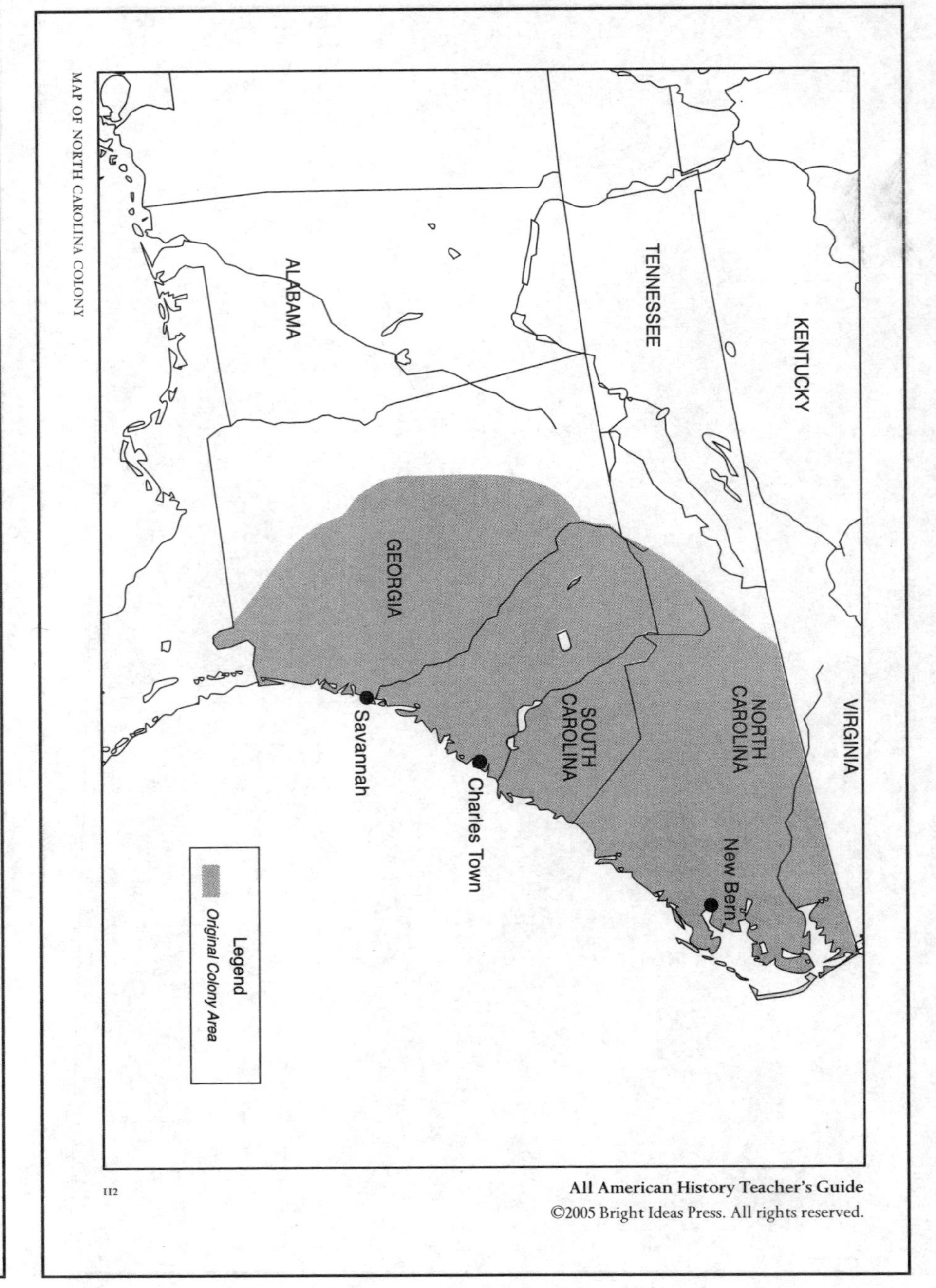

MAP OF NORTH CAROLINA COLONY

112

All American History Teacher's Guide

Name________________ Date ________

LESSON 14: THE SOUTH CAROLINA COLONY

Picture of key figure

Flag of country that played a role in its founding

England

Motivation for founding

$

Year of the first permanent colony settlement **1670**

Founded by a company or proprietor(s); if a company, write its name

proprietors

Name of this colony's key figures **Sir Ashley Cooper, the Eight Lords Proprietor**

List some other individuals who were instrumental in the early years of this colony

Sir Robert Heath

Key settlements **Charles Town**

List any other important facts about this colony or significant events in its development

Inadequate food supplies and threat of Spanish attack for first ten years; rice and indigo crops dependent upon slave labor

Goose Creek Men seeking more local control

Quit rent system

1712 Separation from North Carolina

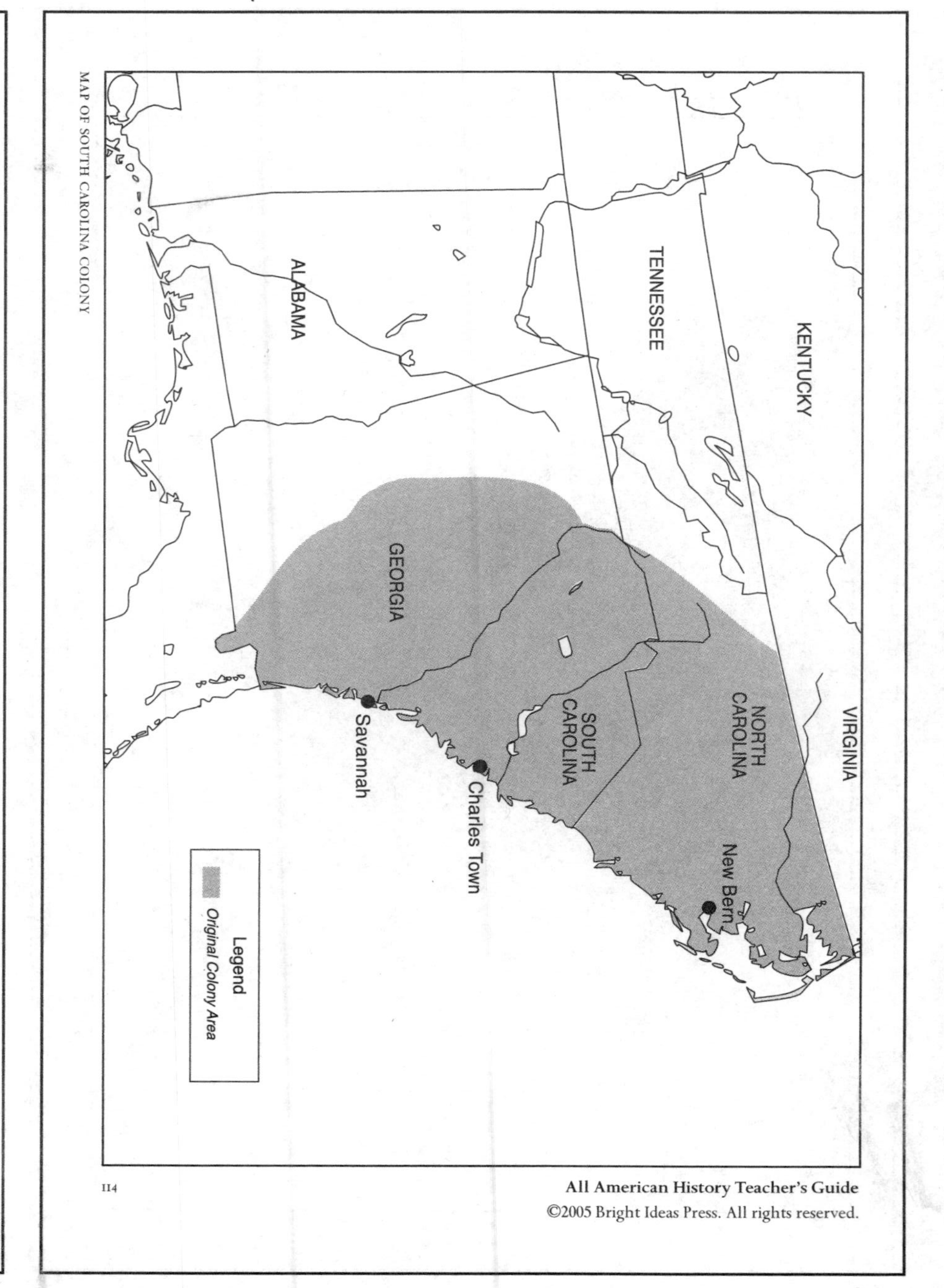

MAP OF SOUTH CAROLINA COLONY

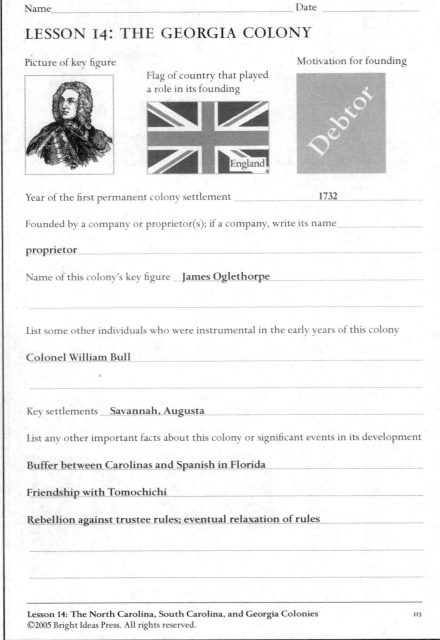

Name ____________ Date ____________

LESSON 14: THE GEORGIA COLONY

Picture of key figure

Flag of country that played a role in its founding

England

Motivation for founding

Debtor

Year of the first permanent colony settlement **1732**

Founded by a company or proprietor(s); if a company, write its name

proprietor

Name of this colony's key figure **James Oglethorpe**

List some other individuals who were instrumental in the early years of this colony

Colonel William Bull

Key settlements **Savannah, Augusta**

List any other important facts about this colony or significant events in its development

Buffer between Carolinas and Spanish in Florida

Friendship with Tomochichi

Rebellion against trustee rules; eventual relaxation of rules

Lesson 14: The North Carolina, South Carolina, and Georgia Colonies 115

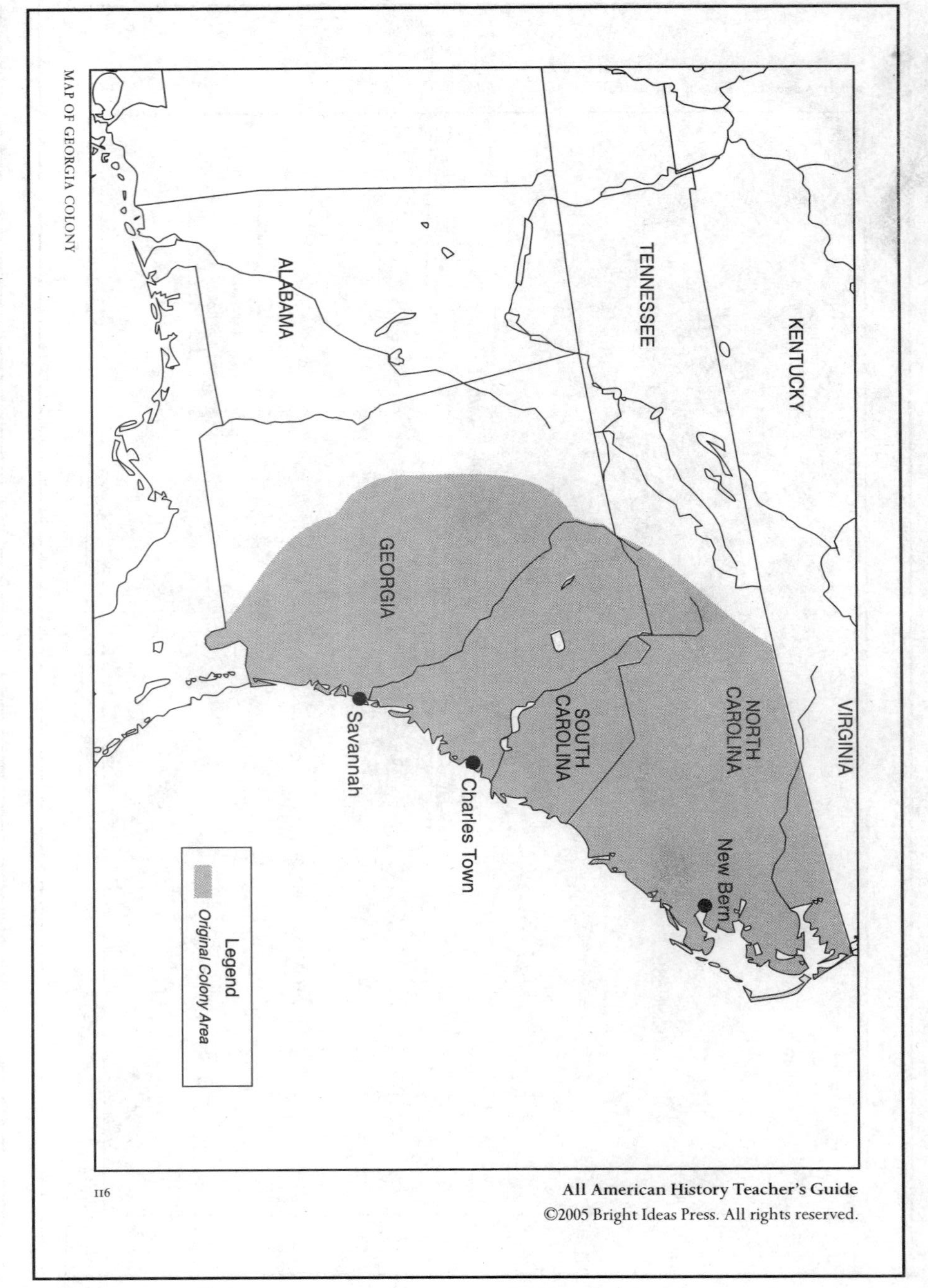

MAP OF GEORGIA COLONY

116

All American History Teacher's Guide

LESSON 14: FOR REVIEW

Write the corresponding letter of the correct answer in the space provided.

A. Colonel William Bull
B. Anthony Ashley Cooper
C. John Culpeper
D. Goose Creek Men
E. Sir Robert Heath
F. James Oglethorpe
G. Tomochichi
H. Tuscarora

H 1. Native American tribe that sought revenge by raiding North Carolina settlements

F 2. Founder of Georgia

B 3. Lord Proprietor who encouraged the printing of pamphlets to advertise Carolina's wonders

C 4. North Carolina settler who led a rebellion against the governor of the colony

G 5. Creek chief who became a good friend of James Oglethorpe

A 6. South Carolinian who helped Oglethorpe lay out Savannah

E 7. Englishman who was given Carolana by King Charles I in 1629

D 8. South Carolina settlers from Barbados who opposed proprietary government and sought more local governmental control

Write the missing word or words in the spaces provided.

1. In 1663, King Charles II gave the land from Virginia to Florida to eight prominent Englishmen known as the **Lords Proprietor**.

2. The colony of Georgia, set up as a charity and administered by twenty trustees, was intended to have the majority of its settlers be **debtors**.

3. For many years, North Carolina's only settlements were small communities of tobacco farmers in the isolated northern Albemarle region. The largest of these settlements was **New Bern**.

4. The Albemarle settlers were primarily former **indentured servants** and other poor whites, who had been squeezed out of Virginia by the low price of tobacco.

5. The first English settlement in South Carolina was at present-day **Charleston**, briefly known as Albemarle Point.

6. For many years, settlers in the Carolinas feared the threat of an attack from the **Spanish** in St. Augustine.

7. The staple crop that ensured Charles Town's prosperity was **rice**. An ideal second crop grown with it was **indigo**, a plant used to dye cloth a rich purple color.

8. By the early 1700s, South Carolina's economy had become based upon **African slave** labor.

9. The proprietors eventually began recruiting religious dissenters to South Carolina—first English Presbyterians and Baptists and later **French Huguenots**, whose tastes and ideas contributed to the creation of an aristocratic Charles Town society.

10. South Carolina settlers were delighted with the arrival of Oglethorpe and his colonists because they hoped that the Georgia settlement would serve as a buffer between them and **the Spanish**.

11. Colonists in Georgia rebelled against the trustees' rules requiring them to grow **mulberry trees**, pay quit rents, and abstain from strong liquor.

12. Eventually both the Carolinas and Georgia became **royal** colonies with their governors appointed by the English crown.

LESSON 14: FOR FURTHER STUDY

1. Research the Stono Rebellion, which occurred in Charles Town in 1739. Who rebelled and where? What did they do? Who put down the rebellion and how long did that take? What changed as a result of this rebellion?

2. Read about the Cherokee tribe. Record the information on a Native American Tribe form.

3. Both the Carolinas faced problems from pirates. Find out about the activities of Edward Teach (Blackbeard) and Stede Bonnet (the Gentleman Pirate). How did they get their nicknames? Why was North Carolina especially ideal for pirates?

4. Early in Georgia's history, the colony became entangled in a war between England and Spain called the War of Jenkins' Ear. How did this war get its name? What role did Oglethorpe and the Georgia settlers play in the war?

Name______________________ Date ______________

LESSON 15: ORIGINAL THIRTEEN COLONIES

List the original thirteen colonies by geographic region.

NEW ENGLAND: New Hampshire
Massachusetts
Rhode Island
Connecticut

MIDDLE: New York
New Jersey
Pennsylvania
Maryland
Delaware

SOUTH: Virginia
North Carolina
South Carolina
Georgia

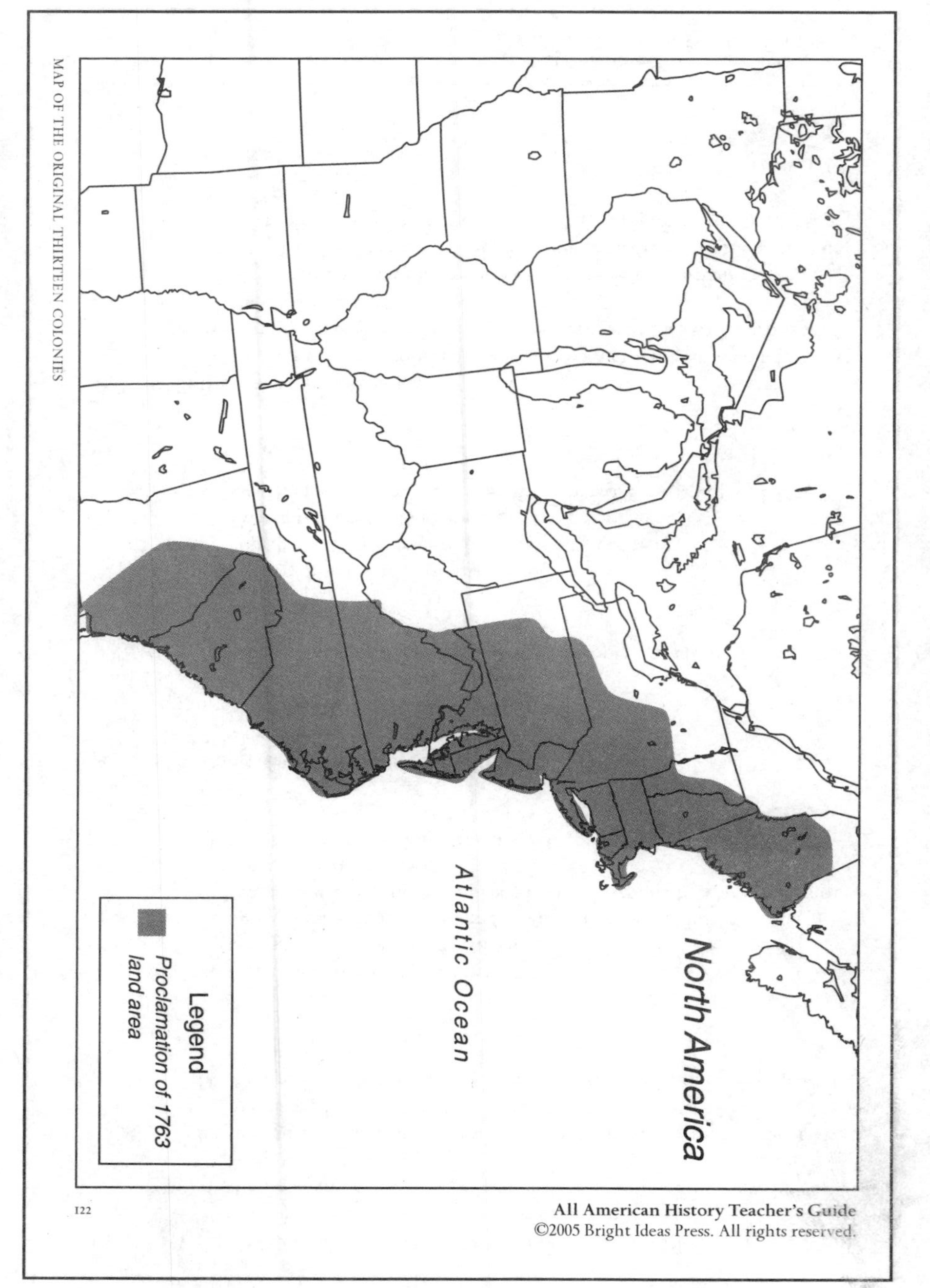

MAP OF THE ORIGINAL THIRTEEN COLONIES

LESSON 15: FOR REVIEW

Write the letter of the correct answer in the space provided.

__C__ 1. In colonial America there were
- A. mostly very small families
- B. quite a few divorces
- C. many remarriages
- D. few blended families

__A__ 2. During the colonial period,
- A. childbirth was quite dangerous for both mother and child
- B. fathers were rarely involved in disciplining their children
- C. children were usually not asked to take on household duties until they reached their teen years
- D. men and women married at a later age than their European counterparts

__B__ 3. Colonial families
- A. rarely ate meals together
- B. relied upon each other for food, shelter, and a sense of belonging
- C. had quite a bit of free time
- D. usually did not spend their evenings at home

__C__ 4. Colonial women
- A. did not generally marry until their mid-twenties
- B. liked to space their children four to five years apart
- C. were not allowed to own property in their name, vote, or run for public office
- D. were equal in status to their husbands

__C__ 5. Which of the following was NOT true of colonial education?
- A. schools varied greatly from region to region
- B. the first American college, Harvard, was founded by New England Puritans
- C. the Quakers in Pennsylvania were not interested in providing elementary education for their children
- D. children in Southern colonies were usually taught at home by parents or private tutors

__B__ 6. Upper-class men in the colonial period
- A. were rarely seen with a waistcoat
- B. were able to import silken and linen clothing from Europe
- C. had narrow cuffs and no ruffles on their shirts and breeches that came down to their ankles
- D. no longer wore leggings, under stockings, or cravats

__A__ 7. Working-class men in the colonial period
- A. wore trousers that covered the leg
- B. had shoes that were fastened by shoe laces
- C. preferred boots with high heels
- D. ordered most of their clothing from Europe

__A__ 8. Upper-class women in the colonial period
- A. considered their corset to be an essential garment
- B. owned primarily silk brocade gowns
- C. saw their skirts grow more and more narrow as the years passed
- D. often wore trousers

__B__ 9. In the American colonies,
- A. women were not concerned about keeping their hair covered
- B. working-class women usually covered their dresses with aprons while they worked
- C. gloves were not considered to be fashionable for women
- D. a typical dress for a working-class woman consisted of a bodice and skirt joined together, with the skirt opening in front to reveal a separate petticoat

D 10. Which of the following was NOT true of clothing for colonial children?
- A. boys wore dresses until they were five or six years old
- B. boys were "breeched" when they were put into their first pair of pants
- C. toddlers had leading strings attached to their clothing to help their parents guide them as they learned to walk
- D. most boys and girls had store-bought shoes with hard soles from Europe

B 11. The average life expectancy for an American during the colonial period was under
- A. ten years
- B. twenty-five years
- C. forty years
- D. sixty-five years

A 12. Illnesses in colonial America
- A. were often caused by contaminated water
- B. were generally treated by doctors trained in medical schools
- C. were rarely treated through "bleedings" using leeches
- D. were usually well understood

D 13. Colonial Americans
- A. usually had running water and septic systems in their homes
- B. had indoor toilets
- C. bathed at least every other day
- D. believed that a layer of dirt provided protection against germs

A 14. Which of the following was NOT true of colonial food?
- A. most European foods grew well in America
- B. food was usually cooked in big kettles over an open hearth
- C. most meals were stews
- D. meat was often preserved by smoking and vegetables by pickling

B 15. American colonists drank
- A. a great deal of water
- B. little milk
- C. few alcoholic beverages
- D. very little cider

D 16. New England colonists
- A. consumed a lot of fresh vegetables and salads
- B. did not cook with molasses or maple syrup
- C. used a lot of sugar
- D. consumed a lot of meat and fish

C 17. In the Middle colonies
- A. there was a very short growing season and rocky soil
- B. the French settlers ate a lot of cabbage and pork
- C. the Dutch enjoyed cookies, cakes, and pastries
- D. there was little baking of pies and breads because of the unavailability of ovens

B 18. White Southerners
- A. ate very little meat and had little variety in the types of foods they consumed
- B. often hid the bad flavor of spoiled food by adding pepper
- C. did not generally enjoy Indian hominy
- D. ate spicier foods than their African slaves

LESSON 15: FOR FURTHER STUDY

1. Try to find pictures of colonial hornbooks and selections from the *New England Primer.* Would you have enjoyed learning using these and other colonial educational methods? The first published book of American poetry was also the first American book to be published by a woman—Anne Bradstreet. See if you can find one of her poems to read.

2. Look for more pictures of colonial clothing. Decide what you like and dislike about the clothes.

3. Read about one or more of the illnesses that took lives during the colonial period—cholera, smallpox, scarlet fever, rickets, and tuberculosis. What are the symptoms of these diseases? Do these diseases cause many deaths today? Why or why not?

4. Find recipes used during the colonial period and try making some of the colonial specialties. See if you can find excerpts from Susannah Carter's *The Frugal Housewife* and from other cookbooks and women's books of the colonial period.

Name ________ Date ________

SUMMARY OF PROJECTS AND SPECIAL ACTIVITIES

READING

What biographies or nonfiction books have you read about this period of history and who were the author(s)?

What historical fiction books have you read about this period of history and who were the author(s)?

What magazine or Internet articles have you read about this period of history?

FIELD TRIPS/VIRTUAL TOURS

What field trips or virtual tours have you taken to sites from this period of history?

Which was your favorite and why?

MOVIES

What movies have you watched that are set in this time period or what documentaries have you watched that are about persons or events from this time period?

Which was the most interesting to you and why? ________

ART

What art projects have you completed that were about this time period or were done in an artistic technique from this time period?

NOTEBOOKS AND OTHER ACTIVITIES

Who has been highlighted in your Native American or African American notebook?

What other fun and creative activities have you done? ________

LESSON 16: FOR REVIEW

Write T for True and F for False in the space provided.

__T__ 1 The vast majority of European settlers in America were yeoman farmers, trades people, shopkeepers, and skilled artisans.

__T__ 2. Most African slaves lived in the South.

__F__ 3. Native Americans formed a highly unified group, identifying not only with their own particular tribe but also feeling linked to other tribes.

__F__ 4. All of the thirteen English colonies in America began as royal colonies.

__F__ 5. From the beginning, the thirteen colonies were not allowed the right to legislative representation in their government.

__T__ 6. In 1686, the English sought to tighten control over the New England colonies by creating the Dominion of New England.

__F__ 7. The New England settlers found it quite easy to make a living from farming.

__T__ 8. Most people in the New England colonies were English immigrants who came over in groups for religious reasons.

__T__ 9. The Middle colonies were settled by immigrants from a variety of European countries, and most of them were established as profit-making enterprises from the earliest years of their existence.

__F__ 10. From the beginning, the South was predominantly industrial.

__F__ 11. There was only a small group of yeoman or subsistence farmers in the South.

__F__ 12. The large population centers in the colonies were primarily found in the Southern colonies.

__T__ 13. During the colonial period, horse-pulled wagons and sleighs provided most land transportation.

Write the corresponding letter of the correct answer in the space provided.

A. The *Bay Psalm Book*
B. blue laws
C. John Cotton
D. Jonathan Edwards
E. the Great Awakening
F. Gilbert Tennant
G. *Pilgrim's Progress*

__D__ 1. Preacher known for his powerful sermons, like "Sinners in the Hands of an Angry God"

__A__ 2. First book ever issued from a press in the American colonies

__C__ 3. Puritan minister who exerted tremendous power in Massachusetts through his use of the pulpit

__G__ 4. Book popular during the colonial period

__F__ 5. Presbyterian minister in the Middle colonies who founded the "Log Cabin" to prepare young men for ministry

__E__ 6. Great religious revival in America from 1730 to 1760

__B__ 7. Puritan rules banning work or play on the Sabbath

LESSON 16: FOR FURTHER STUDY

1. Read the story of John Peter Zenger and his famous trial. What was the significance of his trial for American life? How did many of the American colonies punish those who broke the law? How were these punishments different from those used today?

2. Study the colonial whaling industry. Learn more details about the lucrative triangular trade. See if you can find pictures of colonial furniture and metal work.

3. Read about the life of Jonathan Edwards as well as excerpts from his famous sermon "Sinners in the Hands of an Angry God." How did he deliver his sermons? You might also research the life of Presbyterian minister David Brainerd, who ministered to Native Americans. Look for excerpts from his journal.

4. Learn to do some string games, such as cat's cradle. Find examples of colonial toys, quilts, music, and dances.

UNIT 2: FINAL REVIEW

Write the corresponding letter of the founder of each colony in the space provided.

A. Lord Baltimore
B. Sir George Carteret
C. Anthony Ashley Cooper
D. Thomas Hooker
E. Peter Minuit
F. James Oglethorpe
G. William Penn
H. John Smith
I. Peter Stuyvesant
J. John Wheelwright
K. Roger Williams
L. John Winthrop

E 1. Delaware

D 2. Connecticut

F 3. Georgia

A 4. Maryland

L 5. Massachusetts

J 6. New Hampshire

B 7. New Jersey

I 8. New York

C 9. North and South Carolina

G 10. Pennsylvania

K 11. Rhode Island

H 12. Virginia

Designate in the space provided — R if the colony was founded for religious reasons, P if the colony was founded for profit, B if the colony was founded for both reasons, or D if the colony was founded as a debtor colony.

P 1. Delaware

B 2. Connecticut

D 3. Georgia

R 4. Maryland

R 5. Massachusetts

B 6. New Hampshire

P 7. New Jersey

P 8. New York

P 9. North and South Carolina

R 10. Pennsylvania

R 11. Rhode Island

P 12. Virginia

Write T for True and F for False in the space provided.

T 1. The Massachusetts Bay Colony passed the Olde Deluder Satan Act, which required every town with more than fifty families to establish a grammar school.

F 2. Girls in New England were allowed to attend grammar schools and colleges, while girls in the Mid-Atlantic and Southern colonies were required to attend dame schools.

F 3. Southern planters were strong supporters of public education.

T 4. By the late colonial period, Southern colonies had passed laws making it illegal to teach slaves how to read and white because they feared the possibility of literate slaves succeeding in an uprising.

F 5. At the time of the colonial period, hornbooks were no longer used to teach children how to read.

T 6. The *New England Primer* was the first textbook used in the colonies.

F 7. Most colonial teachers were spinster women.

T 8. The school year for colonial children was short, and many children only attended school when their parents did not need them to work.

T 9. Colonial schools were generally allowed to use various punishments to discipline students who were tardy or negligent in their studies.

T 10. Eighteenth-century men commonly wore wigs when away from home, and certain styles of wigs became associated with particular professionals.

F 11. Puritan men and women in New England were known for their ornate style of clothing.

F 12. American doctors in the colonial period were well informed about the causes and cures of many diseases and had a number of effective painkillers and medicines to give to their patients.

F 13. Colonial homes generally had indoor stoves and refrigerators.

T 14. The *Compleat Housewife* appears to be the first cookbook published in the colonies.

T 15. Two typical New England foods were flapjacks and hasty pudding.

F 16. The Southern colonies generally had a short growing season and a bad climate for crops.

T 17. African Americans in the South generally ate spicier foods than the European colonists there.

F 18. Most colonial homes had separate dining rooms.

F 19. The people of colonial America developed a culture that was completely divorced from their European roots.

T 20. In America an individual's destiny was more closely tied to his accomplishments and less to his family background than it was in Europe.

F 21. American colonial society had a highly developed nobility and a very small middle class.

T 22. The natural conditions of America, as well as the fact that an ocean separated it from the homeland, made it difficult for the English to assert strong control over the thirteen colonies.

F 23. The Dominion of New England lasted until the beginning of the American Revolution.

T 24. American colonists believed that they should enjoy the rights and freedoms of Englishmen.

T 25. The New England colonies were known for their cod industry, shipbuilding, whaling, and triangular slave trade.

F 26. Life in the Middle colonies was not as diverse and cosmopolitan as life in New England.

T 27. Agriculture and manufacturing provided a strong economic base for the Middle colonies.

T 28. The primary crop grown on Southern plantations was tobacco; rice and indigo were also important crops cultivated in the Carolinas and Georgia.

F 29. Before the American Revolution, there was no regular mail delivery in the colonies.

T 30. The thirteen American colonies were primarily populated by Protestants.

Name ____________________ Date ________

LESSON 17: THE FRENCH AND INDIAN WAR

The war was a colonial extension of what European war? **the Seven Years' War**

Flags of the countries involved in the French and Indian War

England

France

With which side did most Native American tribes ally themselves? **France**

Color the square red if the battle was a British victory. Color the square blue if the battle was a French victory. ■ = blue (French) ■ = red (British)

FIRST PHASE

- ■ (blue) Ft. DuQuesne
- ■ (red) Ft. Edward
- ■ (red) Ft. William Henry

SECOND PHASE

- ■ (blue) Ft. Oswego
- ■ (blue) Ft. William Henry

THIRD PHASE

- ■ (red) Ft. Louisbourg
- ■ (red) Ft. Frontenac
- ■ (red) Ft. Ticonderoga
- ■ (red) Montreal
- ■ (red) Ft. DuQuesne
- ■ (red) Ft. Niagara
- ■ (red) Quebec
- ■ (red) Detroit

Pictures of some of the key individuals in the French and Indian War

Washington

Amherst

Wolfe

Montcalm

MAP OF FRENCH AND INDIAN WAR BATTLESITES

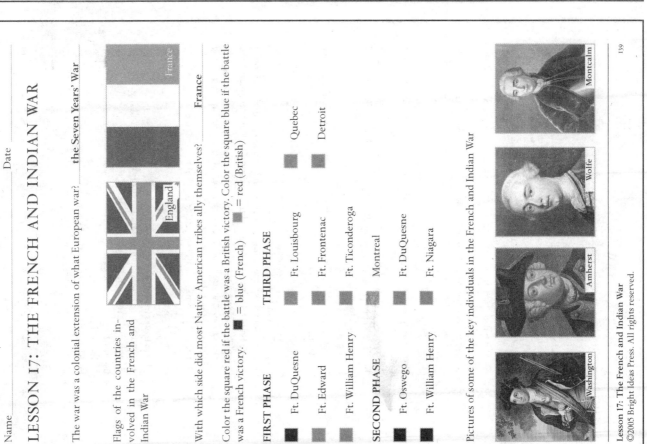

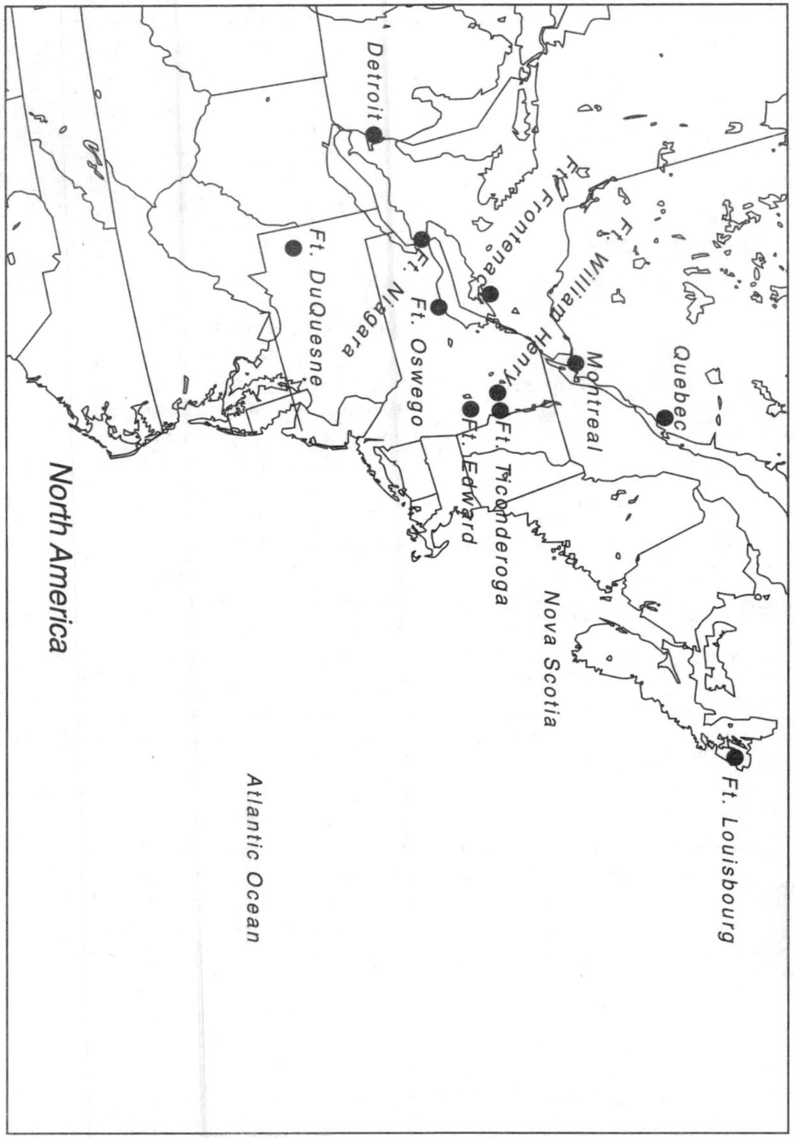

Detroit
Ft. Frontenac
Ft. William Henry
Quebec
Montreal
Ft. DuQuesne
Ft. Niagara
Ft. Oswego
Ft. Ticonderoga
Ft. Edward
Nova Scotia
Ft. Louisbourg
North America
Atlantic Ocean

LESSON 17: FOR REVIEW

Write the letter of the correct answer in the space provided.

__C__ 1. Historical scholars have generally
- A. found little to debate concerning the causes of the American Revolution
- B. believed that the colonists failed to develop a sense of American identity
- C. pointed to parliamentary policies toward the colonies as one of the causes of war
- D. discounted the role of colonial leaders in arousing American anger against the British

__B__ 2. In the years prior to the outbreak of the American Revolution, most colonists
- A. experienced less religious freedom than the British
- B. came to prefer American simplicity and self-reliance rather than the more aristocratic British society
- C. saw their population decline
- D. regarded life in the mother country as superior to life in the New World

__C__ 3. Between 1763 and 1775,
- A. most colonists were ready to form an independent America nation
- B. the British Parliament refrained from passing laws that regulated the colonists' trade or travel
- C. the cry of "no taxation without representation" became a rallying point for the colonists
- D. the British removed all troops stationed in the colonies

__B__ 4. The French and Indian War was a
- A. conflict between French and Indian fur trappers in America
- B. colonial extension of the Seven Years' War in Europe
- C. short conflict, lasting only a couple of years and resulting in little bloodshed
- D. fight primarily between the British and their colonists

__C__ 5. In 1750,
- A. the Spanish still claimed large portions of North America
- B. the British had stripped the French of all of their territory in the New World
- C. the French held eastern Canada and the Louisiana Territory
- D. the British claimed large portions of territory on both the east and west coasts of America

__D__ 6. During the early 1750s, the French had
- A. many more enemies among the Native Americans than the British
- B. settled their previous tensions with the British
- C. little concern about the westward movement of British colonists
- D. fur-trading posts and forts in a region bounded by Quebec, Montreal, Detroit, and New Orleans

__A__ 7. Which of the following was TRUE during the early 1750s?
- A. the French wanted to keep the British from expanding into the Ohio River valley
- B. the British were building a chain of new forts from the St. Lawrence River to the Mississippi River
- C. Fort Duquesne was built by the British in present-day Virginia on land claimed by the French
- D. George Washington defended Fort Duquesne against French attacks

__C__ 8. Fort Necessity was built by
- A. the French near Fort Duquesne
- B. the British in the early 1600s
- C. George Washington and his men when they were unable to take over Fort Duquesne
- D. the Spanish to protect Florida

B 9. During the first phase of fighting in the French and Indian War (1754 – 1755),
- A. almost all of the American native tribes decided to ally themselves with the British
- B. the American colonists managed mostly on their own against the French
- C. the French colonies were able to produce their own food and were protected by their own militias
- D. the Iroquois chose to side with the French because Champlain had helped them in their war with the Huron

A 10. Major General Edward Braddock, sent to oversee British and colonial forces in 1755,
- A. was mortally wounded near Fort Duquesne
- B. succeeded in teaching his soldiers how to use guerilla fighting tactics
- C. was not willing to work with George Washington
- D. led his forces to ultimate victory over the French

D 11. In the second phase of the fighting (1756 – 1757),
- A. Lord Loudon succeeded in getting the colonists excited about the war effort
- B. the British were outnumbered almost two to one by the French
- C. Native Americans scalped many of their French allies
- D. the British were soundly defeated by the French under Montcalm at Fort Oswego and Fort William Henry

B 12. The tide began to turn in favor of the British in 1758 under the leadership of William Pitt, who
- A. coerced the colonists into supporting the war effort
- B. encouraged the British to adapt their war strategies to the American landscape and terrain
- C. enlisted the Spanish as British allies
- D. forced generals Amherst and Wolfe to return to England

D 13. Which of the following was NOT a British victory in 1758 – 1759?
- A. Fort Louisbourg
- B. Fort Niagara
- C. Fort Ticonderoga
- D. Fort William Henry

C 14. On September 13, 1759, just outside the French city of Quebec,
- A. the British suffered a surprising defeat by the French
- B. the British and French fought to a draw
- C. both General Wolfe and General Montcalm were mortally wounded
- D. the French won a decisive victory

A 15. By September of 1760,
- A. the British controlled all of the American frontier
- B. the British had surrendered to the French at Montreal
- C. Detroit remained in French hands
- D. the Treaty of Paris, ending the French and Indian War, had been signed

C 16. The Treaty of Paris, ending the French and Indian War, gave
- A. no territory to the Spanish
- B. New Orleans and lands west of the Mississippi River to the British
- C. all of North America east of the Mississippi River, except for New Orleans, to the English
- D. New Orleans to the French

A 17. In 1764, Pontiac's Rebellion flared up,
- A. and many of the battlefields were the same as those in the French and Indian War
- B. and the fighting continued for more than five years
- C. but eventually the enmity between the British and the Native Americans died down
- D. and the Native Americans were re-energized and unwilling to capitulate to the British

D 18. As a result of the French and Indian War,
- A. the British were able to retire an enormous national debt
- B. the relationship between the British and their colonists was vastly improved
- C. British naval supremacy was diminished
- D. the American colonists united for the first time against a common enemy

LESSON 17: FOR FURTHER STUDY

1. Research the life and military career of the British general Jeffrey Amherst. What position did he take after the French and Indian War as a reward for his success? Read about the controversy surrounding him in the post-war years. Why did Amherst refuse to take a field command in the American Revolution?

2. Visit one or more of the forts in Pennsylvania and New York that were battle sites in the French and Indian War — Fort Duquesne (Fort Pitt), Fort Niagara, Fort Necessity, Fort Ticonderoga, and Fort William Henry. If you can't visit in person, do a "virtual tour" online.

3. Look for the Benjamin West painting from 1770 entitled *The Death of General Wolfe*. What can you learn about the Battle of Quebec from this painting? Can you find out who the people are with him in the painting? Find the lyrics to the song "The Death of General Wolfe." Learn more about Wolfe's life and military career.

4. Read about the early life of George Washington. Look for paintings of him as a young man. Find out more about the role that he played in the French and Indian War and how those war years prepared him for the revolution to come.

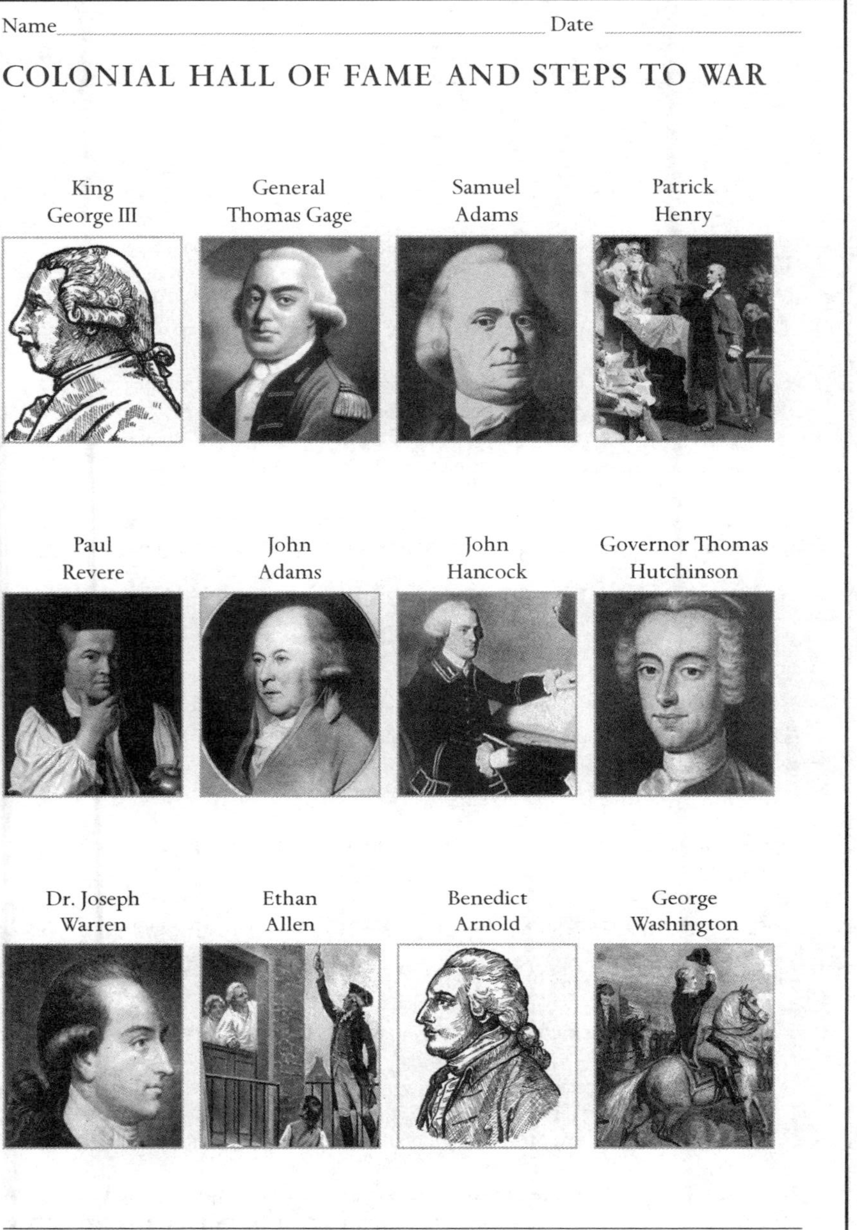

Name ____________ Date ____________

COLONIAL HALL OF FAME AND STEPS TO WAR

King George III | General Thomas Gage | Samuel Adams | Patrick Henry

Paul Revere | John Adams | John Hancock | Governor Thomas Hutchinson

Dr. Joseph Warren | Ethan Allen | Benedict Arnold | George Washington

Lesson 18: A Time of Crisis in Colonial Relations 147

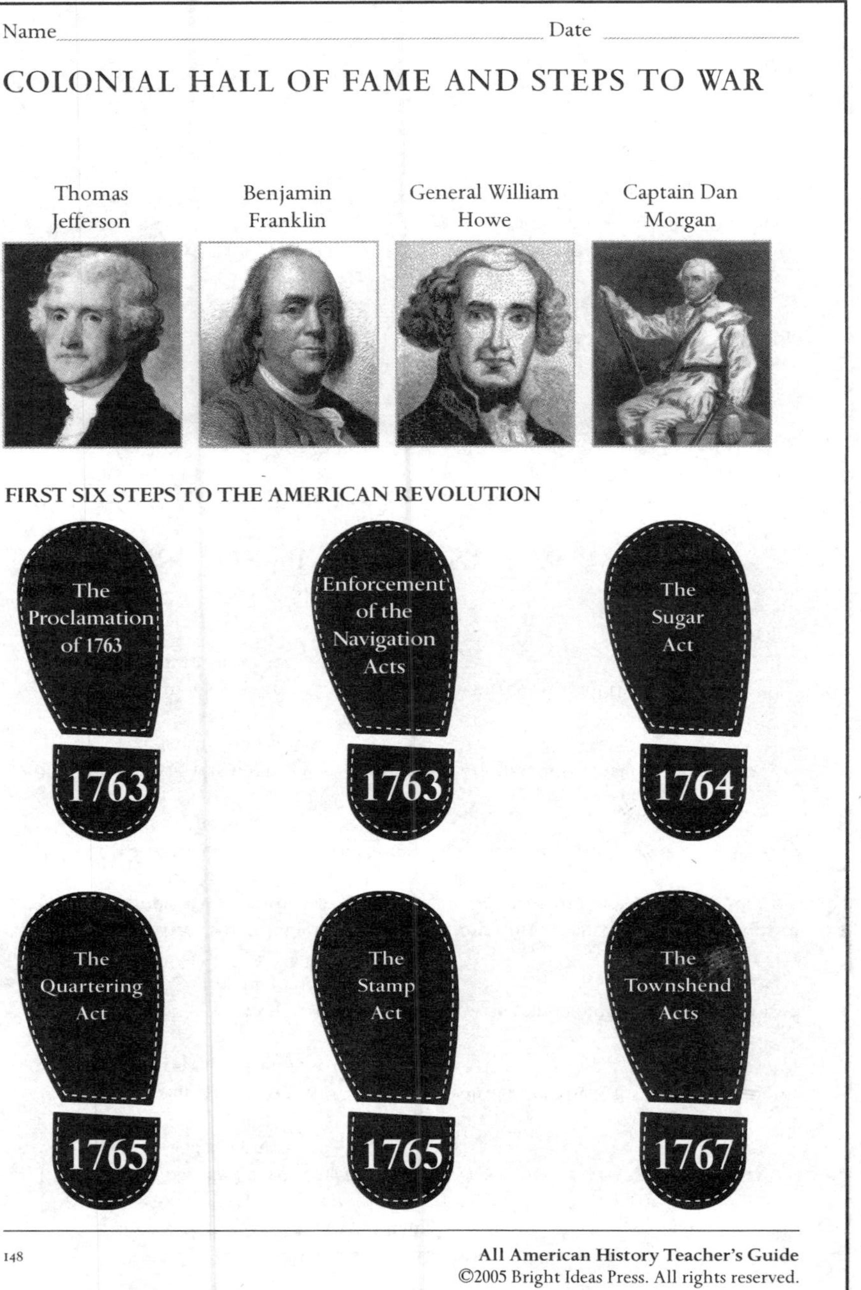

Name ____________ Date ____________

COLONIAL HALL OF FAME AND STEPS TO WAR

Thomas Jefferson | Benjamin Franklin | General William Howe | Captain Dan Morgan

FIRST SIX STEPS TO THE AMERICAN REVOLUTION

The Proclamation of 1763 — 1763

Enforcement of the Navigation Acts — 1763

The Sugar Act — 1764

The Quartering Act — 1765

The Stamp Act — 1765

The Townshend Acts — 1767

148 **All American History Teacher's Guide**

LESSON 18: FOR REVIEW

Write the corresponding letter of the correct answer in the space provided.

A. Navigation Acts
B. Proclamation of 1763
C. Quartering Act
D. Stamp Act
E. Sugar Act
F. Townshend Acts

C 1. Required colonists to provide housing and supplies for British soldiers

F 2. Required colonists to pay a duty on lead, paint, glass, paper, wine, and tea

E 3. Required colonists to pay a three-penny tax on every gallon of molasses imported

D 4. Required colonists to buy stamps to place on newspapers and legal documents

B 5. Prohibited colonists from settling west of the Appalachian Mountains

A 6. Required colonial imports and exports to be carried on British and colonial ships

Write T for True and F for False in the space provided.

T 1. From the 1660s to the 1760s, the thirteen colonies were largely unbothered by the British government.

T 2. The thirteen colonies were not united as a single body. In fact, they usually acted as individual nations.

F 3. The thirteen colonies were ready to declare their independence in 1760.

F 4. After the French and Indian War, France became the dominant European power in North America.

T 5. King George III was the ruler of Britain in the 1760s and 1770s.

F 6. The British government did not need the colonists' help in paying off its war debt from the French and Indian War.

F 7. After the French and Indian War, the British Parliament felt that it needed to loosen the restrictions that it had placed on the thirteen colonies.

F 8. By 1763, the British government was eager for the westward movement of American colonists.

F 9. The Navigation Acts were rigorously enforced by the British government for over one hundred years.

T 10. The Sugar Act especially hurt the New England colonies, which imported molasses for their rum industry.

F 11. The thirteen colonies were grateful for the presence of British troops in America during the years following the French and Indian War.

T 12. Citizens' groups called the Sons of Liberty sprang up to lead the resistance against the Stamp Act.

F 13. George Washington gave a stirring speech in the Virginia House of Burgesses against the Stamp Act.

T 14. Within a few years the British Parliament repealed all the Townshend taxes except those on tea.

LESSON 18: FOR FURTHER STUDY

1. Research King George III, the British monarch during the years leading up to and during the American Revolution. How old was George III when he succeeded his grandfather to the throne in 1760? Describe George III's temperament and personal difficulties. What was George III's attitude toward the colonies?

2. Read about Daniel Boone. How was his boyhood perfect preparation for his wilderness explorations later in life? Which wilderness areas did he explore? How did he help to encourage the westward movement of the American colonists in 1775?

3. Investigate the life of Samuel Adams. What was his educational and business background before he became involved in revolutionary activities? List the political offices that he held and describe his political beliefs. How did the British view Sam Adams?

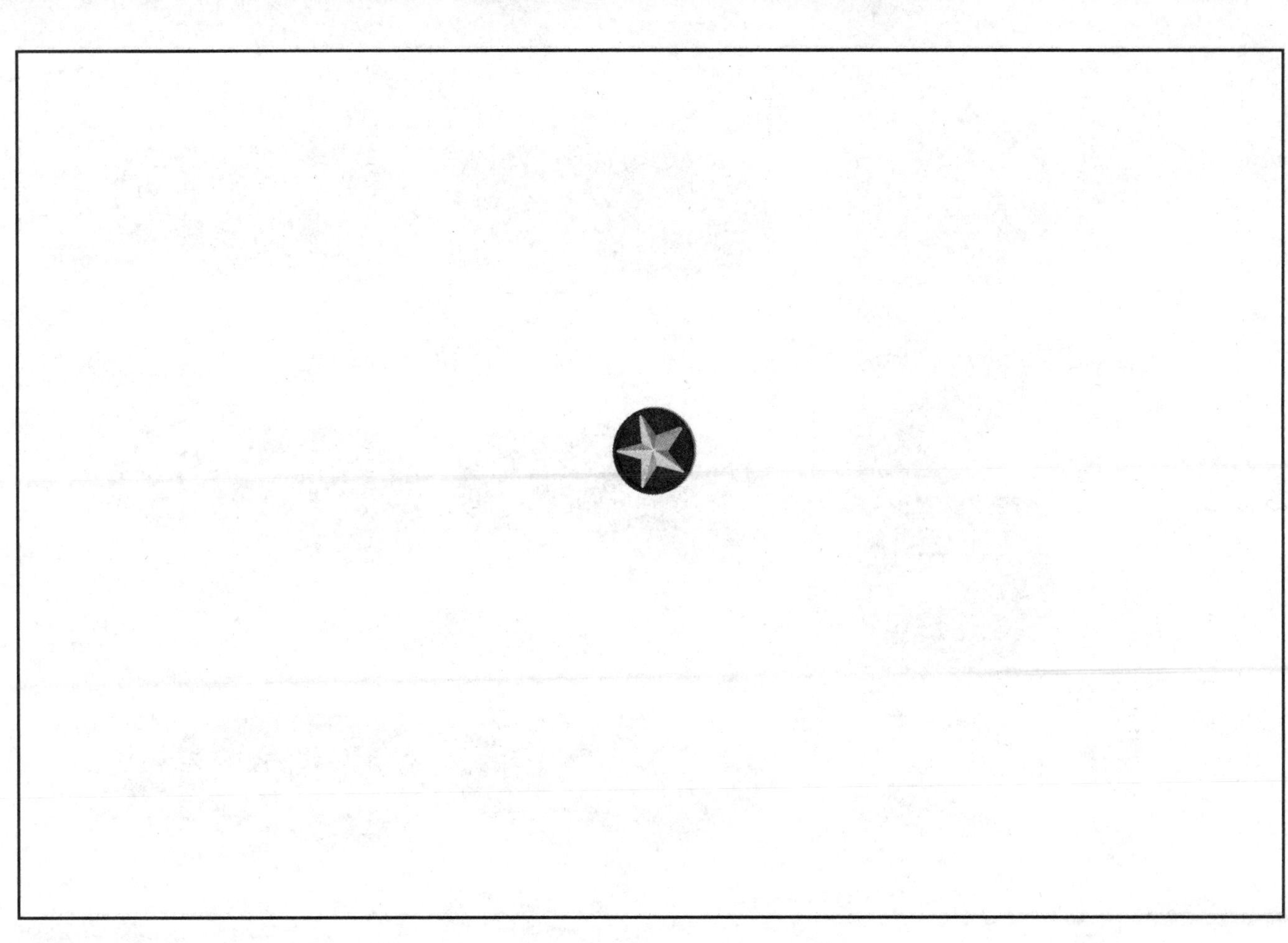

4. Find out more about the Sons of Liberty in Massachusetts and the other colonies. Who were their leaders and in what type of secret activities were they involved? Where and what were the "Liberty Tree" and the "Liberty Pole"?

Name_____________ Date _________

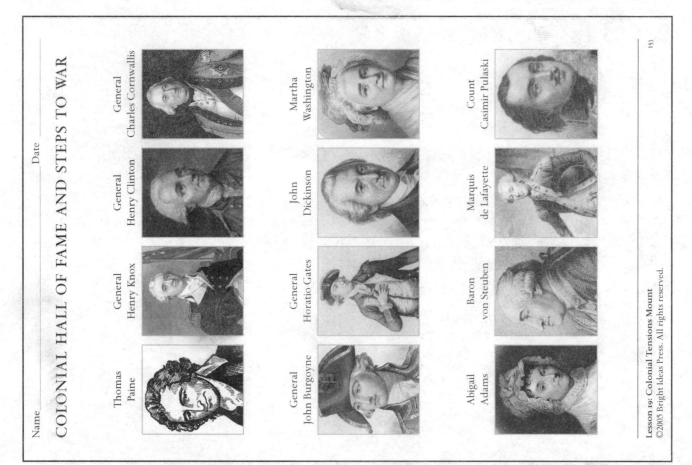

COLONIAL HALL OF FAME AND STEPS TO WAR

Thomas Paine | General Henry Knox  | General Henry Clinton  | General Charles Cornwallis

General John Burgoyne  | General Horatio Gates  | John Dickinson  | Martha Washington

Abigail Adams  | Baron von Steuben  | Marquis de Lafayette  | Count Casimir Pulaski

Lesson 19: Colonial Tensions Mount 153

Name_____________ Date _________

COLONIAL HALL OF FAME

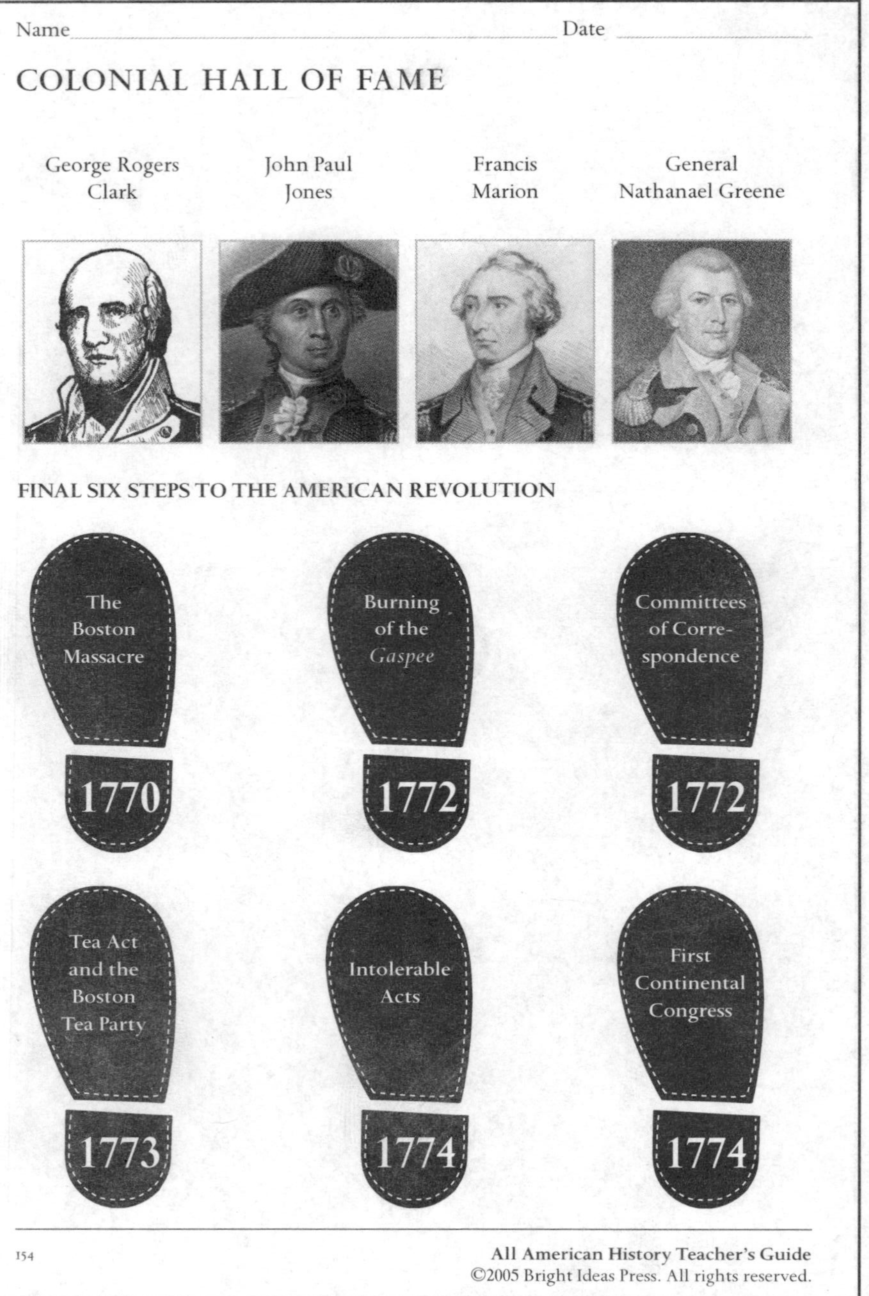

154 All American History Teacher's Guide

LESSON 19: FOR REVIEW

Write the corresponding letter of the correct answer in the space provided.

A. Boston Massacre
B. committees of correspondence
C. First Continental Congress
D. *Gaspee*
E. Intolerable Acts
F. Tea Act

B 1. Groups formed to relay messages about British violation of colonists' rights

D 2. British royal revenue ship burned by Rhode Island colonists

C 3. Assembly that convened in Philadelphia in 1774 to discuss the colonies' relationship with Great Britain

E 4. The closing of Boston Harbor to all shipping and the placing of Boston under martial law

A 5. Conflict between British soldiers and Boston men and boys that led to the death of five Americans

F 6. Permission given to the British East India Company to sell its tea below the price of tea smuggled in by the colonists from the Dutch

Write the missing word or words in the spaces provided.

1. Colonial assemblies held the power of **the purse** and often used this power to gain control over appointments and sometimes even to influence the governor himself.

2. The Sons of Liberty, led by **Sam Adams**, called the Americans killed in the Boston Massacre martyrs for the cause of liberty.

3. The engraving called *The Bloody Massacre Perpetrated in King Street* was produced by **Paul Revere** and was used as a propaganda tool to stir up anti-British sentiments among the colonists.

4. The British soldiers involved in the Boston Massacre were defended by Patriot lawyers Joshua Quincy and **John Adams**.

5. The British revenue ship named the *Gaspee* ran aground while chasing an American merchant ship suspected of **smuggling**.

6. The radical colonial leader Samuel Adams reached the height of his political influence while using the **committees of correspondence** to spread his opposition to the actions of the British government.

7. One of Boston's wealthiest merchants, **John Hancock**, was another Patriot leader instrumental in establishing the Boston committee of correspondence.

8. The most infamous event in the colonies protesting Parliament's tea law occurred in **Boston**.

9. One of the Intolerable Acts of 1774 closed the harbor of **Boston** to punish it for its defiance of the British Parliament.

10. The First Continental Congress adopted the Declaration and Resolves, a list of American rights and grievances to be sent to **King George III and Parliament**.

11. Before adjourning, the First Continental Congress established the **Continental Association**, which called for a pledge from all colonial heads of household to neither export to nor import goods from England.

12. The American Revolution evolved as a confrontation between a cranky "mother," who was **Britain** and a "disobedient child," who was **the American colonies**.

LESSON 19: FOR FURTHER STUDY

1. In 1768, British customs officials seized the *Liberty*, a sloop owned by a Boston merchant named John Hancock. Why did they seize this ship? Research the life of Hancock. How was he significant during the Revolutionary War period?

2. Crispus Attucks, a free black laborer, was one of the five Americans killed in the Boston Massacre. Although his life prior to death was shrouded in mystery, Attucks emerged as one of the most famous of all black men involved in the American Revolution. See what you can find out about the life of Crispus Attucks. Record the information on an African American form.

3. Samuel Adams's cousin, John Adams, became known as Old Sink or Swim. Find out what that expression meant and what role John Adams played in American history during the years leading up to the American Revolution. John Adams stated, "The Revolution was affected before the war commenced. The Revolution was in the minds and hearts of the people." Decide what you think he meant and whether or not you agree with him.

4. Patrick Henry gave a famous speech in the Virginia House of Burgesses on March 23, 1775. See if you can find a copy of that speech and read it. Do you recognize any of Henry's statements? What was Patrick Henry like and what was his involvement in colonial politics in the years leading up to the American Revolution? Describe his speaking style.

Name________________ Date ________

LESSON 20: WAR FOR INDEPENDENCE BEGINS

FIRST BATTLES OF THE AMERICAN REVOLUTION

Color the square blue if the battle was an American victory. Color the square red if the battle was a British victory, or write a *D* in the square if the battle was a draw. Write the name of the colony or geographical region in which the battle took place, and write the name(s) of important American and British leaders involved. ■ = blue (American) ■ = red (British)

■ **Lexington and Concord**

Location: **Massachusetts**

American leaders: **Captain John Parker**

British leaders: **General Thomas Gage**

■ **Ft. Ticonderoga**

Location: **New York**

American leaders: **Ethan Allen, Benedict Arnold**

British leaders: **N/A**

■ **Breed's Hill/Bunker Hill**

Location: **Massachusetts**

American leaders: **Col. William Prescott, Dr. Joseph Warren**

British leaders: **Generals Gage, Howe, Clinton, and Burgoyne**

■ **Quebec/Canada**

Location: **Canada**

American leaders: **General Richard Montgomery, Benedict Arnold, Captain Dan Morgan**

British leaders: **N/A**

MAP OF REVOLUTIONARY WAR BATTLESITES IN THIS REGION

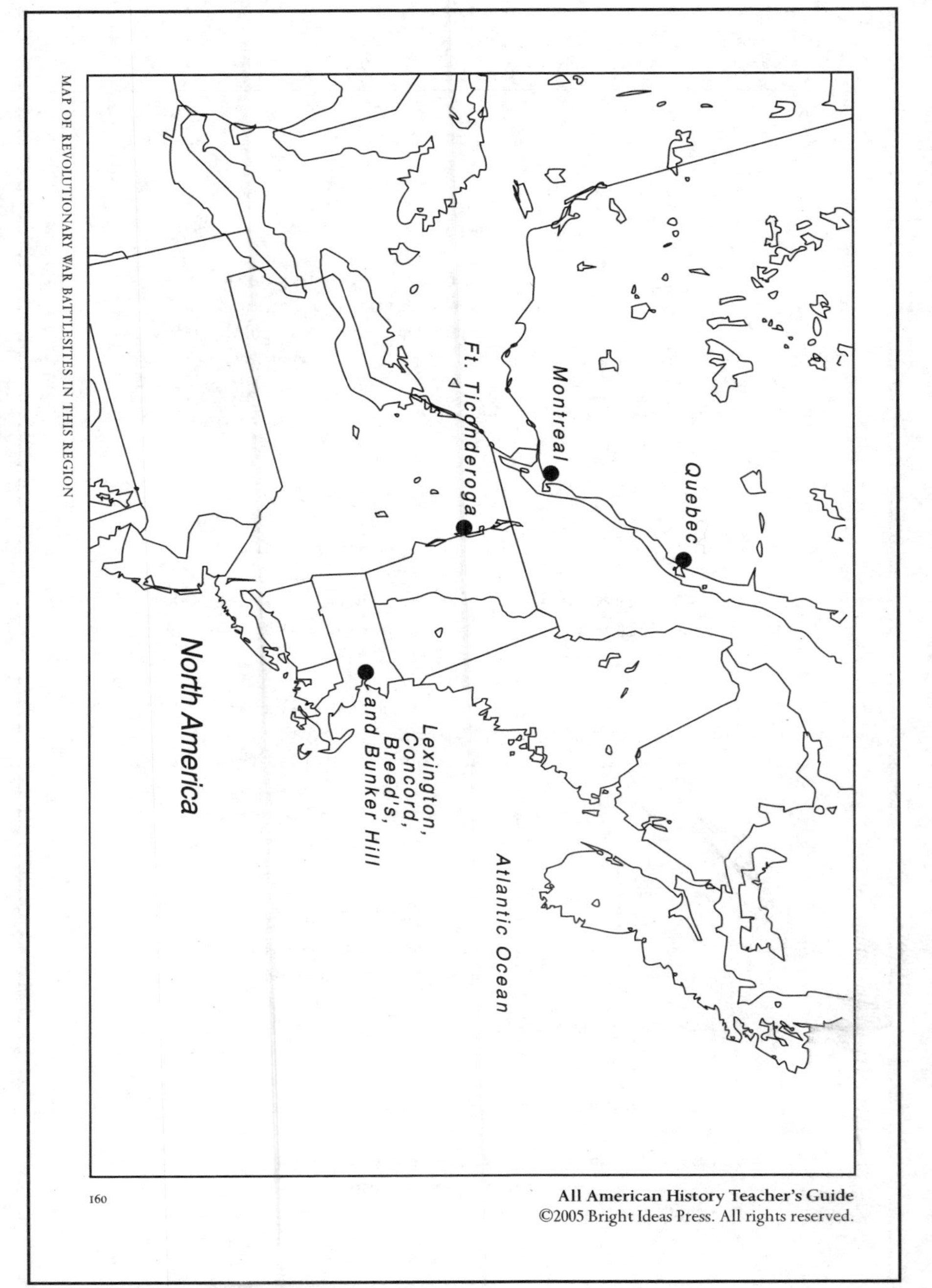

LESSON 20: FOR REVIEW

Write the letter of the correct answer in the space provided.

A 1. In the fall of 1774,
- A. the Massachusetts Committee of Public Safety established a network of spies
- B. the British were worried about the threat posed by colonial minutemen
- C. the colonists had not yet begun to stockpile arms and ammunition
- D. the Sons of Liberty experienced a decline in membership

C 2. Which of the following was NOT an advantage held by the British?
- A. a large, well-trained army
- B. the largest navy in the world
- C. bolder military leaders and their knowledge of a "wilderness strategy"
- D. a larger population base

B 3. British general Thomas Gage received secret orders from the British government in April 1775
- A. to leave Boston and sail to New York
- B. to destroy the colonists' military supplies and capture their leaders
- C. to march to Canada to subdue a French rebellion
- D. to return to Great Britain

B 4. Militia men in Lexington and Concord were roused from their beds the night of April 18, 1775, by the cry, "The British are coming!" The riders bearing this news were
- A. Sam Adams and John Hancock
- B. Paul Revere, William Dawes, and Samuel Prescott
- C. Thomas Gage and John Parker
- D. Joseph Warren, William Howe, and John Parker

C 5. At Lexington and Concord
- A. the colonial minutemen were not ready to fight the British
- B. more Americans were killed than British
- C. the colonists worked hard to move their ammunition to new hiding places
- D. the British and Americans never faced each other in open combat

A 6. The leaders of the American attack on Fort Ticonderoga were
- A. Ethan Allen and Benedict Arnold
- B. George Washington and John Parker
- C. Henry Knox and Benedict Arnold
- D. Joseph Warren and Sam Adams

D 7. The Battle of Fort Ticonderoga
- A. was a British victory
- B. was long and bloody
- C. led to a British invasion of the colonies from Canada
- D. took the British by surprise, making it possible for American forces to plan an invasion of Canada

B 8. In June 1775, a commander of the newly organized Continental Army was appointed by the Second Continental Congress. His name was
- A. John Hancock
- B. George Washington
- C. Sam Adams
- D. Benedict Arnold

A 9. In 1775, the Second Continental Congress sent the Olive Branch Petition to George III. This petition
- A. was the last attempt at reconciliation between the colonies and Britain
- B. called for colonial independence
- C. admitted mistakes made by the colonists
- D. accused the king of treason

D 10. When the Olive Branch Petition arrived in Britain, King George III
   A. burned it
   B. signed it
   C. referred it to Parliament
   D. refused even to consider it

C 11. Which of the following was NOT true of the British forces in Boston in May 1775?
   A. troop reinforcements had arrived from Britain
   B. three new generals had come from the mother country
   C. Gage had received orders to move his troops to New York
   D. plans were being made to fortify the nearby Charlestown peninsula

C 12. At the Battle of Breed's Hill
   A. the British were able to take the hill after one charge
   B. the Americans won a decisive victory
   C. British losses greatly outnumbered American losses
   D. the Americans learned that the British army was invincible

A 13. The two American leaders at the Battle of Quebec were
   A. Richard Montgomery and Benedict Arnold
   B. George Washington and Joseph Warren
   C. Henry Clinton and John Burgoyne
   D. William Howe and William Prescott

C 14. During the Battle of Quebec,
   A. the British were surprised by the double-pronged American invasion and were unable to defend the city
   B. Benedict Arnold led the American forces to a quick and decisive victory
   C. General Montgomery was killed within minutes
   D. Montgomery and Arnold were distinguished by their acts of bravery

C 15. As 1775 turned into 1776,
   A. the British Parliament seemed more open to conciliation
   B. British-appointed governors continued to rule the colonies
   C. the British king had hired thousands of Hessians to fight the colonists
   D. American ships were still trading freely

LESSON 20: FOR FURTHER STUDY

1. Find a copy of "The Midnight Ride of Paul Revere" by Henry Wadsworth Longfellow and "Concord Hymn" by Ralph Waldo Emerson. Read these poems. What new information did you gain from reading them?

2. Discover why Ethan Allen organized the Green Mountain Boys. Where did they get their name? What action did they take after the Revolution was over?

3. Dr. Joseph Warren became known as the martyr of Bunker Hill. Find out why he was called that and how he supported the Patriots' cause before his death.

4. Research Revolutionary War weapons, such as cannon, flintlock muskets, bayonets, and rifles. Find pictures of the weapons that you consider to be most interesting. Which one was the most commonly used weapon? What type of powder was used for the firearms of the period?

Name____________________ Date __________

LESSON 21: WAR IN THE NORTHEAST

List at least three significant events of 1776.

Publication of Thomas Paine's pamphlet *Common Sense*; British evacuation of Boston (after the arrival of the "train of artillery" from Ft. Ticonderoga); signing of the Declaration of Independence in July

FIGHTING CONTINUES

Color the square blue if the battle was an American victory. Color the square red if the battle was a British victory, or write a *D* in the square if the battle was a draw. Write the name(s) of important American and British leaders involved. ■ = blue (American) ■ = red (British)

■ **Battles in New York**

American leaders: **General George Washington**

British leaders: **General William Howe, General Henry Clinton, General Charles Cornwallis**

■ **Battles in New Jersey**

American leaders: **General George Washington**

British leaders: **General Charles Cornwallis**

Lesson 21: War in the Northeast and the Declaration of Independence 165

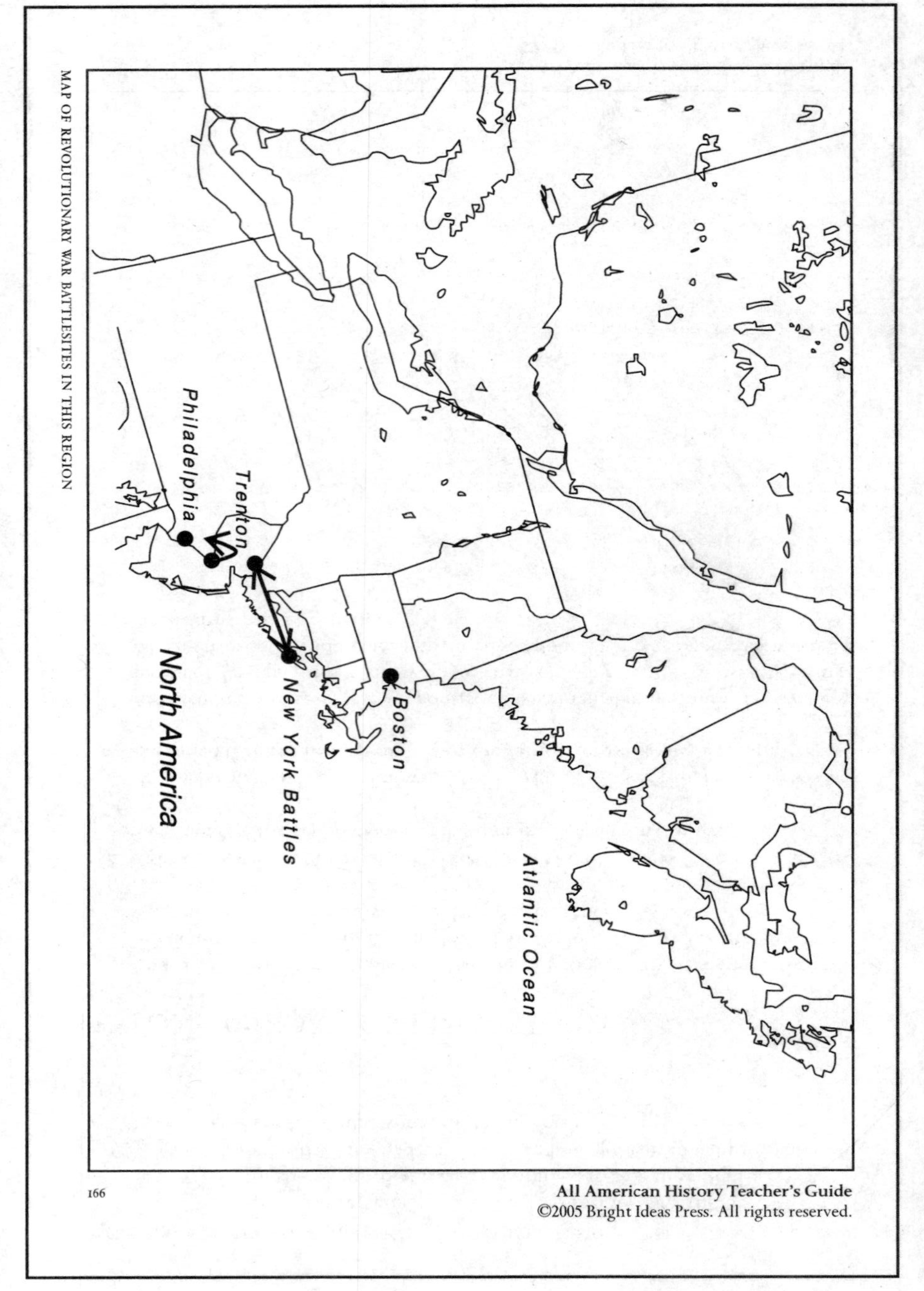

MAP OF REVOLUTIONARY WAR BATTLESITES IN THIS REGION

166 All American History Teacher's Guide

LESSON 21: FOR REVIEW

Write T for True and F for False in the space provided.

F 1. In *Common Sense*, Thomas Paine called upon the American colonists to give up their fight for independence.

T 2. Thomas Paine's pamphlet was written in language that common people could understand and provoked fiery debates among the American colonists.

F 3. Washington decided to keep his troops in Boston after Howe moved his forces to New York.

F 4. The entire Continental Congress worked together to write the resolution calling for American independence.

T 5. In all, forty-seven alterations were made to the Declaration of Independence before it was presented to the Continental Congress.

T 6. The final Declaration of Independence consisted of two parts—justification of the colonists' right to overthrow British rule and a list of colonial grievances against the British king.

F 7. Very few delegates in the Continental Congress were willing to sign the Declaration of Independence.

T 8. The Declaration of Independence made all-out war certain.

T 9. British forces in New York greatly outnumbered American forces.

F 10. A series of battles in Brooklyn, Manhattan, Long Island, Harlem, New York City, and White Plains were won by American forces under Washington.

T 11. By mid-November 1776, Washington and his men had retreated from New York and begun a grueling march through New Jersey.

F 12. General Howe refused to go into winter quarters in December, deciding to press after the Americans who had crossed into Pennsylvania.

Write the missing word or words in the spaces provided.

1. **Thomas Paine** was the author of *Common Sense*, a small volume that served to light the fire of the American Revolution.

2. **General Henry Knox** was responsible for bringing Fort Ticonderoga's artillery to the top of Dorchester Heights in Boston.

3. When the British evacuated their forces from Boston to Canada, they were ultimately bound for **New York**.

4. The first draft of the Declaration of Independence was written by **Thomas Jefferson**.

5. The three generals in charge of the British invasion of New York were generals **Howe**, **Clinton**, and **Cornwallis**.

LESSON 21: FOR FURTHER STUDY

1. Read more about Henry Knox. What roles did he play during the American Revolution and in the first years of our nation?

2. Investigate some of the inventions of Thomas Jefferson (storm windows, polygraph, dumbwaiter, weather vane) and Benjamin Franklin (battery, lightning rod, bifocals).

3. Find a copy of the Declaration of Independence at the National Archives. Read it and see if you can understand it. Look at the signatures. How many of the men's names do you recognize? How many copies of the Declaration written in Jefferson's hand exist today? Where are they located? What were the Dunlap Broadsides? Look

for a copy of John Trumbull's painting, *The Declaration of Independence*, which hangs in the Capitol Rotunda. Who do you recognize in this painting?

4. During the fighting in New York, General Washington sent Captain Nathan Hale behind British lines to gain information about British positions on Long Island. What happened to Hale? What famous saying is attributed to him?

Name ______ Date ______

LESSON 22: MORE WAR IN THE NORTHEAST

MUCH MILITARY ACTION

Color the square blue if the battle was an American victory. Color the square red if the battle was a British victory, or write a *D* in the square if the battle was a draw. Write the name of the colony or geographical region in which the battle took place, and write the name(s) of important American and British leaders involved. ■ = blue (American) ■ = red (British)

■ **Trenton**

Location: **New Jersey**

American leaders: **George Washington**

British leaders: **N/A**

■ **Princeton**

Location: **New Jersey**

American leaders: **General George Washington, General Hugh Mercer**

British leaders: **General Charles Cornwallis, Col. Charles Mawhood**

■ **Bennington**

Location: **Vermont**

American leaders: **Green Mountain Boys**

British leaders: **General John Burgoyne**

■ **Brandywine Creek**

Location: **Pennsylvania**

American leaders: **George Washington**

British leaders: **General William Howe**

■ **Germantown**

Location: **Pennsylvania**

American leaders: **General George Washington**

British leaders: **General William Howe**

■ **Saratoga**

Location: **New York**

American leaders: **General Horatio Gates, Major-General Benedict Arnold, Captain Dan Morgan**

British leaders: **General John Burgoyne**

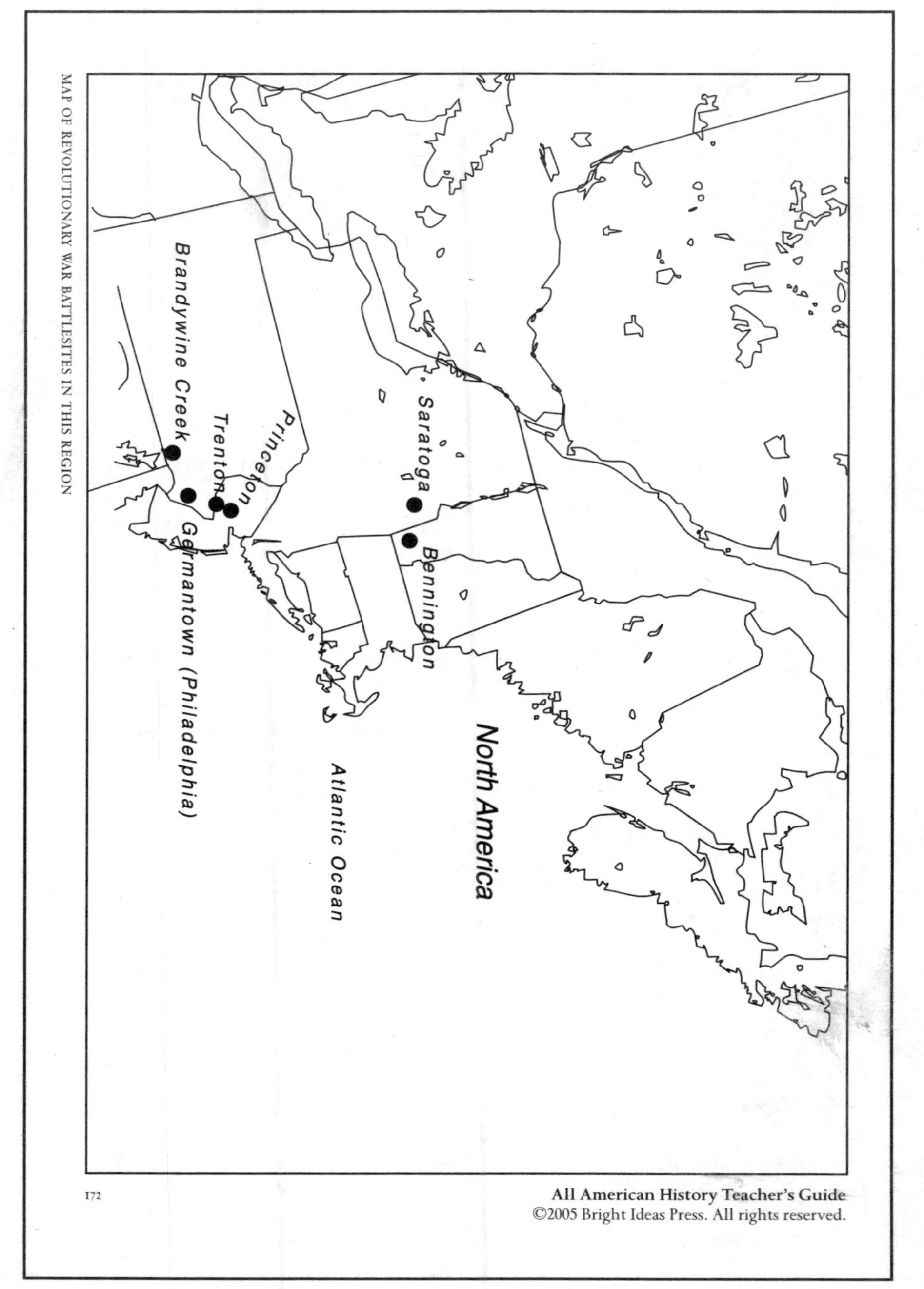

MAP OF REVOLUTIONARY WAR BATTLESITES IN THIS REGION

LESSON 22: FOR REVIEW

Write the missing word or words in the spaces provided.

1. British forces fighting in America during the Revolution included British regulars, **Hessian** mercenaries, **Loyalists**, and **Native Americans**.

2. Washington was interested in building an army of professional American soldiers, called **Continentals (regulars)**.

3. American forces during the Revolution often went without pay, **food**, and **proper clothing** because the Continental Congress had little money to fight the war.

4. On Christmas night, 1776, Washington and his troops crossed the ice-choked **Delaware** River during a sleet storm to surprise the Hessians on the other side.

5. After the battle of Princeton, the Americans moved into winter camp in 1776 – 77 in **Morristown**, New Jersey

6. In early 1777, the British decided to move to take control of **New York** in order to divide the colonies in half. Three British armies would be part of the invading forces.

7. On July 5,1777, the British general Burgoyne recaptured Fort **Ticonderoga**.

8. By the summer of 1777, General Howe had come to believe that the capture of **Philadelphia** was necessary to demoralize the Americans and ensure a final British victory.

9. The near victory of the Americans in the fall of 1777 at **Germantown** prevented General Howe from joining Burgoyne in New York. Instead, British forces occupied Philadelphia for the winter.

10. During the winter of 1777 – 1778, Washington and his men camped at **Valley Forge**.

11. The American victory at Saratoga persuaded **France** to join an alliance with the Americans.

12. On November 15, 1777, the Continental Congress adopted the **Articles of Confederation**, which were an attempt to establish a national government for the united colonies.

Write the corresponding letter of the correct answer in the space provided.

A. Bennington
B. Brandywine
C. Princeton
D. Saratoga
E. Trenton

__A__ 1. American victory that occurred when Vermont and New Hampshire men killed or took prisoner almost all of Burgoyne's troops

__D__ 2. American victory that was the turning point of the American Revolution

__E__ 3. American victory over drunken Hessian soldiers on Christmas Day, 1776

__B__ 4. British victory that led to British occupation of Philadelphia

__C__ 5. American victory when Washington surprised British reinforcements

LESSON 22: FOR FURTHER STUDY

1. In 1777, the Marquis de Lafayette arrived in Philadelphia. Research the life of Lafayette and the role he played in the American Revolution. Which American leader treated Lafayette like a son?

2. The Flag Act of 1777 called for the establishment of an official flag for the new American nation. Read about this flag's design. How was Betsy Ross involved?

3. Find out more about the life of Benedict Arnold, especially his military career. Why did he become disillusioned with the Patriot cause? What steps did he take to betray his country?

4. Look at a copy of the Articles of Confederation. How many articles did it have? What did Article I say that the name of the new Confederacy would be? According to Article II, what did each state retain? For what reason did the states enter into a "firm league of friendship with each other"? (Article III) Read more about the details of the government to be set up under the Articles.

Name______________ Date ______

LESSON 23: WAR IN THE SOUTH AND WEST

FIGHTING SHIFTS FROM THE NORTH

Color the square blue if the battle was an American victory. Color the square red if the battle was a British victory, or write a *D* in the square if the battle was a draw. Write the name of the colony or geographical region in which the battle took place, and write the name(s) of important American and British leaders involved. ■ = blue (American) ■ = red (British)

[D] **Monmouth Courthouse**

Location: **New Jersey**

American leaders: **General George Washington, General Charles Lee, Baron von Steuben**

British leaders: **General Henry Clinton**

■ **Savannah**

Location: **Georgia**

American leaders: **General Benjamin Lincoln, Count Casimir Pulaski**

British leaders: **N/A**

■ **Vincennes**

Location: **Indiana**

American leaders: **George Rogers Clark**

British leaders: **N/A**

Lesson 23: War in the South, in the West, and on the High Seas 177

MAP OF REVOLUTIONARY WAR BATTLESITES IN THIS REGION

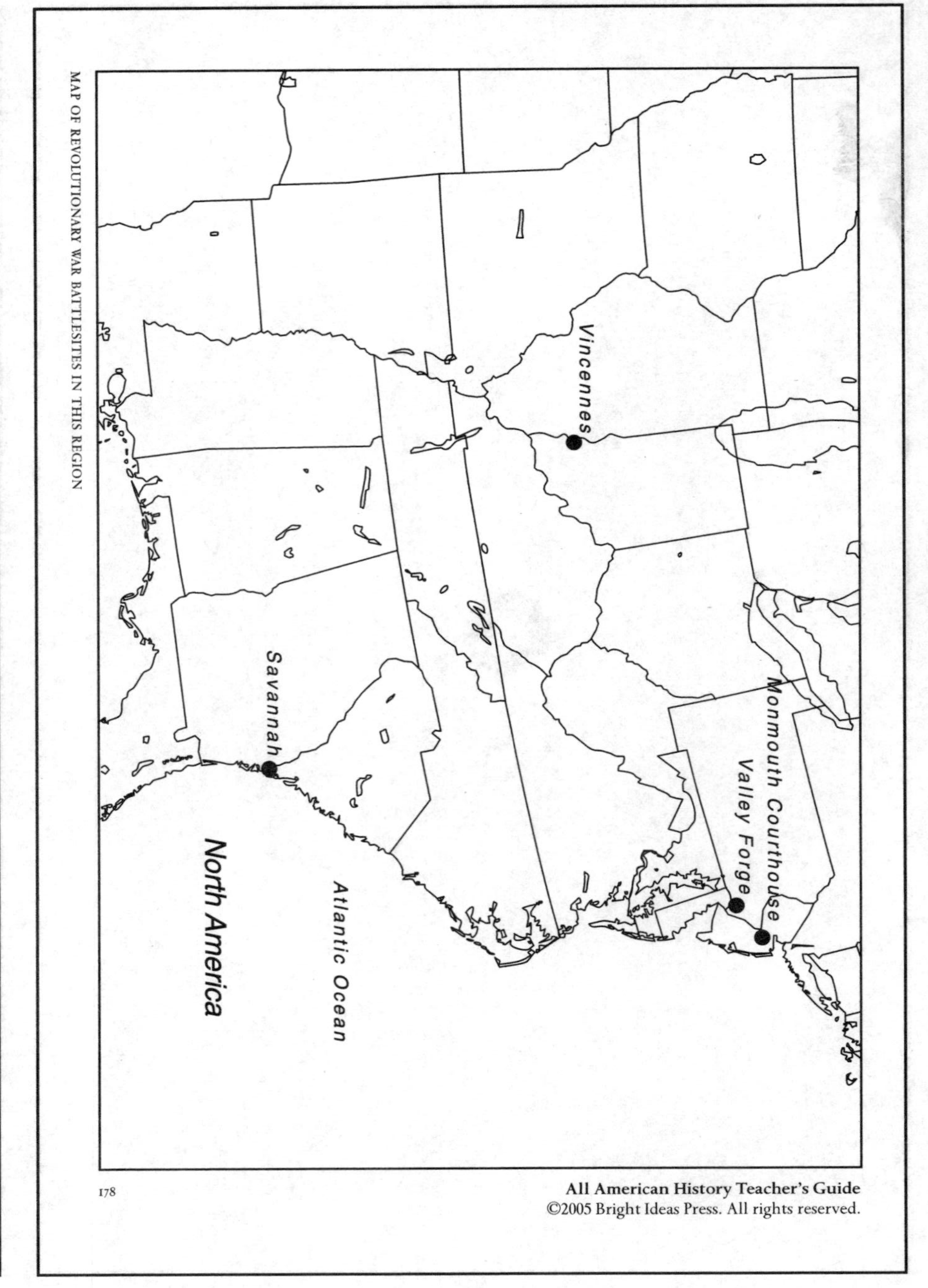

178

All American History Teacher's Guide

LESSON 23: FOR REVIEW

Write the letter of the correct answer in the space provided.

C 1. These people were known as the backbone of the American Revolution
   A. lawyers and merchants
   B. indentured servants
   C. artisans and small farmers
   D. planters

B 2. Which of the following did Patriot women NOT do during the Revolution?
   A. feed and care for the wounded
   B. serve in the Continental Congress
   C. run farms and businesses
   D. make cannonballs and gunpowder

A 3. The woman who fought in the American Revolution but disguised that she was a woman was
   A. Deborah Sampson
   B. Martha Washington
   C. Molly Pitcher
   D. Clara Barton

D 4. During the American Revolution,
   A. no African Americans fought on the Patriot side
   B. Africans were not willing to help the British, even in return for a promise of freedom
   C. most white Americans were eager for African Americans to be supplied with guns to help fight
   D. about five thousand African Americans fought on the side of the Patriots

B 5. Washington and his men spent the winter of 1777 – 1778 at
   A. Philadelphia
   B. Valley Forge
   C. Long Island
   D. Boston

D 6. During the Patriot army's time at Valley Forge, which of the following was NOT true?
   A. many of the men had no shoes
   B. about 1,200 huts were erected to house the men
   C. diseases like typhoid fever and dysentery took a deadly toll
   D. the soldiers decided to mutiny against Washington and his officers

D 7. The man responsible for teaching coordinated maneuvering and drilling to the American troops was
   A. the Marquis de Lafayette
   B. George Washington
   C. John Paul Jones
   D. Baron von Steuben

A 8. By June 1778,
   A. General Howe had resigned
   B. the British had decided to stay put in Philadelphia
   C. the French were no longer willing to send a fleet to America
   D. Washington and his troops had marched South

C 9. During the Battle of Monmouth Court House
   A. General Lee became known for his bravery
   B. the Americans won a decisive victory
   C. Von Steuben helped to prevent an American rout
   D. the fighting was hindered by ice and snow

B 10. The last major battle of the American Revolution in the North was the Battle of
   A. Saratoga
   B. Monmouth Court House
   C. Brandywine
   D. Savannah

C 11. The first stage of the British southern strategy was the capture of
- A. Charleston
- B. Wilmington
- C. Savannah
- D. Charlotte

B 12. The British decided to shift the focus of the war south in 1778. They made this decision because
- A. they had won so many decisive victories in the North
- B. they felt it would be easier to win in the South due to the large number of Loyalists there
- C. Washington and his troops had moved to the South
- D. General Howe preferred the warmer southern climate

D 13. The leader of the American expedition to take the Ohio River valley from the British and their Indian allies was
- A. Davy Crockett
- B. Daniel Boone
- C. John Paul Jones
- D. George Rogers Clark

A 14. An important British fortified fort in the West that fell to the Americans was
- A. Vincennes, Indiana
- B. Chicago, Illinois
- C. Cleveland, Ohio
- D. Louisville, Kentucky

A 15. The most famous American naval hero in the American Revolution was
- A. John Paul Jones
- B. Baron von Steuben
- C. Casimir Pulaski
- D. George Washington

LESSON 23: FOR FURTHER STUDY

1. Look for a famous painting of Baron von Steuben by Charles Wilson Peale. Find out who von Steuben met in Paris to offer the colonies his military services. What training techniques did he use? Why do you think that they were successful?
2. Read more about Count Casimir Pulaski. Why was he known as the Father of American Cavalry?
3. The world's first submarine attack was made by the American *Turtle* during the American Revolution. Read about its construction. Who designed the *Turtle* and how did it work? Did it succeed in its mission?
4. Can you find all the words to "Yankee Doodle"? Who wrote this song and when? Why was it surprising that the Americans "adopted" it?

Name______________________ Date __________

LESSON 24: DECISIVE SOUTHERN VICTORIES

FINAL BATTLE

Color the square blue if the battle was an American victory. Color the square red if the battle was a British victory, or write a *D* in the square if the battle was a draw. Write the name of the colony or geographical region in which the battle took place, and write the name(s) of important American and British leaders involved. ■ = blue (American) ■ = red (British)

■ **Charleston**

Location: **South Carolina**

American leaders: **Benjamin Lincoln**

British leaders: **General Henry Clinton, General Charles Corrnwallis**

■ **Camden**

Location: **South Carolina**

American leaders: **General Horatio Gates**

British leaders: **Charles Cornwallis**

■ **King's Mountain**

Location: **NC/SC border**

American leaders: **Major Patrick Ferguson**

British leaders: **N/A**

■ **Cowpens**

Location: **South Carolina**

American leaders: **Dan Morgan**

British leaders: **Banastre Tarleton**

D **Guilford Courthouse**

Location: **North Carolina**

American leaders: **General Nathanael Greene**

British leaders: **Charles Cornwallis**

■ **Yorktown**

Location: **Virginia**

American leaders: **General George Washington, Lafayette**

British leaders: **General Charles Cornwallis**

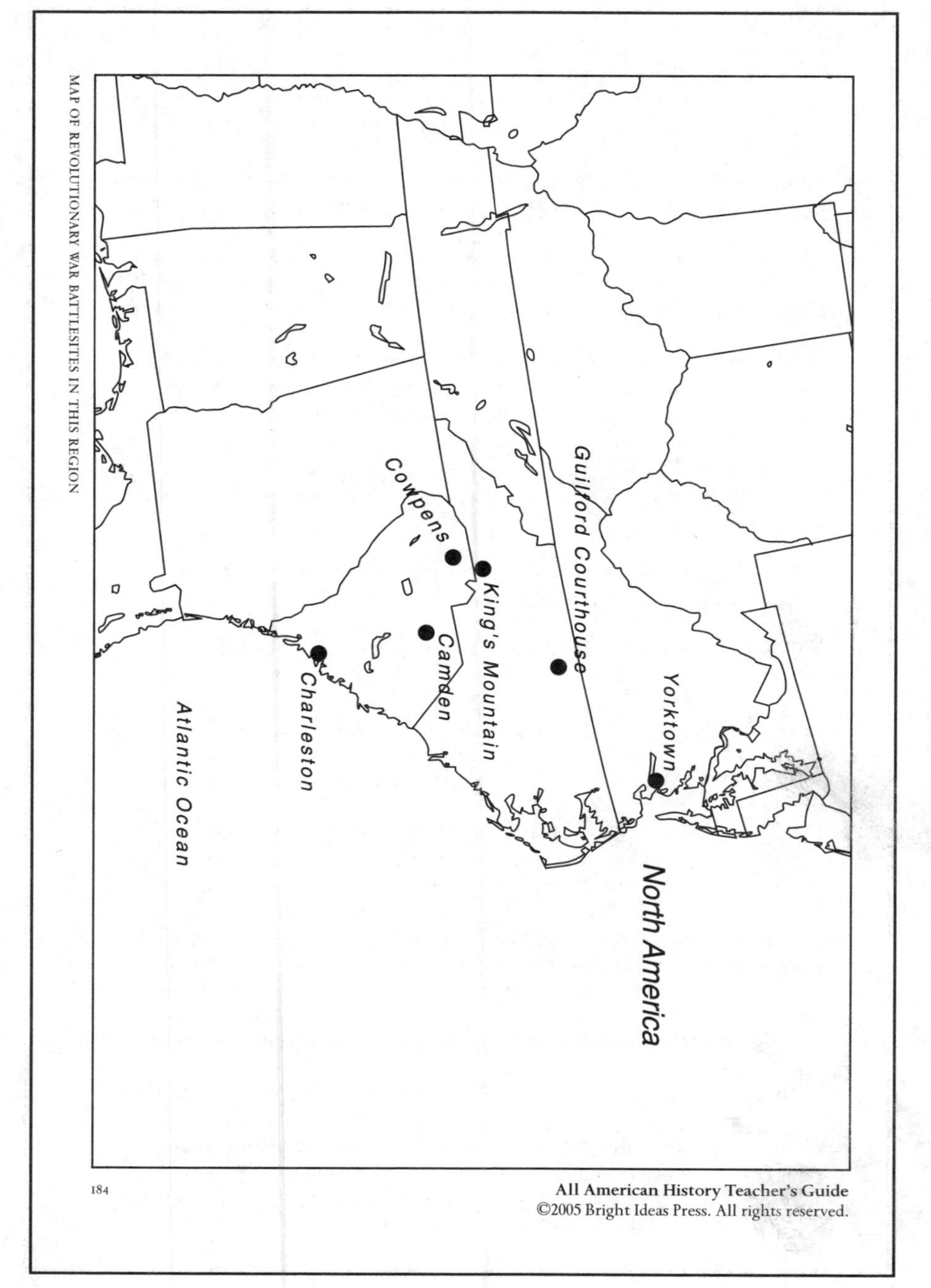

MAP OF REVOLUTIONARY WAR BATTLESITES IN THIS REGION

LESSON 24: FOR REVIEW

Write T for True and F for False in the space provided.

F 1. By 1778, neither the British nor the American forces were strong enough to continue major military operations in the North, but the advantage had shifted to the British there.

T 2. Because the Spanish had joined the French in an alliance with the Americans, Great Britain faced the possibility of a major European war in 1779.

T 3. The British believed that their conquest of the Southern colonies depended on the active participation of Southern Loyalists.

F 4. Savannah and Charleston did not fall quickly to the British.

T 5. Francis Marion, Thomas Sumter, and Andrew Pickens led guerilla bands of Patriots against the British troops and Loyalists in South Carolina.

T 6. The Patriots' defeat at Charleston represented the greatest loss of manpower and equipment of the war for the Americans.

T 7. After the fighting at Charleston ended, General Clinton placed General Cornwallis in charge of British forces in the South and returned to New York City.

F 8. The new Patriot commander, General Gates, led the American forces to a stunning victory at the Battle of Camden.

T 9. The Patriot victory at King's Mountain gave General Nathanael Greene time to reorganize and rebuild the American troops in the South.

F 10. General Cornwallis and his troops soundly defeated Daniel Morgan and his sharp-shooting riflemen at the Battle of Cowpens.

T 11. After suffering heavy casualties in the Carolinas, Cornwallis marched his forces to Virginia.

F 12. Soon after Cornwallis arrived at Yorktown, he received the reinforcements and supplies from New York promised by General Clinton.

F 13. The French fleet never arrived for the Battle of Yorktown.

T 14. Although the British surrendered in October 1781, the peace treaty ending the war was not signed in Paris until September 1783.

Write the corresponding letter of the correct answer in the space provided.

A. Camden
B. Charleston
C. Cowpens
D. Guilford Courthouse
E. King's Mountain
F. Yorktown

B 1. British victory in which almost the entire southern Patriot army surrendered

C 2. American victory in a cattle-grazing area in South Carolina

F 3. Last major battle of the Revolution

A 4. British victory in which many American militiamen panicked and fled without firing a shot

D 5. A bloody battle in North Carolina in which there was no clear winner

E 6. American victory in which a primarily Loyalist force was surrounded and captured just inside the South Carolina border

LESSON 24: FOR FURTHER STUDY

1. In order to finance the Revolution, the Continental Congress began issuing paper currency known as Continental dollars. Find out what the phrase "not worth a continental" meant. How did the Congress raise enough money to wage the war?

2. Read more about the Loyalists (sometimes called the Tories) during the American Revolution. In which colonies was the Loyalist presence strongest? Who tended to be Loyalists? What happened to confiscated Loyalist property after the war was over?

3. See if you can find paintings done by American artists during the American Revolution. Some of the most famous artists included Gilbert Stuart, Charles

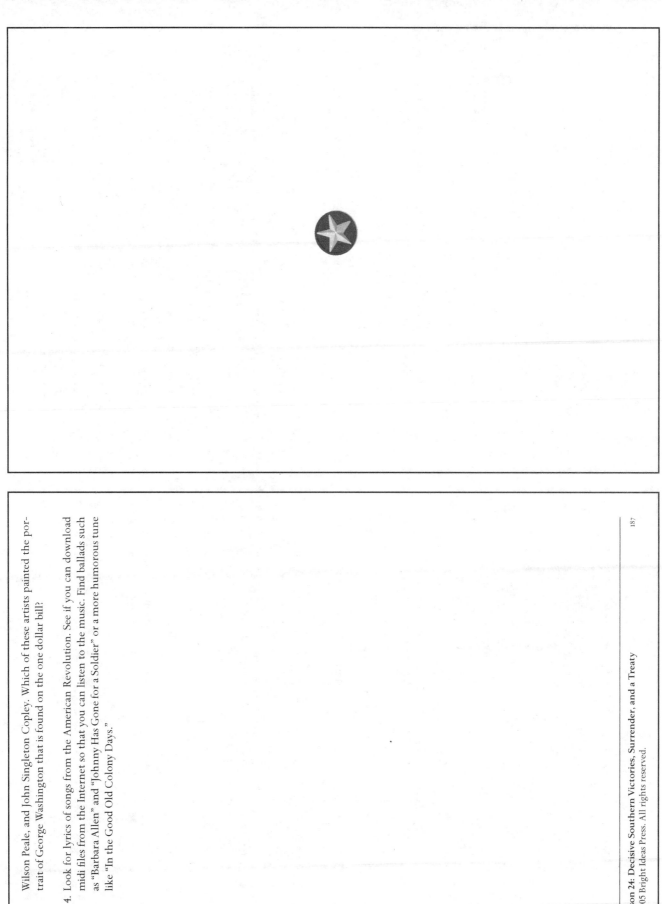

Wilson Peale, and John Singleton Copley. Which of these artists painted the portrait of George Washington that is found on the one dollar bill?

4. Look for lyrics of songs from the American Revolution. See if you can download midi files from the Internet so that you can listen to the music. Find ballads such as "Barbara Allen" and "Johnny Has Gone for a Soldier" or a more humorous tune like "In the Good Old Colony Days."

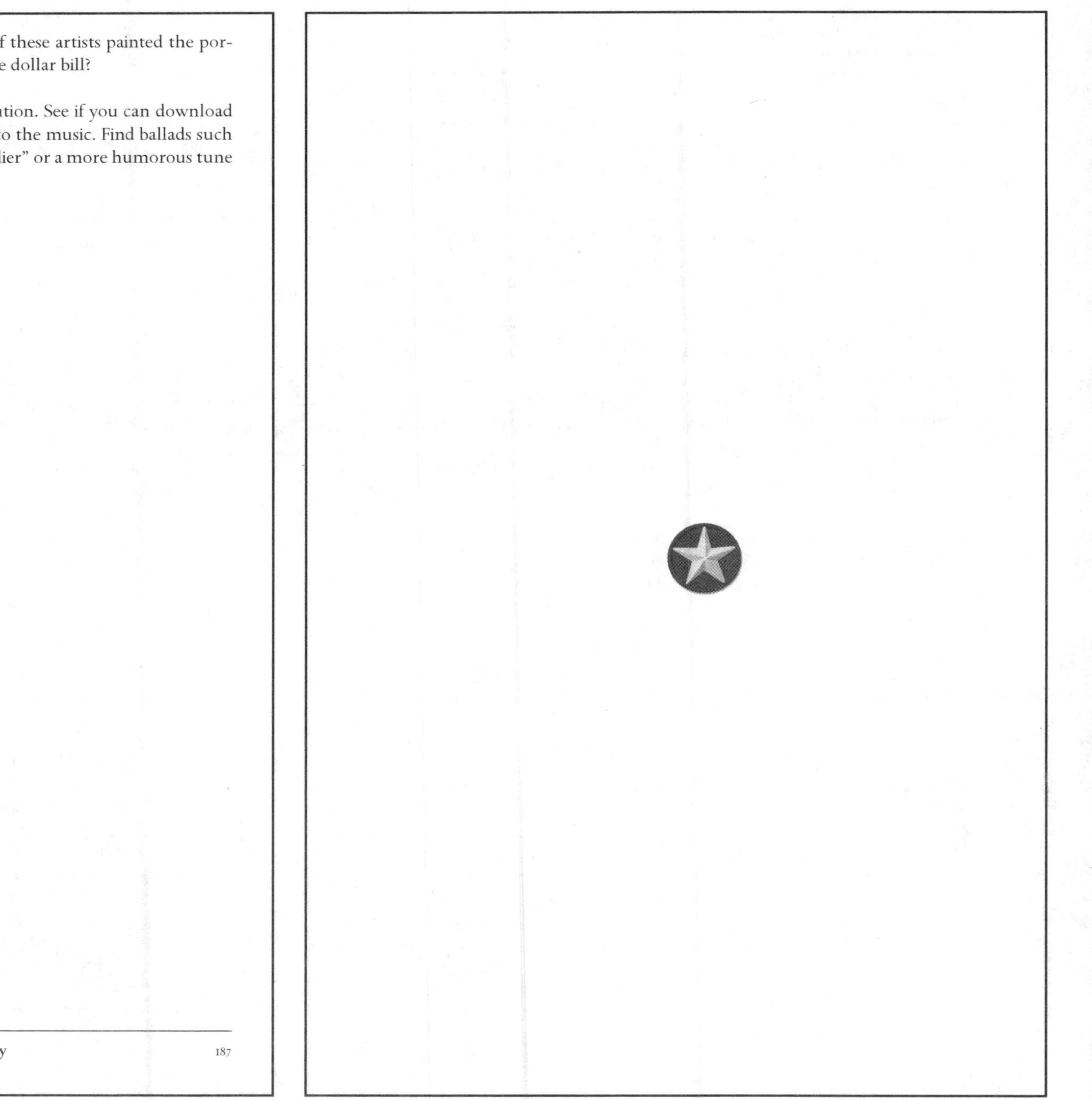

UNIT 3: FINAL REVIEW

Write the corresponding letter of the correct answer in the space provided.

A. Abigail Adams
B. John Adams
C. Sam Adams
D. Ethan Allen
E. George Rogers Clark
F. Benjamin Franklin
G. Nathanael Greene
H. John Hancock
I. Patrick Henry
J. Henry Knox
K. Marquis de Lafayette
L. Thomas Jefferson
M. John Paul Jones
N. Francis Marion
O. Mary Hays McCauly
P. Thomas Paine
Q. Paul Revere
R. Deborah Sampson
S. Baron von Steuben
T. George Washington
U. Martha Washington

H 1. Wealthy Boston merchant who was instrumental in establishing the committees of correspondence and served as president of the Continental Congress

R 2. Woman who disguised herself as a man to fight for the Patriot cause

K 3. French aristocrat who served with the American forces and became like a son to George Washington

P 4. Author of *Common Sense*, a small volume that served to light the fire of the American Revolution

A 5. One of her husband's most trusted advisors and the writer of hundreds of letters to him while he served in the Continental Congress and then as an American ambassador abroad

Q 6. Boston silversmith who did a popular engraving of the Boston Massacre and another of three horsemen who delivered the news that the British were coming to Lexington and Concord

F 7. Pennsylvania newspaper editor and inventor who served on the committee that wrote the Declaration of Independence and served as a diplomat in France

T 8. Unanimously selected by the Continental Congress to serve as commander of the Continental army

A. Abigail Adams
B. John Adams
C. Sam Adams
D. Ethan Allen
E. George Rogers Clark
F. Benjamin Franklin
G. Nathanael Greene
H. John Hancock
I. Patrick Henry
J. Henry Knox
K. Marquis de Lafayette
L. Thomas Jefferson
M. John Paul Jones
N. Francis Marion
O. Mary Hays McCauly
P. Thomas Paine
Q. Paul Revere
R. Deborah Sampson
S. Baron von Steuben
T. George Washington
U. Martha Washington

D 9. Leader of the Vermont Green Mountain Boys at Fort Ticonderoga

C 10. Boston agitator and leader of the Sons of Liberty

U 11. Wife who traveled to stay with her husband while the Continental forces were in winter quarters at Cambridge, Morristown, and Valley Forge

M 12. Most famous American naval hero of the Revolution

L 13. Author of the first draft of the Declaration of Independence

J 14. General responsible for bringing the cannon from Fort Ticonderoga to Boston

O 15. Woman who carried water in a pitcher to her husband and his fellow artillery gunners at Monmouth

E 16. "George Washington of the West" who led the American expedition to take the Ohio River valley from the British and their Indian allies

B 17. Patriot lawyer who defended the British soldiers arrested for murdering Americans in the Boston Massacre

N 18. South Carolina guerilla leader known as the Swamp Fox

G 19. American commander in the South who was successful in chasing Cornwallis out of the Carolinas

S 20. Prussian drillmaster who worked with the troops at Valley Forge

I 21. Virginia orator who gave a famous speech against the Stamp Act in the House of Burgesses

Write the corresponding letter of the correct answer in the space provided.

A. Brandywine Creek
B. Breed's Hill
C. Camden
D. Charleston
E. Cowpens
F. Fort Ticonderoga
G. Guilford Courthouse
H. King's Mountain
I. Lexington and Concord
J. Monmouth Courthouse
K. Princeton
L. Quebec
M. Saratoga
N. Trenton
O. White Plains / Brooklyn / Harlem / Manhattan
P. Yorktown

E 1. American victory in a cow-grazing area in South Carolina won by Dan Morgan and his sharp-shooting riflemen

A 2. British victory that led to the British occupation of Philadelphia

I 3. Place where the first shots of the American Revolution were fired

G 4. Bloody battle in North Carolina in which there was no clear winner

M 5. American victory that was the turning point of the Revolution

J 6. Longest and hottest battle of the Revolution; the last major battle in the North

L 7. Unsuccessful American attempt at an invasion of Canada

O 8. British victory that forced Washington's army to retreat into New Jersey

C 9. British victory in the South that led to the departure of General Gates

B 10. Technically a British victory but became a rallying point for American resistance early in the Revolution

N 11. American victory over drunken Hessian soldiers on Christmas Day 1776

P 12. Last major battle of the Revolution

K 13. Second consecutive American victory that encouraged the French to release supplies to the American war effort and boosted sagging American morale

A. Brandywine Creek
B. Breed's Hill
C. Camden
D. Charleston
E. Cowpens
F. Fort Ticonderoga
G. Guilford Courthouse
H. King's Mountain
I. Lexington and Concord
J. Monmouth Courthouse
K. Princeton
L. Quebec
M. Saratoga
N. Trenton
O. White Plains / Brooklyn / Harlem / Manhattan
P. Yorktown

H 14. American victory in which a primarily Loyalist force was surrounded and captured just inside the South Carolina border

F 15. American capture of a British stockpile of artillery, which forestalled a planned British invasion of Canada

D 16. American defeat that represented the greatest loss of manpower and equipment of the Revolution for the Patriots

Name_______________________ Date ___________

LESSONS 25 — 28: STATES AND THEIR CAPITALS

Order Added	State Name	Capital City
1.	Delaware	Dover
2.	Pennsylvania	Harrisburg
3.	New Jersey	Trenton
4.	Georgia	Atlanta
5.	Connecticut	Hartford
6.	Massachusetts	Boston
7.	Maryland	Annapolis
8.	South Carolina	Columbia
9.	New Hampshire	Concord
10.	Virginia	Richmond
11.	New York	Albany
12.	North Carolina	Raleigh
13.	Rhode Island	Providence
14.	Vermont	Montpelier
15.	Kentucky	Frankfort
16.	Tennessee	Nashville
17.	Ohio	Columbus
18.	Louisiana	Baton Rogue
19.	Indiana	Indianapolis
20.	Mississippi	Jackson
21.	ILLINOIS	Springfield
22.	Alabama	Montgomery
23.	Maine	Augusta
24.	Missouri	Jefferson City
25.	Arkansas	Little Rock
26.	Michigan	Lansing
27.	Florida	Tallahassee
28.	Texas	Austin
29.	Iowa	Des Moines
30.	Wisconsin	Madison

MAP OF STATES IN THE ORDER ADDED TO THE UNION

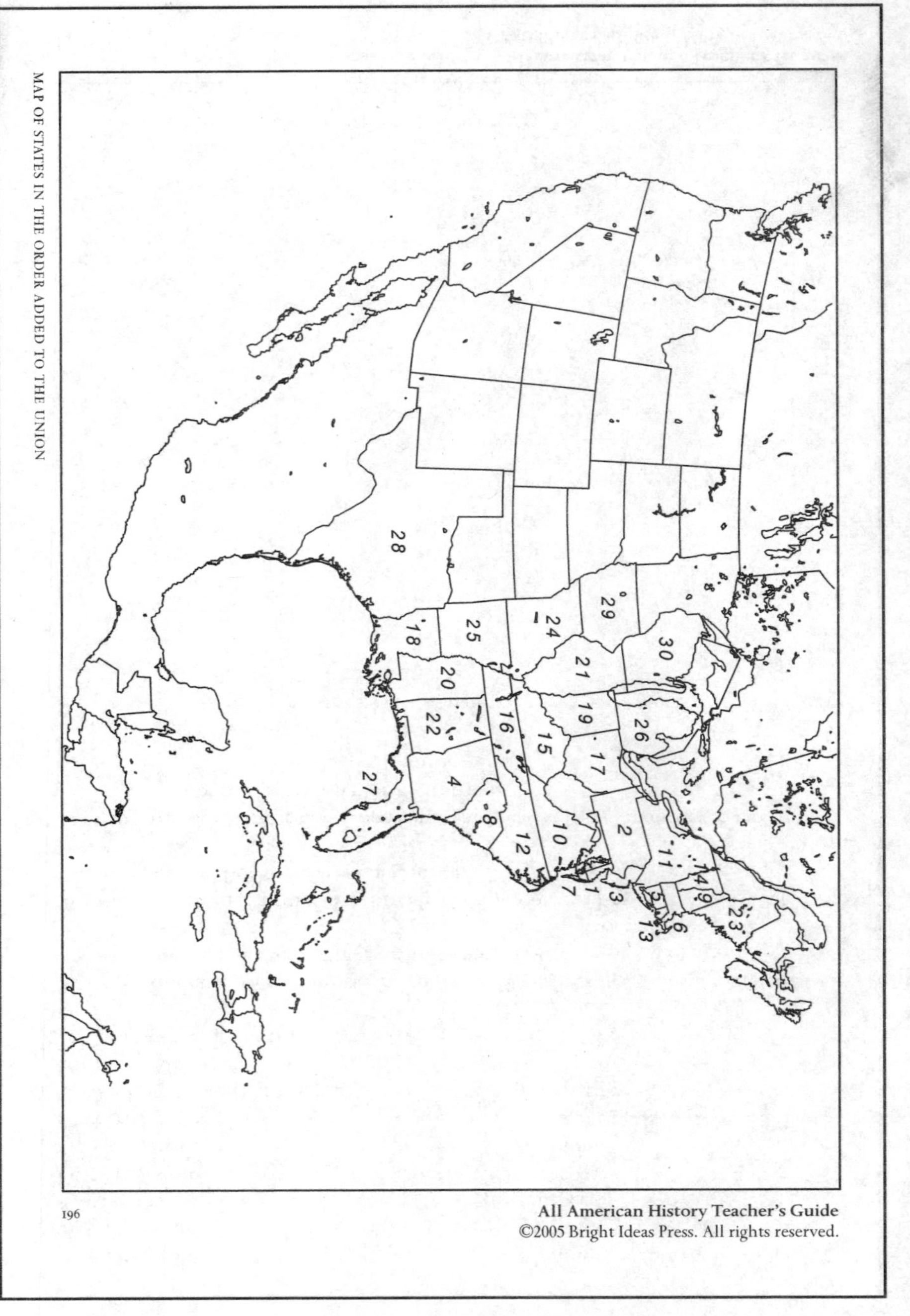

LESSON 25: FOR REVIEW

Write T for True and F for False in the space provided.

F 1. From 1790 – 1848 the new American nation was spared the difficulties of warfare and financial crisis.

F 2. The boundaries of the United States did not change until 1840.

F 3. During the first fifty years of U.S. government, no political parties existed.

F 4. All of America's early leaders favored the development of a strong national government and advocated strict interpretation of the nation's constitution.

T 5. The American colonies were deeply in debt after the Revolution.

T 6. Congress had no power under the Articles of Confederation to tax or regulate interstate commerce.

F 7. From 1783 to 1789, the American colonies worked together to establish a strong central government and gained the respect of other world nations.

F 8. The Continental Congress discouraged the new American states from writing state constitutions.

T 9. Maryland and Virginia called the Mount Vernon Conference to discuss their trade differences.

F 10. All thirteen states sent delegates to the Annapolis Conference, which developed a very specific set of national trade regulations.

T 11. At the urging of James Madison and Alexander Hamilton, the delegates at the Annapolis Conference issued a call for a convention in Philadelphia in 1787.

T 12. A rebellion of Massachusetts farmers and workers led by Daniel Shays attempted to seize control of a federal arsenal in Springfield.

T 13. The Constitutional Convention met in Philadelphia from May until September 1787.

T 14. The delegates at the Constitutional Convention were well-educated members of American's upper and middle classes. Many of them had previous experience in American government.

F 15. George Washington has become known as the Father of the Constitution.

F 16. Jefferson was supportive of the convention's vote to keep all of its proceedings secret.

T 17. The Great Compromise resolved the controversy concerning the representation of the states in the national legislative branch.

F 18. The Constitutional Convention refused to allow slaves to be counted when determining the number of a state's legislative representatives.

T 19. Federalists were American leaders who supported the United States Constitution and worked to get it ratified.

T 20. By 1790, all thirteen states had ratified the U.S. Constitution.

LESSON 25: FOR FURTHER STUDY

1. Read more about Mount Vernon, George Washington's home. Take a virtual tour of the mansion and its grounds online.

2. Obtain a copy of the United States Constitution. Hold on to it because it will be useful throughout the remainder of your study of U.S. history. How many articles are in the Constitution and what is the subject of each article? In which articles do you think the Great Compromise and Three-Fifths Compromise are located? How many times has the Constitution been amended?

3. Choose a delegate from the Constitutional Convention and learn more about his life and role at the Convention. In addition to Washington, Madison, and Franklin, some of the other well-known delegates include Roger Sherman, John Dickinson, Elbridge Gerry, Alexander Hamilton, and Gouverneur Morris, and George Mason.

4. Take a virtual tour of the historic district of Philadelphia (if you can't visit in person). Visit one or more of the following: Independence National Historic Park (Independence Hall, Old City Hall, and Congress Hall), the Liberty Bell Center, and the Betsy Ross House.

Name ________ Date ________

LESSON 26: GEORGE WASHINGTON

Picture of the president

Year born **1732**

Year died **1799**

In which state was he born? **Virginia**

What jobs did he hold before becoming president? **Commander-in-chief of the Continental Army during American Revolution**

With what political party was this president affiliated? **Federalist**

Vice President: **John Adams**

What were the years of his presidency? **1789 – 1797**

List some significant developments during his administration

Establishment of Federal City, Organization of president's cabinet, Establishment of national judiciary, Adoption of Bill of Rights and eleventh Amendment, 1793 Proclamation of Neutrality, Jay Treaty, Whiskey Rebellion, Hamilton's debt-assumption program and national bank, Farewell Address

STATES ADDED TO THE UNION DURING THIS PRESIDENT'S TERM(S)

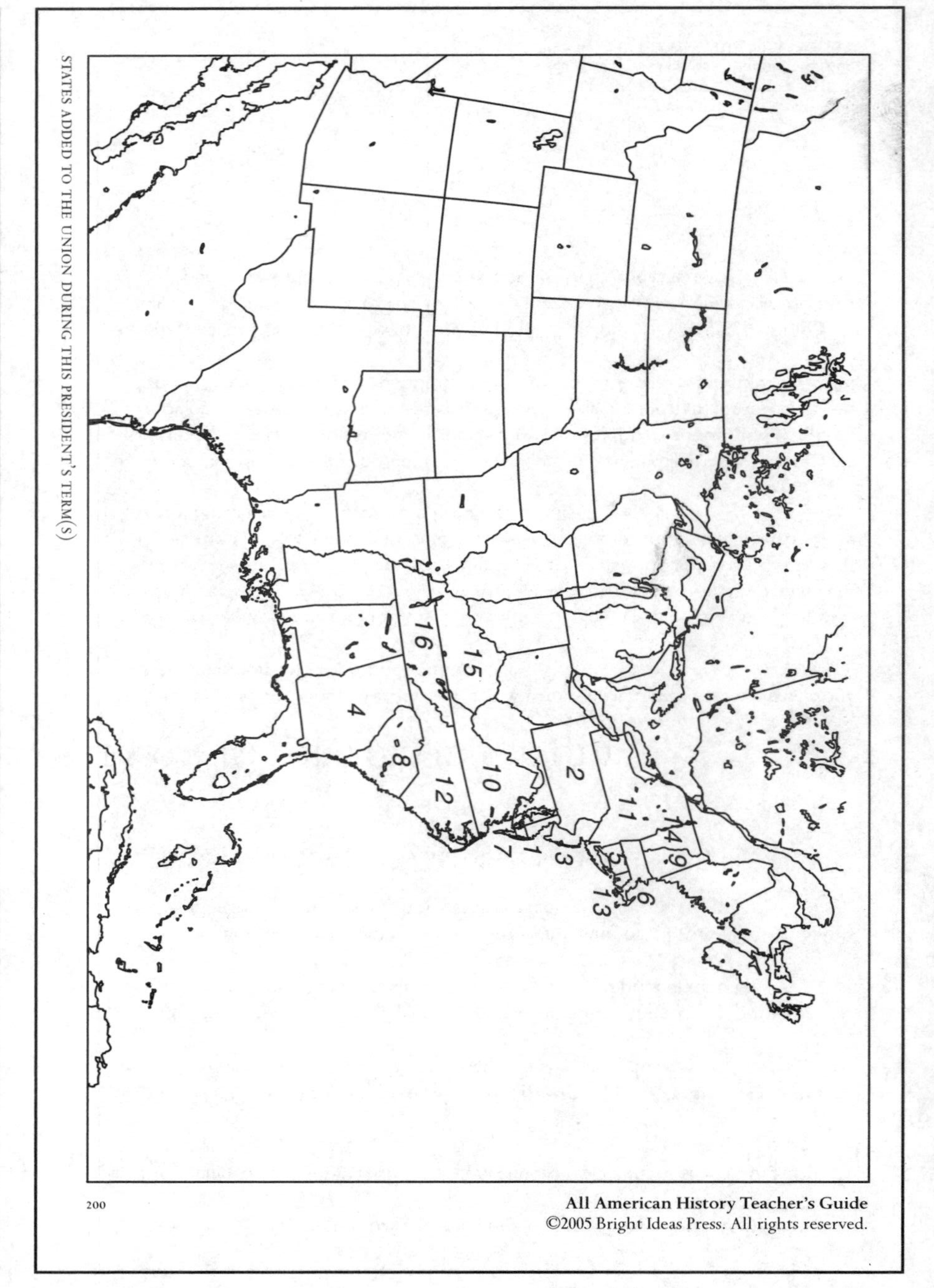

Name ______________________ Date ______________

LESSON 26: JOHN ADAMS

Picture of the president

Year born **1735**

Year died **1826**

In which state was he born? **Massachusetts**

What jobs did he hold before becoming president? **U.S. diplomat to Europe, Vice-President**

With what political party was this president affiliated? **Federalist**

Vice President: **Thomas Jefferson**

What were the years of his presidency? **1797 – 1801**

List some significant developments during his administration

New treaty with France

Alien and Sedition Acts; Kentucky and Virginia Resolutions

Appointment of Federalist John Marshall as chief justice of Supreme Court

Judiciary Act of 1801; midnight court appointments

STATES ADDED TO THE UNION DURING THIS PRESIDENT'S TERM(S)

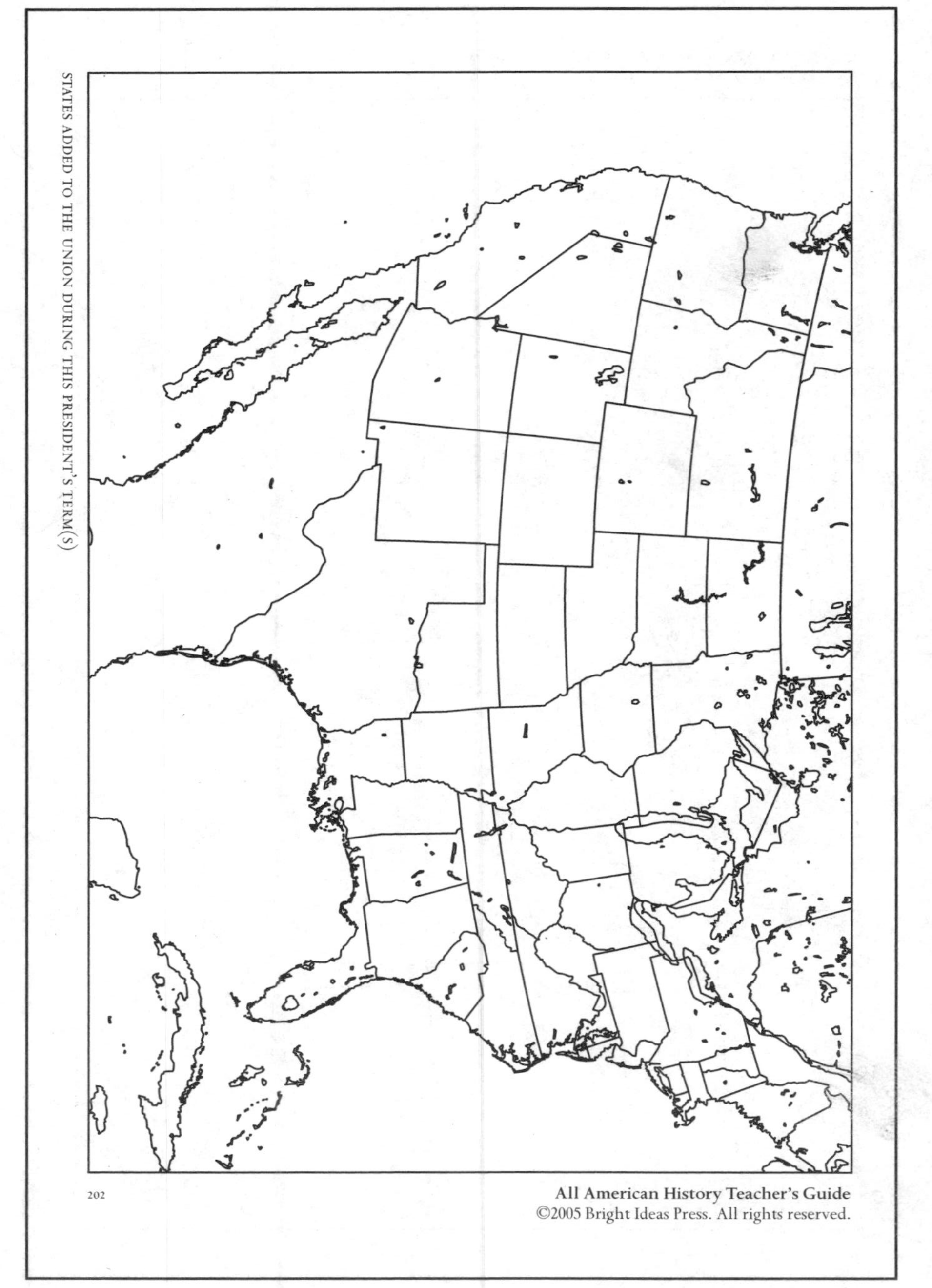

Name ______ Date ______

LESSON 26: THOMAS JEFFERSON

Picture of the president

Year born 1743

Year died 1826

In which state was he born? Virginia

What jobs did he hold before becoming president? **Diplomat to Europe, Secretary of State, Vice-President**

With what political party was this president affiliated? **Democratic-Republican**

Vice President: **Aaron Burr, George Clinton**

What were the years of his presidency? **1801 – 1809**

List some significant developments during his administration

Marbury v. Madison **(right of judicial review)**

Repeal of 1801 Judiciary Act

Twelfth Amendment

Louisiana Purchase; Lewis and Clark expedition

Naval War with Tripoli

Embargo Act; repeal of Embargo Act

STATES ADDED TO THE UNION DURING THIS PRESIDENT'S TERM(S)

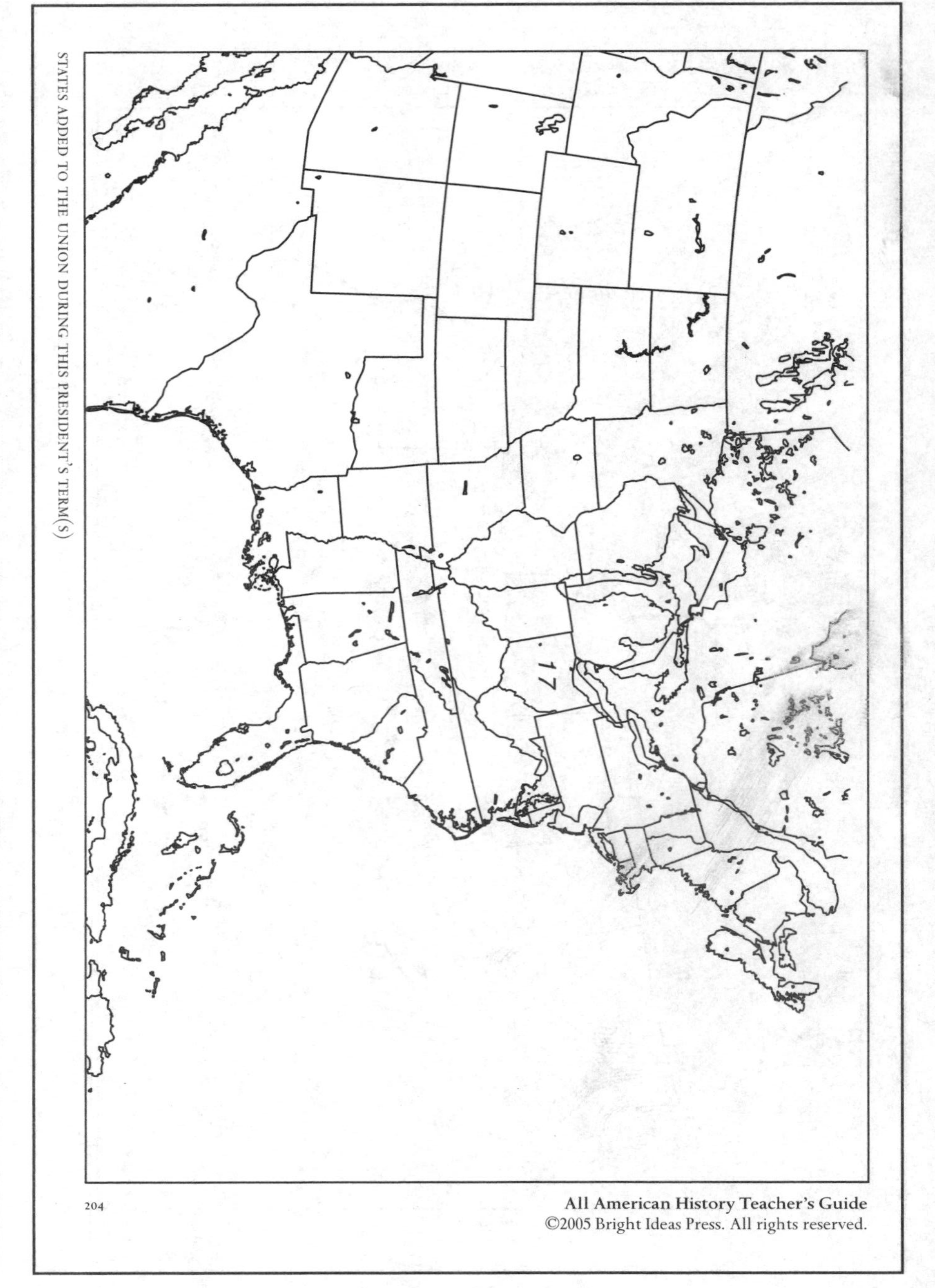

Name ________________ Date ________

LESSON 26: JAMES MADISON

Picture of the president

Year born **1751**

Year died **1836**

In which state was he born? **Virginia**

What jobs did he hold before becoming president? **Secretary of State**

With what political party was this president affiliated? **Democratic-Republican**

Vice President: **George Clinton, Elbridge Gerry**

What were the years of his presidency? **1809 – 1817**

List some significant developments during his administration

War of 1812

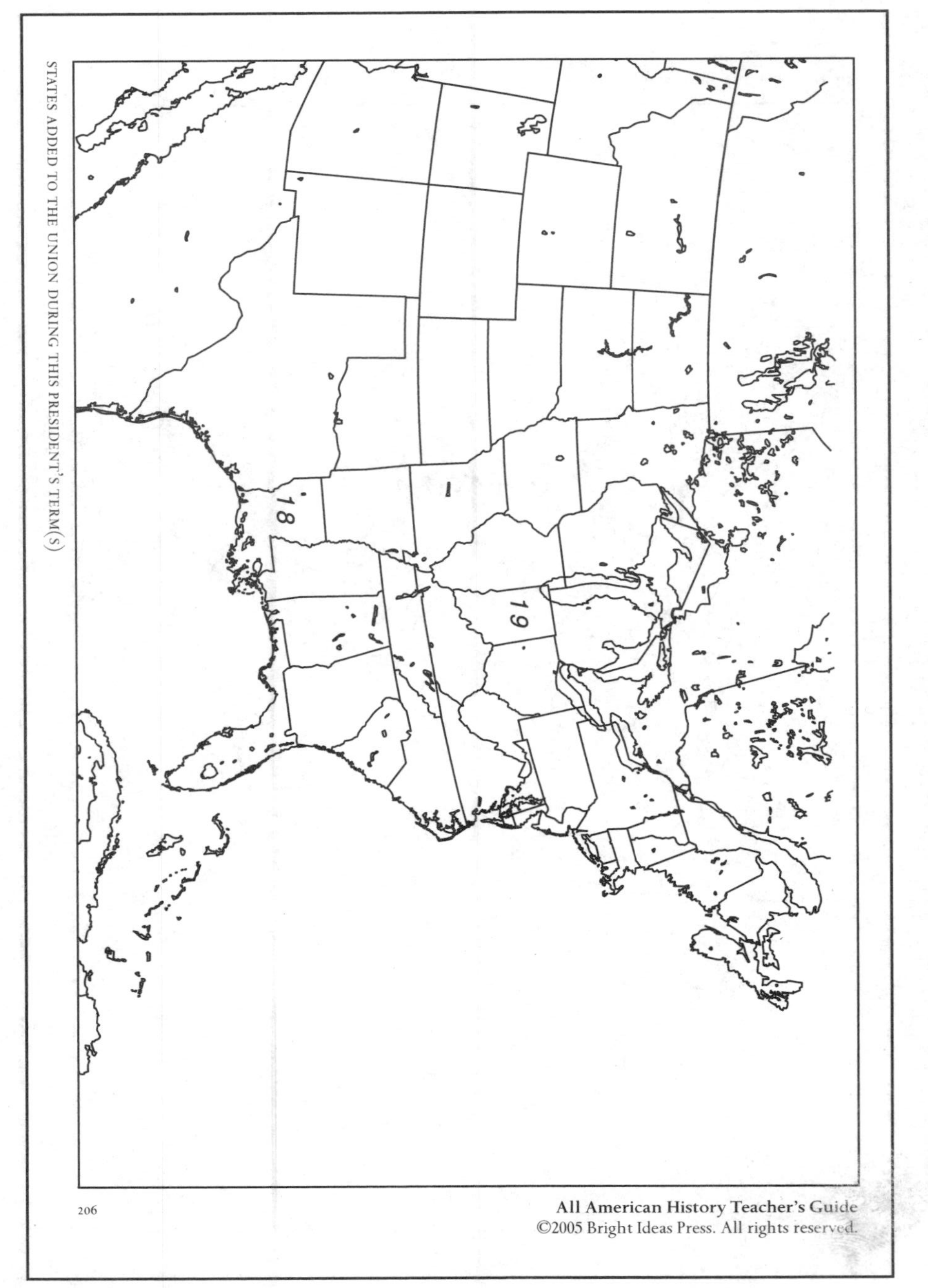

STATES ADDED TO THE UNION DURING THIS PRESIDENT'S TERM(S)

Name ______ Date ______

LESSON 26: JAMES MONROE

Picture of the president

Year born **1758**

Year died **1831**

In which state was he born? **Virginia**

What jobs did he hold before becoming president? **Diplomat to Europe, Secretary of State**

With what political party was this president affiliated? **Democratic-Republican**

Vice President: **Daniel Thompkins**

What were the years of his presidency? **1817 – 1825**

List some significant developments during his administration

Rush-Bagot Treaty

Adams-Onis Treaty

Monroe Doctrine

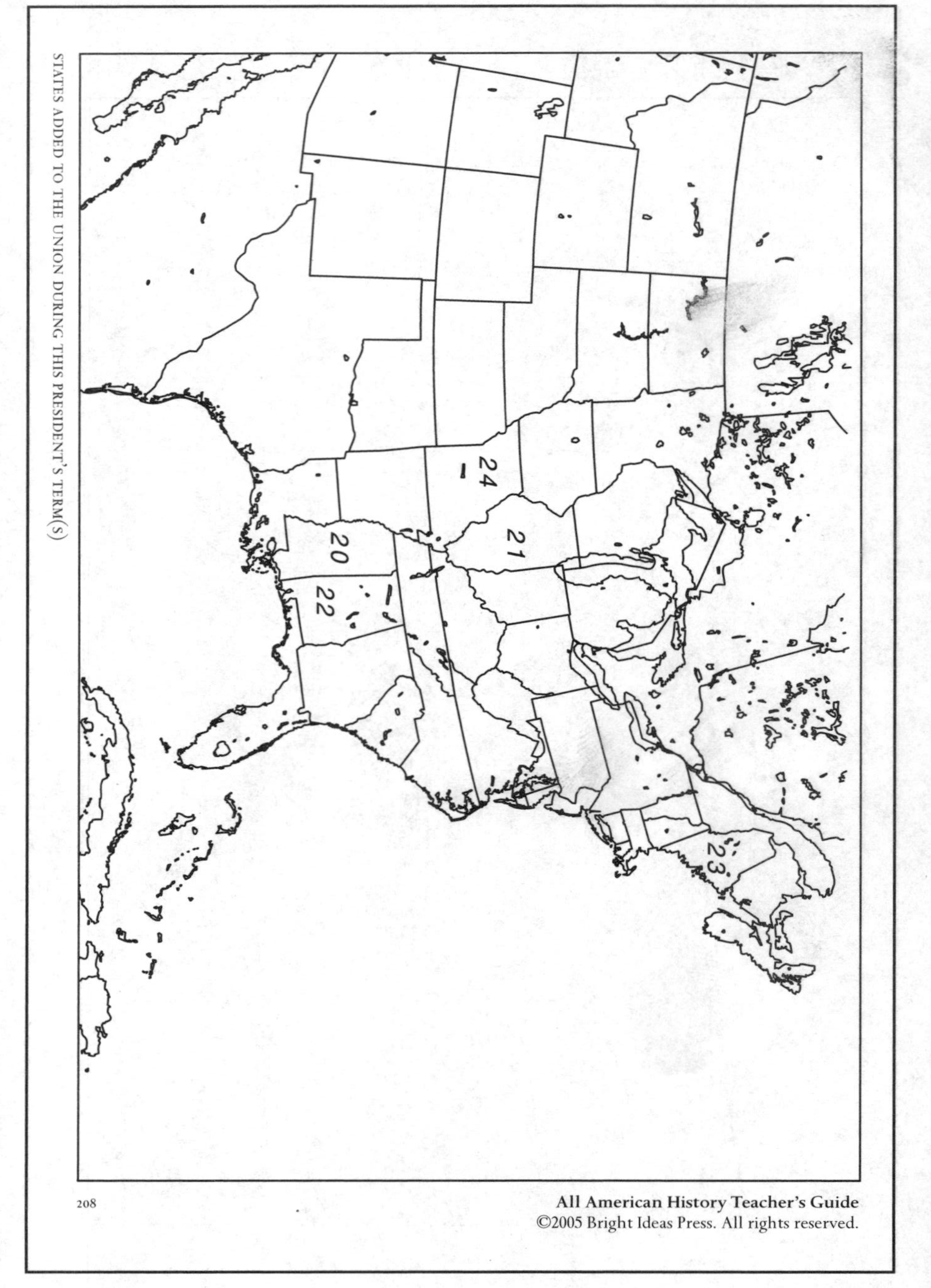

STATES ADDED TO THE UNION DURING THIS PRESIDENT'S TERM(S)

LESSON 26: FOR REVIEW

Write the corresponding letter of the man who was president when each of these occurred.

A. George Washington
B. John Adams
C. Thomas Jefferson
D. James Madison
E. James Monroe

__B__ 1. Passage of the Alien Act and the Sedition Act

__C__ 2. Landmark decision of the Marshall Court, *Marbury v. Madison*

__C__ 3. Lewis and Clark Expedition

__E__ 4. Signing of the Rush-Bagot Treaty and Adams-Onis Treaty

__D__ 5. War of 1812

__A__ 6. Whiskey Rebellion

__A__ 7. Establishment of the presidential cabinet

__A__ 8. Unanimous election in the Electoral College

__B__ 9. Passage of the Virginia Resolutions and Kentucky Resolutions

__C__ 10. Louisiana Purchase

__C__ 11. Naval War with Tripoli

__A__ 12. Passage of the Bill of Rights

__B__ 13. Selection of John Marshall as chief justice and "midnight appointments"

__E__ 14. Announcement of the Monroe Doctrine

__A__ 15. Jay Treaty

__C__ 16. Embargo Act

__A__ 17. Passage of Eleventh Amendment

A. George Washington
B. John Adams
C. Thomas Jefferson
D. James Madison
E. James Monroe

__C__ 18. Twelfth Amendment

__A__ 19. Establishment of national judiciary under 1789 Judiciary Act

__A__ 20. Famous Farewell Address

Write T for True and F for False in the space provided.

__T__ 1. The United States experienced rapid economic and population growth during the first years of its existence.

__F__ 2. Washington's inauguration took place on the steps of the Capitol in Washington, D.C.

__T__ 3. The District of Columbia was built on a piece of land along the Potomac River granted by Virginia and Maryland.

__F__ 4. The Bill of Rights was introduced by Alexander Hamilton.

__T__ 5. When France went to war with Britain, the United States was obligated to come to the aid of the French by the terms of its 1778 Treaty of Alliance.

__F__ 6. The Jay Treaty heightened American tensions with the British.

__F__ 7. Washington sought to affirm states' rights during the Whiskey Rebellion.

__F__ 8. In his Farewell Address, Washington encouraged America to cultivate political ties with Europe and search for foreign alliances.

__T__ 9. The election of 1796 demonstrated that peaceful transfer of power could occur in the new American nation.

__F__ 10. Adams pushed the United States to enter the war between the British and the French.

__T__ 11. Jefferson and Madison believed that the Alien and Sedition acts were unconstitutional violations of First Amendment freedoms.

F 12. The third, fourth, and fifth U.S. presidents, all from Massachusetts, were interested in increasing the power of the national government.

T 13. During Jefferson's presidency, plans were made to reduce taxes and pay off the national debt.

T 14. The Anti-Federalists began to call themselves Democratic-Republicans or Jeffersonians.

T 15. *Marbury v. Madison* established the Supreme Court's right of judicial review.

T 16. The Twelfth Amendment to the United States Constitution called for the casting of separate ballots for president and vice president.

F 17. The Embargo Act was a very popular piece of legislation.

T 18. The major event of Madison's administration was American involvement in the War of 1812.

T 19. Monroe reminded many of George Washington and came within one vote of being the only president besides Washington to be elected unanimously.

F 20. The Monroe Doctrine supported an end to American isolationism.

LESSON 26: FOR FURTHER STUDY

1. Research the Hamilton/Burr duel. Why were Vice President Burr and Alexander Hamilton antagonists? How did the duel end? What was the Burr Conspiracy?

2. Find out more about the Lewis and Clark Expedition. Who were Meriwether Lewis and William Clark? How did their backgrounds prepare them for this expedition? Where did they explore? What did they bring back from their explorations? Who was Sacajawea and what role did she play in the expedition?

3. Examine the life of Benjamin Banneker, a free African American and brilliant scientist from Baltimore. What role did he play in the nation's capital? Record the information on an African American form. Discover the plan that Pierre Charles L'Enfant had for the Federal City.

4. Look up the XYZ and Citizen Genet affairs. During which administrations did they occur? With which European nation(s) were they concerned? How did they end?

Name________________ Date ________

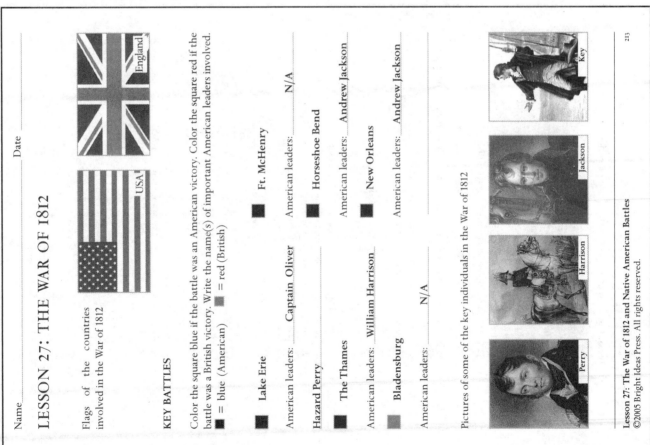

LESSON 27: THE WAR OF 1812

Flags of the countries involved in the War of 1812

USA

England

KEY BATTLES

Color the square blue if the battle was an American victory. Color the square red if the battle was a British victory. Write the name(s) of important American leaders involved.

■ = blue (American) ■ = red (British)

■ **Lake Erie**

American leaders: **Captain Oliver Hazard Perry**

■ **The Thames**

American leaders: **William Harrison**

■ **Bladensburg**

American leaders: **N/A**

■ **Ft. McHenry**

American leaders: **N/A**

■ **Horseshoe Bend**

American leaders: **Andrew Jackson**

■ **New Orleans**

American leaders: **Andrew Jackson**

Pictures of some of the key individuals in the War of 1812

Perry | Harrison | Jackson | Key

MAP OF WAR OF 1812 BATTLESITES

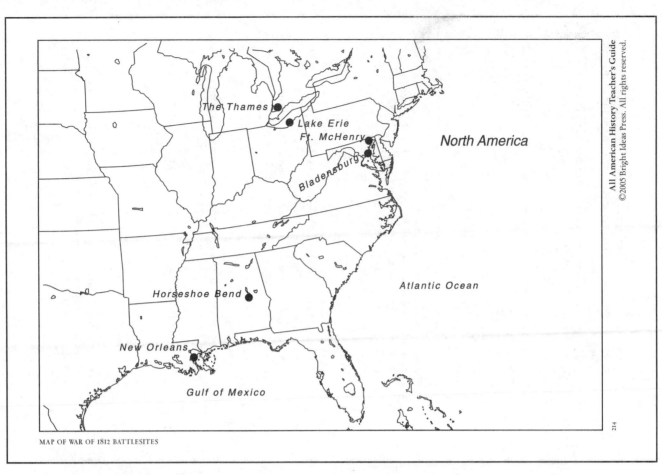

The Thames
Lake Erie
Ft. McHenry
Bladensburg
Horseshoe Bend
New Orleans
Gulf of Mexico
Atlantic Ocean
North America

LESSON 27: FOR REVIEW

Write the letter of the correct answer in the space provided.

__A__ 1. Which of the following statements is true?
- A. The new American nation had tried to stay neutral in the fighting between France and Britain
- B. Most Federalists were War Hawks who favored going to war against Britain
- C. Most westerners and southerners opposed war with Britain
- D. Many New Englanders favored war with Britain

__D__ 2. Which of the following is NOT a reason why the United States declared war on the British?
- A. British impressment of American soldiers
- B. British violation of U.S. territorial waters
- C. British trade restrictions
- D. British execution of Native Americans

__C__ 3. As the United States declared war in 1812, the country
- A. was strongly united behind President Madison
- B. was adequately prepared to fight
- C. was helped by the fact that the British were occupied fighting the French
- D. was ready to pay the costs of war

__C__ 4. In the early 1790s,
- A. the United States faced little resistance from Native Americans
- B. American troops successfully wiped out Native Americans who resisted westward expansion
- C. Indian resistance was fiercest in the Northwest Territory
- D. the Americans just tried to ignore Native Americans

__A__ 5. The Battle of Fallen Timbers
- A. ended in an American victory under General Anthony Wayne
- B. had no effect on Native American claims to land in the Northwest Territory
- C. prevented American settlers from moving into the Ohio region
- D. made a hero of Tecumseh

__B__ 6. The secretary of the Northwest Territory and its first delegate to the United States Congress was
- A. Anthony Wayne
- B. William Henry Harrison
- C. Andrew Jackson
- D. John Quincy Adams

__D__ 7. The Native American leader Tecumseh
- A. worked hard to develop friendly relations with white Americans
- B. did not support the development of the Shawnee Confederacy
- C. failed to emerge as a powerful leader among his people
- D. was supported in his mission by his brother, the Prophet

__B__ 8. The Battle of Tippecanoe
- A. succeeded in diminishing Indian raids on the frontier
- B. made a hero of William Henry Harrison
- C. resulted in few losses among the Americans and Shawnees
- D. was the place where Tecumseh was finally killed

__A__ 9. During the early stages of the War of 1812,
- A. the American army fought poorly in the opening campaign in Canada
- B. the American navy was completely unsuccessful
- C. the *USS Constitution* was shattered by British ships
- D. the American armed forces were enlarged to two hundred thousand men

__C__ 10. At the Battle of the Thames
- A. Andrew Jackson commanded American forces
- B. the Americans and Native Americans fought on the same side
- C. the Shawnee leader Tecumseh was killed
- D. the Americans were defeated by the British

B 11. When the British arrived in Washington, they
   A. killed President Madison
   B. set fire to the president's house
   C. tortured the members of Congress
   D. took many prisoners of war

A 12. Which of the following statements about the Battle of Baltimore is accurate?
   A. Local merchants sank their boats in the harbor to create a barrier
   B. The Americans were unsuccessful in their attempts to dig trenches and put cannon into place
   C. Fort McHenry fell with no shots being fired
   D. The British planned only a sea invasion of the city

A 13. "The Star-Spangled Banner"
   A. was first published as a poem
   B. was set to music written by Francis Scott Key
   C. became the national anthem in 1812
   D. was written during the Battle of Bladensburg

B 14. At the Battle of Horseshoe Bend
   A. General William Harrison led the American forces
   B. Creeks known as the White Sticks sided with the Americans
   C. both the Red Sticks and White Sticks sided with the British
   D. the British were victorious

D 15. During the Battle of New Orleans,
   A. hundreds of Americans died
   B. fighting lasted all day
   C. Andrew Jackson was humiliated
   D. the war was actually already over

C 16. The Treaty of Ghent
   A. added new territory to the United States
   B. settled all boundary disputes between the United States and Britain
   C. made no reference to impressment
   D. gave the British hopes of regaining their American colonies

LESSON 27: FOR FURTHER STUDY

1. Find out why Francis Scott Key was on a ship in the Chesapeake Bay the night that Fort McHenry was bombed by the British. Read all four stanzas of the "Star Spangled Banner." To what tune was this poem set soon after Key wrote it? When was Key's song made the national anthem? Prior to "The Star-Spangled Banner," what was the national anthem? Why do some people want to change our national anthem?

2. Learn more about General William Henry Harrison and General Andrew Jackson. What strategies did they use in pursuing victory? How did their soldiers feel about them?

3. Read about the lives of Tecumseh and the Prophet. Research the Shawnee. Record the information on a Native American Tribe form.

4. Research the Hartford Convention of 1815. Which leaders were involved in this meeting? Why was secession considered there? How did the end of the war affect the convention's work? Why was this meeting such a significant event?

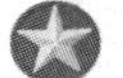

Name________________ Date ________

LESSON 28: JOHN QUINCY ADAMS

Picture of the president

Year born **1767**

Year died **1848**

In which state was he born? **Massachusetts**

What jobs did he hold before becoming president? **Diplomat to Europe, Secretary of State**

With what political party was this president affiliated? **Democratic-Republican**

Vice President: **John C. Calhoun**

What were the years of his presidency? **1825 – 1829**

List some significant developments during his administration

Accusations of a "corrupt bargain"

Promotion of Clay's American System: protective tariff (Tariff of Abominations 1828), national bank, internal improvements

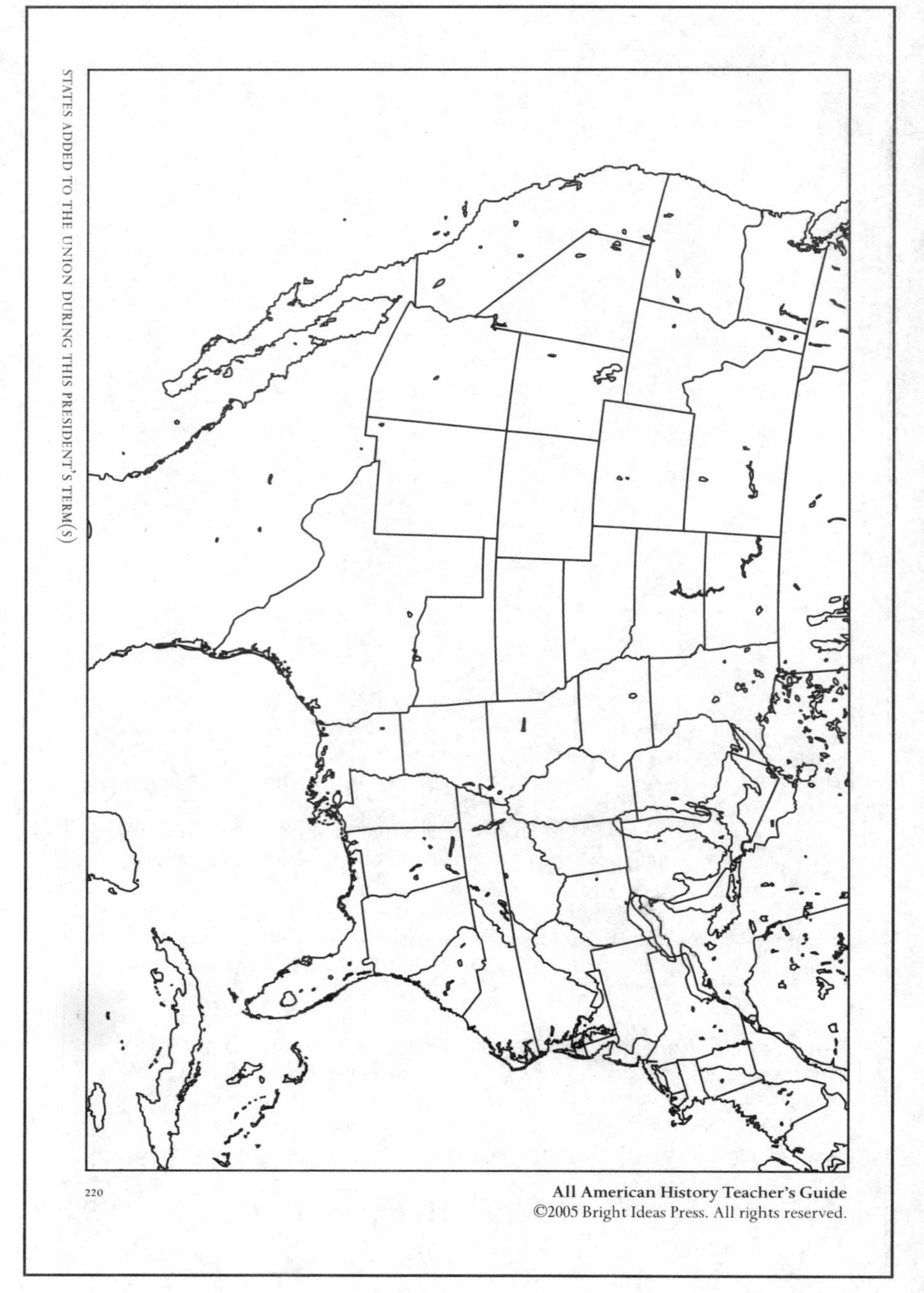

STATES ADDED TO THE UNION DURING THIS PRESIDENT'S TERM(S)

Name ______________________ Date ____________

LESSON 28: ANDREW JACKSON

Picture of the president

Year born **1767**

Year died **1845**

In which state was he born? **North Carolina/South Carolina border**

What jobs did he hold before becoming president? **Military commander, governor of the Florida territory; U.S. Representative, U.S. Senator**

With what political party was this president affiliated? **Democratic**

Vice President: **John C. Callhoun, Martin Van Buren**

What were the years of his presidency? **1829 – 1837**

List some significant developments during his administration

Spoils system

Kitchen cabinet

Tariff of 1832; Compromise Tariff of 1833

Issue of nullification

Pet banks

High inflation, Specie Circular of 1836

STATES ADDED TO THE UNION DURING THIS PRESIDENT'S TERM(S)

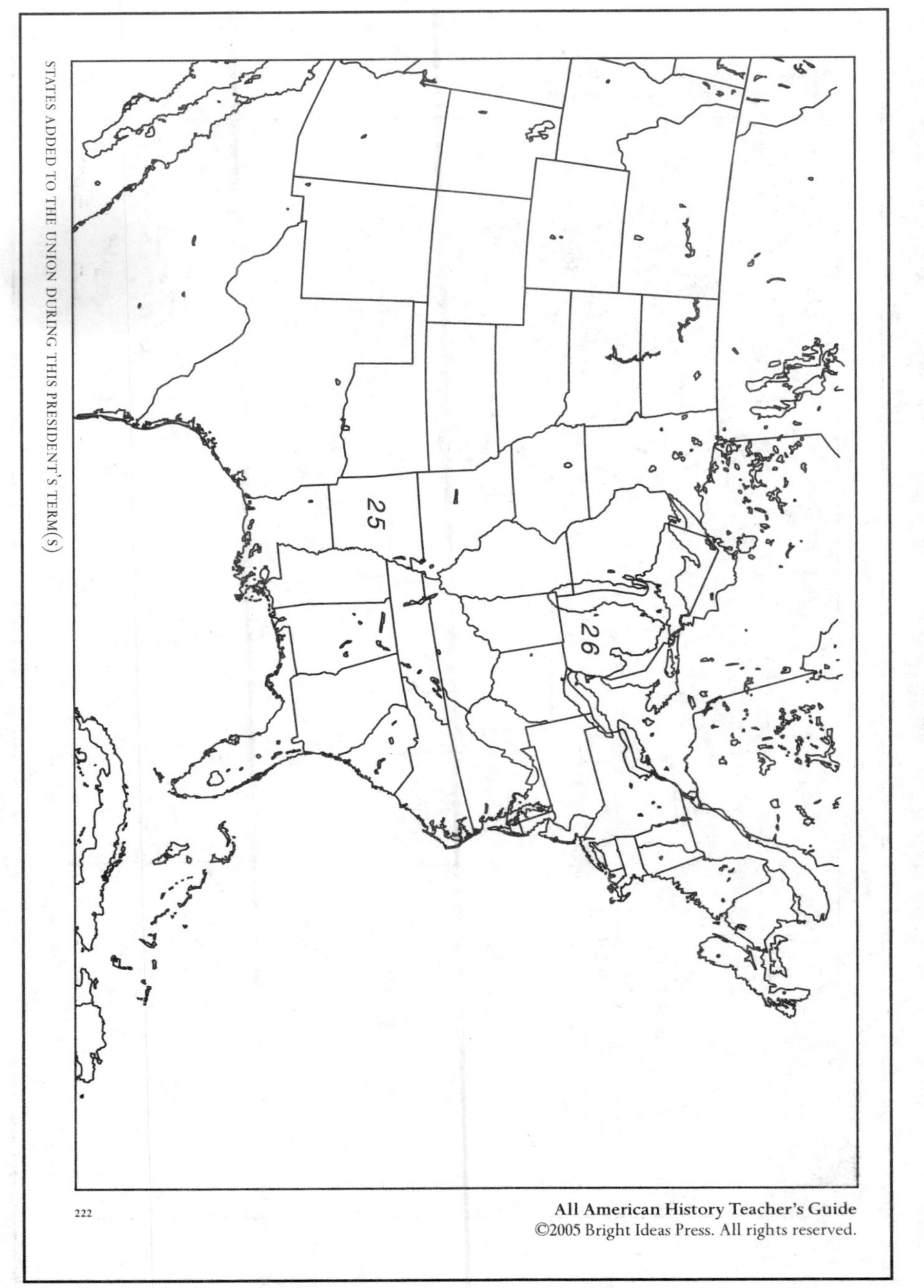

Name ____________ Date ____________

LESSON 28: MARTIN VAN BUREN

Picture of the president

Year born **1782**

Year died **1862**

In which state was he born? **New York**

What jobs did he hold before becoming president? **Governor of New York, Vice-President**

With what political party was this president affiliated? **Democratic**

Vice President: **Richard Johnson**

What were the years of his presidency? **1837 – 1841**

List some significant developments during his administration

Panic of 1837; Depression

Independent treasury

Lesson 28: The Jacksonians and the Whigs

223

STATES ADDED TO THE UNION DURING THIS PRESIDENT'S TERM(S)

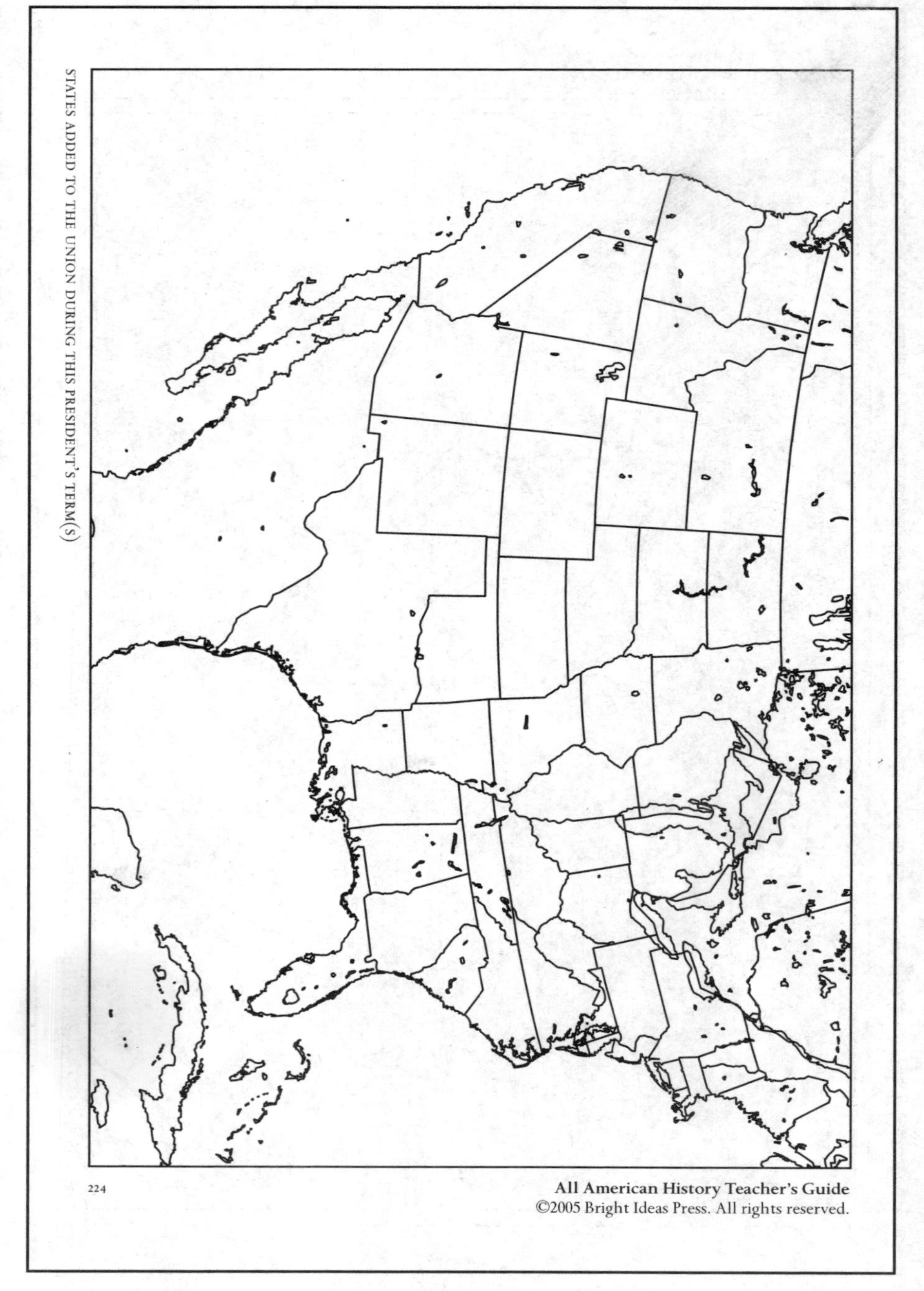

224

All American History Teacher's Guide

Name ______ Date ______

LESSON 28: WILLIAM HENRY HARRISON

Picture of the president

Year born **1773**

Year died **1841**

In which state was he born? **Virginia**

What jobs did he hold before becoming president? **Secretary of the Northwest Territory, Military commander**

With what political party was this president affiliated? **Whig**

Vice President: **John Tyler**

What were the years of his presidency? **1841**

List some significant developments during his administration

Longest inagural speech

Death from pneumonia one month after inauguration

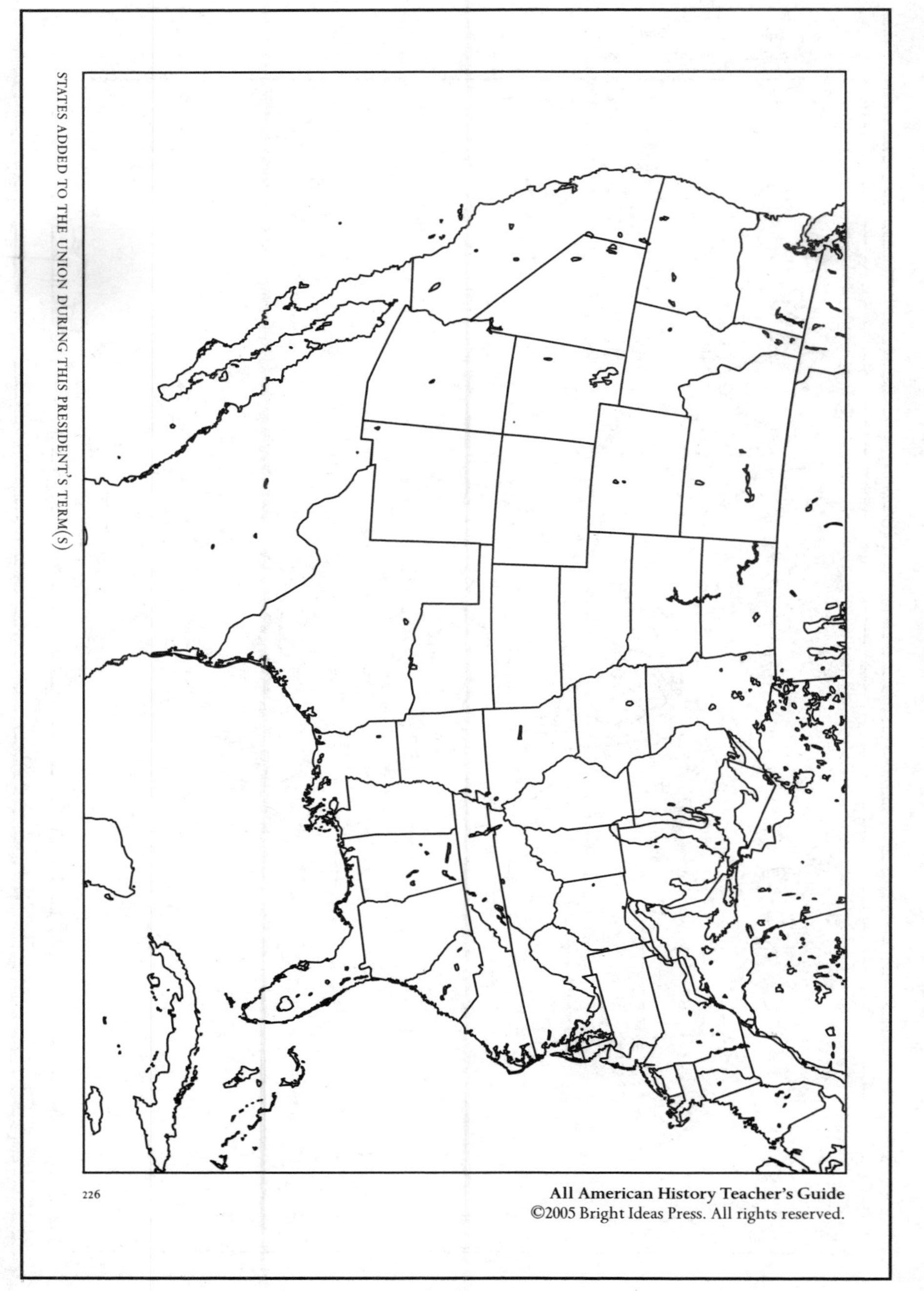

STATES ADDED TO THE UNION DURING THIS PRESIDENT'S TERM(S)

Name______________________ Date ____________

LESSON 28: JOHN TYLER

Year born ______ **1790**

Year died ______ **1862**

Picture of the president

In which state was he born? **Virginia**

What jobs did he hold before becoming president? **Governor of Virginia, U.S. Senator, Vice-President**

With what political party was this president affiliated? **Whig**

Vice President: **None**

What were the years of his presidency? **1841 – 1845**

List some significant developments during his administration

"His Accidency" – resignation of entire cabinet except for Secretary of Sate Webster

Introduction of first impeachment resolution against a president

Webster-Ashburton Treaty

Annexation of Texas

STATES ADDED TO THE UNION DURING THIS PRESIDENT'S TERM(S)

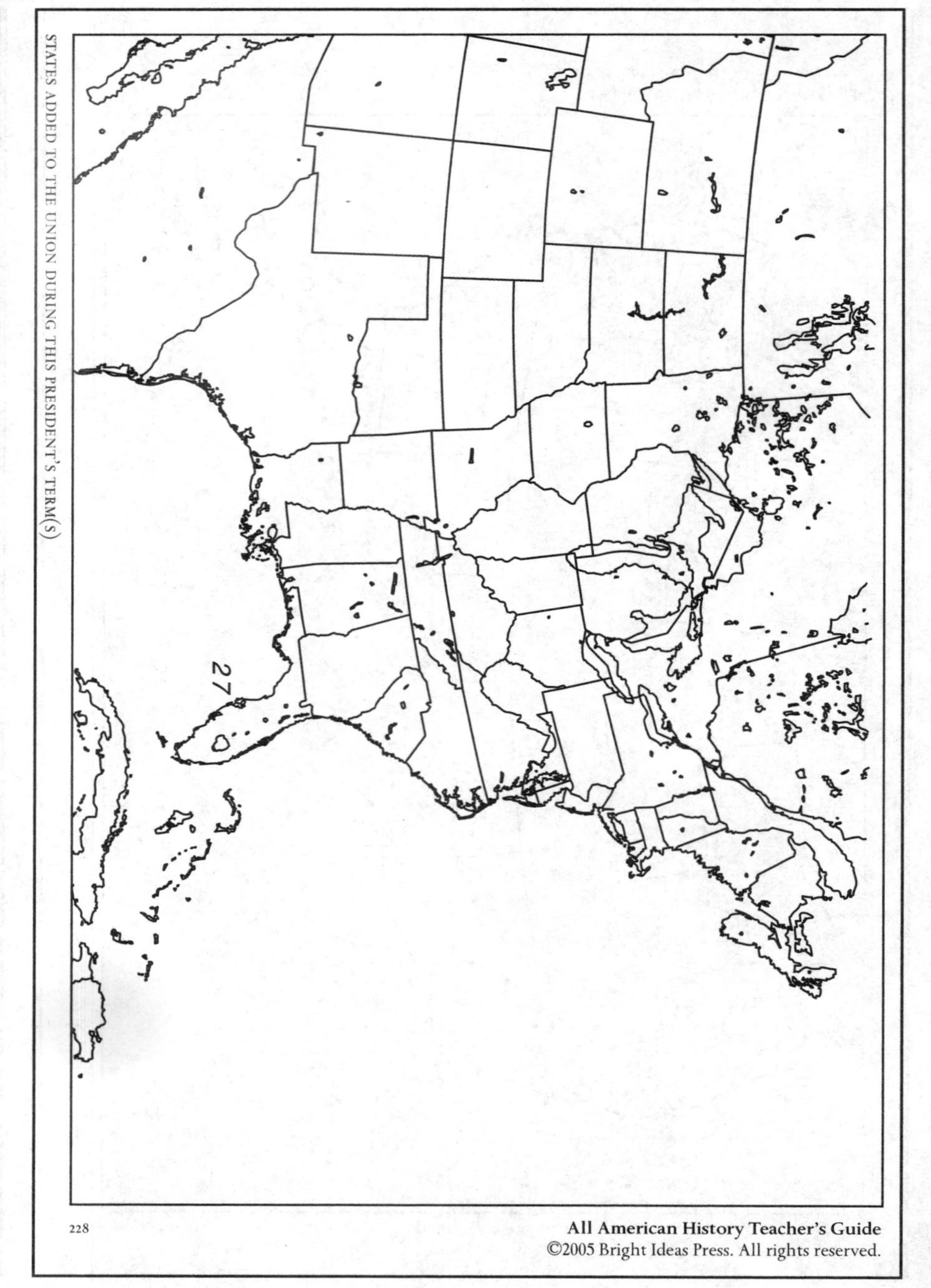

Name ______ Date ______

LESSON 28: JAMES POLK

Picture of the president

Year born **1795**

Year died **1849**

In which state was he born? **North Carolina**

What jobs did he hold before becoming president? **U.S. Representative, Speaker of the House**

With what political party was this president affiliated? **Democratic**

Vice President: **George Dallas**

What were the years of his presidency? **1845 – 1849**

List some significant developments during his administration

Settlement of Oregon boundary with Britain

Restoration of Independent Treasury System

Lower tariffs

Mexican War

STATES ADDED TO THE UNION DURING THIS PRESIDENT'S TERM(S)

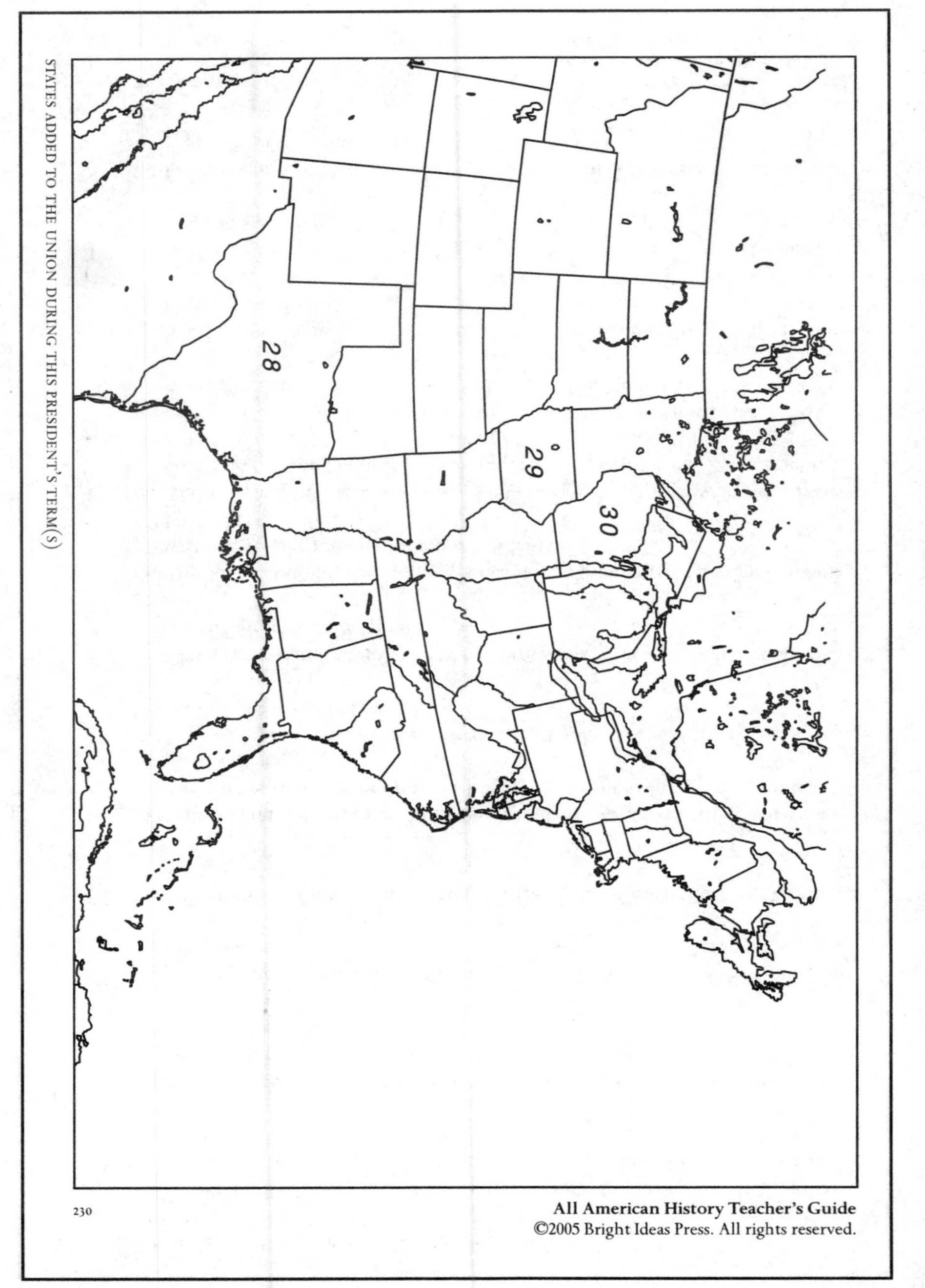

LESSON 28: FOR REVIEW

Write the corresponding letter of the man who was president when each of these occurred.

A. John Quincy Adams
B. Andrew Jackson
C. Martin Van Buren
D. William Henry Harrison
E. John Tyler
F. James K. Polk

__F__ 1. Mexican War

__A__ 2. Tariff of abominations

__C__ 3. Panic of 1837

__E__ 4. First impeachment resolution

__A__ 5. Emphasis on Clay's "American System"

__B__ 6. Specie Circular of 1836

__F__ 7. Settlement of Oregon boundary

__A__ 8. Accusations of a "corrupt bargain"

__D__ 9. First death of a president in office

__B__ 10. Pet banks

__B__ 11. Spoils system

__E__ 12. Webster-Ashburton Treaty

__E__ 13. Resignation of an entire cabinet (except one member)

__C__ 14. Independent treasury system

__B__ 15. Kitchen Cabinet

Write T for True and F for False in the space provided.

__T__ 1. Unlike the Federalist and Democratic-Republican parties, the Jacksonians and Whigs had grassroots organizations and support in every part of the country.

__F__ 2. Andrew Jackson worked hard to negotiate a treaty with the Seminole in Florida that would end hostilities there and protect the future of the Five Civilized Nations.

__T__ 3. John Quincy Adams was chosen to be president by the U.S. House of Representatives.

__F__ 4. The election of John Quincy Adams meant a continuation of the Virginia dynasty.

__F__ 5. Brilliant and well educated, John Quincy Adams was an astute politician who was not above using "political backslapping" to get his programs adopted.

__T__ 6. A key emphasis of the administration of John Quincy Adams was the American System of Henry Clay.

__T__ 7. Clay's American System called for a protective tariff, a national bank, and internal improvement projects.

__F__ 8. The 1828 election focused upon issues rather than personalities and ended with the re-election of John Quincy Adams.

__F__ 9. Andrew Jackson was known as a well-educated aristocrat who feared the common man and opposed democratization of the national government.

__T__ 10. John C. Calhoun, Jackson's first vice president, anonymously published a pamphlet that defended the doctrine of nullification.

__T__ 11. South Carolina nullified the Tariff of 1832 and threatened to secede if forced to pay the tariff duties.

__T__ 12. Jackson considered the Bank of the United States to be unconstitutional and vetoed its petition for recharter.

__F__ 13. Jackson's Specie Circular was highly successful in solving the economic problems of the United States.

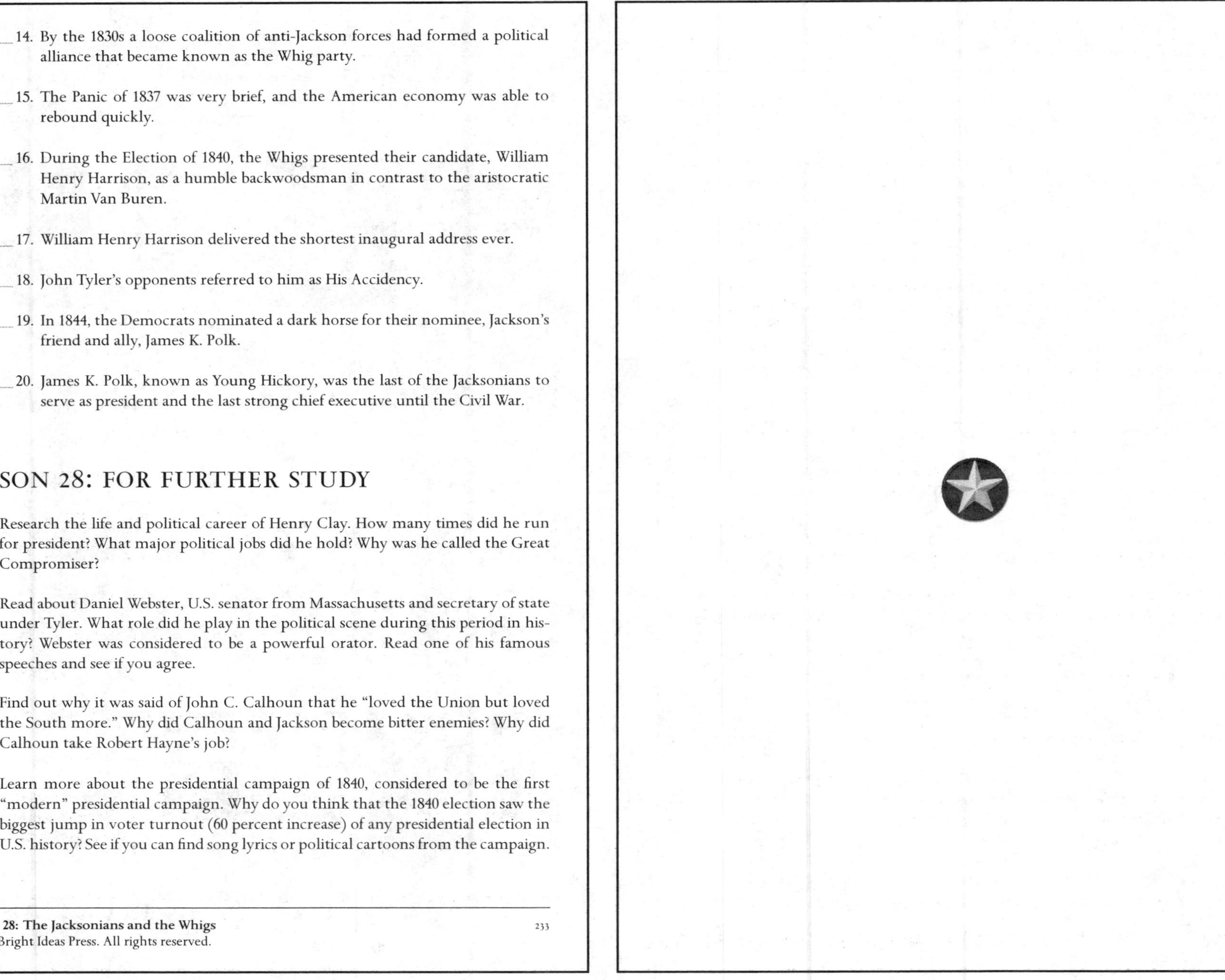

T 14. By the 1830s a loose coalition of anti-Jackson forces had formed a political alliance that became known as the Whig party.

F 15. The Panic of 1837 was very brief, and the American economy was able to rebound quickly.

T 16. During the Election of 1840, the Whigs presented their candidate, William Henry Harrison, as a humble backwoodsman in contrast to the aristocratic Martin Van Buren.

F 17. William Henry Harrison delivered the shortest inaugural address ever.

T 18. John Tyler's opponents referred to him as His Accidency.

T 19. In 1844, the Democrats nominated a dark horse for their nominee, Jackson's friend and ally, James K. Polk.

T 20. James K. Polk, known as Young Hickory, was the last of the Jacksonians to serve as president and the last strong chief executive until the Civil War.

LESSON 28: FOR FURTHER STUDY

1. Research the life and political career of Henry Clay. How many times did he run for president? What major political jobs did he hold? Why was he called the Great Compromiser?

2. Read about Daniel Webster, U.S. senator from Massachusetts and secretary of state under Tyler. What role did he play in the political scene during this period in history? Webster was considered to be a powerful orator. Read one of his famous speeches and see if you agree.

3. Find out why it was said of John C. Calhoun that he "loved the Union but loved the South more." Why did Calhoun and Jackson become bitter enemies? Why did Calhoun take Robert Hayne's job?

4. Learn more about the presidential campaign of 1840, considered to be the first "modern" presidential campaign. Why do you think that the 1840 election saw the biggest jump in voter turnout (60 percent increase) of any presidential election in U.S. history? See if you can find song lyrics or political cartoons from the campaign.

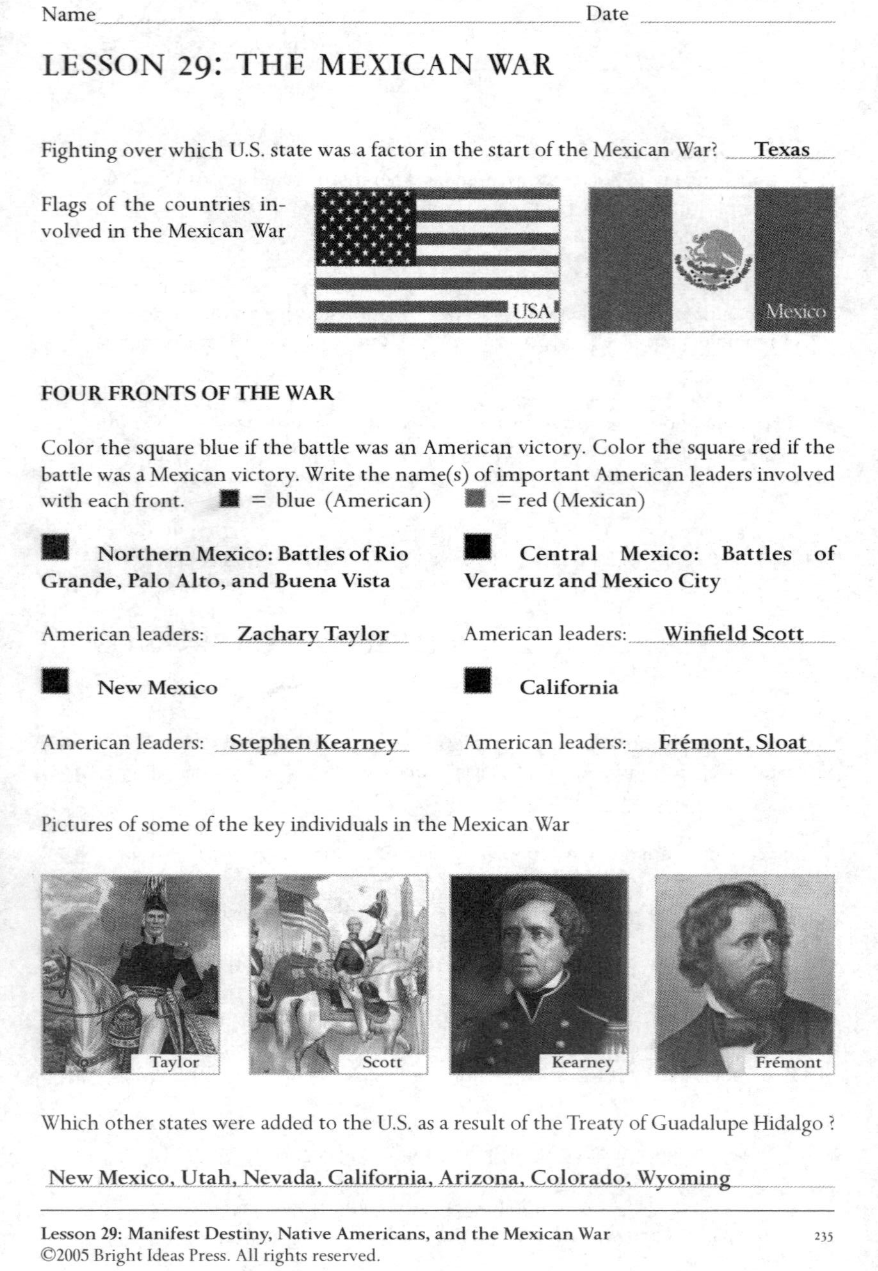

Name____________________ Date __________

LESSON 29: THE MEXICAN WAR

Fighting over which U.S. state was a factor in the start of the Mexican War? **Texas**

Flags of the countries involved in the Mexican War

FOUR FRONTS OF THE WAR

Color the square blue if the battle was an American victory. Color the square red if the battle was a Mexican victory. Write the name(s) of important American leaders involved with each front. ■ = blue (American) ■ = red (Mexican)

■ **Northern Mexico: Battles of Rio Grande, Palo Alto, and Buena Vista**

American leaders: **Zachary Taylor**

■ **Central Mexico: Battles of Veracruz and Mexico City**

American leaders: **Winfield Scott**

■ **New Mexico**

American leaders: **Stephen Kearney**

■ **California**

American leaders: **Frémont, Sloat**

Pictures of some of the key individuals in the Mexican War

Which other states were added to the U.S. as a result of the Treaty of Guadalupe Hidalgo ?

New Mexico, Utah, Nevada, California, Arizona, Colorado, Wyoming

MAP OF MEXICAN WAR BATTLESITES

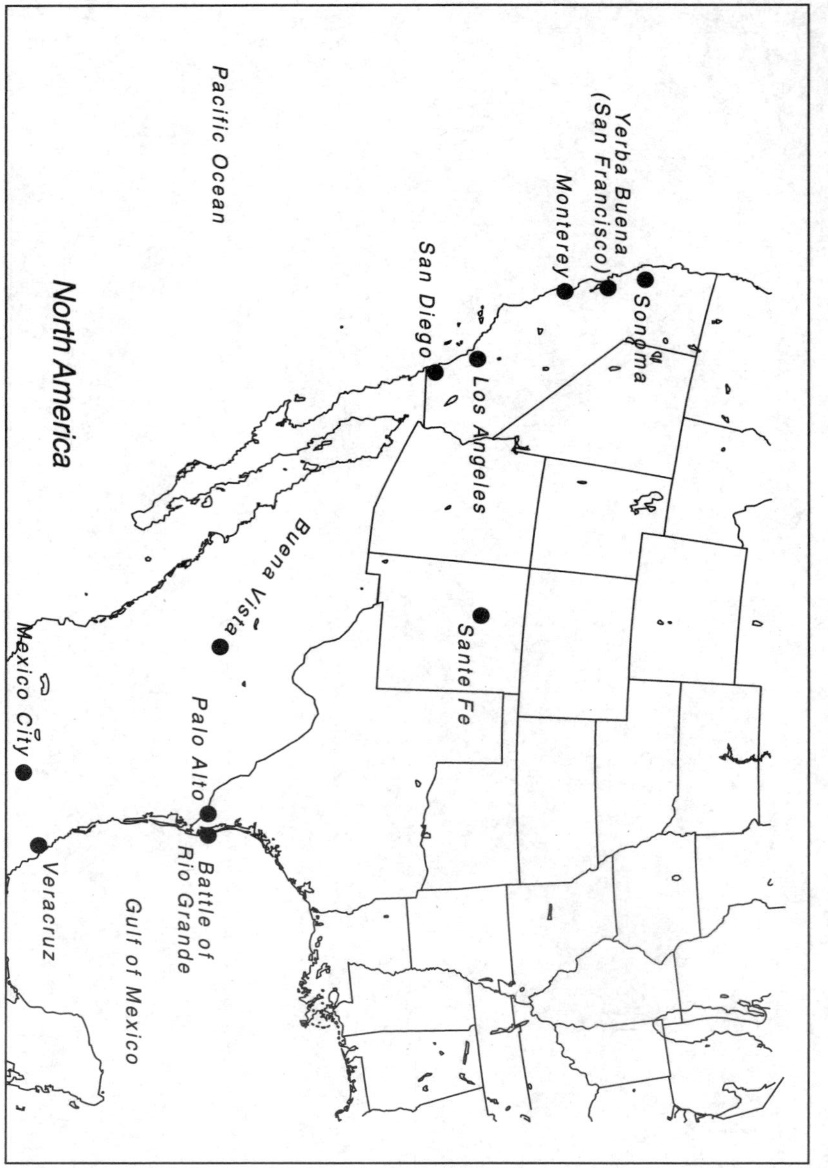

Name ____________ Date ____________

LESSON 29: FOR REVIEW

Write the missing word or words in the spaces provided.

1. **Manifest Destiny** refers to the belief that America had been providentially ordained to posses the North American continent.

2. In 1803, the United States gained significant western territory as a result of **the Louisiana Purchase**.

3. By 1810, the American government had annexed **West Florida** and nine years later it annexed **East Florida**.

4. The United States and Britain agreed to joint occupation of **Oregon** in 1818 with the forty-ninth parallel as the dividing line.

5. American settlers, led by Stephen Austin, had moved into the Spanish-controlled region of **Texas** by 1822.

6. The dictator who controlled Mexico by 1834 and soon declared martial law in Texas was **Santa Ana**.

7. When Texans finally won their independence from Mexico, they had rallied around the battle cry, "Remember **the Alamo**!"

8. The journey of the Cherokee from their homes westward to Indian Territory in Oklahoma became known as the **Trail of Tears**.

Write the letter of the correct answer in the space provided.

C 1. Following the American Revolution,
- A. the U.S. government discouraged westward expansion
- B. Manifest Destiny was supported by millions of Native Americans
- C. the Northwest Territory eventually yielded five states
- D. the Northwest Ordinances failed to develop an orderly process for statehood

A 2. The mountain men of the early 1800s, who paved the way for American settlers to move farther west, included all of the following EXCEPT
- A. Daniel Boone
- B. Zebulon Pike
- C. Jim Beckwourth
- D. Jedediah Smith

C 3. The Oregon territory
- A. was a Spanish possession until 1840
- B. was not considered to be a desirable place to settle
- C. was the location of a missionary outreach to Native Americans in the 1830s
- D. was quite small

A 4. In 1834, Texas was
- A. a state in the Mexican Republic
- B. no longer under martial law
- C. not allowing people from the United States to cross its borders illegally
- D. an independent nation

D 5. When Texas became independent,
- A. it immediately started a war with the United States
- B. President Jackson was eager to annex it to the United States
- C. the United States considered Mexico to be a strong ally
- D. it was established as a republic that lasted for almost ten years

__C__ 6. Which of the following is NOT true of the California Gold Rush?
- A. an estimated eighty thousand people traveled to California in 1849
- B. gold seekers came from the eastern United States and many other countries
- C. a large percentage of prospectors struck it rich
- D. California gold production did not begin to decline for more than fifty years

__C__ 7. President Jackson
- A. was prohibited from moving Indian tribes west by the Indian Removal Act of 1830
- B. was deterred in his aggressive actions again Native Americans by two Supreme Court decisions in 1831 and 1832
- C. seized millions of acres of tribal lands and removed five tribal nations from their homes
- D. agreed with Chief Justice Marshall in his judgment concerning the Cherokee

__C__ 8. The Seminole War (1835 – 1842)
- A. was popular with the American people
- B. made Osceola a national hero
- C. cost more than twenty million dollars and the lives of fifteen hundred American soldiers
- D. led to a stronger Seminole presence in Florida

__D__ 9. As James Polk prepared to take office,
- A. the United States was eager to improve relations with Mexico
- B. the Mexicans agreed to repay the money that they owed Americans
- C. American expansionists had given up on their demands of Mexico
- D. the outgoing president, John Tyler, signed a joint congressional resolution annexing Texas

__B__ 10. John Slidell, sent by President Polk to Mexico City in the fall of 1845,
- A. negotiated a truce with the Mexicans
- B. was never allowed to meet with Mexican governmental leaders
- C. was not authorized to offer Mexico any money in the negotiations
- D. did not intend to ask Mexico for California and New Mexico

__B__ 11. As the United States faced war with Mexico,
- A. the American people were strongly united behind Polk's leadership
- B. the nation possessed only a small army
- C. the country had no navy
- D. its military leaders were unqualified

__A__ 12. General Zachary Taylor, "Old Rough and Ready,"
- A. was successful in defeating the Mexicans in the North
- B. was a disciplined strategist
- C. was despised by his troops
- D. entered the war only in its final stages

__D__ 13. General Winfield Scott, "Old Fuss and Feathers,"
- A. arrived in Mexico with his troops by train
- B. was unsuccessful in capturing either Veracruz or Mexico City
- C. was disorganized and disinterested in military pomp and discipline
- D. outwitted Santa Ana and created jealousy among Polk and the Democrats because of his success

__A__ 14. Colonel Stephen Kearney
- A. succeeded in capturing New Mexico for the Americans
- B. joined Scott in the Mexico City campaign
- C. disagreed with Polk's decision to occupy New Mexico and California
- D. was later elected president

__A__ 15. Captain John C. Fremont
- A. provided leadership for establishment of Bear Flag Republic
- B. served as military governor of New Mexico
- C. commanded naval forces that arrived in California in 1846
- D. was an assistant to Zachary Taylor in his Mexican campaigns

__C__ 16. Under the terms of the Treaty of Guadalupe
- A. Mexico paid the United States fifteen million dollars
- B. the Texas-Mexican border was left undecided
- C. the United States received a large amount of territory from Mexico
- D. Mexico agreed to pay all debts that it owed American citizens

LESSON 29: FOR FURTHER STUDY

1. Research the life and travels of one or more of the following Mountain Men — Jedediah Smith, Zebulon Pike, and Jim Beckwourth. If you research Beckwourth, record the information on the African American form. Who was Davy Crocket and for what was he known? See if you can find the lyrics to the 1955 top-40 hit "Davy Crockett" by Bob Hayes.

2. Look for information about Dr. Marcus Whitman and his wife Narcissa. What role did they play in the settlement of Oregon? How did they die? Find out what it was like to travel the Oregon Trail.

3. Read about what it was like to head west in a wagon train. Find out what started the California Gold Rush. Research the lives of one or more of these former success stories — Levi Strauss, Philip Armour, Henry Wells, William Fargo, and Bret Harte.

4. Learn about Sequoyah and the development of the Cherokee alphabet. Research *Worcester v. Georgia*. Who was Worcester and why was he sentenced to prison? Who was still chief justice of the Supreme Court when this decision was handed down? How did the decision affect the Cherokee? Read more about this tribe and record the information on a Native American Tribe form.

Name________________________ Date __________

LESSON 30: INDUSTRIAL REVOLUTION

MANUFACTURING

What was the major difference between the Rhode Island and Lowell factory systems?

Rhode Island employed whole families, and Lowell employed women and girls.

Why did Lowell employees go on strike in the mid-1830s? **cuts in wages**

List the advantages and disadvantages of a capitalist market economy.

Advantages	Disadvantages
encourages economic growth	**makes the economy more prone to**
leads to provision of more services	**boom and bust cycles that lead to**
promotes interdependence	**panics**

AGRICULTURE

In what ways did the invention of the cotton gin harm the South? **profitability of cotton production revitalized slavery; reliance on one crop hampered growth of other industries**

How did the growing use of farm machinery affect U.S. farmers? **Needed more cash to buy the machinery; could produce more crops**

The U.S. began slowly to become more urbanized. What were the six largest cities in the U.S. in 1790?

Philadelphia, New York City, Boston, Charleston, Baltimore, Salem

How many U.S. cities had populations of at least 200,000 in 1860? **43**

TRANSPORTATION

Identify one of the few road projects subsidized by the U.S. federal government

National or Cumberland Road

What problems were associated with the revolutionary steamboats, and why had the canal craze ended by the 1840s?

They were dangerous to operate and only operable on major rivers

What type of transportation boomed in the U.S. from 1830–1860? **rail roads**

COMMUNICATION

From the 1830s to the 1850s, how long did it take to transport mail by clipper ship from the eastern U.S. to California?

8 – 9 months

How long did it take to transport mail by stagecoach from Missouri to California in the late 1850s?

about 25 days

How long did it take to transport mail by Pony Express from Missouri to California in 1860?

10 days or less

List the requirements to be a Pony Express rider **18 or younger, skinny, willing to risk death**

What development made possible the mass circulation of newspapers? **development of the steam printing press**

LESSON 30: FOR REVIEW

Write the corresponding letter of the correct answer in the space provided.

A. Samuel Colt
B. John Deere
C. Robert Fulton
D. Elias Howe
E. Charles Goodyear
F. Francis Cabot Lowell
G. Samuel F. B. Morse
H. Cyrus McCormick
I. Samuel Slater
J. Eli Whitney

D 1. Developer of the sewing machine

J 2. Inventor of the cotton gin and popularizer of interchangeable parts

A 3. Designer of the six-shooter used by Americans during the Mexican War

I 4. British mechanic who constructed the first successful American cotton-spinning mill

E 5. Inventor of vulcanization (rubber)

C 6. Designer of the first effective American steamboat

B 7. Inventor of a steel plow

F 8. Boston merchant who developed a factory system primarily employing twelve to twenty-five-year-old women and girls

G 9. Inventor of the telegraph

H 10. Developer of a mechanical reaper

Write T for True and F for False in the space provided.

T 1. In the years leading up to the American Revolution, Great Britain had prohibited manufacturing in the colonies as well as the export of industrial machines and emigration of engineers.

T 2. The Rhode Island System and Lowell System were two factory systems that developed in the United States during the early years of the nation.

F 3. The American textile industry flourished in both the North and the South.

F 4. Secretary of the Treasury Alexander Hamilton published a report that listed the disadvantages of American industrial development.

T 5. Federal assistance to American manufacturing included protective tariffs and patent protection to inventors.

F 6. Protective tariffs were designed to help the American consumer—making it possible for him to pay less for a higher quality product.

T 7. During the period of early American industrialization, the nation was developing a capitalistic market economy based on money and jobs.

T 8. American industrialization in the first half of the nineteenth century occurred unevenly, and the "putting out" system of workers producing goods at home still existed.

T 9. At the end of the American Revolution, most Americans still lived on farms.

F 10. Eli Whitney's invention of the cotton gin almost led to the end of slavery in the South.

F 11. American agriculture was barely affected by the Industrial Revolution in the first half of the nineteenth century.

F 12. Before 1830, the major form of transportation in America was railroads.

T 13. In the first half of the nineteenth century, many corduroy and macadamized roads were constructed by private developers, who then charged tolls for the use of their roads.

T 14. The National or Cumberland Road was one of the few road projects in the United States subsidized by federal money.

F 15. The Erie Canal fueled a canal craze in the 1820s and 1830s, and many canals became even more successful than the Erie.

T 16. The Baltimore and Ohio Railroad built a steam-powered train named the *Tom Thumb* by 1830.

T 17. Like canals and turnpikes, railroads were first developed with private capital.

__T__ 18. Both stagecoaches and clipper ships were used to deliver mail in the United States during the first half of the twentieth century.

__T__ 19. The Pony Express lasted less than two years, put out of business by the transcontinental telegraph.

__F__ 20. The number of American newspapers and magazines did not increase significantly during the first half of the nineteenth century.

LESSON 30: FOR FURTHER STUDY

1. Read more about the Rhode Island system of factory management (Samuel Slater) and the Lowell system of factory management. Would you have liked to have lived and worked under these systems?

2. Research the construction of the Erie Canal. Why did people call it Clinton's Ditch? What impact did the canal have on the state of New York? Can you find the words to a familiar American folk song about the Erie Canal?

3. Look for information about the beginning of railroads in the United States. Who was considered to be the father of American railroads? Research the construction of the B & O Railroad and find photos of trains from this era.

4. Find out more about Samuel F. B. Morse and his development of the telegraph. What was Morse like? Where did he construct the first telegraph line in the U.S? What was the first message sent on his telegraph?

Name ______________________ Date ____________

LESSON 31: REVIEW OF STATES AND CAPITALS

Order Added	State Name	Capital City
1.	Delaware	Dover
2.	Pennsylvania	Harrisburg
3.	New Jersey	Trenton
4.	Georgia	Atlanta
5.	Connecticut	Hartford
6.	Massachusetts	Boston
7.	Maryland	Annapolis
8.	South Carolina	Columbia
9.	New Hampshire	Concord
10.	Virginia	Richmond
11.	New York	Albany
12.	North Carolina	Raleigh
13.	Rhode Island	Providence
14.	Vermont	Montpelier
15.	Kentucky	Frankfort
16.	Tennessee	Nashville
17.	Ohio	Columbus
18.	Louisiana	Baton Rogue
19.	Indiana	Indianapolis
20.	Mississippi	Jackson
21.	Illinois	Springfield
22.	Alabama	Montgomery
23.	Maine	Augusta
24.	Missouri	Jefferson City
25.	Arkansas	Little Rock
26.	Michigan	Lansing
27.	Florida	Tallahassee
28.	Texas	Austin
29.	Iowa	Des Moines
30.	Wisconsin	Madison

MAP OF THE STATES AND THEIR CAPITALS

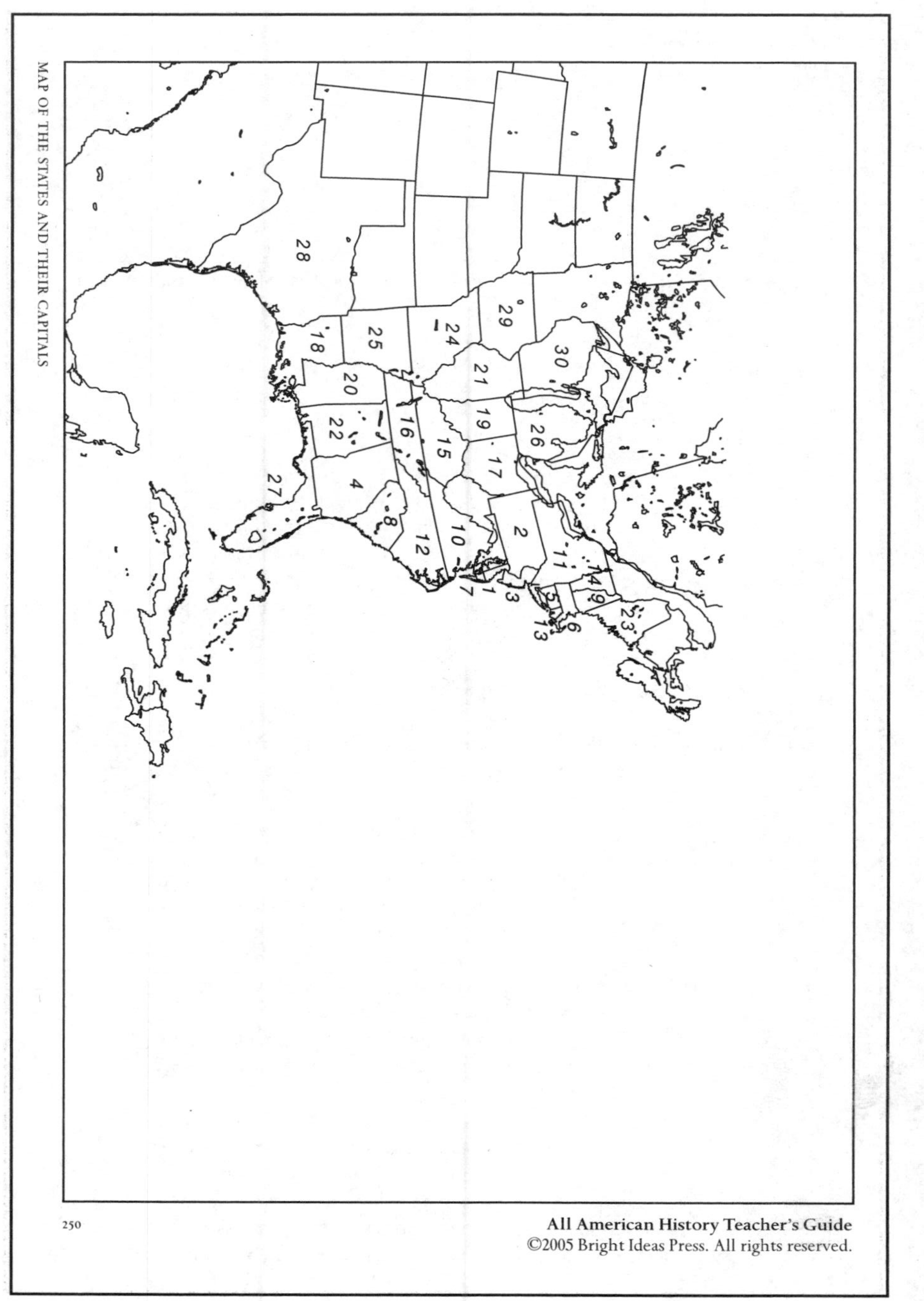

LESSON 31: FOR REVIEW

Write the letter of the correct answer in the space provided.

__B__ 1. At the beginning of the nineteenth century, the average life span in the United States was
- A. less than thirty years
- B. less than forty years
- C. less than fifty years
- D. less than sixty years

__D__ 2. During the nineteenth century, when an American woman married, she
- A. was allowed to own property
- B. no longer was required to give up her legal identity
- C. was still allowed to vote
- D. knew that everything she had would now belong to her husband

__A__ 3. The 1848 Seneca Falls convention
- A. called for the reform of marital and property laws that kept women in an inferior status
- B. was a small meeting, attended by only twenty-five to thirty people
- C. was commended for its work by many pastors
- D. was uniformly praised by the press

__A__ 4. In the first half of the nineteenth century,
- A. almost one-half of the children in the United States did not attend a school
- B. there were only a few free public schools outside of the South
- C. few children who did not attend school learned to read
- D. the United States had an extremely low literacy rate

__B__ 5. Which of the following is NOT true of clothing styles for American men during the first half of the nineteenth century?
- A. men's everyday trousers were held up by suspenders, not belts
- B. men almost always wore frock coats, and overcoats had not been introduced
- C. leather boots served as everyday shoe wear for men
- D. a variety of men's hat styles were available

__D__ 6. During the first half of the nineteenth century, American women
- A. no longer kept their heads covered most of the time
- B. wore dresses that opened down the front when outside the home
- C. experimented with wearing trousers
- D. were expected to wear a corset year round

__B__ 7. During the first half of the nineteenth century, clothing styles for American children included all of the following EXCEPT
- A. dresses for girls and boys until the age of six
- B. increasingly restrictive outfits and the introduction of corsets for children by 1830
- C. skeleton suits for boys
- D. military style uniforms for boys

__C__ 8. Medical practices from 1800 to 1860
- A. emphasized surgical procedures
- B. never experimented with any type of anesthesia
- C. still had little regard for cleanliness, leading to the continuing spread of infectious disease
- D. led to enactment of physician licensing laws in every state

__A__ 9. American cuisine before the Civil War
- A. included four principal food traditions and remained grounded in British roots
- B. emphasized green vegetables and fruits
- C. did not make use of native American ingredients
- D. was hardly influenced at all by the influx of European immigrants

Write the missing word or words in the spaces provided.

1. Two American women who worked to make the Seneca Falls convention a reality were Lucretia Mott and __**Elizabeth Cady Stanton**__.

2. **Horace Mann**, head of the Massachusetts Board of Education, eventually became known as the Father of American Education.

3. Although he worked for years as an educator, **William McGuffey** has primarily been remembered as the compiler of a set of eclectic readers.

4. Perhaps the foremost medical practitioner of the period was **Dr. Benjamin Rush**.

5. *Not by Bread Alone*, an American cookbook published in this period, had a patriotic cover and distinctly native approach to food.

6. During the first half of the nineteenth century, American cooking was influenced by the influx of European immigrants, especially those from **Germany**, who brought with them an emphasis on beer, wursts, marinated meats, and sour flavors.

LESSON 31: FOR FURTHER STUDY

1. Discover what provoked Elizabeth Cady Stanton and Lucretia Mott to begin planning for the Seneca Falls convention. Find a copy of the Seneca Falls *Declaration of Sentiments* and read it. How did Mr. Stanton feel about this declaration? What famous abolitionist(s) attended the convention?

2. Why were the *McGuffey Readers* known as "eclectic" readers? Find excerpts from these readers to look over.

3. Research the life of Noah Webster, author of the "Blue-backed Speller" (*A Grammatical Institute of the English Language*). Webster's book, written in 1783, was

used for one hundred years to teach American children how to read, spell, and pronounce words. Why did he write this book? What other important book did Webster author? See if you can find original texts from his works.

4. Look for American recipes from the first half of the nineteenth century. They might include directions on how to make apple fritters, molasses gingerbread, sweet potato pie, chicken or jackrabbit stew, and roasted pig. Try to bake one of these dishes.

Name ____________________ Date __________

SUMMARY OF PROJECTS AND SPECIAL ACTIVITIES

READING

What biographies or nonfiction books have you read about this period of history and who were the author(s)?

What historical fiction books have you read about this period of history and who were the author(s)?

What magazine or Internet articles have you read about this period of history?

FIELD TRIPS/VIRTUAL TOURS

What field trips or virtual tours have you taken to sites from this period of history?

Which was your favorite and why?

MOVIES

What movies have you watched that are set in this time period or what documentaries have you watched that are about persons or events from this time period?

Which was the most interesting to you and why? __________

ART

What art projects have you completed that were about this time period or were done in an artistic technique from this time period?

NOTEBOOKS AND OTHER ACTIVITIES

Who has been highlighted in your Native American or African American notebook?

What other fun and creative activities have you done? __________

LESSON 32: FOR REVIEW

Write the letter of the correct answer in the space provided.

A 1. American society during the first half of the nineteenth century was characterized by
- A. tremendous growth in the working class in the North
- B. a shift away from an emphasis on one's gentlemanly honor in the South
- C. less tension and concern about European immigration
- D. the end of duels and mob justice in the South

B 2. The Cane Ridge Revival
- A. was soon repudiated by its Presbyterian sponsors due to poor attendance
- B. took place on the American frontier in Kentucky
- C. was an isolated event that had little lasting impact in the United States
- D. did not permit dancing, jumping, or shaking

C 3. Charles Finney
- A. refused to advertise his revival meetings
- B. criticized the anti-slavery movement
- C. provided an "anxious bench" for those responding to his public invitation
- D did not see large numbers of conversions

B 4. Transcendentalism
- A. taught that man is born a sinner
- B. glorified nature as a creative force for discovering one's true self
- C. emphasized the death and resurrection of Christ
- D. carefully adhered to biblical principles

A 5. The Church of Jesus Christ of Latter-Day Saints
- A. was founded by Joseph Smith
- B. did not grow very quickly
- C. repudiated the Book of Mormon
- D. never faced persecution

A 6. Which of the following is NOT true of nineteenth-century American children?
- A. they rarely owned their own dolls
- B. they enjoyed dominoes, checkers, and marbles
- C. they experimented with tops and Jacob's ladder
- D. they played hopscotch, blind man's bluff, and kick the can

D 7. A typical night at an American theater during the first half of the nineteenth century would
- A. never have featured a melodrama
- B. have probably been a quiet and subdued experience
- C. never have included the drinking of alcoholic beverages
- D. have involved a great deal of audience participation and sometimes led to riots

B 8. Minstrel shows
- A. were not a uniquely American form of entertainment
- B. introduced many enduringly popular songs
- C. rarely included any form of comedy
- D. were not popular until after the Civil War

C 9. Stephen Foster
- A. composed fewer than twenty songs in his lifetime
- B. received little acclaim for his music
- C. wrote songs that reflected nostalgia for a simpler era
- D. exhibited little diversity in his compositions — mostly writing sad ballads

A 10. The style of architecture that became identified with the political ideals of the new American republic (1780 – 1820) was known as
- A. Federal
- B. Romantic
- C. Baroque
- D. Modern

D 11. The model for the American architectural style known as the National style (1820 – 1850) was
   A. the Roman coliseum
   B. the French chateau
   C. the British palace
   D. the ancient Greek temple

B 12. As a result of the Industrial Revolution, the American middle class
   A. could spend less money on housing
   B. often chose to build attractive homes outside the city
   C. could no longer afford indoor plumbing
   D. wanted to build townhouses in the city

Write the corresponding letter of the correct answer in the space provided.

A. John James Audobon
B. James Fenimore Cooper
C. Charles Finney
D. Ralph Waldo Emerson
E. Nathaniel Hawthorne
F. Washington Irving
G. Henry Wadsworth Longfellow
H. Herman Melville
I. John Trumbull
J. Charles Wilson Peale
K. Edgar Allan Poe
L. Walt Whitman

I 1. Artist known for his realistic historical paintings, such as *The Battle of Bunker Hill* and *The Signing of the Declaration of Independence*

D 2. Transcendentalist who wrote of the glory of nature in works such as *Nature* and *Self-Reliance*

H 3. Author of *Moby Dick* and part of the Young America literary circle

C 4. Leader of a series of American revivals from 1824 to 1837

F 5. Author of *Knickerbocker History*, a comic fictional history of Dutch New York, and *Sketch Book*, stories from the Hudson Valley

K 6. Poet and creator of detective novels and horror tales

E 7. Author of the *Scarlet Letter*, dealing with the problem of sin and the effects of guilt

A. John James Audobon
B. James Fenimore Cooper
C. Charles Finney
D. Ralph Waldo Emerson
E. Nathaniel Hawthorne
F. Washington Irving
G. Henry Wadsworth Longfellow
H. Herman Melville
I. John Trumbull
J. Charles Wilson Peale
K. Edgar Allan Poe
L. Walt Whitman

L 8. Poet whose lengthy volume of poetry entitled *Leaves of Grass* was unconventional in style, using free verse

J 9. Painter known for his portraits of famous American officers and for his establishment of America's first museum of the natural world

B 10. Creator of the American frontier hero archetype in the *Leatherstocking Tales*

A 11. Painter of American birds

G 12. Poet known for his narrative poems about important national figures

LESSON 32: FOR FURTHER STUDY

1. Find a list of Stephen Foster's songs. Pick several songs and look at the words. Listen to a recording of them if you can find one. What do you learn about American culture of the period from these songs?

2. Pick a literary work of the period to read in its entirety or excerpts, such as *Rip Van Winkle* by Washington Irving or one of Longfellow's poems. Try some recipes from a period cookbook, such as *Not By Bread Alone.*

3. Look for paintings by one or more painters of the period, such as Thomas Cole, George Caleb Bingham, and George Catlin.

4. Find photographs of American buildings and homes built in the Federal and Greek Revival (National) architectural styles. Take a virtual tour of a southern plantation home; or if you live near one, tour it in person.

UNIT 4: FINAL REVIEW

Match the person to the event.

A. George Washington
B. John Adams
C. Thomas Jefferson
D. James Madison
E. James Monroe
F. John Quincy Adams
G. Andrew Jackson
H. Martin Van Buren
I. William Henry Harrison
J. John Tyler
K. James K. Polk

K 1. Mexican War

C 2. Lewis and Clark Expedition

F 3. Tariff of abominations

A 4. Passage of the Bill of Rights

J 5. Webster-Ashburton Treaty

B 6. Virginia and Kentucky Resolutions

H 7. Panic of 1837

C 8. Louisiana Purchase

I 9. First presidential death in office

C 10. *Marbury v. Madison*

G 11. Kitchen Cabinet

G 12. Spoils system

C 13. Embargo Act

E 14. War of 1812

K 15. Settlement of Oregon boundary

B 16. "Midnight" judicial appointments

A. George Washington
B. John Adams
C. Thomas Jefferson
D. James Madison
E. James Monroe
F. John Quincy Adams
G. Andrew Jackson
H. Martin Van Buren
I. William Henry Harrison
J. John Tyler
K. James K. Polk

E 17. Rush-Bagot and Adams-Onis treaties

A 18. Whiskey Rebellion

G 19. Specie Circular of 1838

A 20. Jay Treaty

F 21. Clay's "American System"

Match the war to the corresponding person or event.

A. War of 1812
B. Mexican War

B 1. Battle of Veracruz

B 2. General Zachary Taylor

A 3. Impressment of sailors

A 4. Battle of the Thames

B 5. Stephen Kearney

B 6. Bear Flag Republic

B 7. Battle of Buena Vista

A 8. President Madison

A 9. Treaty of Ghent

B 10. John Slidell

A. War of 1812 B. Mexican War

_A_ 11. Battle of New Orleans

_A_ 12. USS *Constitution*

_A_ 13. General William Henry Harrison

_B_ 14. President Polk

_A_ 15. Battle of Tippecanoe

_A_ 16. Burning of Washington D.C.

_B_ 17. John C. Fremont

_B_ 18. Treaty of Guadalupe Hidalgo

_B_ 19. General Winfield Scott

_A_ 20. Battle of Horseshoe Bend

Write T for True and F for False in the space provided.

_T_ 1. Child mortality rates were still high in the early 1800s.

_F_ 2. The majority of American parents no longer needed their children to work in order for their family to survive financially.

_F_ 3. In the first decades of the nineteenth century, American women were never allowed to work outside the home.

_T_ 4. Wealthy children in the South were usually taught by private tutors or attended private academies.

_T_ 5. Horace Mann believed that public schools made it possible to improve and equalize educational opportunities for American children.

_F_ 6. The *McGuffey's Readers* were criticized for failing to teach children traditional moral values.

_T_ 7. Sewing machines were not invented until 1850 and were expensive to own.

_T_ 8. Wool and linen were the most common fabrics used for clothing.

_T_ 9. Americans during this period did not launder their clothing frequently.

_T_ 10. Most men did not own enough shirts to set one or more aside as just night-shirts.

_F_ 11. Women's dresses were always closed with hooks and eyes.

_T_ 12. Upper-class American women had their dresses made to reflect current trends in London, Paris, and large eastern U.S. cities.

_T_ 13. During the first half of the nineteenth century, surgery was usually the last resort for any medical problem because it was always painful and usually fatal.

_F_ 14. Hydropathy and homeopathy are two alternative medical treatments that were not used until the twentieth century.

_T_ 15. Meats and breads predominated in nineteenth-century American cuisine.

_T_ 16. Much American corn was converted into whiskey.

_T_ 17. The dominant form of Christian religious expression in early nineteenth-century America was revivalism, and the period became known as the Second Great Awakening.

_T_ 18. The most famous American camp meeting revival of this period occurred at Cane Ridge, Kentucky.

_F_ 19. Revivals in the West were more subdued than those in the East.

_F_ 20. Charles Finney cautioned his listeners against the use of emotional and informal prayers and would not use choirs in his revivals.

_F_ 21. Unitarianism affirmed the Trinity and the deity of Christ.

_T_ 22. Deists denied the essential doctrines of orthodox Christianity and taught that God created the universe, set it in motion, and stood back to allow it to work.

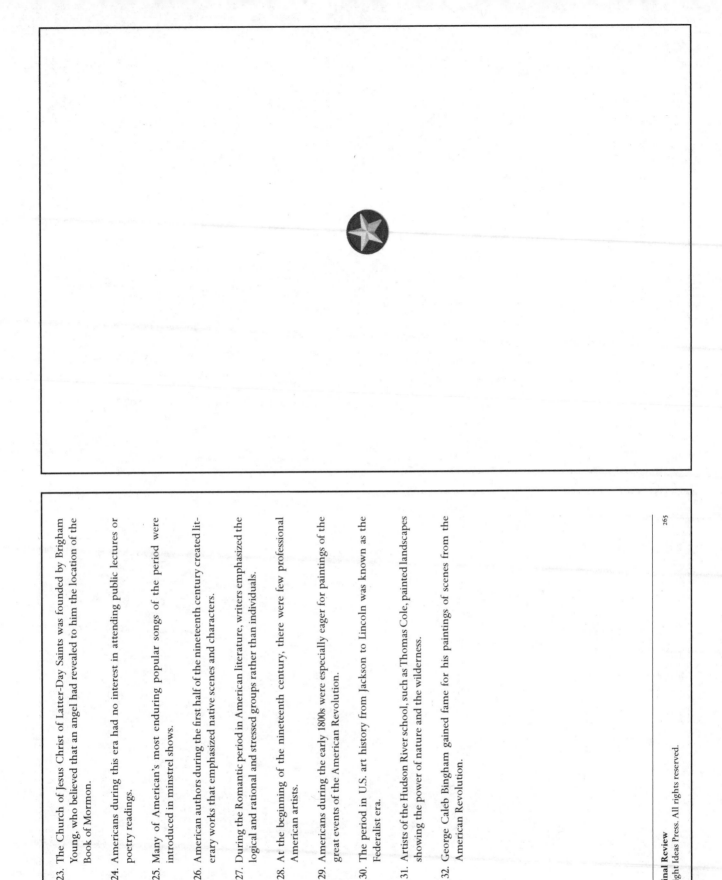

F 23. The Church of Jesus Christ of Latter-Day Saints was founded by Brigham Young, who believed that an angel had revealed to him the location of the Book of Mormon.

F 24. Americans during this era had no interest in attending public lectures or poetry readings.

T 25. Many of American's most enduring popular songs of the period were introduced in minstrel shows.

T 26. American authors during the first half of the nineteenth century created literary works that emphasized native scenes and characters.

F 27. During the Romantic period in American literature, writers emphasized the logical and rational and stressed groups rather than individuals.

T 28. At the beginning of the nineteenth century, there were few professional American artists.

T 29. Americans during the early 1800s were especially eager for paintings of the great events of the American Revolution.

F 30. The period in U.S. art history from Jackson to Lincoln was known as the Federalist era.

T 31. Artists of the Hudson River school, such as Thomas Cole, painted landscapes showing the power of nature and the wilderness.

F 32. George Caleb Bingham gained fame for his paintings of scenes from the American Revolution.

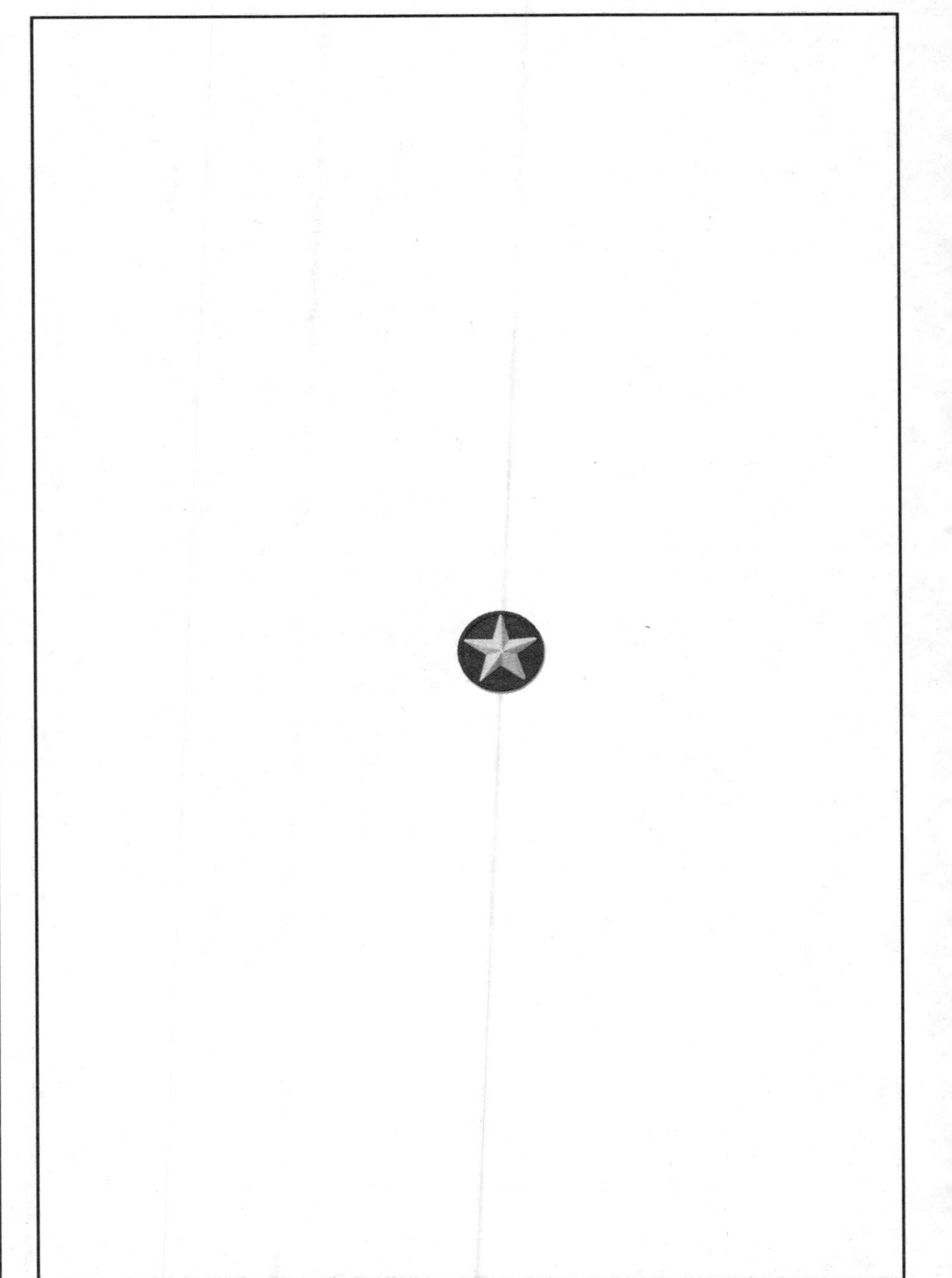

Section Seven

OPTIONAL FORMS

Name________________________________ Date ____________

NATIVE AMERICAN TRIBE

Name of the tribe ________________________________

In what region of the United States did this tribe live? ________________

Pictures of important tribal leaders

Paste image here	Paste image here	Paste image here

What explorer(s) or colonist(s) interracted with this tribe? ________________

____

____

Were relations friendly? ________________________________

What kind of food did this tribe eat? ________________________________

____

What language did they speak? ________________________________

____

Write about about this tribe's religious customs, transportation methods, and recreation.

____

____

____

Name ______________________ Date ____________

TRIBAL LIFE

Draw some pictures based on your research.

Man in tribal clothing

Woman in tribal clothing

Draw a picture of typical tribal housing and some tribal tools or weapons.

Name ______________________ Date __________

NATIVE AMERICAN

Picture of this individual

Name ______________________

____

Paste image here

Year born ______________________

Year died ______________________

Tribe into which he or she was born ______________________

What job or jobs did this person hold? ______________________

____

Explain about the type of obstacles he or she needed to overcome ______________________

Name______________________________________ Date ________________

Explain the role that this individual played in the history of the United States.

Locate a picture of a significant event or place from this individual's life, photocopy it, and paste it here. Or draw a scene if no picture is available.

Name ______________________ Date __________

AFRICAN AMERICAN

Picture of this individual

Name ______________________

____

Paste image here

Year born ______________________

Year died ______________________

State in which he or she was born ______________________

What job or jobs did this person hold? ______________________

____

Explain about the type of obstacles he or she needed to overcome ______________________

Name____ Date ______________

Explain the role that this individual played in the history of the United States.

____

____

____

____

____

____

Locate a picture of a significant event or place from this individual's life, photocopy it, and paste it here. Or draw a scene if no picture is available.

Name ________________ Date ________

EUROPEAN EXPLORER

Name of the explorer ________________

Picture of the explorer

Paste image here

Year born ________________

Year died ________________

Flag of country for which he did exploration

Paste image here

Flag of country for which he did exploration

Paste image here

Flag of the country where he was born

Paste image here

How many voyages did he take? ________________

During what years did he participate in exploration? ________________

What area(s) of the world did he explore? ________________

List the achievement(s) for which he should be remembered

VOYAGES OF

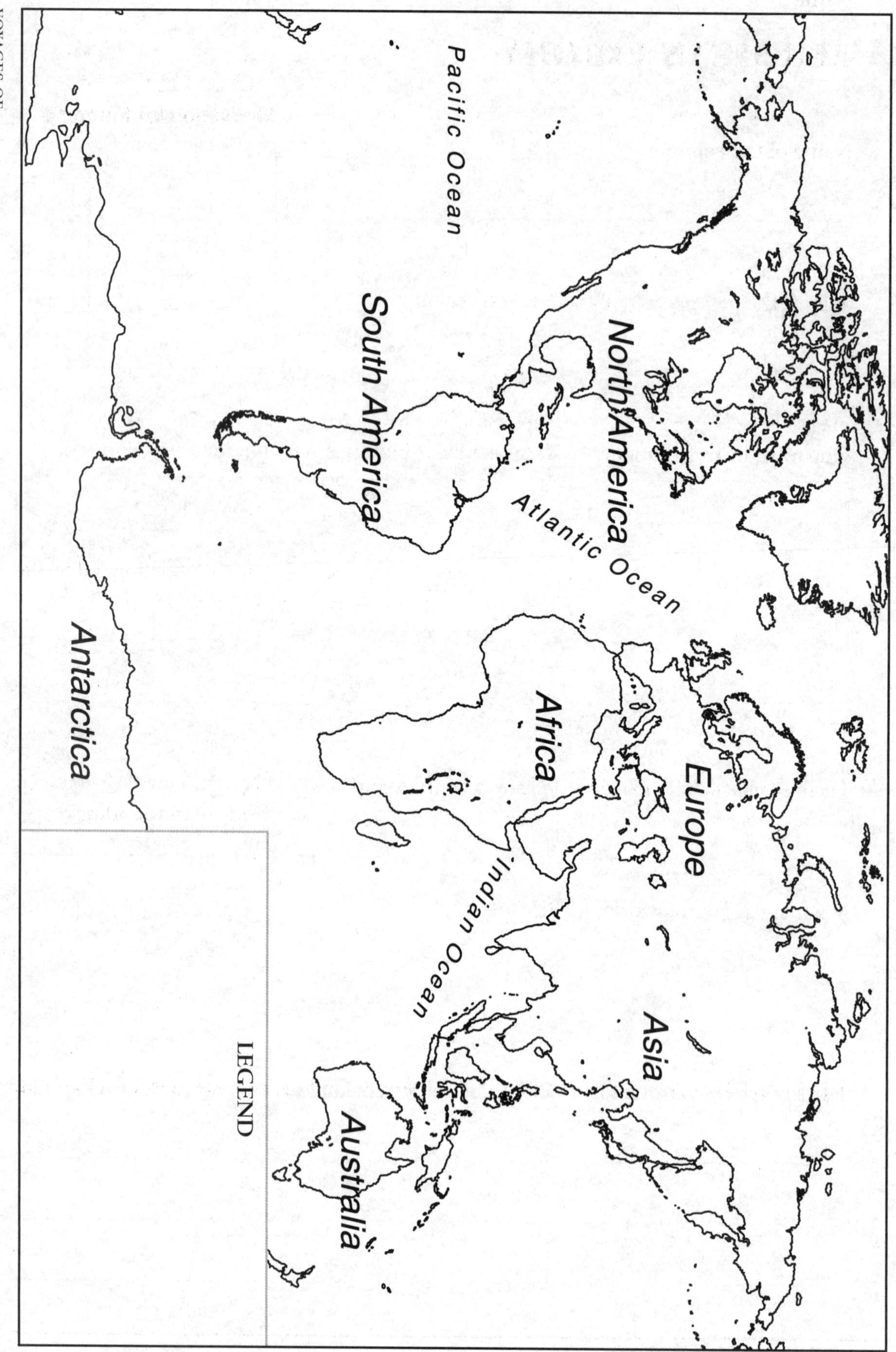
Pacific Ocean
South America
North America
Atlantic Ocean
Antarctica
Africa
Europe
Indian Ocean
Asia
Australia
LEGEND

Name ______________________________ Date ______________

AMERICAN COLONY

Name of the colony ______________________________

____

Year of the first permanent colony settlement

____

Motivation for founding

Paste image here

Picture of colony's founder

Paste image here

Name of this colony's primary founder?

____

List some other individuals who were instrumental in the early years of this colony

____

Flag of country that played a role in its founding

Paste image here

Flag of country that played a role in its founding

Paste image here

Flag of country that played a role in its founding

Paste image here

List any other important facts about this colony or significant events in its development

____

____

____

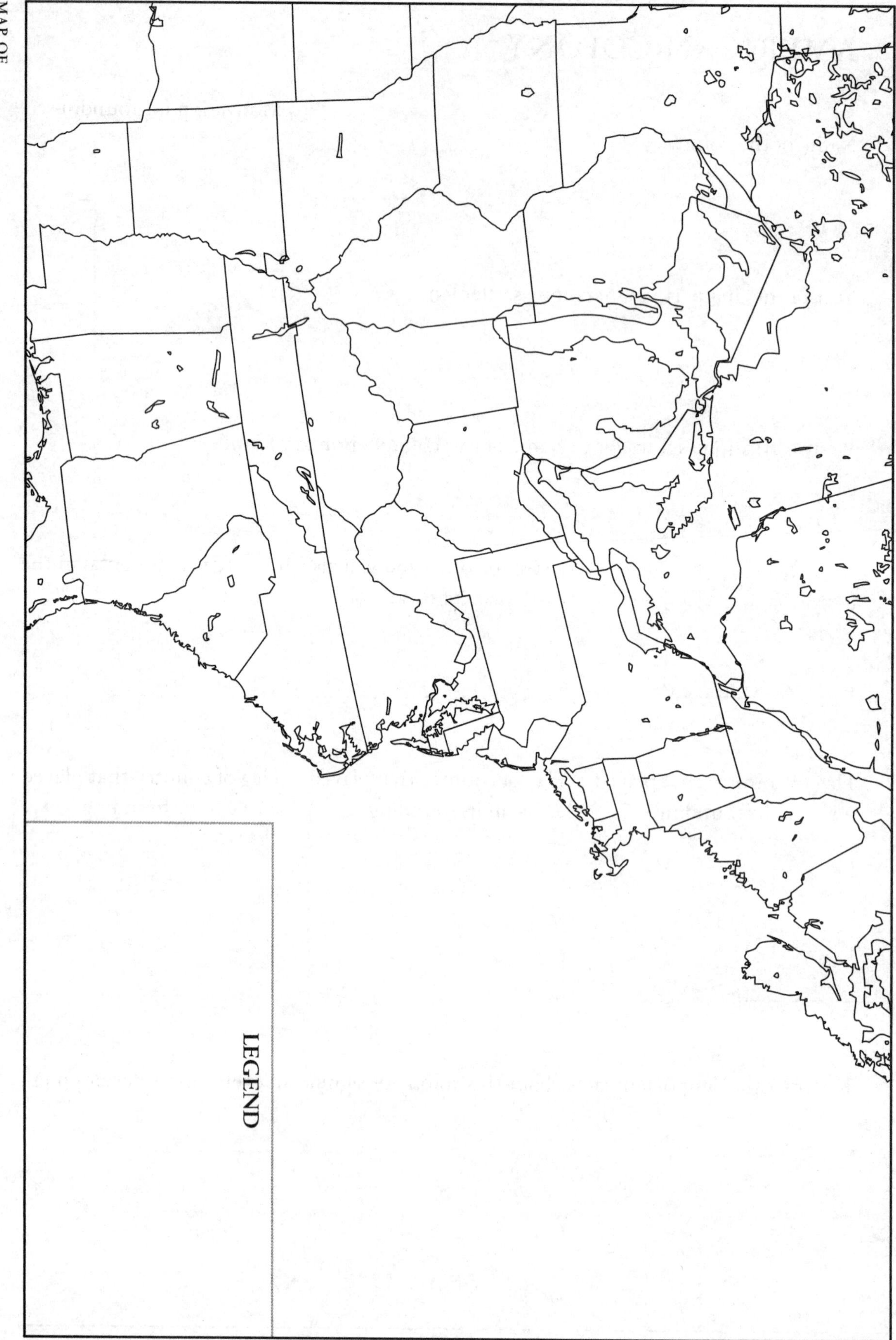
MAP OF
LEGEND

Name ______________________ Date ____________

UNITED STATES PRESIDENT

Name of the president ______________________

____

Year born ______________________

Year died ______________________

What political party was this president affiliated with?

____

What jobs did he hold before becoming president?

____

Picture of the president

Paste image here

Picture of vice president

Paste image here

What state was he born in? ______________________

List some significant developments in domestic policy during his administration

____

____

____

____

____

____

____

____

STATES ADDED TO THE UNION DURING THIS PRESIDENT'S TERM(S)

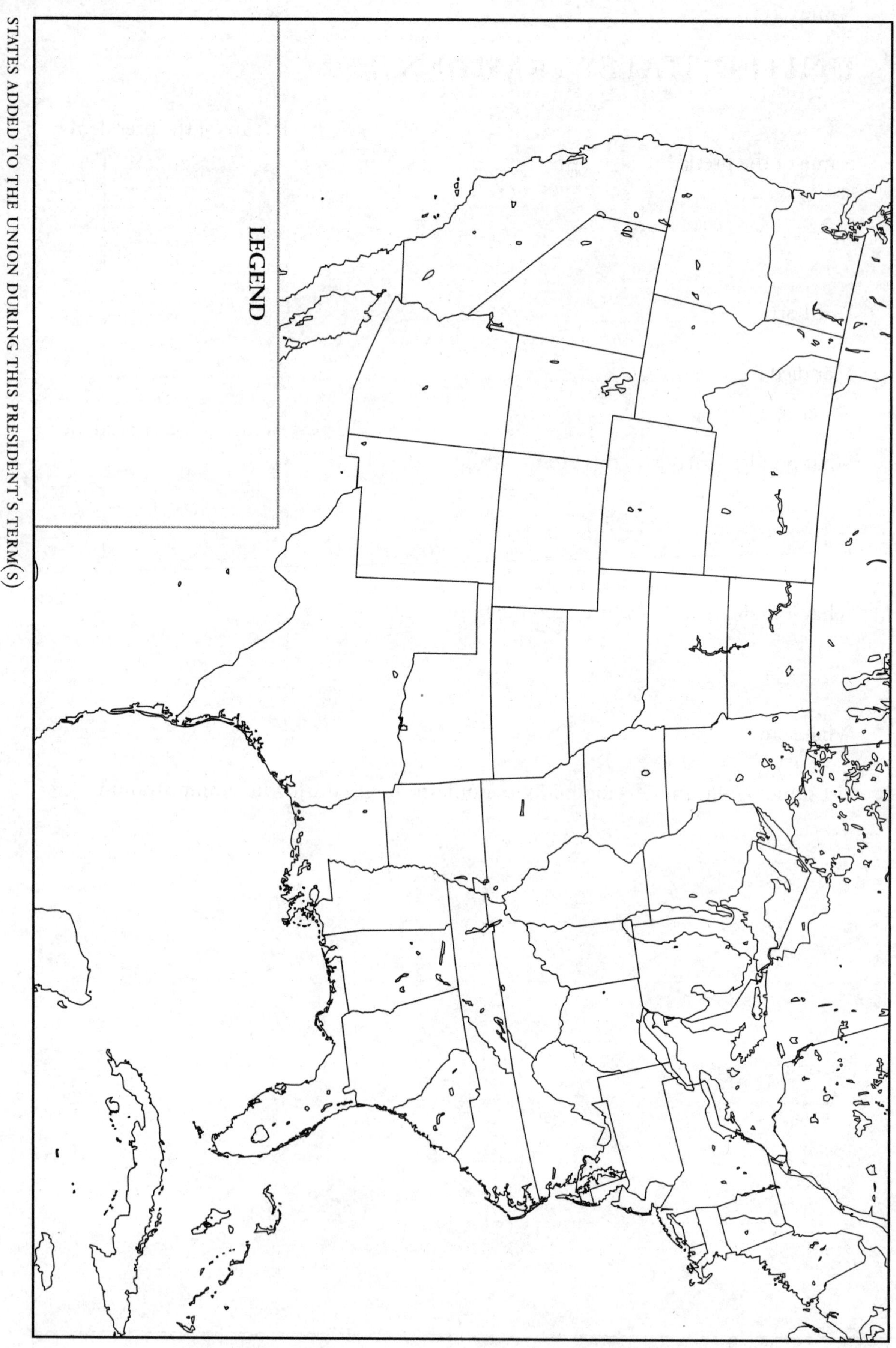

Name ______________________ Date ______________

REVOLUTIONARY WAR BATTLE

Name of the battle? ______________________

Date(s) of the battle ______________________

Location of the battle ______________________

Pictures of some of the key individuals in this battle

Paste image here

Paste image here

Paste image here

Paste image here

Paste image here

What was the purpose of this battle? ______________________

____

List any other important facts about this battle ______________________

____

____

How was this battle significant to the Revolutionary War? ______________________

____

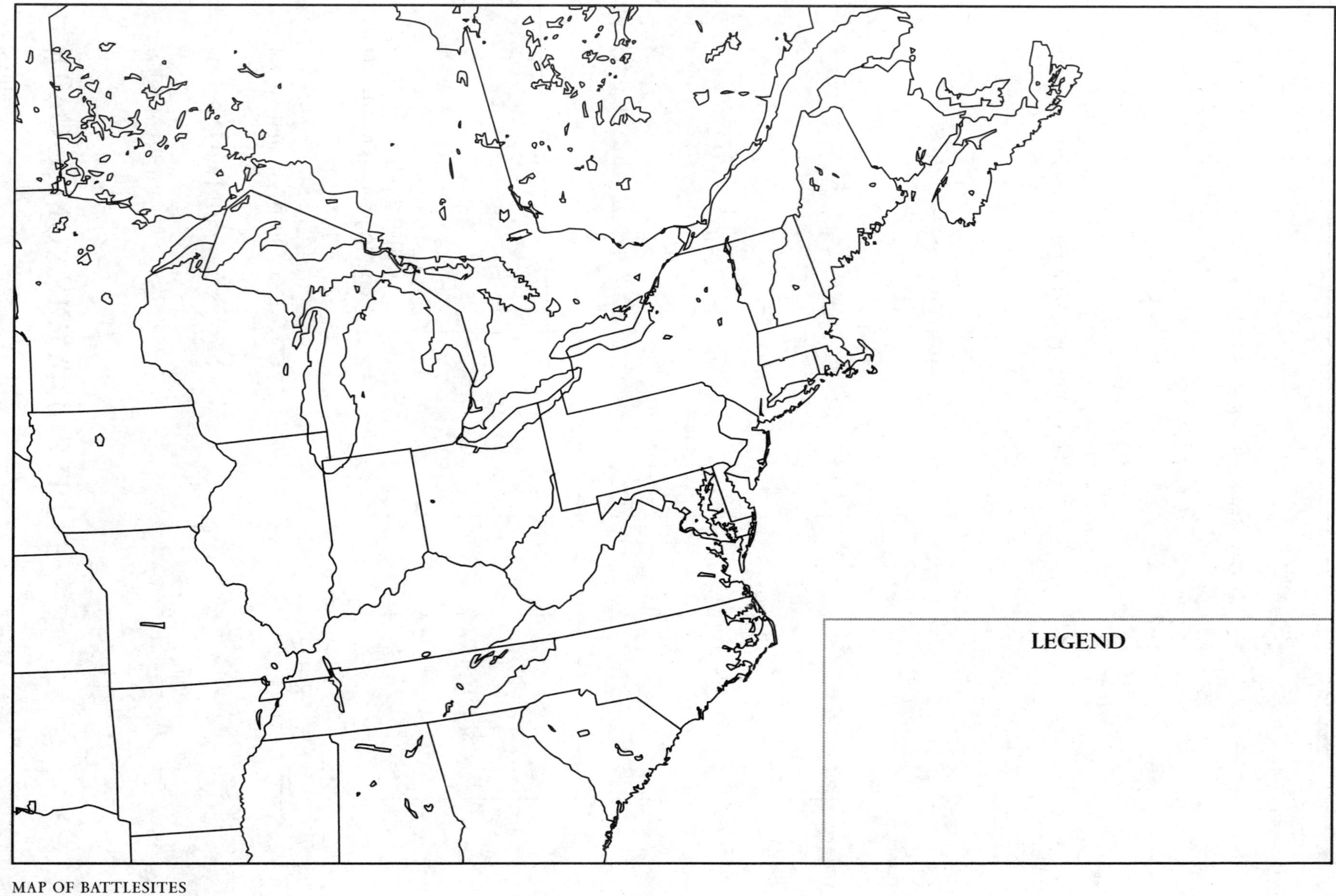

MAP OF BATTLESITES

Name______________________________ Date ____________

WAR OF 1812 BATTLE

Name of the battle? ______________________________

Date(s) of the battle ______________________________

Location of the battle ______________________________

Pictures of some of the key individuals in this battle

Paste image here

Paste image here

Paste image here

Paste image here

Paste image here

What was the purpose of this battle? ______________________________

List any other important facts about this battle ______________________________

How was this battle significant to the War of 1812? ______________________________

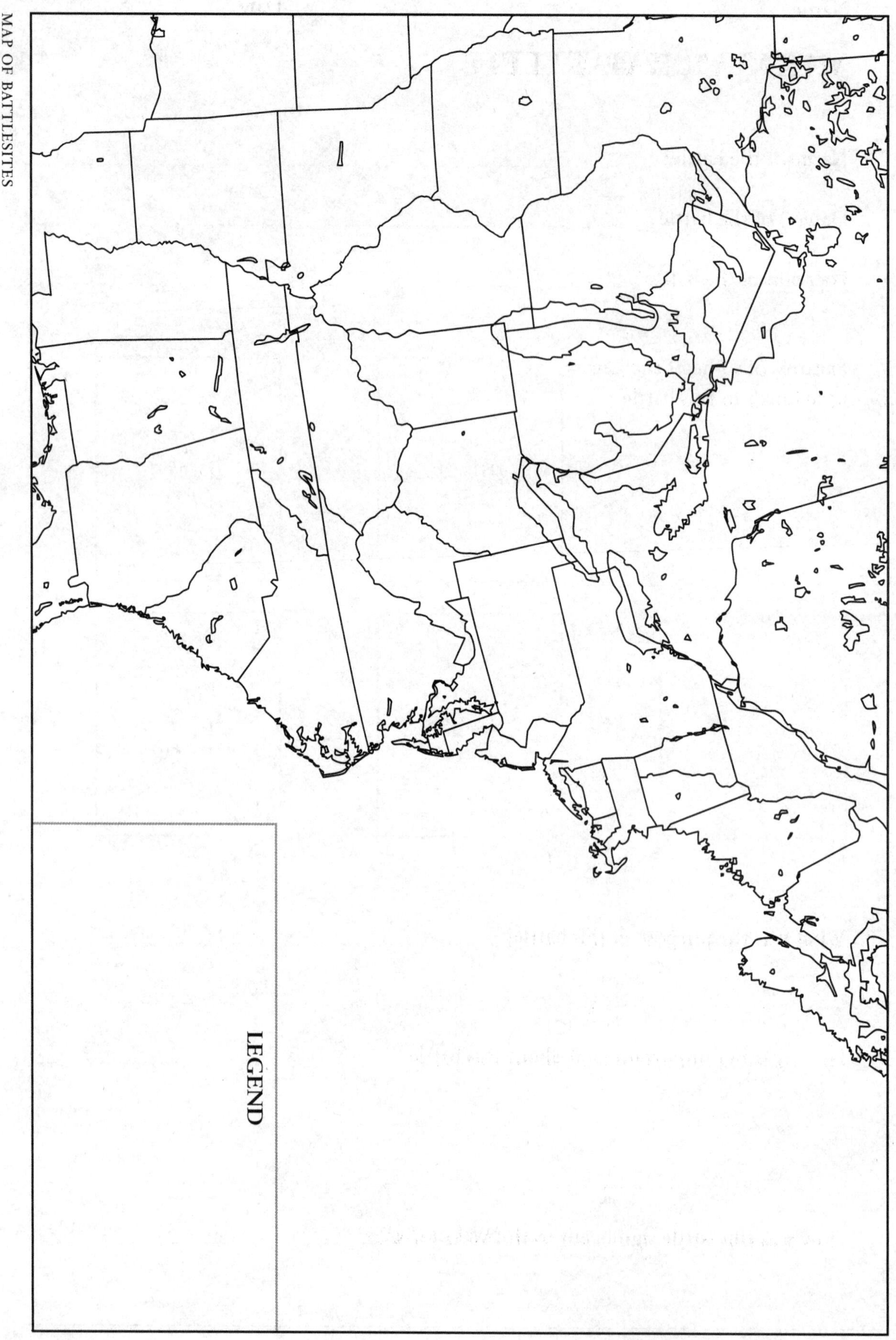
LEGEND

Name________________________________ Date ____________

MEXICAN WAR BATTLE

Name of the battle? ________________________________

Date(s) of the battle ________________________________

Location of the battle ________________________________

Pictures of some of the key individuals in this battle

Paste image here

Paste image here

Paste image here

Paste image here

Paste image here

What was the purpose of this battle? ________________________________

____

List any other important facts about this battle ________________________________

____

____

How was this battle significant to the Mexican War?________________________________

____

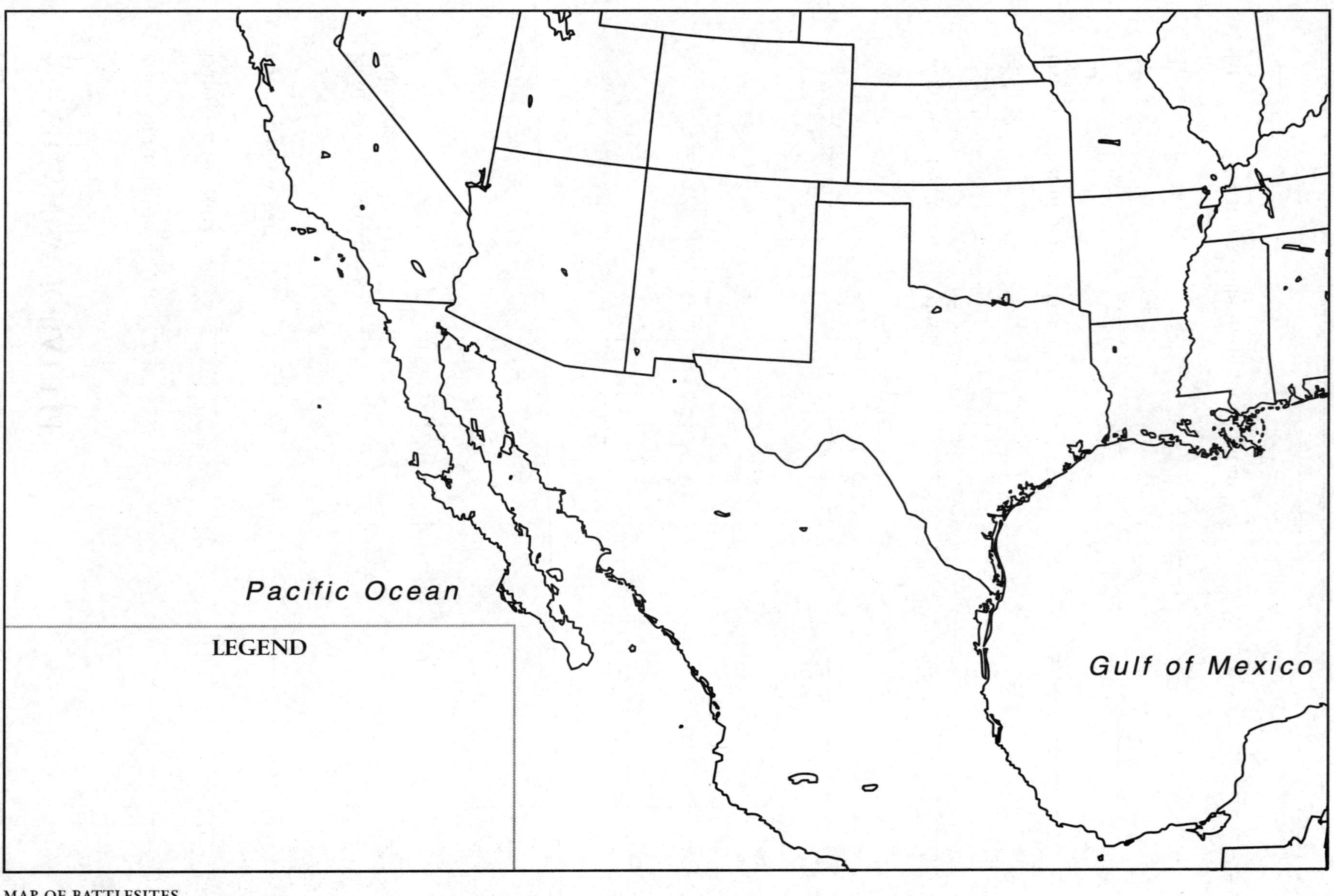

MAP OF BATTLESITES

Name____ Date ____________________

COLONIAL FAMILY LIFE

How is colonial family life the same as life with your family? ____________________

How is it different? ____________________

List some similarities and differences between colonial education and your current education

What do you think your favorite food would have been if you had lived in colonial times?

What would have been your least favorite food?____________________

Name____ Date ____________________

COLONIAL CLOTHING

Draw a picture of a man and a woman in some kind of colonial clothing, or locate a picture, photocopy it, and glue it in place.

Man in colonial clothing

Woman in colonial clothing

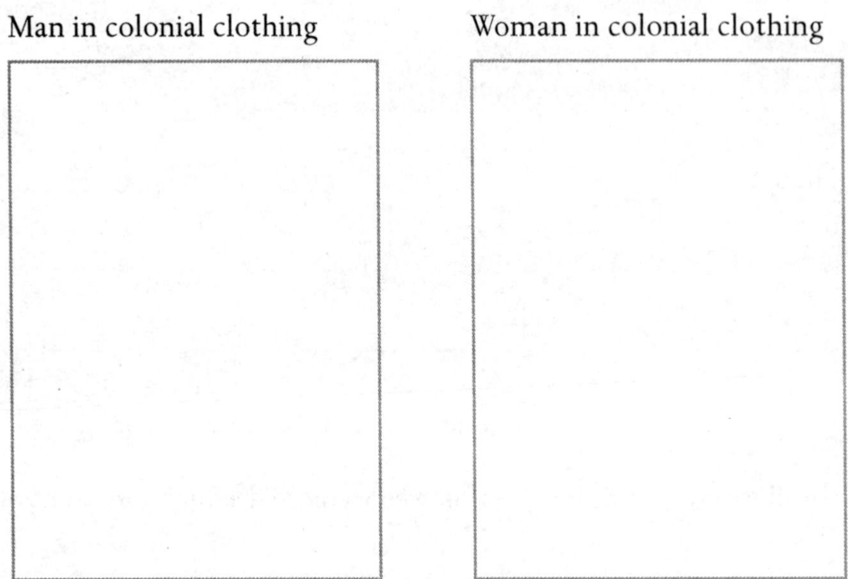

Draw a picture of a boy and a girl in some kind of colonial clothing, or locate a picture, photocopy it, and glue it in place.

Boy in colonial clothing

Girl in colonial clothing

Name _______________ Date _______________

COLONIAL CULTURE

What elements of colonial culture are the same as today's? _______________

What elements of colonial culture are different from today's? _______________

Many industries today are very different than colonial industries were. After reading about the colonial industries, what industry do you think you would have liked to work in if you had lived in colonial times and why?

How were the colonial religious services different than the religious services you attend?

Name____ Date ________________

Transportation has changed radically from colonial times. Draw a picture of what you think your faviorite mode of transportation would have been.

If you had lived in colonial times, what do you think your favorite game or activity would have been?

____

____

Are there any books or songs that people read or sang in colonial times that we still read and sing today?

____

____

Which ones?____

____

Do you have a favorite and what is it? ______________________________________

Name_______________________________ Date ____________

NINETEENTH CENTURY FAMILY LIFE

How is nineteenth century family life the same as life with your family? ____________

How is it different? ____________

List some similarities and differences between nineteenth century education and your current education

What do you think your favorite food would have been if you had lived in the nineteenth century?

What would have been your least favorite food? ____________

Name________________________________ Date ____________

NINETEENTH CENTURY CLOTHING

Draw a picture of a man and a woman in nineteenth century clothing, or locate a picture, photocopy it, and glue it in place.

Man in nineteenth century clothing

Woman in nineteenth century clothing

Draw a picture of a boy and a girl in some kind of nineteenth century clothing, or locate a picture, photocopy it, and glue it in place.

Boy in nineteenth century clothing

Girl in nineteenth century clothing

Name____ Date ________________

NINETEENTH CENTURY CULTURE

What elements of nineteenth century culture are the same as today's? ____________

____

____

____

____

What elements of nineteenth century culture are different from today's? ____________

____

____

____

How did the Industrial Revolution change where Americans lived and why? ____________

____

____

____

How were nineteenth century religious services different than the religious services you attend?

____

____

____

____

____

Name____ Date ____________________

If you had lived in nineteenth century times, what do you think your favorite game or activity would have been?

____

____

Many of the American novelists who wrote in the nineteenth century created stories that are now considered classics. Do you have a favorite? If so, what is it and who is the author?

____

____

____

Draw a building that has features of a nineteenth century architectural style and identify the style.

Section Eight

IMAGES FOR REQUIRED FORMS

UNIT ONE

Christopher Columbus	Prince Henry the Navigator	Marco Polo	Leif Eriksson
Hernando Cortés	Vasco Nuñez de Balboa	John Cabot	Amerigo Vespucci
Giovanni da Verrazano	Ferdinand Magellan	Juan Ponce de Leon	Francisco Pizarro
Sir Francis Drake	Francisco Vasquez de Coronado	Hernando de Soto	Jacques Cartier
	Samuel de Champlain	Henry Hudson	Sir Walter Raleigh

UNIT TWO

Clarendon
Albemarle
Craven
John Berkeley
Ashley
Will Berkeley

	William Bradford		John Smith
	John Wheelwright		John Winthrop
	Thomas Hooker		Roger Williams
Carteret and Berkeley		Peter Stuyvesant	
	William Penn	Peter Minuit	

Fatti Maschii Parole Femine
ARMS OF THE CALVERT FAMILY

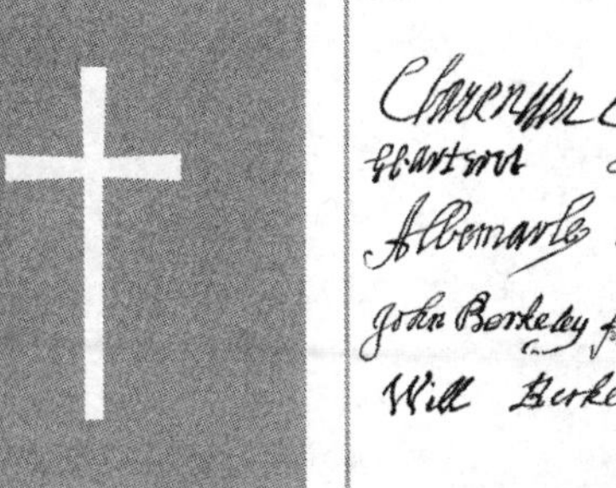

Debtor

	The Lords Proprietor		Cecil Calvert
	James Oglethorpe		Sir Ashley Cooper

UNIT THREE

Louis Montcalm	James Wolfe	Jeffrey Amherst	George Washington
Patrick Henry	Samuel Adams	General Thomas Gage	King George III
Governor Thomas Hutchinson	John Hancock	John Adams	Paul Revere
George Washington	Benedict Arnold	Ethan Allen	Dr. Joseph Warren
Captain Dan Morgan	General William Howe	Benjamin Franklin	Thomas Jefferson

General Charles Cornwallis	General Henry Clinton	General Henry Knox	Thomas Paine
Martha Washington	John Dickinson	General Horatio Gates	General John Burgoyne
Count Casimir Pulaski	Marquis de Lafayette	Baron von Steuben	Abigail Adams
General Nathanael Greene	Francis Marion	John Paul Jones	George Rogers Clark

UNIT FOUR

James Madison	Thomas Jefferson	John Adams	George Washington
Andrew Jackson	William Henry Harrison	Captain Oliver Perry	James Monroe
Martin Van Buren	Andrew Jackson	John Quincy Adams	Francis Scott Key
General Zachary Taylor	James Polk	John Tyler	William Henry Harrison
	John C. Frémont	Brig. Gen. Stephen Kearney	General Winfield Scott

UNIT THREE

The Proclamation of 1763
1763
Enforcement of the Navigation Acts
1763
The Sugar Act
1764
The Quartering Act
1765
The Stamp Act
1765
The Townshend Acts
1767
The Boston Massacre
1770
Burning of the *Gaspee*
1772
Committees of Corre-spondence
1772
Tea Act and the Boston Tea Party
1773
Intolerable Acts
1774
First Continental Congress
1774

UNIT ONE

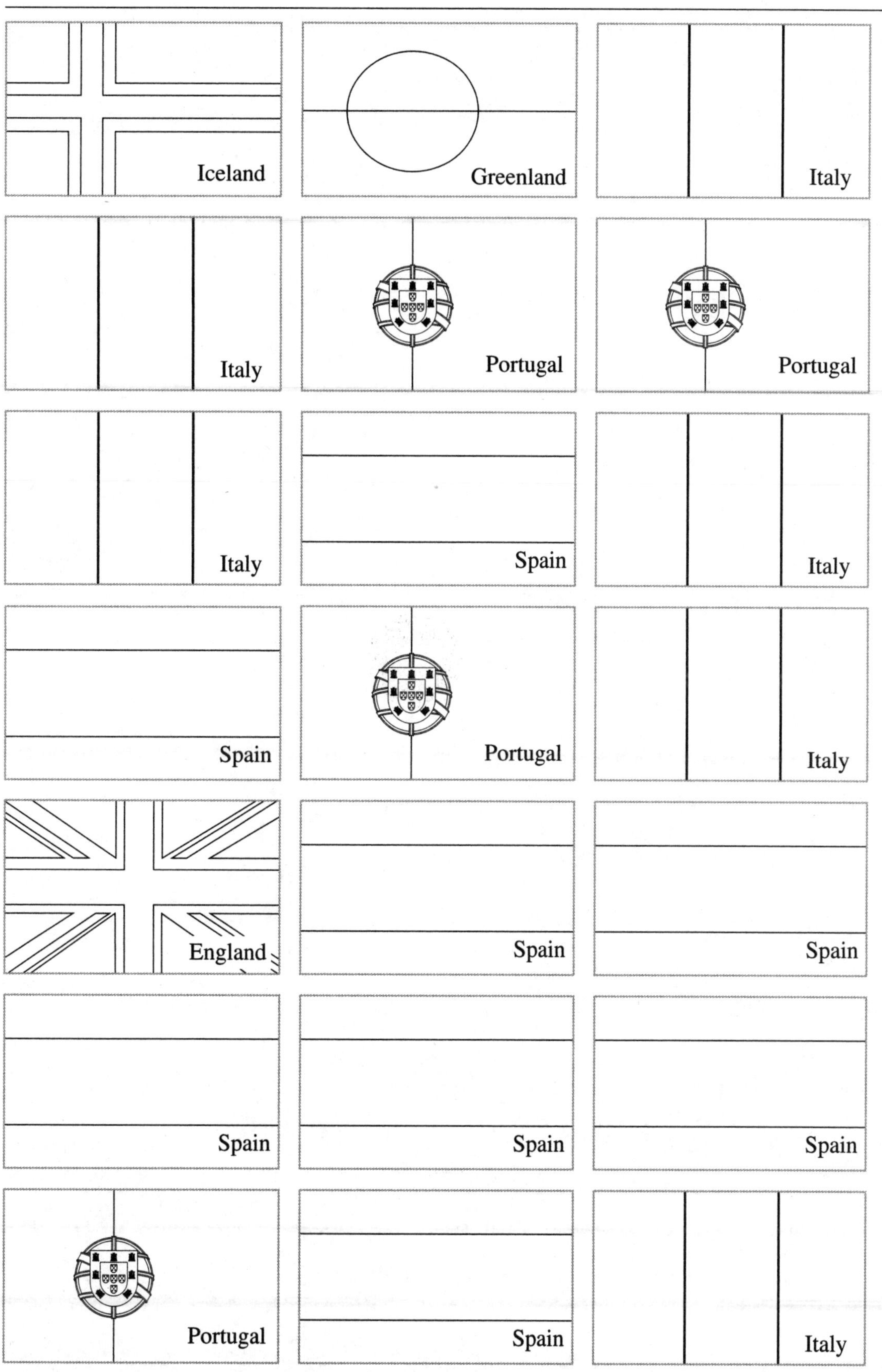

Iceland
Greenland
Italy
Italy
Portugal
Portugal
Italy
Spain
Italy
Spain
Portugal
Italy
England
Spain
Spain
Spain
Spain
Spain
Portugal
Spain
Italy

Italy	Greenland	Iceland
Portugal	Portugal	Italy
Italy	Spain	Italy
Italy	Portugal	Spain
Spain	Spain	England
Spain	Spain	Spain
Italy	Spain	Portugal

France France France

Spain Spain Spain

Spain England England

England England England

England Netherlands France

France

France	France	France
Spain	Spain	Spain
England	England	Spain
England	England	England
France	Netherlands	England
		France

UNIT TWO

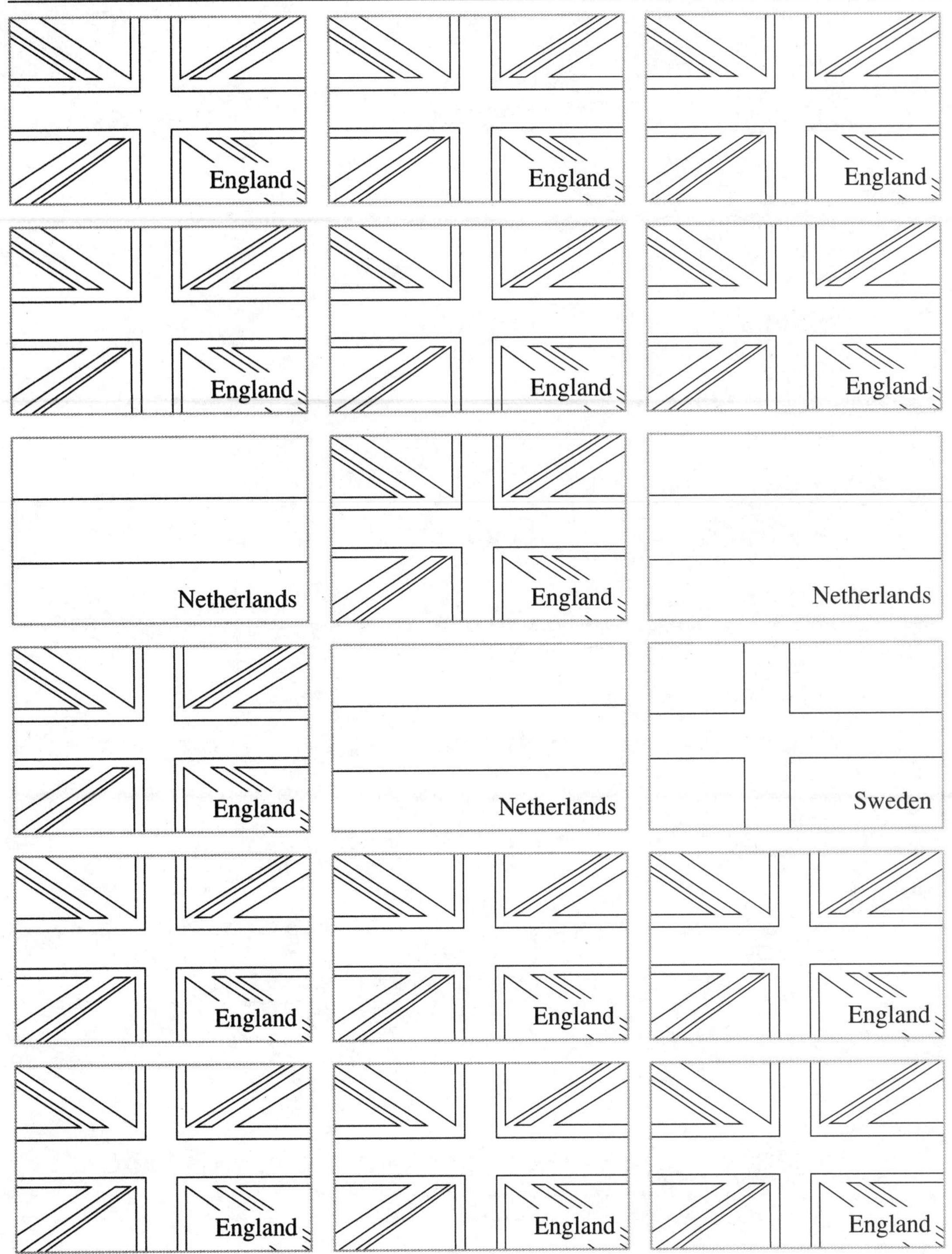
England
England
England
England
England
England
Netherlands
England
Netherlands
England
Netherlands
Sweden
England
England
England
England
England
England

England	England	England
England	England	England
Netherlands	England	Netherlands
Sweden	Netherlands	England
England	England	England
England	England	England

UNIT THREE

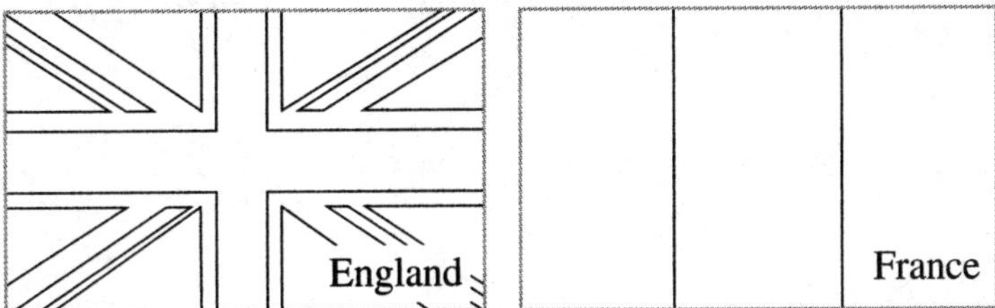

France

England

UNIT FOUR

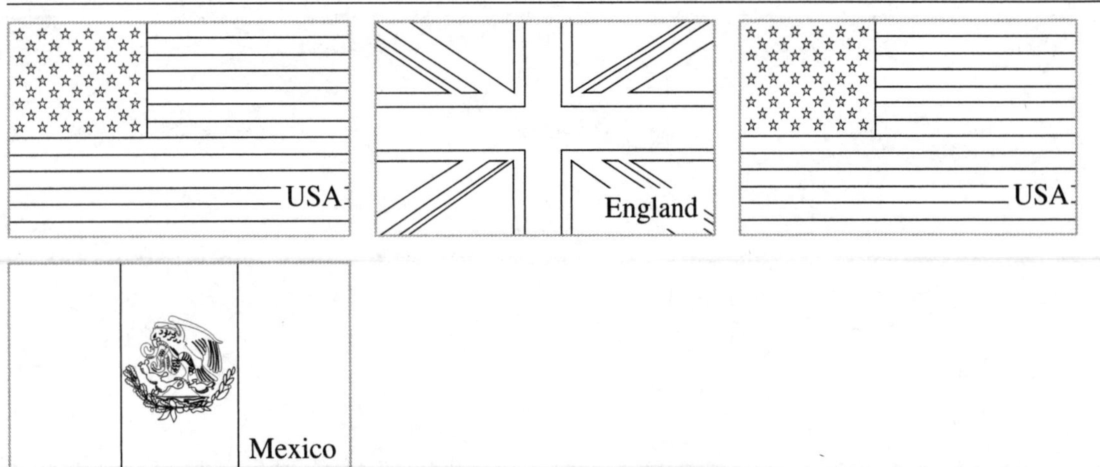

USA

England

USA

Mexico

Appendix

SELECT BIBLIOGRAPHY

UNIT ONE

Arnold, Eric. *Christopher Columbus: Sailing the Sea of Darkness.* Middletown: Weekly Reader Books, 1992.

Baker, Susan. *Tales of Courage: Explorers of North America.* Austin: Steck-Vaughn, 1989.

Barker, Felix, Malcolm Ross-MacDonald, and Duncan Castlereagh. *The Glorious Age of Exploration.* Garden City: Doubleday and Company, 1973.

Blassingame, Wyatt. *Ponce De Leon.* Philadelphia: Chelsea House, 1991.

Cesarani, Gian Paolo. *Marco Polo.* New York: G. P. Putnam's Sons, 1977.

Chubb, Thomas. *Prince Henry the Navigator and the Highways of the Sea.* New York: Viking Press, 1970.

Cullen, Derek and John Murray-Robertson. *Exploring the Oceans.* Needham: Schoolhouse Press, 1988.

Donaldson-Forbes, Jeff. *Amerigo Vespucci.* New York: PowerKids Press, 2002.

Dyment, John. *Meet the Men Who Sailed the Seas.* New York: Random House, 1966.

Fisher, Leonard Everett. *Prince Henry the Navigator.* New York: Macmillan Publishing Co., 1990.

Flowers, Sarah. *The Age of Exploration.* San Diego: Lucent Books, 1999.

Fradin, Dennis. *Explorers: New True Book.* Chicago: Children's Press, 1984.

Gallagher, Carole. *Christopher Columbus and the Discovery of the New World.* Philadelphia: Chelsea House, 2000.

Gallagher, Jim. *Ferdinand Magellan and the First Voyage Around the World.* Philadelphia: Chelsea House, 2000.

Gallagher, Jim. *Hernando de Soto and the Exploration of Florida.* Philadelphia: Chelsea House Publishers, 2000.

Ganeri, Anita. *Focus on Vikings.* New York: Shooting Star Press, 1993.

Gleiter, Jan and Kathleen Thompson. *First Biographies: Christopher Columbus.* Austin: Raintree Steck-Vaughn, 1995.

Goetzmann, William and Glyndwr Williams. *The Atlas of North American Exploration.* New York: Prentice Hall, 1992.

Goodman, Joan Elizabeth. *Beyond the Sea of Ice: The Voyages of Henry Hudson.* New York: Mikaya Press, 1999.

Goodnough, David. *Christopher Columbus.* Mahwah: Troll Communications, 1979.

Goodnough, David. *Francis Drake.* Mahwah: Troll Communications, 1979.

Goodnough, David. *John Cabot and Son.* Mahwah: Troll Communications, 1979.

Harley, Ruth. *Ferdinand Magellan: Adventures in Discovery.* Mahwah: Troll Communications, 1979.

Harley, Ruth. *Henry Hudson.* Mahwah: Troll Communications, 1979.

Harmon, Dan. *Juan Ponce de Leon and the Search for the Fountain of Youth.* Philadelphia: Chelsea House, 2000.

Hewitt, James. *Famous Names in World Exploration.* Hove: Wayland Publishers, 1979.

Hoose, Phillip. *We Were There, Too! Young People in U.S. History.* New York: Farrar, Straus, and Giroux, 2001.

Hopkins, Andrea. *Vikings: the Norse Discovery of America.* New York: PowerKids Press, 2002.

Humble, Richard. *The Age of Leif Eriksson: Exploration through the Ages.* New York: Franklin Watts, 1989.

Humble, Richard. *The Explorers.* Alexandria: Time-Life Books, 1978.

Humble, Richard. *The Voyage of Magellan: Exploration through the Ages.* New York: Franklin Watts, 1988.

January, Brendan. *Explorers of North America.* New York: Grolier Publishing, 2000.

Jensen, Malcolm C. *Leif Erikson the Lucky.* New York: Franklin Watts, 1979.

Kent, Zachary. *The World's Great Explorers: Marco Polo.* Chicago: Children's Press, 1992.

Kerby, Elizabeth. *The Conquistadors.* New York: G. P. Putnam's Sons, 1969.

Knoop, Faith Yingling. *Vasco Nunez de Balboa.* Champaign: Garrard Publishing, 1969.

McCall, Edith. *Explorers in a New World.* Chicago: Children's Press, 1960.

MacDonald, Fiona. *Timelines Explorers: Expeditions and Pioneers.* New York: Franklin Watts, 1994.

Maestro, Betsy and Giulio. *The Discovery of the Americas.* New York: Lothrop, Lee, and Shepard, 1991.

Marcovitz, Hal. *Francisco Coronado and the Exploration of the American Southwest.* Philadelphia: Chelsea House, 2000.

Marcovitz, Hal. *Marco Polo and the Wonders of the East.* Philadelphia: Chelsea House, 2000.

Marshall, Peter and David Manuel. *The Light and the Glory.* Old Tappan: Fleming H. Revell Co., 1980.

Matthews, Rupert. *Explorer: Eyewitness Books.* New York: Alfred A. Knopf, 1991.

Millard, Anne. *Explorers and Traders.* San Francisco: Time-Life Books, 1996.
Moore, Judy Hull and Laurel Hicks. *The History of Our United States.* Pensacola: Abeka Publishing, 1990.
Poole, Frederick King. *Early Exploration of North America.* New York: Franklin Watts, 1989.
Roop, Peter and Connie. *I Columbus.* New York: Walker and Company, 1990.
Ross-MacDonald, Malcolm and Duncan Castlereagh. *The Glorious Age of Exploration.* Garden City: Doubleday and Company, 1973.
Ross, Stewart. *Fact or Fiction: Conquerors and Explorers.* Brookfield: Aladdin Books, 1996.
Ryan, Peter. *Explorers and Mapmakers.* New York: E. P. Dutton, 1989.
Sandak, Cass. *Explorers and Discovery.* New York: Franklin Watts, 1983.
Sims, Lesley. *Voyage to the Edge of the World.* London: Usborne Publishing, 1994.
Strong, Stacie. *The Voyage of Columbus in His Own Words.* Los Angeles: Intervisual Communications, Inc., 1991.
Wilbur, C. Keith. *Early Explorers of North America.* Chester: Globe Pequot Press, 1989.
Williams, Brian. *Tales of Courage: Voyages of Discovery.* Austin: Steck-Vaughn, 1989.

UNIT TWO

Alderman, Clifford. *The Story of the Thirteen Colonies.* New York: Random House, 1966.
Barrett, Tracy. *Growing Up in Colonial America.* Brookfield: Millbrook Press, 1995.
Blow, Michael. *The American Heritage History of the Thirteen Colonies.* New York: American Heritage Publishing Company, 1967.
Coleman, Brook. *The Colony of Virginia.* New York: PowerKids Press, 2000.
Corwin, Judith Hoffman. *Colonial American Crafts — the Home.* New York: Franklin Watts, 1989.
Corwin, Judith Hoffman. *Colonial American Crafts — the School.* New York: Franklin Watts, 1989.
Dean, Ruth and Melissa Thomson. *Life in the American Colonies.* San Diego: Lucent Books, 1999.
Draper, Allison Stark. *What People Wore in Colonial America.* New York: PowerKids Press, 2001.
Erdosh, George. *Food and Recipes of the Thirteen Colonies.* New York: PowerKids Press, 1997.
Fradin, Dennis. *From Sea to Shining Sea: Georgia.* Chicago: Children's Press, 1991.
Fradin, Dennis. *From Sea to Shining Sea: Maryland.* Chicago: Children's Press, 1997.
Fradin, Dennis. *From Sea to Shining Sea: Massachusetts.* Chicago: Children's Press, 1991.
Fradin, Dennis. *From Sea to Shining Sea: New Hampshire.* Chicago: Children's Press, 1992.
Fradin, Dennis. *From Sea to Shining Sea: New York.* Chicago: Children's Press, 1993.
Fradin, Dennis. *From Sea to Shining Sea: North Carolina.* Chicago: Children's Press, 1992.
Fradin, Dennis. *From Sea to Shining Sea: South Carolina.* Chicago: Children's Press, 1992.
Fradin, Dennis. *From Sea to Shining Sea: Virginia.* Chicago: Children's Press, 1992.
Fradin, Dennis. *The Connecticut Colony.* Chicago: Children's Press, 1992.
Fradin, Dennis. *The Delaware Colony.* Chicago: Children's Press, 1992.
Fradin, Dennis. *The Georgia Colony.* Chicago: Children's Press, 1990.
Fradin, Dennis. *The Maryland Colony.* Chicago: Children's Press, 1990.
Fradin, Dennis. *The Massachusetts Colony.* Chicago: Children's Press, 1987.
Fradin, Dennis. *The New Jersey Colony.* Chicago: Children's Press, 1991.
Fradin, Dennis. *The New York Colony.* Chicago: Children's Press, 1988.
Fradin, Dennis. *The North Carolina Colony.* Chicago: Children's Press, 1991.

Fradin, Dennis. *The Pennsylvania Colony.* Chicago: Children's Press, 1988.
Fradin, Dennis. *The Rhode Island Colony.* Chicago: Children's Press, 1989.
Fradin, Dennis. *The South Carolina Colony.* Chicago: Children's Press, 1992.
Fradin, Dennis. *The Virginia Colony.* Chicago: Children's Press, 1986.
Fradin, Dennis. *From Sea to Shining Sea: Connecticut.* Chicago: Children's Press, 1997.
Fradin, Dennis and Judith. *From Sea to Shining Sea: Delaware.* Chicago: Children's Press, 1994.
Fradin, Dennis and Judith. *From Sea to Shining Sea: Rhode Island.* Chicago: Children's Press, 1995.
Gleiter, Jan and Kathleen Thompson. *Pocahantas.* Austin: Raintree-Steck-Vaughn, 1995.
Hakim, Joy. *Making Thirteen Colonies.* New York: Oxford University Press, 1993.
January, Brendan. *Colonial Life — A True Book.* New York: Children's Press, 2000.
January, Brendan. *The Thirteen Colonies — A True Book.* New York: Children's Press, 2000.
Kalman, Bobbie. *Colonial Crafts.* New York: Crabtree Publishing, 1992.
Kalman, Bobbie. *Early Schools.* New York: Crabtree Publishing, 1982.
Kalman, Bobbie. *Games from Long Ago.* New York: Crabtree Publishing, 1995.
Kalman, Bobbie. *A One-Room School.* New York: Crabtree Publishing, 1994.
Kent, Deborah. *African-Americans in the Thirteen Colonies.* New York: Children's Press, 1996.
King, David C. *American Kids in History: Colonial Days.* New York: John Wiley and Sons, Inc., 1998.
Lukes, Bonnie L. *Colonial America.* San Diego: Lucent Books, 2000.
McCall, Barbara. *The European Invasion.* Vero Beach: Rourke Publications, 1994.
McGovern, Ann. *If You Lived in Colonial Times.* New York: Scholastic, 1964.
Maxson, H. A. and Claudia Young. *Zwaanendael: Valley of the Swans.* Dover: Dover Litho, 2000.
Miller, Brandon Marie. *Dressed for the Occasion: What Americans Wore 1620 – 1970.* Minneapolis: Lerner Publication Company, 1999.
Nobleman, Marc Tyler. *We the People: The Thirteen Colonies.* Minneapolis: Compass Point Books, 2002.
Quasha, Jennifer. *Jamestown: Hands-On Project about One of America's First Communities.* New York: PowerKids Press, 2001.
Reische, Diana. *Founding the American Colonies.* New York: Franklin Watts, 1989.
Schlesinger, Jr., Arthur M. *John Smith — English Explorer and Colonist.* Philadelphia: Chelsea House, 2000.
Scott, John Anthony Scott. *Settlers on the Eastern Shore: The British Colonies in North America 1607 – 1750.* New York: Facts on File, 1991.
Thompson, Kathleen. *Portrait of America: Connecticut.* Austin: Steck-Vaughn, 1996.
Thompson, Kathleen. *Portrait of America: Delaware.* Austin: Steck-Vaughn, 1996.
Thompson, Kathleen. *Portrait of America: Georgia.* Austin: Steck-Vaughn, 1996.
Thompson, Kathleen. *Portrait of America: Massachusetts.* Austin: Steck-Vaughn, 1996.
Thompson, Kathleen. *Portrait of America: Maryland.* Austin: Steck-Vaughn, 1996.
Thompson, Kathleen. *Portrait of America: New Hampshire.* Austin: Steck-Vaughn, 1996.
Thompson, Kathleen. *Portrait of America: New Jersey.* Austin: Steck-Vaughn, 1996.
Thompson, Kathleen. *Portrait of America: New York.* Austin: Steck-Vaughn, 1996.
Thompson, Kathleen. *Portrait of America: North Carolina.* Austin: Steck-Vaughn, 1996.
Thompson, Kathleen. *Portrait of America: Pennsylvania.* Austin: Steck-Vaughn, 1996.
Thompson, Kathleen. *Portrait of America: Rhode Island.* Austin: Steck-Vaughn, 1996.
Thompson, Kathleen. *Portrait of America: South Carolina.* Austin: Steck-Vaughn, 1996.
Thompson, Kathleen. *Portrait of America: Virginia.* Austin: Steck-Vaughn, 1996.
Whitehurst, Susan. *The Colony of Connecticut.* New York: PowerKids Press, 2000.
Whitehurst, Susan. *The Colony of Delaware.* New York: PowerKids Press, 2000.
Whitehurst, Susan. *The Colony of Georgia.* New York: PowerKids Press, 2000.

Whitehurst, Susan. *The Colony of Maryland.* New York: PowerKids Press, 2000.
Whitehurst, Susan. *The Colony of Massachusetts.* New York: PowerKids Press, 2000.
Whitehurst, Susan. *The Colony of New Hampshire.* New York: PowerKids Press, 2000.
Whitehurst, Susan. *The Colony of New Jersey.* New York: PowerKids Press, 2000.
Whitehurst, Susan. *The Colony of New York.* New York: PowerKids Press, 2000.
Whitehurst, Susan. *The Colony of North Carolina.* New York: PowerKids Press, 2000.
Whitehurst, Susan. *The Colony of Pennsylvania.* New York: PowerKids Press, 2000.
Whitehurst, Susan. *The Colony of Rhode Island.* New York: PowerKids Press, 2000.
Wilmore, Kathy. *A Day in the Life of A Colonial Schoolteacher.* New York: PowerKids Press, 2000.

UNIT THREE

Benchley, Nathaniel. *George the Drummer Boy.* New York: Harper and Row, 1977.
Brand, Oscar. *Songs of '76 — A Folksinger's History of the Revolution.* New York: M. Evans and Company, Inc., 1972.
Branse, J. L. *A Day in the Life of a Colonial Soldier.* New York: PowerKids Press, 2002.
Carter, Alden. *Colonies in Revolt.* New York: Franklin Watts, 1988.
Colby, C. B. *Revolutionary War Weapons.* New York: Coward McCann Geoghagen, 1963.
Cooper, Jason. *Valley Forge.* Vero Beach: The Rourke Corporation, 1999.
Davis, Burke. *Heroes of the American Revolution.* New York: Random House, 1971.
Dolan, Edward. *The American Revolution: How We Fought The War of Independence,* Brookfield: Millbrook Press, 1995.
Edwards, Pamela Duncan. *Boston Tea Party.* New York: G. P. Putnam's Sons, 2001.
Erdosh, George. *Food and Recipes of the Revolutionary War.* New York: The Rosen Company, 1997.
Feuerlicht, Roberta Strauss. *A Free People.* New York: Messner, 1969.
Graff, Stewart. *John Paul Jones.* Champaign: Garrard Press, 1961.
Grant, R. G. *The American Revolution.* New York: Thomson Learning, 1995.
Hakim, Joy. *From Colonies to Country.* New York: Oxford University Press, 1993.
Haley, Gail. *Jack Jouett's Ride.* New York: Viking Press, 1973.
Hall-Quest, Olga. *The Bell That Rang for Freedom.* New York: Dutton, 1965.
Hiscock, Bruce. *The Big Tree.* New York: Atheneum, 1991.
Hughes, Libby. *Valley Forge.* New York: Dillon Press, 1993.
Johnson, Neil. *The Battle of Lexington and Concord.* New York: Four Winds Press, 1992.
Jones, Michael Wynn Jones. *The Cartoon History of the American Revolution.* New York: G. P. Putnam's Sons, 1979.
Ketchum, Richard M. *The American Heritage Book of the Revolution.* New York: American Heritage Publishing Company, 1971.
Lawson, Robert. *Ben and Me.* Boston: Little, Brown, and Company, 1939.
Lukes, Bonnie. *The American Revolution.* San Diego: Lucent Books, 1996.
Martin, Joseph. *Yankee Doodle Boy.* New York: Harmony House, 1995.
Maurois, Andre. *Lafayette in America.* Boston: Houghton-Mifflin, 1960.
Miller, Natalie. *The Story of the Liberty Bell.* Chicago: Children's Press, 1995.
Morris, Richard. *The Constitution.* Minneapolis: Lerner Publication, 1985.
Moss, Marissa. *Emma's Journal — the Story of a Colonial Girl.* San Diego: Silver Whistle, 1999.
Nolan, Jeannette. *George Rogers Clark — Soldier and Hero.* New York: Messner, 1954.

Nordstrom, Judy. *Concord and Lexington.* New York: Dillon Press, 1993.
O'Connor, Richard. *The Common Sense of Thomas Paine.* New York: Prentice-Hall, 1969.
Richards, Norman. *The Story of the Declaration of Independence.* Chicago: Children's Press, 1968.
Sandak, Cass. *The John Adamses.* New York: Crestwood House, 1991.
Sandak, Cass. *The Washingtons.* New York: Crestwood House, 1992.
Schackburg, Richard. *Yankee Doodle.* Englewood Cliffs: Prentice-Hall, 1965.
Schleifer, Jay. *Our Declaration of Independence.* Brookfield: The Millbrook Press, 1992.
Silverman, Jerry. *Songs and Stories from the American Revolution.* Brookfield: The Millbrook Press, 1994.
Stein, R. Conrad. *The Story of the Boston Tea Party.* Children's Press, 1984.
Stein, R. Conrad. *The Story of Valley Forge.* Children's Press, 1985.
Todd, Anne. *The Revolutionary War.* Mankato: Capstone Books, 2001.
Winnick, Karen B. *Sybil's Night Ride.* Honesdale: Boyds Mill Press, 2000.

UNIT FOUR

Adler, David. *A Picture Book of George Washington.* New York: Holiday House, 1989.
Beyer, Mark. *The Election of 1800.* New York: Rosen, 2004.
Brown, Warren. *John C. Calhoun.* New York: Chelsea House, 1993.
Carter, Alden. *The Mexican War.* New York: Franklin Watts, 1992.
Clare, John. *Industrial Revolution.* San Diego: Gulliver Books, 1994.
Colman, Warren. *The Bill of Rights.* Chicago: Children's Press, 1987.
Davis, Lucille. *Elizabeth Cady Stanton.* New York: Bridgestone Books, 1998.
Gay, Kathleen and Martin Gay. *War of 1812.* New York: Henry Holt Company, 1995.
Glubok, Shirley. *The Art of America from Jackson to Lincoln.* New York: Macmillan Company, 1973.
Glubok, Shirley. *The Art of the New American Nation.* New York: MacMillan Company, 1972.
Goodman, Susan E. *Ultimate Field Trip 4 — A Week in the 1800s.* New York: Atheneum, 2000.
Hakim, Joy. *The New Nation.* New York: Oxford University Press, 1993.
Harness, Cheryl. *George Washington.* Washington, D.C.: National Geographic Society, 2000.
Henry, Joanne Landers. *Robert Fulton — Steamboat Builder.* New York: Chelsea House, 1991.
Jones, Vera Boyd. *Alexander Hamilton — First U.S. Secretary of the Treasury.* Philadelphia: Chelsea House, 2000.
Kozar, Richard. *Meriwether Lewis and William Clark — Explorers of the Louisiana Purchase.* Philadelphia: Chelsea House, 2000.
Lake, A. I. *Gold Fever — the Wild West in American History.* Vero Beach: Rourke Publications, 1990.
Laughlin, Florence. *Skyrockets for the President.* Chicago: Rand-McNally, 1973.
Miller, Natalie. *The Story of the White House.* Chicago: Children's Press, 1966.
Nash, Carol Rust. *The Mormon Trail and the Latter-Day Saints in American History.* Springfield: Enslow, 1999.
Peterson, Helen Stone. *Henry Clay.* Champaign: Garrard Publishing, 1964.
Prolman, Marilyn. *The Story of the Capitol.* Chicago: Children's Press, 1969.
Quackenbush, Robert. *Quick, Annie, Give Me A Line: the Story of Samuel F.B. Morse.* Englewood Cliffs: Prentice-Hall, 1983.
Quasha, Jennifer. *Gold Rush: Hands-On Projects About Mining the Riches of California.* New York: PowerKids Press, 2001.
Richards, Caroline. *A Nineteenth Century Schoolgirl — the Diary of Caroline Cowles Richards, 1852 – 1855.* Mankato: Blue Earth Books, 2000.

Sandak, Cass. *The Jacksons.* New York: Crestwood House, 1992.
Sandak, Cass. *The Jeffersons.* New York: Crestwood House, 1992.
Sandak, Cass. *The John Adams.* New York: Crestwood House, 1992.
Sandak, Cass. *The Madisons.* New York: Crestwood House, 1992.
Sandak, Cass. *The Monroes.* New York: Crestwood House, 1993.
Sandak, Cass. *The Washingtons.* New York: Crestwood House, 1001.
Smith-Baranzini, Marlene and Howard Egger-Bovet. *Book of the New American Nation.* Boston: Little, Brown, and Company, 1995.
Tibbets, Alison Davis. *James K. Polk: Manifest Destiny.* Springfield: Enslow Publishers, 1994.
Todd, Anne. *The War of 1812.* Mankato: Capstone Press, 2001.
Whitman, Walt. *I Hear America Singing.* New York: Philomel, 1991.

ALSO AVAILABLE FROM BRIGHT IDEAS PRESS...

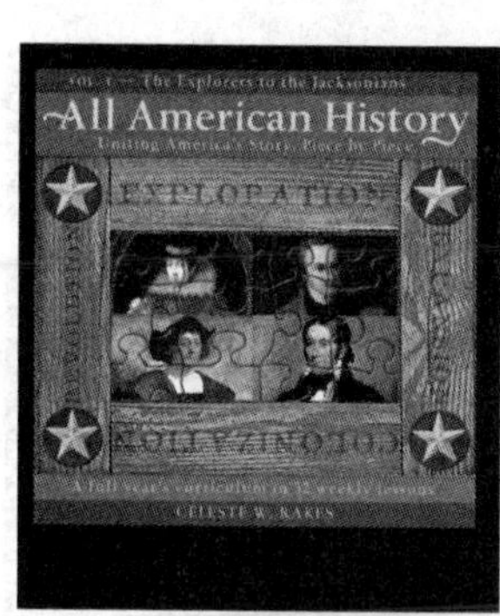

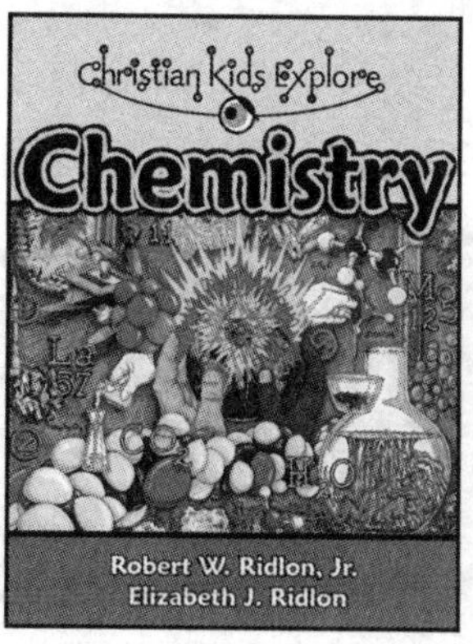

All American History by Celeste W. Rakes
Containing hundreds of images and dozens of maps, *All American History* is a complete year's curriculum for students in grades 5 – 8 when combined with the Student Activity Book and Teacher's Guide (yet adaptable for younger and older students).

There are 32 weekly lessons, and each lesson contains three sections examining the atmosphere in which the event occurred, the event itself, and the impact this event had on the future of America.

- Student Reader — ISBN: 1-892427-12-5
- Teacher's Guide — ISBN: 1-892427-14-1

The Mystery of History Volumes I & II by Linda Hobar
This award-winning series provides a historically accurate, Bible-centered approach to learning world history. The completely chronological lessons shed new light on who walked the earth when, as well as on where important Bible figures fit into secular history. Grades 4 – 8, yet easily adaptable.

- Volume I: Creation to the Resurrection — ISBN: 1-892427-04-4
- Volume II: The Early Church & the Middle Ages — ISBN: 1-892427-06-0

CHRISTIAN KIDS EXPLORE... SERIES

Christian Kids Explore Biology by Stephanie Redmond
One of Cathy Duffy's 100 Top Picks! Elementary biology that is both classical and hands-on. Conversational style and organized layout makes teaching a pleasure.

- ISBN: 1-892427-05-2

Christian Kids Explore Earth & Space by Stephanie Redmond
Another exciting book in this award-winning series! Author Stephanie Redmond is back with more great lessons, activities, and ideas.

- ISBN: 1-892427-19-2

Christian Kids Explore Chemistry by Robert W. Ridlon, Jr., and Elizabeth J. Ridlon
Another great book in this award-winning series! Authors Robert and Elizabeth Ridlon team up for 30 lessons, unit wrap ups, and even coloring pages all about the fascinating world of chemistry.

- ISBN: 1-892427-18-4

FOR ORDERING INFORMATION, CALL 877-492-8081 OR VISIT WWW.BRIGHTIDEASPRESS.COM

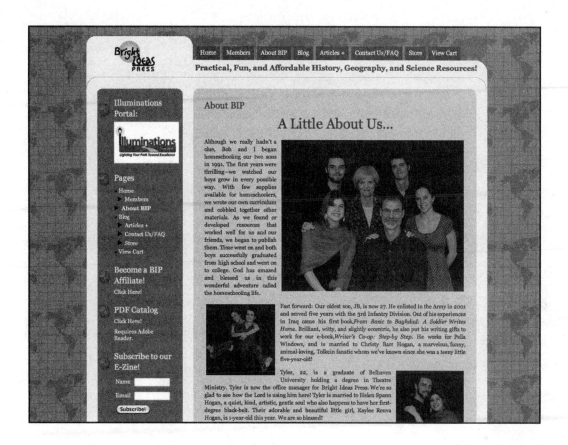

All American History